Susan Gittins

CTV

The Television Wars

Published in 1999 by Stoddart Publishing Co. Limited
34 Lesmill Road, Toronto, Canada M3B 2T6
180 Varick Street, 9th Floor, New York, New York 10014

Distributed in Canada by:
General Distribution Services Ltd.
325 Humber College Boulevard, Toronto, Canada M9W 7C3
Tel. (416) 213-1919   Fax (416) 213-1917
Email customer.service@ccmailgw.genpub.com

Distributed in the United States by:
General Distribution Services Inc.
85 River Rock Drive, Suite 202, Buffalo, New York 14207
Toll-free Tel. 1-800-805-1083   Toll-free Fax 1-800-481-6207
Email gdsinc@genpub.com

03   02   01   00   99   1   2   3   4   5

Canadian Cataloguing in Publication Data

Gittins, Susan
CTV: the television wars

ISBN 0-7737-3125-3

1. CTV Television Network — History.   2. Baton Broadcasting — History.   I. Title.

HE8700.9.C3G58   1998   384.55'4'06571   C98-931467-7

Jacket design: Angel Guerra
Design and typesetting: Kinetics Design & Illustration

Printed and bound in Canada

*We acknowledge for their financial support of our publishing program the
Government of Canada through the Book Publishing Industry Development
Program (BPIDP), the Canada Council, and the Ontario Arts Council.*

Contents

Preface

"A network is a group of people quarrelling."
— DOUG BASSETT

For almost four decades, CTV's boardroom battles provided better and certainly far more original Canadian drama than anything the network aired for its viewers. Marked by bitter personal rivalries, the off-screen tug-of-war for control of the country's first private television network was one of the longest-running series in history. It starred such memorable characters as Big John Bassett, the flamboyant patriarch of Baton Broadcasting, which owned the flagship Toronto station CFTO. Big John called most of the shots for more than twenty years, but a cooperative ownership structure, which gave each CTV member station one vote, regardless of size, thwarted his ambition of running the entire show.

Out on the west coast, Frank Griffiths and Ray Peters, of WIC Western International Communications, were not content with Big John's virtual monopoly on the production of network programming. Again and again, they blocked Baton's efforts to expand its influence. The Baton-WIC slugfest intensified when Doug Bassett, Big John's middle son, replaced his father at the CTV boardroom table, but WIC was not alone in opposing Baton's domination. As many as eighteen feuding affiliates packed the directors' meetings, each one shouting — often profanely — to be heard as they fought tooth and nail to stake out their turf from Victoria, British Columbia, to St. John's, Newfoundland.

As Baton and WIC pieced together their rival fiefdoms, new players, including the upstart CanWest Global Communications System, clouded the broadcasting horizon. Baton never ceased to view the CTV trademark as a prize worth capturing, but that goal remained elusive until the demise of the network's one-member, one-vote principle, and the arrival (seemingly from central casting) of Ivan Fecan. He began to swap stations like baseball cards, ultimately gained control of the network, and launched the process of Canadianizing its prime-time schedule.

☆

Most of the information in this book comes from personal interviews conducted over the course of a year. A prime resource was the transcripts of public hearings stored in Ottawa's National Archives, or at regional offices of the Canadian Radio-television Telecommunications Commission in Ottawa, Vancouver, and Montreal. Many of CTV's former and current directors were generous enough to speak with me at length. I thank particularly Doug Bassett, Allan Beattie, Ivan Fecan, Doug Holtby, Senator Finlay MacDonald, Jim Macdonald, Bill McGregor, Ray Peters, John Pollock, Fred Sherratt, and Allan Slaight. John Bassett agreed to be interviewed but ill health intervened. Fortunately, Fred Eaton, Eddie Goodman, the Right Honourable Brian Mulroney, and Ted Rogers contributed their memories of Baton's founding father. Allen Lambert, Dr. Reginald Roy, and Peter Paul Saunders provided similar recollections of the late Frank Griffiths.

I would also like to acknowledge the thoughts and comments of Tony Allard, Susanne Boyce, Paul Bronfman, Mike Buzzell, Murray Chercover, Pauline Couture, Suzette Couture, Drew Craig, Tom Curzon, Mike Duffy, Sandra Faire, Jon Festinger, Allan Fotheringham, Peter Grant, Julia Keatley, Peter Kent, Ed King, Michael Levine, Gary Maavara, Ian Morrison, Dr. Catherine Murray, Knowlton Nash, Craig Oliver, Tony Parsons, Robert Patillo, Lloyd Robertson, Carole Taylor, Pamela Wallin, and many, many unnamed others.

Of all the people whom I considered integral to the story, only George Eaton and John Cassaday, a former president of CTV, declined to be interviewed.

My thanks as well to my agent, Perry Goldsmith, and his colleague, Robert Mackwood, of Contemporary Communications, for suggesting the subject matter. Stoddart Publishing's managing editor Don Bastian, along with senior editor Marnie Kramarich and copy editors Kathleen Richards and Wendy Thomas, helped steer the manuscript towards its final form, and Jack Stoddart, the firm's president, offered key support from the beginning.

Finally, a special word of thanks to my friends Natasha and Drummond in Toronto and my family in the Vancouver area — my sister Debbie and my parents, Roy and Christina.

SUSAN GITTINS
Bowen Island, British Columbia

Prologue — 1997

December 17 was an unseasonably warm and sunny day in Agincourt, a sprawling suburb northeast of Toronto. Inside CFTO's Studio 6, a packed audience of on-air personalities, shareholders, directors, and journalists had gathered for the first annual meeting of Baton Broadcasting Incorporated ever to be held in the place where its programming was made.

Baton's chairman Allan Beattie rose to introduce the company's wunderkind chief executive officer, Ivan Fecan, who earlier that year had achieved what his Bassett predecessors never quite managed to do. At long last, he'd secured for Baton what he called "the best television trademark in the country" — the CTV Television Network.

Fecan considered the CTV logo so valuable that he'd been slapping it all over non-network programs like the Dini Petty, Camilla Scott, and Vicki Gabereau talk shows; American syndicated programs like *Wheel of Fortune*; and individual Baton stations' local newscasts. Of course, it appeared as well (lurking annoyingly in the lower-right corner of the screen) on forty hours a week of actual network programming, anchored by *CTV National News*, *W Five*, *Canada AM*, and the Canadian Mountie drama series *Due South*. Depending on your point of view, it was either an example of brand-identification overkill, or the latest smart move by one of Canada's smartest broadcasters.

Despite Fecan's achievements, however, he remained largely unknown outside broadcasting circles. Six months earlier, the Vancouver *Province* had run a story headlined: "Who the hell is Ivan Fecan?" The answer was: a real-live television prodigy, who'd started out on the creative side of the business as a programmer and proved to be equally talented as a corporate strategist, moving all of Baton's puzzle pieces around until they formed a cohesive whole.

An hour earlier, Baton's shareholders had begun to arrive in CFTO's marble-floored main lobby. This area had changed very little in the thirty-seven years since the station's ribbon-cutting ceremony. The only permanent addition was an oil portrait of the station's founder, John White Hughes Bassett, which commanded the west wall. As the guests entered, they were scooped up and led through a labyrinth of windowless, cement-block corridors on quickie tours of the sets, newsrooms, and editing facilities. Their first impression of the CFTO complex, referred to by long-suffering employees as "the regional detention centre," was that it looked ready to burst at the seams. What had started life in 1960 as a purely local station in the middle of nowhere had grown to house a national television network's entire office and production facilities, national and local news services, and national public affairs and morning shows. Scattered throughout the station and adjacent buildings were a twenty-four-hour headline news service (CTV News 1); a comedy service (The Comedy Network); an outdoor sports service (Outdoor Life); and three specialty channels (CTV Sportsnet, CTV Direct, and Talk TV) that weren't yet up and running. All were catered to by a single and long-out-moded source of food — a cafeteria known as the Niner Diner, which radiated all the ambience of a department-store restaurant, circa 1960.

After their whirlwind visit, the shareholders were ushered into Studio 6 and seated according to rank. Baton's directors occupied two rows of seats, off to one side. The first row had readily identifiable bookends: Fredrik and George Eaton of the troubled department store chain. Next to Fred sat Douglas Bassett, who'd stepped aside as Baton's CEO the year before.

In the central section, the first two rows were reserved for the cream of CTV's on-screen talent. Lloyd Robertson, the aging but immensely popular chief news anchor, took pride of place. Next to him sat his weekend replacement, Sandie Rinaldo. In front of them was the host of Baton's *Sunday Edition*, Mike Duffy, a consummate Parliament Hill insider who later received the most prolonged applause from the assembled directors when the full roster of Baton/CTV local and network stars stood up to take a bow. These were the people who brought news, sports, and entertainment to millions of Canadians every day. On this particular Wednesday, however, the executives were eager to take centre stage.

Allan Beattie completed his introductions of Ivan Fecan and his team, which included Baton's vice-president of strategic planning, Henry Eaton, the son of John Craig, eldest of the four next-generation brothers. Then the studio lights dimmed and an absent star appeared on the Cineplex-size screen. Here shone the image of the legendary John W. H. Bassett, filmed several weeks earlier leaning back in his desk chair, a huge smile beneath the signature bushy eyebrows of his still handsome eighty-two-year-old face, as he recalled the humble beginnings of his station.

"Oh heavens, the day" — he permitted himself a chuckle — "before we went on the air, getting everything ready because we'd set the target for New Year's Eve, can only be described in two words: total chaos." A wave of affectionate laughter rippled through the studio for "Big John," so called because of his almost six-foot, five-inch height, and larger-than-life personality.

Watching Bassett's video self regale the studio audience with nostalgic tales was a bittersweet moment for his son Douglas and others who knew that the real Big John — or "Uncle John," as the Eaton brothers called him — lay ill in a downtown hospital. Indeed, the meeting's organizers had feared that their tribute would become an obituary instead. But fearsome competitor that he was, Bassett clung to life.

And so, as the screen went dark that triumphant December morning in the station that he had built, it was easy to go back almost forty years in time and imagine Big John Bassett in his prime, striding through his hospitality suite at Toronto's Royal York Hotel, champagne glass in hand, as he boasted to anyone who'd listen that the Baton Aldred Rogers Broadcasting Ltd. application for the city's first private television licence was "in the bag."

One

The
Originals

Big John's Flagship — 1958–60

In 1958, Prime Minister John Diefenbaker decided to change the ground rules of Canadian broadcasting. The Chief had been thinking along these lines for more than a decade, prodded by a cross-section of Progressive Conservative supporters. They included the owners of private radio stations, newspaper publishers, and sundry other business interests who wanted a piece of a medium that, while still in its adolescence, appeared to offer the potential of huge riches. According to a study prepared by the Bank of Commerce, broadcasting (including both radio and television) ranked third in profitability among 140 leading Canadian industries. Radio was pretty good: the expatriate media baron Roy Thomson had declared that his Canadian stations played the sweetest music available — "the sound of the thirty-second commercial at thirty dollars a time." But television was bigger and better. In Thomson's most famous phrase, owning a station was "just like having a licence to print your own money." That was in Scotland, but many people wanted to learn whether his maxim would hold true at home in Canada.

In fact, Diefenbaker needed little urging from anybody. As leader of the Opposition, he had looked with approval to the United States, where broadcasting was overwhelmingly a matter of private enterprise. He did not like or trust the Canadian Broadcasting Corporation (CBC), which

— when it came to television — was the only game in town. (Television, by the way, came to Canada in 1952, more than a decade after its introduction in the States.) When Diefenbaker ousted the federal Liberals from power five years later, the CBC owned (along with numerous radio stations) six television stations, in Vancouver, Winnipeg, Toronto, Ottawa, Montreal, and Halifax, and provided programming to an additional thirty-one privately owned affiliates in smaller centres. There was no such thing as a privately owned and non-affiliated television station; you had to join the CBC club.

But that's not all. Since its creation in 1936, the CBC's Board of Governors had ruled and regulated both public and private outlets, both radio and television stations. It was intolerable to Diefenbaker that they should be empowered to function as "litigant and judge, investigator and jury." Accordingly, in 1958, his Tory government passed a new Broadcasting Act, which established a new and independent regulatory body, the Board of Broadcast Governors (BBG). More important, it permitted the establishment of what were known as second television stations in the six cities where CBC-owned service already existed (the most lucrative markets from an advertising standpoint), as well as in Calgary and Edmonton. Here was where the money would be made — but not immediately. Aside from massive capital costs, there were one or two hurdles to be overcome. For example, second stations would be subject to the same Canadian content rules as the CBC. These rules stated that, by 1961, Canadian-produced programs had to account for 40 per cent of a station's output between 6 p.m. and midnight, and 45 per cent of its total daily programming. The latter figure would rise to 55 per cent the following year. That presented no problem for the CBC; it was already at sixty-plus per cent. Whether a start-from-scratch station could possibly comply remained to be seen.

It was obvious as well that these stations would eventually combine to form a second English-language television network, but that was in the future — they had to be licensed first. To this end, the BBG proposed to receive licence applications at public hearings in the eight cities involved, after which, its three full-time and twelve part-time members would make recommendations to the minister responsible — in this case, the Minister of Transport, George Hees. Later, they'd hold further hearings into subsequent new-licence applications, licence renewals, transfers of ownership, and affiliations or disaffiliations within a network (either the CBC, or the as-yet-nonexistent private one, whose anticipated formation they'd also oversee). Throughout these proceedings, it would be their job to set and enforce the rules. For example, they might threaten to lift an existing licence, or to renew it only under certain conditions and on promises of performance.

Unfortunately, the BBG was ill suited to the tasks at hand. Most of its members knew little about broadcasting and owed their appointments to the fact that they were well-known Tory loyalists. Dr. (later Senator) Eugene Forsey was an exception to this rule. Although a Diefenbaker appointee, he was also the research director of the Canadian Labour Congress and often expressed a dissenting view. But only the BBG's chairman, Dr. Andrew Stewart, the president of the University of Alberta, was considered politically impartial. In all, critics feared that the Diefenbaker regime was handing over Canada's public airwaves to be exploited by their wealthy friends. Nowhere was this fear more palpable than in Toronto, the country's largest television market, where the competition would therefore be fiercest for the new private licence.

On St. Patrick's Day, 1960, Toronto was well on its way to setting a sixty-year snowfall record. Big John Bassett swept out of the Oak Room at Union Station, where his Baton Aldred Rogers Broadcasting team had just succeeded in dazzling the BBG with a closed-circuit television presentation of news, entertainment, and sports programming — the centrepiece of their hard-fought effort to win the licence sweepstakes. Bassett had been magnificent, electric, in full possession of his forty-four-year-old self, particularly when he single-handedly kept the show going during a power failure that plunged the cavernous meeting room into pitch darkness for five interminable minutes.

The swashbuckling publisher of the Toronto *Telegram* was bursting to proclaim his certainty that Baton Aldred Rogers had prevailed, but he was under strict orders from his lawyer, Eddie Goodman, to keep his mouth zipped. Given the group's highly publicized Tory connections, Goodman was worried that the BBG, in a fit of reverse discrimination, might favour one of the eight other applicants, simply to avoid charges of political patronage. Going in, Goodman knew the application would have to be good enough to withstand close scrutiny, and he thought it had succeeded. All Bassett had to do now was keep quiet. In Goodman's words, "I told him the only way we could lose was if he talked."

Not talking, though, was totally out of character for Big John Bassett. The week-long hearings were the biggest event in town, and the Baton Aldred Rogers suite across the street at the Royal York Hotel was *the* place to gather afterwards for a drink. At the centre of these convivial get-togethers was the extra-tall, blond, and handsome Bassett, who cruised above the cocktail crowd on his own oral jet stream, fuelled by four-letter Irish charm. Over and over, he voiced his belief that "the licence is in the bag." Another favourite expression was "Piece of cake, baby," accompanied by a flash of his 100-watt smile.

One rival applicant later claimed that Bassett had gone so far as to yell across at him that he'd been promised the licence by both Diefenbaker and George Hees. This was not a possibility that outraged belief. Former prime minister Brian Mulroney, then vice-chairman of the Youth for Diefenbaker Movement, recalls that Bassett, Goodman, and Hees (dubbed "Gorgeous George" by the Liberal opposition) were all "cut from the same cloth," and that "George was their guy in Cabinet." John David Eaton, the big money behind Baton's application, was the Tory party's largest financial backer. Other members of the Baton group were well connected also. Joel Aldred, the radio and television announcer, was a long-time Diefenbaker supporter; Ted Rogers chaired the Youth for Diefenbaker Movement; and Goodman and his fellow lawyer Charles Dubin had organized and raised funds for the Chief's 1958 campaign. A too-close-for-comfort aura pervaded the hearings and did not dissipate when — a scant three days later — the BBG awarded the Toronto licence to Baton Aldred Rogers. An immediate outcry arose that the fix was in. Joseph Sedgwick, the lawyer for a losing application backed by Argus Corporation, sent a letter to the *Globe and Mail*, noting that the BBG's decision appeared "not to be explained by any ordinary process of thought or reason." He then quoted a doggerel verse that clearly alleged favouritism on the board's part. Eugene Forsey was so incensed that, the next few times Sedgwick appeared before the BBG, Forsey would leave the room and not return until Sedgwick had finished speaking.

In fact, the matter arose in the House of Commons the following month, when Douglas Fisher, a CCF member of Parliament, asked Diefenbaker if there had been "any communication from him or his Cabinet associates" to the BBG that "suggested or indicated a preference for any particular applicant for a television station licence in Toronto, notably the successful Bassett application."

"May I say with all emphasis, *no*," the Chief replied.

The object of all this controversy let it roll off his back — at least until July, when the issue cropped up again in Parliament. Jack Pickersgill, the Liberal broadcasting critic, complained that "months before the application was heard," Bassett had opined that "there was no need of holding any hearing because he already had it in the bag." Bassett dismissed the charge as "absolutely untrue. I haven't spoken to Mr. Pickersgill about anything important for the last ten years — just a few how-do-you-do's." As for the BBG's decision-making process, Bassett maintained that his application had simply been the best and that detractors were indulging in "goddamn" belly-aching. Goodman agrees: "There was no fix; we won that application on merit. The only reason why there was such a big fuss about it was that Bassett was such an outspoken Tory." Finlay MacDonald, Big John's long-time friend (and Brian Mulroney's first appointment to the Senate), puts it the same way, but differently: "Bassett won it fair and square, in spite of his braggadocio."

In his heyday, John White Hughes Bassett was considered, above all, a "man's man," one who loved sports, sexual high jinks, and carousing with his pals at watering holes such as the ill-reputed Berkley Hotel. Less acknowledged was his equally ardent patriotism — even if, as some critics later charged, Big John's Canada began just east of Montreal and ended just west of Toronto.

Big John was bred to success by his father, John Bassett Sr., also a strikingly handsome man and a Tory newspaper publisher of legendary charm and combative temper. Bassett Sr. had set sail from Ireland in 1909, landed in Montreal, and obtained his first low-level job at a Liberal newspaper. Four months later, he took time off for a crash course in French, which prepared him for a fluently bilingual cub reporter's job at the solidly Tory *Gazette*. As the brash young journalist rose through the ranks to become its publisher, he met, and cultivated intimate friendships with, the most powerful men of his age — including fellow publishers, international politicians, and a Prince of Wales. Later Big John would form his own bonds with three of these high-profile newspaper men: George McCullagh (who'd oversee the merger of two Toronto newspapers into the *Globe and Mail*), Roy Thomson (later Lord Thomson of Fleet), and Max Aitken (later Lord Beaverbrook, or — as the Bassett family called him — the Beaver).

Big John inherited his looks and height from both his parents. His mother, Marion Avery, a daughter of the Ottawa establishment who bore a distinct resemblance to Katharine Hepburn, was almost as tall as her husband. Later, Big John would tell Mike McManus, the host of an Ontario Educational Communications Authority television program called *Journeys in Time*, that he clearly remembered her leaving for a party or social event, resplendent in a formal gown, leaning over to kiss him goodnight and instruct him to be good.

When Big John was sent to the elite Bishop's College boarding school in Quebec's Eastern Townships, he'd had plenty of exposure to rich and famous people at the family dinner table. At six feet tall, he was a trifle clumsy, but nonetheless made the football and hockey teams, played tennis, and excelled at debating. Confidence and self-assurance were not in short supply. He'd return home for the holidays and spend summer vacations at Tyrone, the family's lakefront country retreat not far from Bishop's. Here, the hormone-driven Big John developed a keen interest in the opposite sex. This would later entangle his life as he conducted numerous extramarital affairs until he met his true love, his second wife, Isabel.

After graduation from the college, Big John moved smoothly into Bishop's University, where his family hoped that there'd be less scope for wild escapades than at McGill University in sinful Montreal. Little did they know that he already had his eye on the biggest catch at Bishop's, a popular girl named Moira Bradley, whose father was a former mayor of nearby Sherbrooke. Big John met her about six weeks after his eighteenth birthday. She was two and a half years older, but that didn't matter — it was love at first sight on his part. He rushed back and informed his roommate that he was bent on marriage. The roommate accurately pointed out that Moira was engaged to someone else. "Well," said Big John, "she soon won't be." He began to court her, aided by the fact that her fiancé had graduated and was working out of the country. By Christmas, he was also out of the picture.

His love life in order, a smitten Big John hit the books, managing the university magazine and graduating with first-class honours, which earned him a promised Mercury convertible from Bassett Sr. He also wrote a sports column for his father's latest acquisition, the *Sherbrooke Record* — just as, later on, he'd write opinion pieces and other articles under his own byline for the *Telegram*. "I was a conformist," he later explained. "I used to argue with Father, but I wasn't really rebellious. I accepted the status quo in those pre-war years. But then, the status quo was very good for me."

Quite so. While not as wealthy as his friends, John Bassett Sr. lived well. He wanted his son to be a lawyer, but Big John aspired to be a newspaper man like his father and his father's glamorous associates. In hopes of broadening Big John's vistas, Bassett Sr. suggested that he go to Europe to study post-graduate French. Big John dropped out after a single day of classes and began to tour with a semi-professional hockey team.

Later, in London, he met up with his father and the young press baron George McCullagh, who offered Bassett, ten years his junior, an entry-level reporting job at the *Globe and Mail*.

Thus the newly married Big John made his way to Toronto, where he charmed the *Globe* newsroom with his ability to laugh at his own screw-ups. He joined a clique dubbed "McCullagh's Hussars," who rode horses every Sunday at their boss's country estate, or gathered of a weeknight to watch movies in his home theatre. As a result, Moira frequently found herself alone, which Big John admitted "must have been extraordinarily difficult for her."

Shortly after the birth of their first son, John Frederick, World War II erupted, and Big John took his family back to Sherbrooke. There he enlisted in the Black Watch of Canada, but that regiment wasn't sent overseas for several years. While waiting to be called into active service, he and Moira had two more sons, Douglas Graeme and David Eaton. Then, in 1941, a battalion of the Queen's Own Royal Rifles was decimated in Hong Kong. Bassett rushed to volunteer and sailed for Europe the next year. Once abroad, he fought in North Africa and Italy, winding up attached to another regiment, Vancouver's Seaforth Highlanders. When their ship was torpedoed in the Mediterranean Sea, Big John was rescued, and his commanding officer promoted him to major on the spot.

As a Seaforth Highlander, Major Bassett helped liberate Holland with accustomed style. According to Finlay MacDonald, "he opened up all the tennis courts and hotels in Amsterdam" — then awoke with a splitting hangover to learn that he'd been nominated back in Sherbrooke as a candidate in the 1945 federal election. Big John caught the first available military flight and "stepped off the bomber in Montreal, covered in lipstick and wearing his kilt." He must have cut a fine figure, but he wasn't elected. He did, however, realize his teenage ambitions by borrowing $280,000 and buying the *Record* from his father.

"The war changed me from a boy to a man," Big John later told *Journeys in Time*. "It set my priorities and sense of values, which have never really changed since. It made me recognize that if you were alive and in good health, not crippled or badly wounded, nothing could look so blue or grim, no problem could be so dreadful, that you couldn't face it and solve it." These were not empty words. Having witnessed firsthand the horrors of the Holocaust, Big John became a foe of despotism in all its forms, a strong Zionist, and a founding member of the Canadian Council of Christians and Jews. His efforts were recognized. He was the first Gentile to be honoured at a Jewish National Fund Tribute dinner, the first Gentile member of Toronto's Primrose Club, and one of very few Gentiles invited to plant trees in the Jewish homeland.

But all this was far in the future. For the moment, Sherbrooke was proving to be too small a pond. Fortunately, in 1948, Big John received an offer he couldn't refuse: the position of advertising director at the Toronto *Telegram* under its new owner, his mentor and friend George McCullagh. One year later, he was general manager of the pro-Tory newspaper — and, aided by McCullagh, he began his climb up the ladder of the Toronto establishment. At its top was the department store–chain owner John David Eaton, then the richest man in the country.

The Eatons are surely the closest thing to a Canadian aristocracy, and members of the Toronto retailing dynasty have always lived more extravagantly than most crowned heads. Despite their recent fall from grace, the Eaton's department stores must qualify as one of the country's cultural touchstones, right up there with hockey and the Mounties.

At the root of the Eaton's mythology was Timothy himself — a teetotalling Irish immigrant turned dry-goods dealer who opened Toronto's first department store in 1869. As business grew, he distributed the first mail-order catalogue for rural customers in 1884 and opened a second store in Winnipeg in 1905. All the while he stood behind his merchandise with the unequivocal pledge "Goods Satisfactory or Money Refunded." He died in 1907, leaving an estate worth more than $5 million — whereupon the company's two stores, 9,000 employees, two factories, and two European offices passed to his youngest son, John Craig, known as Jack.

Unlike his pious father, Jack Eaton considered his big-bucks lifestyle a birthright. He developed a drinking problem, and his parents admitted him to Toronto's turn-of-the-century equivalent of the Betty Ford Clinic, where his future wife, the young Flora McCrea, nursed him back to sobriety. They enjoyed the comforts of a fifty-room mansion called Ardwold, near Casa Loma in Toronto, and an Italianate summer mansion named Kawandag, built on forty-four acres at Lake Rosseau, in the Muskoka region. Jack owned three Rolls-Royces, a private rail car, and a 172-foot ocean-going yacht christened *Florence*, after his wife. During World War I, he signed it over to the navy and was knighted for his patriotism.

Following Sir John Craig's untimely death at the age of forty-six in 1922, an Irish-born Eaton nephew assumed the presidency for twenty years. Sir John's widow, Lady Eaton, remained a vice-president until the executors chose their second son, John David, to take over the company in 1942. During that time, she condemned women's suffrage and praised the Italian dictator Benito Mussolini, but partially redeemed herself during World War II by converting her thirty-five-room French-style chateau called Eaton Hall, newly built on 300 acres to the north of Toronto, into a temporary home for wounded naval servicemen and displaced children.

John David grew up in Ardwold and was educated at Upper Canada College and Trinity College School in Ontario and Stow in England, later studying at Cambridge. At Eaton's, he started at the bottom by selling men's underwear, then went west to manage the Winnipeg store. There he met his Icelandic-Canadian wife, Signy Hildur Stephenson. At the beginning of his presidency, Eaton's boasted 32,000 employees and fifty-two stores, but John David embarked on a policy of aggressive expansion, pushing into suburban areas. Like his parents, he lived exceedingly well, maintaining a house on Dunvegan Road in Toronto's Forest Hill, a country home in the Caledon Hills, a villa in Antigua, and cottages decorated with Group of Seven paintings on his private island in Georgian Bay, Ontario. On land he too travelled by Rolls-Royce; on water he cruised aboard diesel-powered yachts; in the air he flew either by private plane or private helicopter, which he piloted himself.

John David's privileged lifestyle offered everything, except a bit of cheap fun. Enter Big John Bassett, six years younger than, and the reverse image of, the quiet, reserved Eaton. "He was Mr. Eaton to me," recalls Doug Bassett, Big John's middle son. "He was my father's best friend. They complemented each other, trusted each other. My parents and the Eatons often travelled together." True enough — and Big John was fond of teasing Signy Eaton until she giggled like a schoolgirl. Indeed, Toronto wags had a field day, gossiping about a supposed affair between the two and examining the features of the four Eaton boys for a Bassett likeness. To no avail. Big John was no stranger to extramarital sex, but Signy Eaton wasn't among his conquests.

Nevertheless, Bassett's high spirits would sometimes take him too far, and John David would have to slap him down. One such incident was recounted by Maggie Siggins, Bassett's biographer. While aboard Eaton's 104-foot yacht *Hildur* on Lake Huron, Big John proposed a toast and then flung his glass into the water. Eaton informed him that he'd get neither glasses nor cutlery for the rest of the voyage. His words were law: Big John ate with his fingers.

Usually, though, John David enjoyed his friend's exuberance. Bassett brought the introverted third-generation Eaton out of himself in business too. When George McCullagh killed himself in 1952, John David backed Bassett's plan to buy the *Telegram* for $4.25 million from McCullagh's estate. Eaton took a loan for half that sum and co-signed Bassett's loan for the rest — then offered Big John 30 per cent of the company to stick around and manage the paper. ("In 1952, my old man didn't have a pot to piss in, when — thanks to Mr. Eaton — he bought a newspaper that was losing a million dollars a year," noted Big John's son Johnny F. in a later interview with *Toronto Life* magazine.) At this same time, Bassett put his ownership of the *Sherbrooke Record* into the new Telegram Corporation Ltd., a trust formed to avoid succession duties for the three Bassett and four Eaton children.

The trustees gave Big John a $30,000-a-year management contract and complete voting control of all the trust's shares, of which 30 per cent were held by his sons, John Frederick, Douglas, and David; and 70 per cent by the Eaton sons, John Craig, Fredrik Stefan, Thor, and George. Big John therefore held sway over the management of the publishing assets, but could not profit by any appreciation in their value. This didn't seem to trouble him. He never tired of saying that he had no wish to die a millionaire as long as he could live like one. True to this credo, he charged the running expenses of his Forest Hill home and his Rolls-Royce, along with his chauffeur's salary and unparalleled entertainment bills, to the *Telegram* account.

Professional sports presented the next opportunity to intertwine the fortunes of the Bassett and Eaton families, when Big John succeeded George McCullagh to the board of Maple Leaf Gardens, also known as the Carlton Street Mint, in March 1953. A few years later, Bassett was named to a seven-man committee that would, it was hoped, improve the fortunes of the team. He and his cohorts were nicknamed the Silver Seven for their tabloid-style exploits involving whisky, women, and wild times. In early 1958, as they tried to wrest control of the Gardens from its president Conn Smythe, Bassett and Harold Ballard bought minority interests in the hockey palace, and Bassett put his shares into the Telegram trust.

Meanwhile, Big John had been eyeing the Toronto Argonauts football club and had teamed up with two partners named Erik Cradock and Charlie Burns, in hopes of persuading one or more of the franchise's owners to sell. In 1956, they succeeded. Bassett's initial investment (a little less than 20 per cent of the team) went into the Telegram trust as well. Two years later, Cradock, who'd first proposed the scheme, sold out in disgust. He claimed that Bassett needed to run the whole show — which Bassett went on to do, replacing Cradock as the Argos' chairman.

The year 1958 was significant for Bassett for two other reasons. First, it was the year that John Bassett Sr. died. As Big John later told *Journeys in Time*, "I would hope that I would leave my children the legacy my father left me — to appreciate that one must meet one's responsibilities, make the decisions that one is required to make, and be prepared to live with them and face the consequences." Second, it was the year that Diefenbaker ushered in the new Broadcasting Act.

☆

Baton Broadcasting was formed in mid-1958, well in advance of the first licence hearings. Big John derived the name either from the intersection of BAy and WellingTON streets, or from the surnames BAssett and EaTON.

Its original outside partner was Roy Thomson, who agreed to take a minority interest in the venture. He loaned Baton the able services of Rai Purdy, a former program director of Thomson's Scottish television network, and Don Williamson, a senior engineer with his Canadian radio and television operations. Williamson found a twenty-acre parcel of land for sale just north of Highway 401 in the wilds of Agincourt and declared that it would serve as the site of the proposed transmitter, studios, and offices. Baton took an option on the property, hoping that the licence would be granted before they had to close the deal. But the option ran out, and they were compelled to buy, paying the sum of $132,084.

The Baton-Thomson alliance was only a few months old when Thomson got word from Andrew Stewart, the chairman of the Board of Broadcast Governors, that his name on Baton's application would doom its chances of success. The BBG had no intention of piling "privilege upon privilege" by handing a new television licence to Thomson, who had (in Stewart's view) more than enough media outlets already. Indeed — as we shall see — the board generally opposed the chain ownership of broadcasting and publishing interests and could be expected to give Bassett a hard time also, because of his position at the *Telegram*.

"Thomson was a brusque, no-bullshit fellow," Eddie Goodman recalls. "He told Bassett, 'John, you won't get it if I'm your partner. I'm going to retire from this.'"

"The hell you are," replied Bassett. "We're going to fight them." The two men argued for a while, and Bassett went to consult with Goodman, whom he'd retained when he'd decided to go after the licence.

"This thing is going to be difficult enough," Goodman cautioned him. Finally, Big John accepted the situation and went hunting for other partners, with his friend's blessing. "Anything else you need, let me know," Thomson said.

Baton had concluded that by far the biggest threat to its application was radio station CFRB, controlled through Standard Broadcasting by the mighty Argus Corp. — which was controlled in turn by E. P. Taylor, Wally McCutcheon, Col. W. Eric Phillips, and Bud McDougald. Here was a force to be reckoned with. "They owned the best radio station in the country. They had prominence and money," Goodman says.

Bassett approached Argus about joining forces, and soon Goodman got a call from Wally McCutcheon, the hard-nosed lawyer of the four Argus partners.

"I understand you guys wanna be our partners," McCutcheon said. Goodman said that this was true, and a secret meeting was arranged at the Royal York Hotel. It proved to be short and to the point.

"Let's get one thing straight," the arrogant McCutcheon began. "In any application my company makes, we are going to have control."

"My instructions are that we are delighted to have you as partners, but *we* gotta have control," Goodman replied. This was true. The equally arrogant Bassett had instructed Goodman to offer McCutcheon 35 per cent of a joint venture in which Baton would hold 45 per cent of the equity and would exercise control through a preferred-share voting arrangement. Goodman tried this on, with predictable results.

"There's no deal," McCutcheon said.

"You're right," Goodman agreed. "There's no deal."

On his way out, McCutcheon remarked that CFRB didn't need partners, because it was going to win. "How could the BBG refuse Argus?" he asked imperiously.

Not long after this discussion, Big John heard from a twenty-six-year-old law student named Ted Rogers, the son of the late Edward Samuel Rogers, who'd invented the batteryless radio and founded CFRB (which stood for Canada's First Rogers Batteryless). "I'm a great believer in the cold call," Rogers remembers, "so I phoned John Bassett. Fortunately, he's my kind of guy. He answers his own phone. I introduced myself and [said I] was interested in the Toronto television licence. He replied: '(a) [I've] never heard of you, and (b) Macy's doesn't talk to Gimbels.'" Nonetheless Rogers convinced Bassett to meet him.

Rogers had been trying to drum up $3 million for his own application, but with little success. He lacked funds, because when his father had died twenty years before, "everything was sold or closed or stolen." His widowed mother married a lawyer named John Graham, whom

Rogers admired and respected. But Ted never forgot what he had lost. Consumed by "bitterness and drive," he was determined to get the family back into communications and thought he saw a way.

Through Graham's law partner, Ted had met Joel Aldred, one of North America's most famous television announcers, known as "the man with the $100,000 voice." Like Big John, Aldred had served in World War II. He was a former squadron leader in the Royal Canadian Air Force and had won the Distinguished Flying Cross. In his spare time, he'd also produced a variety show called *Wings of Rhythm* and studied at London's Royal Conservatory of Music. The war over, he returned home and worked for the CBC, but was fired for criticizing its artsy programming. No problem. Two American networks (CBS and NBC) bid for his services, and he wound up working for both of them, appearing eventually with Bob Hope, Perry Como, and Dinah Shore. These duties kept him busy in New York and Hollywood, but he maintained a connection with Toronto and cultivated his own friendships with influential political figures.

"[Aldred] thought I had money. I thought he had money," Ted Rogers recalls. At least both men had some, and they managed to cobble together $1.5 million, which encouraged them to form their own company, Aldred Rogers Ltd. But they obviously needed a third partner, preferably one with access to the remaining $1.5 million. Having checked out the licence-application situation, Rogers concluded that Baton was the front runner and approached CFRB with a let's-stop-Bassett pitch. But Argus didn't think it needed any help to stop Big John or anybody else and rebuffed Rogers's overtures. So, with nothing to lose, he'd made the call to Bassett.

At their 9:30 meeting the next morning in the *Telegram*'s boardroom, the tall skinny youth told Big John that Aldred Rogers could guarantee the application's success. Neither he nor Aldred had conflicting ownership interests, and would strike the BBG as a happy alternative. "We'll merge for 50/50," he said. "You guys have a hell of a nerve!" Bassett bellowed. "You're suffering from the disease of self-importance. You're going to get 37 per cent." Rogers explains why he and Bassett hit it off: "We're both bullshitters and it takes one to know one."

Meanwhile, Bassett had not been idle, recruiting his friend Foster Hewitt, who'd been broadcasting hockey games from Maple Leaf Gardens since the early 1920s. His trademark phrase "He shoots, he scores" had made him perhaps Canada's best-known voice. Hewitt had been trying to put together his own licence application, but agreed to come in with Bassett for 10 per cent — an interesting pairing, because the two men were polar opposites when it came to spending money. The fifty-two-year-old Hewitt, a canny self-made millionaire, liked to keep a low profile and adopt homespun ways, travelling by Greyhound bus, even as far as Florida.

But Bassett continued to slice the Baton pie. Eddie Goodman had been recommended to him by Charles Dubin, who acted for the Telegram trust. Big John suggested that both lawyers could buy 8 per cent of the newly formed company. Goodman replied, "Well, . . . we gotta pay for it. We're not taking this as fees." Accordingly, he and Dubin formed yet another company called Heathcourt Boulevard Investments Inc. to hold their shares — the first time Goodman had taken a position in a client's firm.

Lastly, in order to make room for the final partner, the very wealthy Paul Nathanson of Sovereign Film Distributors, Bassett had to cut the Telegram trust's interest from 45 per cent to 40 per cent, Aldred Rogers's from 37 per cent to 34 per cent, and Heathcourt Boulevard's from 8 per cent to 6 per cent. Bassett wanted Nathanson in for 10 per cent as well, for two reasons: he had solid expertise in distributing films, and his lawyer, Paul Martin Sr., had been a Cabinet minister in the Liberal government of Louis St. Laurent. This, Bassett believed, would make Baton look slightly less Tory-blue and help deflect the inevitable charges of patronage.

And so, in December 1959, Baton Broadcasting became Baton Aldred Rogers Broadcasting Ltd. Of its 1,000 issued common shares, 400 were held by the Telegram trust; 340 by Aldred Rogers; 100 by Foster Hewitt; 100 by Sovereign Film; and 60 by Heathcourt Boulevard Investments. The Telegram held 51 per cent voting control through the class B preference shares.

Of its roughly $3 million of proposed capital, once the application was approved, Telegram Publishing would invest $1,277,025; Aldred Rogers Ltd. would invest $1,085,240; Foster Hewitt and Sovereign Film would each invest $319,200; and Heathcourt Boulevard would invest a token $590.

Toronto's York Club became the temporary headquarters for the brand new company's board meetings. Big John took the chair as chief executive officer; Joel Aldred was president; Ted Rogers and Foster Hewitt were vice-presidents; Charles Dubin acted as secretary; Delbert Perigoe was treasurer; and the remaining directors — Allan Beattie, John Graham, Paul Nathanson, and Rai Purdy — tried to make their presence known. "It was totally a Bassett deal," Rogers says. "We were lucky to get a word in. But we insisted, and he probably had more dialogue with us than he's ever had in his life."

With the ongoing counsel of Eddie Goodman, the team worked hard on their application. They planned to spend $2 million for the studio, the transmitter, and all the necessary equipment. Another $1 million was allotted for the first year's operating costs. Enclosed with the application (which included detailed blueprints) was a supplementary brief, leather-bound and printed on expensive paper, which featured an artist's renderings of the proposed station and its facilities.

After a literally last-minute glitch (Don Williamson, the engineer, had offered to hand-deliver the application to the Department of Transport in Ottawa, but was delayed, and came racing in an hour before the filing deadline), Baton Aldred Rogers debated the best way to mount their presentation at the hearings. Finally, it was decided that Big John, Eddie Goodman, Joel Aldred, Ted Rogers, Foster Hewitt, Paul Nathanson, and Rai Purdy would all take turns speaking. "My triumph was, I managed to stop either Bassett or Aldred from thinking they could stand up there by themselves," says Goodman. "I wanted the BBG to [see] that our expertise was widespread, not that we had a couple of big shooters."

Before the hearings, Ted Rogers's stepfather, John Graham, insisted on taking the prickly Bassett through some practice question-and-answer sessions, grilling him as would the BBG's counsel. "He was deliberately trying to infuriate Bassett," remarks Rogers, "which wasn't hard." All Graham had to do was put the words "yellow journalism" and "*Telegram*" together in the same sentence, and Bassett would hit the roof. There were other flashpoints, too. For example: "Mr. Bassett, you enjoy partying. Do you think you have the stuff to run a television station? Describe for us again your concept of 'public interest.'" Eventually, Bassett was unfazed by anything Graham threw at him. "We worked until three in the morning," Rogers remembers, with Big John swearing a blue streak all the way.

Meanwhile, Eddie Goodman and Rai Purdy were busy scouting out the licence hearings in Winnipeg, Vancouver, and Montreal, which preceded those in Toronto. They wanted to watch the BBG operate and try to determine how it reached its decisions.

At one point during their travels, Purdy said, "I think we're making a mistake. We should make the presentation through our own medium, closed-circuit television."

Goodman called Bassett and pitched the concept. Big John saw the point at once and said he'd speak to Joel Aldred. "Don't ask him, tell him," Goodman said.

A little while later, Bassett was back on the phone. "He's against it," he reported.

"Tell him to give up his shares," Goodman growled.

Possibly in response to this suggestion, Aldred got behind the idea. He and Purdy hastened to produce a videotape that showed highlights of Baton Aldred Rogers's proposed programming schedule. Bell Telephone laid four and a half miles of coaxial cable to connect thirteen television monitors at Union Station with the Meridian Video Tape Centre in east-end Toronto and hooked everything up for a dry run the night before Baton's pitch. When John Bassett said, "Others have promised, Mr. Chairman, but we want to show you what we have done," Ted Rogers signalled Meridian to roll tape. The rehearsal went perfectly. Nothing, it seemed, could mar the drama of the following day.

The following morning — St. Patrick's Day — found Toronto knee-deep in snow. The streets were gridlocked, and people could barely get into Union Station. When Rogers pushed the button to signal Meridian, he blew a fuse. The Oak Room was plunged into darkness. Bassett sailed on, unscripted, in his usual high-flying elocutionary style: "Mr. Chairman, show business has to deal with unexpected eventualities, and while we had not scheduled this brief interlude, . . . I'm sure we'll get the show back on the road." And so forth. The reporter whose task it was to take down a verbatim transcript pleaded with Big John to stop, because he couldn't see to write. Bassett didn't hesitate, holding the room spellbound with his oratory, dropping occasional one-liners like "This is the kind of thing that separates the men from the boys." He could have talked for days, but fortunately the lights came back on within five minutes.

Eddie Goodman took his place at the podium and treaded water for a while, making asides about leprechauns and the luck of the Irish, until he was certain that the link to Meridian had been re-established. Then (this time successfully) the tape presentation got under way.

It was, for its era, not a bad effort. During the mock newscast, a *Telegram* reporter delivered a timely update on the city's snow-removal plans. The broadcast governors watched a clip of themselves presiding at the Montreal hearings. Then followed brief snippets of cooking demonstrations, children's shows, a proposed hospital drama, a light variety show called *The Goofy Gang*, a barbershop quartet, a jazz band, and a church choir. Foster Hewitt outlined the station's proposed sports programming, which included Toronto Maple Leafs hockey. Big John had learned that the Leafs' president Conn Smythe was furious with the CBC for dropping its broadcasts of the junior Marlboroughs games on Sunday afternoons, so had made a deal to air them — in return for which, CFTO got the rights to the Leafs' Wednesday night home contests.

But it was Big John Bassett's performance during the blackout that

saved the day. "We won, in part, because the show must go on," Ted
Rogers argues. Few people could out-talk Bassett, except in French —
and even there, he held his own. Midway through the presentation, he
broke into his second language to tell the board what Baton Aldred
Rogers would provide (one dubbed program, but it was a start) for its
francophone audience.

So far, so good, but a major obstacle remained: the BBG's antipathy
towards the concentrated ownership of mass communication outlets.
This had been made plain during the two previous licence hearings
(described in the next chapter). In particular, as Andrew Stewart had intimated to Roy Thomson, the board was opposed to granting a new licence
to an individual who already had one. Foster Hewitt, for example, had
a 10 per cent interest in the Toronto radio station CKFH (F for Foster
and H for Hewitt). Bassett argued that this wasn't a problem, since
Hewitt was only a minority shareholder in Baton Aldred Rogers. He and
his partners were aware of the board's concerns, he said, but the need
remained for men of "practical experience."

Hewitt seemed likely to squeak by under the wire. A greater problem
was Paul Nathanson's recent acquisition (unknown to Eddie Goodman)
of a 25 per cent interest in CHCH Hamilton, a CBC affiliate controlled
by none other than Goodman's uncle, Ken Soble. Upon learning of this
investment, Goodman was, in his words, "plenty pissed off." Worse still,
Nathanson also owned 10 per cent of yet another station in Windsor,
Ontario, so Bassett had a harder time arguing that to grant his group the
Toronto licence wouldn't pile privilege upon privilege.

Of course, Bassett had troubles of his own. The *Telegram* had no radio
or television interests, but the board's earlier decisions had showed that it
wanted to keep things that way. Big John decided to tackle this one head-
on. He correctly described Toronto as one of the most competitive
media markets in North America, with three daily newspapers, six radio
stations, two CBC television stations (one local and the other down the
road in Hamilton), and three American television stations beaming in
from across the border in Buffalo. Any new private television enterprise
would need all the help it could get, especially when it came to newscasts. Fortunately, the *Telegram* could provide much needed support in
this regard. And, he added, its participation would "ensure that the same
principles of public service which apply to that newspaper will apply to
the operation of this television station."

A week later, when the BBG recommended that Baton Aldred Rogers
be granted the Toronto licence, many observers complained that the board
had gone back on its word, but there was little dispute over the merits of

the application. The minority of board members who opposed it, among them Andrew Stewart, objected because they wanted to keep newspaper publishers well away from television stations, not because they felt that Bassett and Company wouldn't be up to the job. (In all the BBG's judgements, by the way, the majority ruled, and Stewart's vote as chairman carried no extra weight.)

"It was a terrific application. We were never ranked less than second by our competitors," says Ted Rogers. "Naturally, they put themselves first, but they put us second." Eddie Goodman recalls similar reactions: "Three or four applicants came [up] and said, 'Great application, it's me or you.'" Other than that, he utterly discounts any suggestion of a political payoff, noting that several other applicants had friends in high places: "The trouble with most people, *especially* lawyers, is that they think you can get something simply because of connections." He has a point. Joseph Sedgwick was a prominent Conservative, and Argus Corp. was no stranger to the corridors of power, but that didn't help them in their attempts to gain the licence.

☆

Now that the licence was more or less in the bag, Joel Aldred had big plans for the new station, starting with a clean sheet of paper — or, more accurately, an empty field. He'd been sketching out designs for years, taking the best elements from all the facilities he'd worked in, particularly NBC's and ABC's studios in Burbank, California. At the hearings, he showed slides of an artist's conception of a split-level station with 100,000 square feet of space. Its five studios would be filled, if he had his way, with state-of-the-broadcast-art equipment.

In June, Aldred signed a contract with RCA Victor for almost $3 million, more than a third of which went towards the purchase of colour cameras and transmitters. To many observers, it seemed like madness to spend $1.3 million setting up as a colour production centre. At this time, colour transmission wasn't allowed in Canada (and wouldn't be approved until 1966), thanks in part to chronic heel-dragging on the part of the CBC, which said it couldn't afford the conversion costs. While Aldred lobbied the BBG to lift its colour ban, he had to content himself with the thought of producing commercials and programs for use in the United States, where colour had been available since the late 1950s. But Aldred's remarkable foresight would pay off in the end and enable CFTO to be the first Canadian television station to break the black-and-white barrier.

Another of Aldred's innovations was to create a separate production company to develop programs that the station could exchange with or sell to other Canadian outlets, and (if possible) market in the United States and abroad. Bassett supported the idea. While flying over Buffalo, New York, he'd noticed an almost total absence of rooftop antennas. But during descent to the Toronto airport, he'd counted so many he described them as a sea, and they were all pointed to the south. This, of course, was at a time when no one had cable service. What Bassett saw meant that Buffalo residents were watching American channels only, which they could receive by means of rabbit's-ears antennas attached to their sets. They had no desire to watch the CBC, so had no need of a contraption on the roof. Torontonians did, because they were happily tuned in to the U.S. stations. Big John decided that CFTO could win "The Battle of Buffalo" only by developing Canadian programming that was "at least competitive with some of the American programming that [was] pouring in to us." If those home-grown programs could wean a Toronto audience from American fare, they'd be good enough to sell south of the border. If Aldred could produce them, Paul Nathanson could distribute and sell them, through his company Sovereign Film and his interest in Screen Gems.

This prospect excited Aldred, who continued to spend lavishly on outfitting the new facility. By his telling, industry peers were bowled over by CFTO's out-of-the-gate capabilities. "By gosh," he says, "the guys [from] Buffalo nearly dropped dead when they [came] up to take a look."

Somehow, Aldred and his team got the building up and CFTO on the air in just a little over six months. Their target was January 1, 1961, and they made it — but barely — because the equipment they'd expected from RCA Victor didn't show up. When it did, it didn't work, so they had to borrow some from the Ryerson Institute of Technology. But this time, when they pushed the button, no fuse blew.

"I was so proud in the morning when we stood there and John opened the station," recalls Ted Rogers. "[My sister] and the Eaton family were there. We all looked an awful lot younger [then]."

CFTO kicked off its programming with an eighteen-hour telethon for developmentally handicapped children on New Year's Day, 1961. John David Eaton's second-born son, Fred, remembers watching the broadcast with his "Uncle John" and Moira Bassett at his parents' country estate. "My father went to the ribbon-cutting, then he came back and we watched the thing. It was twelve hours, . . . maybe twenty-four hours long. I'm sure I didn't watch all of it," he says. (Fred was to be forgiven for losing track of the time. He was home for Christmas and New Year's from the University of New Brunswick in Fredericton, where he'd elected to pursue his studies because that province had accepted his Grade 12 marks for university entrance. The young scion had partied so hard during his final year at Toronto's Upper Canada College that he'd failed to complete Grade 13.)

So CFTO was on the air, confounding critics who'd called it the Great White Elephant of Agincourt. It looked imposing, but a trifle forlorn — a massive red-brick complex rising out of the underdeveloped countryside, with its 925-foot-high transmitter tower and acres of parking lots, all surrounded by an eight-foot-high chain-link fence. The BBG had wondered aloud whether it might be too remote for performers used to working in the downtown core. "Mr. Aldred will be there," quipped Bassett, and so he was. But Big John preferred to remain in his office at the *Telegram*, leaving Aldred to enjoy a free hand north of the 401. This isolation would soon prove more costly than could be imagined.

Nonetheless, as Aldred had maintained, the station was miles ahead of the competition, public or private. During the Toronto hearings, Bassett admitted that he and his partners envisioned an exchange of videotapes among (and possibly a future association of) independent stations that would "ultimately lead to the creation in Canada of a second network, of which we see the Toronto station as the anchor." Not only did Toronto have the best facilities, Bassett argued, it had the greatest pool of performing and writing talent. He conceded that his Montreal friends might not agree with him, and then had the wit to skirt the network issue. The time was not yet ripe for on-the-record discussion or in-depth BBG interrogation. But well before the Toronto hearings began, Baton Aldred Rogers had quietly contacted the two competing applicants in Montreal, as well as the successful applicants in Winnipeg and Vancouver, along with several privately owned CBC affiliates, with a view to forming what they called a "cooperative group." Bassett admitted that such an arrangement would be "very desirable both from the point of view of cost, [and] from the point of view of Canadian content programming." Out of these tentative overtures, the Independent Television Organization would be born.

The Independent Television Organization versus Spence Caldwell — 1960

The mad scramble for private television licences had brought out the country's business who's who at every stop. More than thirty-five applications would eventually be heard, as the BBG's trans-Canada roadshow moved from Winnipeg and Vancouver in January, to Montreal and Toronto in March, to Edmonton and Calgary in April, and to Halifax and Ottawa in June.

The first stop was the Fort Garry Hotel in Winnipeg. The first applicants were Ralph Misener, a member of the wealthy Ontario shipping family and part-owner of the Winnipeg Blue Bombers football franchise, and his partner, Lloyd Moffat, the owner of CKY, a local radio station. Moffat had come a long way from Prince Albert, Saskatchewan, where he'd started out three decades earlier as a movie projectionist. This proposed expansion into television marked the real beginnings of the Moffat communications empire.

The independent Misener-Moffat group's main competitor was a consortium led by Clifford Sifton of Armadale Communications Ltd. (which owned one television station, two newspapers, and three radio outlets, split among Saskatchewan, Manitoba, and Ontario) and his brother Victor Sifton, who owned the *Winnipeg Free Press*. They were supported by several prominent members of the Winnipeg establishment, including

James and Kathleen Richardson. The BBG listened politely to all concerned and reserved its decision for a week or so.

The board's next destination was Vancouver's Hotel Georgia, where the first of five applicants vying for the second-station licence was Metropolitan Television, led by the forty-three-year-old Frank Griffiths, who had risen from humble beginnings. His father had emigrated from England to the Vancouver suburb of Burnaby and become a chartered accountant. An only child, Frank attended local public schools before following his father's career path. Indeed, he joined his father's firm and proved instrumental in facilitating its expansion.

Frank's great enthusiasm throughout his teenage years was power boating. He'd save his money and bolt outboard motors on whatever makeshift craft he could afford. He attempted to enlist in the navy during World War II, but was rejected because of poor eyesight, so he had to be content with helping Griffiths & Griffiths take advantage of a booming wartime economy. To maintain a high profile, he joined the Vancouver Club (the city's premier gathering place) and the famously difficult-to-infiltrate Capilano Golf Club. Here, in 1948, he met the avid yachtsman and pet food mogul Dr. W. R. Ballard, who was about to launch his latest toy, a refurbished naval vessel. Frank was invited to the party, where he bumped into Ballard's daughter Emily. Mistaking him for a gate-crasher, she tried to have him thrown out. Once she realized that Griffiths had a craft of his own moored nearby, she needled her father into taking her there the following weekend, so that she and Frank could meet again by accident. ("He chased me until I caught him," she later told Dr. Reginald Roy, the author of an unpublished biography of Griffiths.) They married a year later, living aboard Frank's boat until their house was built in the wealthy British Properties subdivision of West Vancouver. Their first son, Frank Jr., was born in 1950.

"Frank, as an accountant, was doing fairly well," explains Dr. Roy. "But he was not a wealthy man until he married a woman who [had] a lot of family money." Griffiths & Griffiths prospered during the post-war years, opening numerous satellite offices throughout the Lower Mainland before merging with Thorne & Riddell. Frank became the managing partner of its Vancouver office in the early 1950s and continued to demonstrate the skills he'd honed in partnership with his father. Even as a young man, he'd acted as a rainmaker, incorporating several companies for his clients, and was adept at obtaining advantageous financing and spotting opportunities in the marketplace.

Griffiths's first entrepreneurial adventure outside the accounting firm was his 1953 investment in Vancouver's first Mercedes-Benz dealership.

Although he later sold out his interest, he continued to drive the cars. His next flyer was buying shares in Queen Charlotte Airlines. When he sold out in 1955, he pocketed a $32,000 capital gain, the first he'd ever made, and began to turn his thoughts to broadcasting.

Griffiths's first acquisition was CKNW, a radio station in the Vancouver suburb of New Westminster. Its signal was so weak that if the wind in the Fraser Valley was blowing the wrong way, you couldn't tune it in. Nevertheless, a pair of local businessmen had hired Frank to examine the finances of its owner, the International Broadcasting Co.

"When Frank looked at the books, his eyes popped," his biographer says. "It was a cash cow." Frank's clients were getting nowhere in their attempts to acquire it, so Griffiths asked them if he could organize a bid of his own. They agreed, but Griffiths was short of funds, so he brought in two friends for a third of the $850,000 purchase price. The remaining two-thirds was raised by him, his wife, Emily, and her two sisters. They formed a new company called Inglewood Investments, owned 25 per cent by Frank, 25 per cent by Emily, and 50 per cent by her siblings. (Emily and her sisters later fell out and didn't speak for years, because Frank kept ploughing their dividends back into the media business.)

Emily approached her father for a loan, but Dr. Ballard refused. Instead, he offered to guarantee a bank loan, which the couple obtained by dropping his well-known name. They also mortgaged their home, boat, and car. "We didn't own anything at that point," Griffiths told his biographer. "It was a tremendous risk and a tremendous opportunity."

The bid succeeded, and Frank was proved right about CKNW's potential. In short order, he was able to buy out his friends' one-third share and pay down the bank loan to boot. Griffiths therefore felt entitled to claim CKNW as a personal success — but Emily never let him forget that her father's reputation was pivotal in its purchase. From then on, whenever broadcasting decisions were made, she expected an equal say. (This rankled Griffiths, who took pains to tell his biographer that Ballard's money had *not* financed his start in the business, as many people believed.)

In 1957, Griffiths formed Metropolitan Television, preparatory to bidding for the Vancouver private licence. Again, Emily and her two sisters bought shares. Together the four of them owned almost one-quarter of Metropolitan, with Frank holding the biggest single interest, roughly 10 per cent. Other members of the Griffiths group included the publisher of *The Province* (a Southam Co. publication), the assistant publisher of the *Sun*, the general manager of CKNW, and his counterpart at CKWX, a long-established rival station.

"All 100 per cent Canadian content," quipped Griffiths, who considered the combined media experience of his team an asset. Whether the BBG would view it in this light remained to be seen. At the hearings, he presented a formidable $1.4-million application, including a scale model of the proposed studio and transmitter, to be built atop Burnaby Mountain. From there, he claimed, the signal would reach one-fifth of Vancouver's population.

During his pitch, Griffiths struck a patriotic note: "We are young Canadians," he said, "with the imagination and expanding spirit of the west. Our programming is directed at encouraging and developing a national Canadian consciousness." He emphasized that Metropolitan was "interested in the long-term future of Canada, . . . not in short-term profit" and promised that its news operation would be "entirely divorced" from the owners' newspapers and radio stations.

Intervenors took issue with this arm's-length posture, pointing out that Griffiths and his partners represented exactly the kind of chain media ownership that the BBG ought to discourage. The provincial branch of the Retail Merchants of Canada warned that Metropolitan could bring pressure to bear, forcing advertisers to buy into print, radio, and television by refusing to accept their ads in any single medium. The British Columbia Federation of Labour had its own axe to grind. It said that, if Metropolitan received a licence, the dissemination of news would fall under what it called a monopolistic control. It noted glumly that, while Vancouverites might see two newspapers for sale, there was in fact only one: "*The Province* is simply a morning edition of the *Sun*." In labour's view, an even wider monopoly "would be dangerous and unrealistic. Such a group would be in a position to condition the public to the opinions and views of editorial writers who have over the years demonstrated a marked hostility to labour."

And so forth. B.C. Labour reserved its greatest ire for Metropolitan, but opposed all five private applications on similar grounds. It felt instead that the CBC should be granted a second licence to operate yet another station in Vancouver. This clearly was not the mandate the BBG had been handed by Diefenbaker. It thanked the various intervenors and turned to the next applicant.

On the second day of the hearings, Vantel Broadcasting, in the person of a young man named Art Jones, presented what would prove to be the winning application. Jones, a University of British Columbia science graduate, had worked for the *Sun* as a news photographer, and later formed Artray Film Productions Ltd., which dealt in television programs and commercials. Although an artistic success, Jones was virtually unknown among Vancouver's high-powered business community. The unpretentious thirty-four-year-old drove an American convertible, not the requisite Mercedes. But here he was, with $2.6 million in backing for his venture, identified by its as-yet-unassigned call letters CHAN.

CHAN had been conceived the previous May, when a New Westminster militia commander named Col. Edward Eakins, whose wife was friendly with Jones's wife, started talking about erecting a television transmitter atop Artray's studios in downtown Vancouver. Next, Mrs. Eakins approached her cousin, Peter Paul Saunders, the president of Imperial Investments, about raising money for a second-station licence application. Saunders was agreeable and contacted a number of potential investors who eventually came up with the funds.

By the time Vantel's three-inch-thick brief was handed to the Board of Broadcast Governors, Jones's group had enlarged its plans. It proposed to spend more money than any other applicant (nearly double the sum mentioned by Griffiths and his partners) to build state-of-the-art studios and offices out near the Vancouver-Burnaby boundary line and to erect a transmitter on Burnaby Mountain.

Jones treated the BBG to a thirty-minute feature film demonstrating the types of programs Vantel would air. He stated that Vantel would concentrate on local and regional subjects, aim to foster home-grown talent, and recapture the Canadian advertising dollars that were flowing south to KVOS in Bellingham, Washington. To achieve the final goal, he proposed a rate structure that was considerably lower than that of KVOS — or, for that matter, the rates charged by Vancouver's CBC television outlet.

Jones made much of the fact that Vantel's owners were not embroiled in other media, with three exceptions: he owned Artray Productions, and two other directors had minor interests in a New Westminster radio station and a television series that was about to start filming that year. This went down well with a majority of the board members — except for Eugene Forsey and Edward Dunlop (George Hees's brother-in-law). They voted against Vantel's application, fearing that Jones had neither the financial strength nor the ability to "make good."

But the deciding factor was Vantel's no-strings status. Ten days later, when the BBG announced its recommendations, it said it had taken into consideration the losing applicants' associations with other media. Misener and Moffat in Winnipeg, and Vantel in Vancouver, came out the winners. Plainly, the Southam-Sifton and Griffiths groups' links with newspapers and radio stations had killed their chances. The Siftons' support of the Liberal party probably hadn't advanced their cause, either —

but the board's political bent, if one existed, failed to reward either Frank Griffiths's group or Pacific Television, yet another Vancouver applicant that, like Griffiths's Metropolitan Television, was packed with well-known Tories.

☆

In March, however, at the Queen Elizabeth Hotel in Montreal, the BBG faced a choice between two of the city's radio station operators for the new English-language television licence. (A second round of hearings would deal with CFTM, the French-language independent.)

Canadian Marconi, the winning applicant, was an honoured veteran. Its forty-year-old outlet, CFCF, had been the first regularly operated broadcasting station in the world. Canadian Marconi's president Stuart Finlayson informed the board that he and his two partners were "very antique," with combined experience totalling ninety-eight and one-half years. He hoped, though, that "antiquity does not denote either senility or any other frailties of old age." Besides, experience counted for something: Marconi's parent, the English Electric Co., had been in the radio business since 1902. Finlayson said his firm had no partners in its $4.5-million application, which (as explained by station manager Dick Misener — no relation to Winnipeg's Ralph Misener) involved building new studio facilities on land they'd optioned in the Park of Jean Talon area. However, Vic George, the station's general manager, told the board that they'd already opened discussions with the Winnipeg and Vancouver licensees in attempts to initiate and develop an exchange of taped and filmed programs.

The unsuccessful Montreal applicant, the Mount Royal Independent Co., lost out for a variety of reasons. It was partly owned by the notoriously eccentric Newfoundland broadcaster Geoff Stirling, who also operated Montreal's newest radio station, CKGM. Stirling's partner was Don Jamieson, a well-known journalist. Together, they'd used their Liberal connections (including Jack Pickersgill, Louis St. Laurent's secretary of state) to obtain a licence for CJON, Newfoundland's first CBC television affiliate, which opened in 1955.

Granting Stirling the Montreal television licence would probably have qualified as piling "privilege upon privilege," but Finlay MacDonald was nonetheless surprised when Stirling was turned down. He was, MacDonald says, "absolutely shameless at working the BBG." For example, Stirling used to fly his wife and children to Prince Albert, Saskatchewan, as many as three times a year, so as to have their teeth fixed by one of the broadcast governors, a woman named Dr. Mabel Connell, who also happened to be John Diefenbaker's family dentist. Once, Don Jamieson found himself sitting next to Dr. Connell aboard an airplane. She opened her purse and showed him snapshots of Stirling's well-polished progeny. Meanwhile, in Toronto, another BBG member, a Baptist minister named the Reverend Emlyn Davies, would sometimes look up from his sermon to find Stirling sitting in the front pew of his church. Back in the Maritimes, Stirling established a journalism prize in the name of yet another member, the Sydney newspaper owner Roy Duchemin. "Geoff Stirling is a character, a rogue. He got in all kinds of trouble," Finlay MacDonald says with affection.

Stirling definitely had plenty of trouble with the BBG in Montreal that March. First, the governors wondered whether Don Jamieson could conceivably commute from St. John's, to act (as had been promised) as programming consultant. Stirling assured them that Jamieson would be in the air so much that his arms would be tired. Next, and more seriously, the board expressed concern that Mount Royal's bid demonstrated an inadequate financial structure. This may have revealed the members' lack of knowledge when it came to the dollars-and-cents business of television. Canadian Marconi's revenue projection for their proposed station, for example, was more than two times higher than Mount Royal's, but the board took that figure at face value. Stirling stood his ground. "I would say that I am definitely very conservative, and I would say [also that others] are maybe extremely optimistic about the number of viewers they are going to have the minute they go on the air," he defended himself. Events would prove that he had a valid point.

For the sheer volume of characters, nothing could match the Toronto licence hearings, where, before capacity crowds, the BBG heard from nine different groups over the course of six days in March. Bassett triumphed, as we know, but he had plenty of competition.

The *Toronto Daily Star*'s Beland Honderich led off the festivities. He was the first of five applicants with extensive publishing interests. The others were Baton Aldred Rogers Broadcasting; Maclean Hunter Publishing; the *Globe and Mail* in association with the J. Arthur Rank film company; and a Southam newspaper–backed group led by Henry Borden, a nephew of the former prime minister, Robert Laird Borden.

Following Honderich in the line-up on March 15 was Spence Caldwell, a fifty-year-old "super-salesman" and former CBC executive, who'd begun life as a radio engineer. A self-made millionaire, he currently headed up his own firm, which had numerous involvements with the television and film industries. Caldwell had decided against a flashy closed-circuit presentation, like the one mounted later by Baton Aldred Rogers. He remarked that his group had the facilities and experience to stage anything it wanted to, but had opted instead for a short and simple pitch. He then launched into a tedious recitation, reeling off the names and positions of his ninety-five investors, as if to overwhelm the board with the importance of the people who'd chosen to back him. At least Caldwell didn't read his entire list. "I'll stop here in the interests of conserving the board's time," he said, about two-thirds of the way through. "I hope that the [others] who are equally prominent in business and our community will understand why they were not read into the record."

To illustrate his $4.4-million application, he displayed slides showing architectural drawings of a six-storey building he proposed to erect on Jarvis Street, just north of the existing CBC headquarters. Caldwell's group felt confident that they could strike a deal with the CBC, paying to share its transmission tower. When the CBC moved to new premises, as was expected to happen in four or five years, Caldwell hoped to take over that tower and quite likely some of their studio facilities.

Caldwell's ex-CBC boss and old friend Ernie Bushnell had spent twenty-five years with the public corporation until his resignation three months earlier. Now he appeared at Caldwell's side as a consultant. This was a familiar role for Bushnell, but his track record was nothing to write home about. Earlier, he'd advised both the unsuccessful Southam-Sifton application in Winnipeg and the failed Pacific Television application in Vancouver, charging each group $3,000 for his services.

Rounding out Caldwell's team was his second-in-command, Gordon Keeble, a former CBC announcer who'd once managed radio station CFCF in Montreal. If the application proved successful, Keeble would take charge of production at the new Toronto station.

Thus, CBC alumni were well represented in the Caldwell group, which wore its independence on its sleeve. It too had been in touch with the Winnipeg and Vancouver licensees about a possible videotape exchange, but otherwise Caldwell stressed that the successful licensee should be free of any connection with other mass media. "We have heard today of the largest radio station in Canada, . . . the largest magazine publishing company — the largest everything," he cried. "Even the richest man in Canada [John David Eaton] is involved. Surely they have enough! Is it not time that somebody else had a chance? Isn't it our turn now at success?"

The following morning, Stuart Griffiths appeared on behalf of the next applicant, Upper Canada Broadcasting. Griffiths — no relation to Frank Griffiths of Vancouver — had been a television executive for sixteen years, first as program director of the CBC, and most recently as program controller of Britain's Granada television network, Upper Canada's majority shareholder. He was described as so full of energy that he "bounced like India rubber when he walked." But Griffiths was merely the emcee of Upper Canada's show. Wayne and Shuster were the personalities the crowd had come to see.

For thirty years, Johnny Wayne and Frank Shuster had served as Canada's comedic ambassadors to Britain and the United States, where they set a record of sixty-seven appearances on *The Ed Sullivan Show*. Although firmly associated with the CBC, they had a minor stake in Upper Canada, for which they prophesied a bright future.

Wayne began by recalling the duo's classic Shakespearean baseball sketch: "When we decided to take it down to the U.S., I was approached by a number of intelligent Canadians, who said, 'You are not going to throw that stuff at them down there — they will never get it!' [But] we took a gamble, . . . and afterwards our American friends came to us and said, 'You mean to say those idiots up there understand this?'"

"I saw the show and I understood it," Andrew Stewart volunteered in his dry Scottish burr.

Wayne went on to declare that his and Shuster's job would be to discover and develop Canadian talent in the "field of light entertainment and variety" — because these genres attracted the largest audience. "Where is this Canadian talent coming from?" he asked. "It is coming from all over the place. My parents could not afford to send me through burlesque, [so] I had to go to university." And so on, which at least brightened the BBG's day.

Wayne and Shuster were a hard act to follow, even for the veteran broadcaster Jack Kent Cooke. Cooke had a reputation for breathing fire and brimstone on anyone at his radio station CKEY who didn't measure up 100 per cent of the time. The Consolidated Frybrook Industries' application, named after his holding company, was strictly a one-man affair. As Consolidated Frybrook's sole owner, Cooke stated that he would also be solely responsible for the new television station if the licence was granted. Broadcast governor Emlyn Davies asked him what provisions he'd made for operations to continue in the event of his death. Cooke replied, without visible humour, that "I come from an almost indestructible line and I have no intention of dying within the next twelve months."

As they had done with Geoff Stirling in Montreal, the BBG questioned Cooke about his pessimistic revenue projections. In a prescient warning, he replied that Robbie Burns's line "The best laid schemes o' mice and men gang aft a-gley" might very well apply to the other applicants' hopes for early-blooming profits.

On March 17, Big John Bassett's Baton Aldred Rogers presented their winning application. Bassett's victory must have infuriated Cooke, who'd lost out to him on many previous occasions, most recently in the battle to control the Toronto Argonauts. (His television schemes having ganged a-gley, Cooke left Toronto and achieved fame and fortune in the United States, as the billionaire owner of the Los Angeles *Daily News* and the Washington Redskins football franchise.)

Their presentation over, the Baton Aldred Rogers team had to cool their heels for two days, waiting to see how their major competitor would perform. The Argus-controlled group were making their application through radio station CFRB's Rogers Radio Broadcasting, a company named after Ted Rogers's father. What they really needed, however, was Ted Rogers's stepfather John Graham to prepare them for their grilling by the BBG lawyer, as he had done with Big John Bassett.

At one point, the lawyer not unnaturally wanted to know who constituted Argus Corp.

"Argus is owned by more than 400,000 shareholders," Wally McCutcheon said. "Seventy-six per cent of the shares are held by Canadians."

The BBG lawyer insisted on knowing who held control.

"No group that I know has a majority of stock," McCutcheon replied.

"But who holds effective control?" the lawyer persisted.

"There is a group that holds less than 30 per cent of the stock," admitted McCutcheon.

"But who exercises effective control over Argus?" the lawyer repeated.

"I will give you the names if the chairman considers it appropriate that I do," McCutcheon answered.

Andrew Stewart indicated that he did, and McCutcheon identified four men — E. P. Taylor, Col. W. Eric Phillips, Bud McDougald, and himself.

The BBG lawyer said it was evident, then, that with its own 49.5 per cent holding of Standard Radio and CFRB, the Argus Corp. and the four men named could exercise control over CFRB in combination with any other shareholder.

"I always regarded 49.5 per cent as effective control," McCutcheon said, eliciting a laugh that eased some of the tension.

But the damage had been done. McCutcheon's reluctance to (as he put it) "publish . . . one's domestic affairs" had made the four men's public identification with the Argus Corp. and the group's holdings in Standard Radio and CFRB seem both mysterious and ominous.

"There's no overall Argus Corp. policy," McCutcheon said later. "It's not a spider sitting in the middle of a web." But that's exactly the impression he had created. Eddie Goodman, who was sitting in the audience with Foster Hewitt, remembers turning to him with a big smile and saying, "Foster, we've just won the application."

That weekend, the board members began sifting through the submissions and shaping their decision. A rebuttal session on Monday morning apparently added nothing new to the applicants' cases. The board met again in camera on Monday afternoon and on Tuesday, March 22, recommended that Canadian Marconi be granted the English-language Montreal licence and Baton Aldred Rogers receive the Toronto licence.

The speed of this announcement surprised many observers, who hadn't expected a decision to be forthcoming for another two weeks. It also surprised and disheartened Spence Caldwell — but only briefly. As Caldwell later recalled for Bassett's biographer, Maggie Siggins, at his moment of deep despair, "I said to myself, 'Wait a minute! How are these stations going to exist if they are not tied together? Can you imagine a station in Vancouver or Halifax running news film which had been sent from New York and processed in Toronto, broadcasting a hot news story three days after every other station had it on?' I phoned Gordon Keeble and told him to get a good night's sleep, because tomorrow we were applying for the network."

Twenty days later, in mid-April 1960, Spence Caldwell did exactly that, pitching the first independent or second-station network proposal to the Board of Broadcast Governors. He said he planned to form a company in which 51 per cent of the shares would be sold to the same group of Bay Street investors who'd backed his own station licence application. Only 49 per cent would be made available to the licensees. This, as Finlay MacDonald remembers, seemed "all back-asswards." For one thing, the station licence hearings were still ongoing. Only four decisions had been made, so Caldwell had no idea who the rest of the recipients would be, let alone whether they'd want to sign up for any network he might devise.

Unfortunately for John Bassett, Andrew Stewart saw merit in Caldwell's proposal. Stewart believed that Baton's CFTO, simply by virtue of the fact that it was in Toronto, would come to dominate any private network. He didn't like the prospect — and over time, he'd do everything he could to support Caldwell.

In early May, the BBG began to edge up on the inevitability of some kind of network. It issued a press release, which noted that an exchange of videotaped programs between the new television licensees, as had been discussed, didn't constitute a network. Instead, the board suggested linking the new stations as soon as possible, by means of microwave transmission. It promised to address this point and others in a further statement the following month, which would set out a number of general conditions that a private television network would have to meet. Then the board would hear full-scale network applications in September.

But Big John jumped the gun, requesting a meeting with the BBG at the end of May. On behalf of the Winnipeg, Vancouver, Montreal, and Toronto licensees, he informed the board that the new stations would probably be making an application in the fall. Preliminary discussions suggested that the four would set up a mutual company, a cooperative, in which they — not outside investors — would hold all the shares. Then they would bring in a management group to operate the network on a fee basis, reporting to the cooperative's board. Bassett argued that any new network, even a Spence Caldwell network, would probably have to avail itself of CFTO's facilities. Programs had to be produced some-where, and Toronto was the logical place, for all sorts of reasons. It would be too expensive to set up a new and separate facility, just to dis-tribute programming to the affiliated stations.

There was a certain logic to that position — but the board didn't pursue the point. Instead, they objected to the whole concept of a sta-tion-owned network. CFTO, in their view, would be bound to seize control of it. So, lo and behold, when the BBG announced its twelve general conditions, one of them was that the stock held by a minimum of six, geographically dispersed stations in the network company should not exceed 49 per cent of the voting stock authorized. Outside investors would hold the controlling 51 per cent. In other words, the board was issuing as policy Spence Caldwell's proposal. Additionally, the board said, the network company would have to provide proof that it could link these stations by microwave for a minimum amount of time per week, and that the mandatory affiliation agreements between the network and its stations would specify a certain number of hours per week reserved for programming provided by that network company.

☆

But all these comings and goings were premature, because the BBG still had four cities to go in its trans-Canada roadshow. In May, the governors headed for Edmonton, to confront a unique situation. Here they awarded the new licence to the CBC, which had decided that it wanted to own an outlet, rather than continue to operate through its long-standing affiliate CFRN, controlled by Dick Rice of Sunwapta Broadcasting. The fifty-five-year-old Rice was a radio pioneer who'd worked his way through AM and FM radio stations into television. Now that the CBC had forced disaffiliation upon him, he'd have to try his luck in the private sector and would surface as an independent, still in possession of a valid licence, at the first meetings of the second-station owners later that year.

Next, in Calgary, yet another radio pioneer, Gordon Love, aged seventy-one, assisted by his sons James and William and his son-in-law, Gordon Carter, handily defeated a group of oil tycoons in the contest for the new television licence. Thirty-two years earlier, Love had bought control and become president of radio station CFCN, "The Voice of the Prairies." At that time, it was one of the most powerful stations on the continent, with a signal that could be received as far south as San Francisco and as far north as the Yukon. In 1954, CFCN and two rival radio stations joined to establish the company that obtained Calgary's first television licence. Love was elected president of the resulting CBC affiliate, but sold out two years later, and in 1960 formed CFCN, which became the seventh recipient of a second-station licence.

By June, the governors were on the east coast, setting up shop in the Lord Nelson Hotel in Halifax, to listen to their thirtieth application. At least, that's what the young Finlay MacDonald calculated the number to be. The prematurely grey MacDonald, who otherwise looked startlingly like the actor Jimmy Stewart, had started off as a radio announcer after studying law and journalism at St. Francis Xavier and Dalhousie universities. He served in the Canadian Army during World War II, then joined the staff of the newly opened CJCH Halifax and was soon its manager, rising to the position of president. MacDonald also became president of the Canadian Association of Broadcasters, a lobby group composed of private radio, television, and (later) cable operators. In 1958, the Tory activist was commissioned by his Nova Scotian friend, the Minister of Revenue, George Nowlan, who was Diefenbaker's man responsible for the CBC, to conduct a sweeping study of Canadian broadcasting. This study led to the new Broadcasting Act, which had set the second-station wheels in motion.

Initially, MacDonald had supported the idea of a separate regulatory board, but changed his mind. Rather than recommend disbanding the CBC's Board of Governors, he instead suggested that it continue, but with diminished powers over the private sector. Nowlan shared these views, but met with opposition in Cabinet from George Hees, who'd been listening to the hopes and dreams of his friends John Bassett and John David Eaton. Now MacDonald found himself following in their footsteps, pitching a second-station application on behalf of CJCH.

First, he had to overcome false allegations on the part of a local labour leader, who was convinced that a labour-bashing car wash owner named McCurdy was the real power behind CJCH Ltd. The reason? McCurdy was said to have a fancy office at the radio station. The smooth-talking MacDonald burned up a fair amount of his allotted rebuttal time refuting this notion. "To begin with," he said, "I would like to . . . state categorically that I am not now, nor have I ever been, a member of the Halifax Auto Car Wash in any [shape or] capacity. . . . I am a little hurt, because Mr. McCurdy has not the fanciest office in the station. *I* have, and I extend a cordial invitation to [the labour leader] to come up and visit us anytime, and I will give him a complete tour of our plant and tell him anything he wishes to know." After a good deal more along these lines, MacDonald won the bid, primarily because the other applicant lacked adequate financing.

A few days later, the BBG held court in the hot and steamy Diocesan Hall of the Charities Establishment in Ottawa, where the trans-Canada hearings came to an end in late June, as Ernie Bushnell and Stu Griffiths (last seen supporting separate applications at the Toronto hearings), teamed up to win the city's first private television licence.

"I spent the first sixteen years of my career being cursed, kicked, and cuffed by Ernest Bushnell," said Griffiths, "and despite the bruises, I love him still. Most of the people [who've] worked with him do, and that is pretty rare in broadcasting, so when the opportunity occurred for Granada to join with him in this application it was very easy for me to recommend that we do so."

"I don't think I can agree with everything you said about me," Bushnell replied. "I am a reformed character."

Actually, "Mister Broadcasting" was a reformed drinker, who'd risen through the CBC ranks to become vice-president of English-language programming. In 1959, he was appointed acting president for six months. The stress pushed him over the edge and he was often seen falling-down-drunk in public. In June of that year, the CBC board decided that he should be pensioned off and asked him to take a two-month leave of absence. The CBC's austere president, Alphonse Ouimet, who'd been recovering from a heart attack and a gall bladder operation, returned to work in August and set about hiring a whole raft of new vice-presidents. This effectively demoted Bushnell, who returned from his leave to find himself barred from the board meeting that had been called to approve the changes. He handed in his resignation, sobered up, and formed his own management consulting company.

In fact, Bushnell was long overdue for a move into private television. He'd never really fit the CBC culture. He loved entertainment shows and had little interest in serious information programs. Knowlton Nash, in his book *The Microphone Wars*, calls Bushnell "a lovable, infuriating old rascal" who feared his epitaph would be that he'd invented the singing commercial. (He was a gifted jingles writer and — before joining the sober-sided corporation — had established Canada's first radio-advertising agency.)

At the hearings, the sixty-year-old Bushnell promised to provide Ottawa with a "people's station" that would spend 18.4 per cent of its gross income on program talent. He himself would become its general manager. To ensure that control remained in local hands, a voting trust agreed to by the thirty-seven mainly local shareholders of E. L. Bushnell Television Co. would not allow a change of ownership without the approval of the broadcasting board. (This seemingly innocuous stipulation would prove crucial many years later, when Bushnell Communications — as it would then be named — became the object of a takeover bid.)

Stu Griffiths, described by his future employee Harvey Kirck as a "rotund, balding little man with buck teeth and pebble glasses," was an integral part of Bushnell's plan. Griffiths was then the controller of programs for Britain's Granada television network and was committed to spending much of his time abroad. But Bushnell told the BBG that Griffiths was prepared to "help us in getting soundly established on an interim basis at least," as assistant general manager. (In fact, Griffiths soon left Granada to become Bushnell's full-time second-in-command.)

When the BBG recommended that the Ottawa television licence go to Bushnell Television, the other four applicants, some of whom were prominent Liberals, raised the familiar spectre of a political fix. They said George Nowlan had backed Bushnell's application, just as Diefenbaker and Hees were said to have done with John Bassett. Bushnell was quick to deny these charges, harking back to his previous appearance before the board on behalf of another applicant. "What about my client, Pacific Television [in Vancouver], which was loaded with big-shot Tories? They didn't get the licence. Art Jones did, and God knows what his politics were. It was suggested that the Conservative government owed me something. For what? For getting them into one juicy mess while I was vice-president of the CBC? Maybe Mr. Bassett was somewhat indiscreet when he intimated that the prime minister had more or less assured him that the application in which he was involved would receive sympathetic consideration. Undoubtedly it did, but not because of the fact that John Bassett was a Tory. I attended the public sessions in Toronto. I heard Joel Aldred make the finest presentation of all the applicants. [After] he had finished I came away with the feeling that if he wasn't successful, there was something more going on than that which met the eye or struck the ear."

Bushnell's admiration for the CFTO contingent, however, went only so far. He said his Ottawa station would be happy to cooperate with any group that planned to form a network, but he didn't want to see any more media concentration in Toronto. At the very least, he thought that Ottawa would be the logical source for a national newscast. In general, he said, Bushnell Television would be a maker, not a taker of network programs, even if Joel Aldred had two or three shows in pilot condition that were ready to be syndicated all across Canada. Dick Misener, the winning licence applicant in Montreal, joked that he "would be very glad to suggest a two-way fight . . . between Mr. Aldred and Mr. Bushnell if I could own the film rights." And a fight was looming — but it would be more diverse than that.

Andrew Stewart, the BBG chairman, didn't want to see any more media concentration in Toronto either, if it meant (as he feared) that Big John Bassett's station would control the new network. He noted that Joel Aldred was asking the other new stations to reserve times for CFTO's programs. In a memorandum to his fellow governors, Stewart wrote, "However, there is no evidence of willingness on the part of the Toronto station to reserve time for programs that can be made available by other stations; and it should be a matter of concern to the board that the Toronto station seems to be . . . endeavouring to develop its activities as, in effect, a network." Stewart was determined this would not happen.

On July 18, 1960, representatives from the newly licensed English-language stations in Vancouver, Calgary, Winnipeg, Toronto, Ottawa, Montreal, and Halifax, together with the station in Edmonton that was about to disaffiliate from the CBC and the newly licensed French-language station in Montreal, formed the Independent Television Organization (ITO) at a meeting in Ralph Misener's Winnipeg boardroom. The nine stations chose Montreal's Dick Misener as president and began to plot a cohesive strategy, with an eye to Spence Caldwell's attempts to set up a network proposal of his own.

This strategy focused, among other matters, on the means by which the stations would exchange their programming. The owners hoped they could simply ship videotapes and film around the country on commercial airline flights and return them by rail express. Dick Misener thought they could get away with this, at least at first. He believed that "an interconnected network in the accepted formal sense of the word" — that is, a group of stations linked by microwave — was less essential in 1960 than it had been in 1952, when the CBC started broadcasting. "Surely the primary function of a network is to move programs or program material to various parts of the country. [Today,] with the facility of videotape and vastly improved recording techniques and with the ever increasing speed of jet travel, it is possible to move most kinds of program material quickly and much more economically."

The ITO owners wanted to believe that this was true — out of financial necessity. They were spending vast sums of money on their studio facilities ("Taj Mahals," as Spence Caldwell called them), as well as on transmitters, staff, programming, and everything else they'd promised in order to get their licences. At this point, they were looking for the quickest, easiest, and cheapest way out. As Ray Peters (who'd just come on the scene in Vancouver as Vantel's newly hired manager) puts it, "The stations didn't want a network," if only because they thought they couldn't afford one.

What they wanted was the ITO, a not-quite-ready-for-network-status compromise. At a second meeting in Montreal on August 21, the member stations agreed to its incorporation. It was to have its headquarters in Winnipeg. Most important, it was to be wholly owned, in equal proportions, by the nine members only. No outside investors or partners could participate — an idea the BBG had already indicated wouldn't fly, insofar as a network was concerned. Each station would be represented by a director, each of whom would have one vote, no matter how large the outlet or its viewing audience. In other words, it was a true cooperative.

The ITO's stated purpose was to share sales efforts, share buying of foreign programming, and share production of some Canadian programming. This constituted a step in the direction of a network, so the member stations also resolved to apply to form one. But, despite Dick

Misener's hopeful premise, a network would require a microwave connection, so they opened discussions with Bell Telephone in Montreal.

In this pre-satellite era, microwave was the most advanced television transmission medium. Various carriers were in on the act, but the major provider was Bell and its provincial counterparts, collectively known as the Trans-Canada Telephone System. By 1958, a line of towers, each one bristling with antennas, stretched from Victoria to Halifax. It was the longest such system in the world, and increased in length a year later, when service was extended to Newfoundland. The towers relayed microwave signals on line of sight; that is, they had to be built up one side of a mountain and down the other. Not only did they carry telephone service and radio signals as well, but a finite number of circuits was available, and the CBC had long-standing contracts for the exclusive use of one of them during certain time periods. There were additional circuits available — in effect, a second microwave service, although it involved the same string of towers — but only in the area bounded by Quebec City and Windsor, Ontario, with Ottawa thrown in for good measure. Trans-Canada Telephone planned to install additional circuits right across the country, but hadn't done so yet.

This presented a problem for the ITO. Many programs could be distributed via microwave at off-peak times. A given station would videotape the transmission and broadcast the show later on. But a national newscast or an important sports event would have to be broadcast live, usually at a time when the CBC had prior claim. Depending on how much programming the ITO proposed to transmit, and when it proposed to do so, there might not be room in the microwave pipeline at any price. And price was a consideration. To connect the eight stations from Vancouver to Halifax for about four hours a day would cost more than $1,000 an hour on a monthly contract basis, once the second microwave system was completely installed. By comparison, linking Toronto, Montreal, and Ottawa under the same terms would be a mere $125, but that wasn't the object of the exercise. The question was — who was going to pay the bills? The ITO's member stations were already crying poor, and everyone, for the moment at least, was stumbling around in the dark.

The ITO therefore confined itself to wait-and-see statements. "At the moment we cannot become a fully interconnected national network because of the present lack of available facilities," Dick Misener concluded. "We will achieve interconnection as and when it is available and within our means. In every other way, it is our primary objective to become a network."

One thing at least was clear. If the ITO had its way, that network would also be controlled by its member stations, not by outside investors. Nor did the ITO plan to have a separate production facility. The stations themselves, along with independent producers under contract, would come up with the necessary programs. Within the next month or so, the ITO did plan to hire a general manager and a management group, with headquarters in Toronto, who would be responsible, among other duties, for setting up the program exchange.

Meanwhile, Spence Caldwell had been travelling to and fro across the country, visiting the ITO member stations and trying to persuade them to join his network instead. He later claimed that they'd asked him if he would agree to manage their network if they succeeded in creating it, but Caldwell wasn't interested. He said his backers insisted on having control. "I am their only contact with the broadcasting industry," he said, "and they want to be able to talk to me."

At the beginning of September, the ITO and Spence Caldwell squared off in front of the BBG in the Court Room of Ottawa's Union Station. Caldwell later took issue with the media's portrayal of the event as "some kind of fight between the stations and myself." Instead, he called it "just an honest . . . difference of opinion — and thank God we have that in this country. But I feel [the network] should be a separate company and they feel that they should own it."

Quite so. Dick Misener emphasized that the ITO's member stations were "unanimous in their conviction" that the only way to go was a "mutual network," wholly controlled by its components. Nor did they feel up to providing a microwave connection right off the bat. Otherwise, they had no problem with the twelve private-network ground rules laid down by the BBG.

"I know there has been a suggestion that broadcasters are a bunch of rugged individualists and non-cooperators," he said, "but there are strong co-ops or mutuals and there are weak or bad co-ops or mutuals. To be effective, we must have a strong mutual." This, he explained, would enable the ITO to fully control its program output. He then went on to describe its efforts to set up a program exchange and touched upon its discussions with Bell Telephone about a microwave connection. To Misener, the most efficient method was the best: "Whether this program material is moved by microwave, [by tape] or film, [by] carrier pigeon, . . . is not the point," he said.

He explained that ITO members would certainly consider investing in a national microwave interconnection — assuming it was available — when they were out of the red. At the moment, though, "neither this organization or any other group can prove to the board that it can obtain microwave connection with its affiliated stations on any practical basis except on a most limited regional basis," Misener said. This translated as: "Spence Caldwell is in the same boat we are. We're both talking about limiting ourselves to the Quebec City–Windsor corridor and to occasional use of an overloaded national system at ungodly hours."

At this point, a BBG governor wondered whether the lack of a national microwave linkage would make the ITO "look like a pale horse against the CBC, if you have no current news, no major sports to offer to your viewers."

Misener admitted that this posed a difficulty, then did his best to dance around it. "We are fully aware . . . that without such interconnection ITO cannot be fully competitive in the area of hot, topical national news pictures, or in providing . . . sports specials [such as] the Grey Cup, NHL [games] or the World Series," he said. "We do feel, however, that the bulk of the program material . . . would not suffer in any way or be any less attractive or useful to the viewer by being either taped or film-delayed. An increasing amount of program content on the major American networks is on film."

Besides, he added, the ITO stations were under the impression that one of the reasons they'd been licensed at all was to provide an alternative to CBC network programming in the form of distinctive local or regional productions. If they were to fulfil this mandate, Misener suggested, the private network might supply a "relatively small part" of their programming — meaning that it wouldn't matter all that much how that network's contribution got from A to B.

That didn't mean, however, that a second network should be a purely commercial or profit-making one with fully sponsored programming, like the one Spence Caldwell proposed. "There is program material that we will all want to carry that will not be readily saleable," Misener said. "I think we [as a group] might very well produce some outstanding public affairs programs. . . . We like money; we must have money; we have . . . large capital investments and operating commitments; we must show a profit, or . . . we cease to exist. But we would like to underline some of our high-sounding promises to the board when applying for licences and say that we still mean it and say that this network would help us to accomplish some of these aims." In fact, Misener added, the ITO stations had become increasingly irritated at the suggestion that commercial broadcasters were somehow "less Canadian" than CBC broadcasters. So saying, he yielded the floor to Spence Caldwell.

Caldwell opened his presentation with a sales pitch: "We want a network. We are enthusiastic about it, we think we should have it, we think we could make it a success, we think it would be profitable and I am very surprised at people who say, 'There is no money in networks, but please, give one to us.'"

And he wanted his Bay Street investors to own it. "The company that is going to take over the network must have adequate capital to finance the whole thing and not rely . . . on the stations," he said. "I think it should be a public company [with shareholders] selected from business and industry across the country to give us a good representation of people and opinions. Our board of directors can be selected from this group of businessmen and from the stations."

The BBG had seen this movie before. Caldwell was rehashing his failed application for the Toronto television licence — the same shareholders (although he was having trouble tracking them down in Nassau, Rome, or wherever else they had scattered to) and the same amount of money (roughly $1.5 million in investment capital). He had budgeted $5 million in revenue against $1 million in expenses for the network's first year of operation. "If we cannot get $5 million, [when] the CBC does $32 million, then I don't think we are very effective," Caldwell said. "Other than the microwave connection and a staff, we do not have any large permanent expenses." Caldwell was assuming that advertisers would cover all his programming costs, but his remark infuriated the station owners, who wondered what he was going to bring to the party. All together, they'd already spent more than $30 million on twenty-seven studios, fifty-four cameras, twenty videotape recorders, and nine fully equipped mobile units. At CFTO, Joel Aldred had one pilot on tape (for a hospital drama series titled *Call Emergency*), and other stations were edging up on production as well. They resented the idea that Caldwell was going to waltz in and make a profit from their investments with what amounted to a bookkeeping service and central clearing house.

The microwave connection was another matter. The member stations couldn't possibly afford it, and Caldwell considered it essential: "A network, to be a real network, has to have a national news service. It has to have special events, elections, and sports. [Otherwise] it will be 'the second stations' and 'the second network' forever." Later he expanded on his argument: "If you don't have the microwave, you are going to be a second-rate news station. You are going to be carrying [items] after [everybody else has]. You are not going to be able to carry any of the sports events —

there is no use airing [a game] after the score is known." He was right, of course. Tossing videotapes onto a plane would not suffice; no one would tune in to watch a foregone conclusion.

Caldwell also took issue with the ITO's views on the cost of a microwave connection. In his estimation, it was expensive, but no more so than a patchwork videotape exchange. If he got a network licence, he pledged to immediately open negotiations with Bell Telephone and hang the expense.

The ITO didn't want to move that quickly. "If there were no limitations of economics, we would certainly love to have a fully interconnected network of vast dimensions," Dick Misener said in his closing statement. "[But] we have to be limited in this entire matter . . . by economics. We could find ourselves bankrupt as a group of individuals or as a network company in very short order, by going into it on an over-large scale. [We] cannot afford . . . an operation of the size the Canadian Broadcasting Corporation is running today. We would hope to have something approaching this ultimately, but at the outset, it would be completely impossible from [the standpoint of] cost."

Misener closed his remarks by reiterating that the ITO's caution should not be misinterpreted as lack of interest or commitment: "As far as the station group itself is concerned, . . . we are rather more than busy this summer, [and] we would like to take a few preliminary steps in this network, without having to erupt fully grown."

At the next round of public hearings, held three weeks later in the Railway Committee Room of the House of Commons, Spence Caldwell kicked off by pushing his luck with the BBG. This seems odd, given that he was having trouble persuading the ITO stations to fall in line and needed all the friends he could get, but he tried it on anyway. In essence, he objected to being regulated in any way, shape, or form: "We do not feel that the new arrival on the Canadian broadcasting scene represented by the proposed second television network should have restrictions or limitations placed upon its activities. All broadcasting operation is virtually in a goldfish bowl." This would prove to be a constant refrain in times to come, but did Caldwell no initial good and got at least one board member's back up.

"Tell us what it is that a private network has to offer the stations to make them want to affiliate with it," a broadcast governor named Edward Dunlop asked.

"I imagine, a gun," Caldwell quipped. "We will know later on."

Over the next two months, Caldwell found out. In his draft affiliation agreement, he offered to retain only 25 per cent of the money his network would make from selling airtime the affiliates set aside for network shows. That was far less than the CBC's 50 per cent, not to mention the 70-plus per cent that was the norm in the United States.

"Can we get along with so little?" Caldwell wondered. He thought so, because the independent stations were in fact intended to be primarily local outlets. They could do anything they wanted to for most of the broadcast day — buy syndicated programs from other sources or produce shows themselves and swap them as they pleased. They could sell advertising day and (for that matter) night. Caldwell saw no need for an "all-embracing network that swallows up to 70 per cent or 80 per cent of their airtime and a similar percentage of their time revenue." His plan was always to provide a limited amount of network programming — somewhere between eight and ten hours a week. That would be enough for him to make money, if — a rather big if — he could sell out each and every commercial minute to national advertisers.

☆

By the time Spence Caldwell got around to making his formal application for a network licence at the beginning of December 1960, he believed that he had the support of a silent majority of the independent English-language stations. No one can be sure whether this was correct. Officially, the stations were soldiering on as members of the ITO, and Caldwell had signed affiliation agreements with none of them. Nor had he worked out an arrangement with CFTO, at which he wanted to produce the majority of his programs, because he didn't plan on having a production facility.

In his presentation, Caldwell promised to raise $1.8 million in capital for his company, to be called the Canadian Television Network, or CTN. It would be owned 51 per cent by Caldwell and his investors. The remaining 49 per cent was set aside for the stations, but it was up to them whether they wanted to come in on the share allotment. If so, they could, according to a formula based on the size of their viewing populations. If not, his investors would simply take more shares.

Next, just as he'd done in Toronto, Caldwell read another long and tedious list of these investors. He then declared he'd made arrangements with the Imperial Bank for a loan, if needed, of as much as $500,000, to cover the cost of the microwave contract. (Unfortunately for Caldwell, this figure would prove to be nowhere near enough.)

Caldwell also tried to make his purely commercial enterprise sound like more than the sum of its parts: "Just as it takes more than a few cents' [worth] of chemicals and a few gallons of water to make a man, it takes more than microwave connections, videotape recordings, and advertising contracts to make a network. A network is a living thing, . . . with a separate animating spirit that gives it life and stature of its own."

The ITO had decided not to submit a competing application at the December hearings, but CFTO made a surprise intervention. Big John Bassett had spoken with Andrew Stewart the day before the hearings opened and asked if he might address the board. He wished to make it clear that CFTO opposed linking up with Caldwell, but he was double-booked in Toronto, so Joel Aldred had to appear in his stead, assuring the BBG that "we are of one mind on the various points that I will bring up."

Aldred disputed Caldwell's assumption that he'd have no trouble obtaining a microwave contract. A new network would find it "extremely difficult" to connect stations west of Toronto and east of Montreal, he said, because the CBC had a lock on the national microwave system's capacity. Nor would Bell look with favour on the idea of the CBC sub-letting or "brokering" its allotted time to a third party, even if that sort of deal could be reached.

More important, Aldred didn't think that Caldwell was promising the stations anything that CFTO couldn't do for itself. Caldwell wanted the network to produce popular programs such as game and variety shows, distribute them to its affiliates, and retain 25 per cent of the national advertising revenue. But CFTO could produce those programs just as easily, keep 100 per cent of the local advertising revenue, then sell the programming to other stations for negotiated fees. In other words, CFTO didn't need a network; it could become a centre of power and influence without one. There was "nothing personal" in this, concluded Aldred, who said he'd known Caldwell for years and wished him every success in his endeavour. "It is purely a matter with us of business practices at the moment."

CFTO's reaction greatly dismayed Caldwell. He was keen to use its studios as his network production centre and was confident that CFTO would see the light "when they realize that this is their network and that it will help with the costs of their operation and their studios." Now he had to counter Aldred's charges. He disposed of the microwave objection by arguing that the CBC would not be brokering its time to his network. He was asking for time outside the CBC's contract, before 2 p.m. and after midnight. Next he addressed the notion that CFTO could peddle its own programming. "I don't know where Joel got these easy-to-sell programs," Caldwell said. "Some of them will be easy and some will be hard. Some of them, [as] I have said, we will have to subsidize to sell."

A week later, on December 8, the BBG decided to give Spence Caldwell a "hunting licence." If he wanted to take his network concept any further, he would have to persuade six of the ITO stations to sign affiliation agreements. And he had to commit in those agreements to a minimum "network reserve time." That is, he'd have to agree to provide not less than ten hours a week of network programming. Some could be bought from American and foreign sources, but the rest (to comply with content rulings) would have to be made in Canada. With Big John and Joel Aldred poised to go their own way, Caldwell faced the prospect of looking elsewhere for his flagship station.

3

Spence Caldwell's CTV — 1961–63

In January 1961, Big John Bassett set the CBC spinning when his single station outbid the public network for the rights to televise the Canadian Football League's Eastern Conference regular-season and playoff games, and a right of first refusal on the Grey Cup. Alphonse Ouimet, the CBC's president, demanded that the neophyte broadcaster give them back, complaining quite accurately that Bassett had no microwave, no network, and no sponsors. Bassett refused to back down. What mattered was that he had the rights, and he was going to exercise them, come what may. And so began the Great Canadian Football Fiasco, which would wind up pushing Big John into the arms of Spence Caldwell's network.

That wasn't what Bassett had in mind. As chairman of the Argonauts and the Maple Leafs, he was convinced that football and hockey were the real "licence to print money." They would attract viewers to CFTO and prove that the station was ready for big-league broadcasting. Accordingly, in the fall of 1960, he got in touch with the CFL's television committee. By Bassett's telling, they were "delighted" to have an alternative to the CBC, which had been airing the games since 1955. Bassett was invited to attend a meeting with the committee in Toronto — not to submit a bid yet, but to explain how Baton Aldred Rogers intended to air the games.

That session lasted two hours. Bassett apparently told the league that the independent stations in Montreal (both French- and English-language) and Ottawa were eager to participate with CFTO in broadcasting the games. To this end, he intended to apply to the Board of Broadcast Governors for a temporary network licence.

Bassett knew nothing about the technical aspects of broadcasting, so he passed the ball to Joel Aldred, who'd approached Bell Telephone about buying time on its Quebec City–to–Windsor microwave service. Aldred claimed that Bell saw no problem in linking the three football cities. He also claimed that he'd received a letter from Andrew Stewart, confirming that the BBG would consider the matter.

Whatever was said, Bassett and Aldred must have satisfied the CFL's concerns, because the league asked him to put a bid in writing. After discussions with Baton Aldred Rogers's finance people, Bassett indicated to his board of directors that he thought the bid should be $375,000 a year, on a two-year basis. "I am familiar with how football works," Bassett explained, "and there is no question that this knowledge was of value to me."

Meanwhile, the CBC, confident that its arrangement would be renewed, bid $355,000 on a one-year basis — $30,000 more than it had paid in 1960, but not enough to prevent the league from handing the rights to Bassett. This enraged Ouimet, who was nonetheless comforted by the possibility that Bassett had bitten off more than he could chew.

For one thing, Spence Caldwell had quietly signed an option agreement with Bell on the second microwave link, looking forward not only to sports events but also to all sorts of network programming. Whether this left room on the microwave for Big John's games remained to be seen. For another, the CBC, in previous years, had provided a wider-ranging service through its affiliates: people could see the games in smaller centres such as Kingston. Bassett was obviously trying to force viewers in Hamilton (who wanted to see the Tiger-Cats in action) to watch CFTO, but if he had his way, a lot of sports fans elsewhere would be cut out of the action — unless, as he hoped, the CBC rolled over and released its affiliates to carry his feed. Lastly, under the terms of the Broadcasting Act, licences for temporary networks were good for only thirty days, with the possibility (though not the certainty) of renewal. The football season lasted for at least three months, and Baton Aldred Rogers's rights covered a two-year period.

In short, if Bassett couldn't get his temporary licence, he'd just committed to pay $750,000 for the rights to games that he could show only in Toronto, via direct transmission from CFTO. Worse yet, some of these games would be "blacked out" by the league. In Finlay MacDonald's words, Bassett was "like a kid [who'd bought] every seat in the stadium. It was lunacy!"

There was, however, a degree of confusion about Spence Caldwell's agreement with Bell Telephone. Eddie Goodman believed that Baton Aldred Rogers could avail themselves of the second microwave link when Caldwell wasn't using it — and Caldwell didn't have a network yet. Also, it seemed unlikely that Caldwell's deal covered the afternoons, when the games were played. Goodman thought the chances were "at least nine out of ten" that the microwave would be available. Thus, buying the rights "wasn't really a big gamble. What were they gonna do?"

By "they," Goodman meant both the BBG and the CBC. This posture doubly infuriated Ouimet. He thought that Bassett was trying to "create a public climate that would force" both the regulators and the corporation to let him have his way. In Ouimet's mind, Bassett's strategy was to let it be known that he had the rights and was ready to broadcast the games, thus gaining the support of sports-minded viewers. If the CBC (or Caldwell) tried to block Bassett's access to the microwave, they'd be seen as villains. So would the BBG, if it failed to endorse Bassett's temporary licence application.

Ouimet kept offering to buy back the rights from Baton Aldred Rogers, though not at the price Bassett had paid. Not surprisingly, Bassett turned him down. He was having fun. Already, CFTO was going head to head with the CBC on the ice, by airing Wednesday-night Maple Leafs games. And, unlike the CBC, it provided whistle-to-whistle coverage. Until Bassett provided competition, the CBC had joined the Saturday-night games late; viewers missed the entire first period and some of the second. Big John told Maple Leaf Gardens' president Conn Smythe, "This is ridiculous. We're going to start at eight o'clock." Bassett said later, "And he agreed. And we did. Well, the CBC, of course, shortly had to follow." Bassett thought that CFTO's hockey coverage was as good as or better than the CBC's and made a convincing argument (which he planned to spring on the BBG) that his camera crews and producers could handle the technical aspects of broadcasting football games. As well, Bassett was fortunate in having on his staff the shrewd and experienced football announcer Johnny Esaw, who had signed up as CFTO's sports director. His skills would prove to be invaluable when it came time to expand the station's — and later the CTV network's — sports coverage in all directions.

And a network was still very much on Bassett's mind. Although he had no intention of selling the football rights, he did have a meeting with

Ouimet, who lectured him long and loud about network responsibilities. It was this discussion that Bassett later said made him receptive to the idea of striking a deal with Caldwell. As he put it, "It is too tough for one station continually to take on a network all the time."

Others, like Finlay MacDonald, argue that Bassett was "forced to join Spence's network against his will. It wasn't his idea." The fact remains that if Caldwell hadn't had certain rights to the microwave link, and Bassett hadn't been so eager to get his football games on the air, CFTO would never have become the Toronto flagship of Caldwell's network, and Baton might have developed its own national network, based primarily on its successful sports coverage.

As the Football Fiasco was getting under way, Spence Caldwell was in England, calling on the British networks and program contractors. Then he went to New York and visited their U.S. counterparts. It wasn't until the end of January 1961 that Caldwell began criss-crossing Canada, trying to persuade at least six affiliates to join his private network. He and Gordon Keeble spent two or three days at each of the ITO stations, discussing plans and fine-tuning the affiliation agreement. At issue were what programs the stations would supply, what they expected the network to provide, and what their investment, if any, in the network company would be.

In Vancouver, Caldwell met with two of Vantel's minority shareholders, Peter Paul Saunders and Andrew Saxton. He did so because Art Jones was about to be replaced. Jones had hired upwards of a hundred people and succeeded in putting CHAN on the air at the end of October 1960, but the numbers didn't look good. At one of the board meetings, a director asked how much money the station would make if its advertising time were completely sold out at the prices established on its rate card. Jones replied that there'd still be a loss and named the figure. This response sealed his fate. Saunders recalls that "Art was not a businessman. He had no financial background."

By contrast, Ray Peters, who took over from Jones in February 1961, was an experienced broadcaster who'd started in show business at the age of eight, as a member of his elder brother's band. He'd sung in Vancouver night spots and later appeared as a singer, musician, and actor in radio musicals, dramas, and comedies. When his voice broke, Peters got a part-time job organizing a radio station's library. This led to a job as promotion manager for the Canadian arm of Britain's Decca Records.

Just out of high school, Peters moved to Montreal and set up distribution systems to get radio stations to play Decca's latest releases. When the British head office moved in its own people in 1949, Peters became the radio director of an advertising agency. Three years later, he took charge of both its radio and television business, dividing his time between Montreal and New York, where he oversaw the production of commercials. "I had a good friend at CBS," Peters recalls, "and I used to go there . . . and watch on weekends. That's where I learned the business of television."

He put his observations to good use in 1954, when Ken Soble (Eddie Goodman's uncle) hired him to help put the newly licensed CHCH Hamilton on the air. Soble was recovering from a heart attack, so Peters had "lots of responsibility," even if he had "no authority and no money." He remained as the station's commercial manager for its first six years of operation. By 1960, he was juggling a number of offers, including one from CBS in New York. But he decided to return home to Vancouver. "I'm thought of as an easterner," he says, "but I'm really a west coast guy."

Peters was hired on the understanding that he would be "groomed as an understudy for Art Jones," but it quickly became apparent that CHAN "was not going to work" with the free-spending Jones in charge. In fact, Peters was about to return to Hamilton when Vantel's directors begged him to stay and run the place.

"When I took over, [Vantel] was in deep difficulty," Peters says. "The bank was calling its loan and we couldn't pay staff. Personally, I was going through a disastrous divorce. I was a single parent [with three young sons] before it was popular." One of the first things the thirty-four-year-old Peters had to do as managing director was to recruit two new financial backers: the American-controlled Famous Players and Britain's Associated Television (now ITV). Each bought 12 per cent of Vantel's equity. That summer, Peters had to axe a quarter of Vantel's staff, including a young woman named Heidi Sohnel, who let it be known that she was going to move to Toronto. Peters had succeeded in finding new jobs for about half the laid-off personnel, so he offered to use his connections to help her land a position there. "No, thank you," she replied. "I've always managed to find my own." And so she did — producing documentaries for the CBC.

At the height of this financial crisis, Vantel's shareholders asked Peters what he thought about Spence Caldwell's network proposal. "Forget it, it's going to fail," he told them. "Spence can't run anything." Peters had met Caldwell for the first time in 1950 and was "unimpressed." Later, when Caldwell had "stars in his eyes" over his network prospects, Peters was equally unimpressed by his backers — the "Bay Street boys," as Peters referred to them. As a result, CHAN never became an affiliate or shareholder of Spence Caldwell's network, although it agreed to carry a number of network programs, retaining most of the ad revenue for itself.

But Caldwell enjoyed greater success elsewhere. Several stations gave him letters of intent, stating that they were prepared to meet and talk things over. Encouraged by this response, Caldwell set up a gathering in Toronto for late March.

By then, he'd given up on CFTO as his network's flagship station and was in discussions with CHCH Hamilton. Still, Caldwell thought he'd take one last run at Bassett, just in case, and scheduled a get-together in early March with Baton Aldred Rogers.

This meeting took place in the *Telegram* boardroom and quickly degenerated into farce. Ted Rogers remembers that he'd been assigned the job of rattling Caldwell. "John Bassett said to me, 'You're a great goddamned debater. I'll be the nice guy and you be the disturber.'" Rogers rehearsed his bad-cop persona and thought he'd worked out a suitably menacing routine. There was only one catch. Bassett was so desperate to air his precious football games that — the night before the meeting — he too had signed a letter of intent with Caldwell, but had forgotten to inform Ted Rogers of the fact.

During the meeting, Rogers thought everything was going well. He'd succeeded in infuriating Caldwell by continually interrupting his presentation. Caldwell was ready to storm out, when Bassett suddenly turned to Rogers and told him to shut up. "You're being rude to our guest!" Bassett bellowed — then politely turned back to Caldwell and asked him to continue. Later, he filled Rogers in on what had happened and gave his young partner a hug.

All Spence Caldwell's pieces were finally falling into place. Twenty-five representatives from eight independent stations attended his big March meeting at Toronto's Park Plaza Hotel. (Montreal's French-language station played no part in Caldwell's plans.) The executives discussed every aspect of network broadcasting, including the elusive microwave connection, BBG regulations, and the question of "option" or "reserve" time — that is, how much network programming they'd accept, and exactly when these programs would be broadcast. Finally, they agreed to set aside a minimum of ten hours a week, as had been suggested in Caldwell's original brief. The absolute maximum reserve time was pegged at twenty-eight hours weekly. This was a commitment on the stations' part only; Caldwell did not commit to provide that many hours. Option time was a matter of concern to the stations, because they wanted to ensure that the network feed wouldn't interfere with their local programs or advertising sales opportunities.

At 11:30 p.m. on the second day, everyone agreed to form a network. In the days that followed they formed committees and began to work on a revised affiliation agreement. It took them seven drafts to get it right. Caldwell immediately sent copies to the stations themselves, so that local shareholders could see what was going on. More copies went to the secretary of the BBG.

And what *was* going on, when it came to ownership of the network? Caldwell's position from the start had been that his investors would control 51 per cent of the share allotment, and that 49 per cent would be offered to the stations, who could come aboard or not, as they pleased. There were few takers, which Caldwell attributed to lack of funds, not any lack of confidence. Of the eight station owners, only John Bassett, Lloyd Moffat from CJAY Winnipeg, and Finlay MacDonald from CJCH Halifax availed themselves of the share offer, and their combined holdings were only 16 per cent of the total. Majority control of Caldwell's new network company rested with its founder and his "Bay Street boys." Still, Baton was in a strong position, with 13 per cent. "In the question of money investment," Bassett said, "we were the largest [single] shareholder."

☆

With his Toronto flagship station and six other signed affiliation agreements in hand, a full-of-himself Spence Caldwell was back before the Board of Broadcast Governors in mid-April to get permission to operate his network. (There were a total of seven affiliates because CHAN, leery of Caldwell, didn't sign.)

This time around, though, there were no high-flown phrases about "animating spirits." Caldwell even refused to guarantee to the BBG that his network would broadcast at least ten hours of programming a week.

"I think [we] will start with more than ten hours," he said. "What I am reluctant to agree to is that we have to. We could wreck the whole audience structure if we put on second-rate sustaining programs just because we have to fill the time periods to conform to a regulation."

Broadcast governor Carlyle Allison reminded Caldwell that the board had made it clear from the outset that it expected the network to have a "skeleton" of at least that much program material.

Caldwell took umbrage at this. "I think we said this before and were scolded, but I think we have all the regulations that we need and I would hate to see us regulated more . . . because this puts a financial responsibility on the network where we would be forced possibly to go to the government and ask them for a grant to do it — like the railways or somebody else."

This was outrageous, coming from the man who'd denigrated the ITO's contention that networks weren't profitable. Allison sternly pointed out that a network licence was a privilege, not a right. "If you get it, you are being given something and I think this board is trying to exact something on behalf of the people of Canada in return," he said.

Andrew Stewart asked why there seemed to be nothing in Caldwell's affiliation agreements about his responsibilities regarding the minimum ten-hours-a-week reserve time. "You tell us you are quite convinced you will do more than this, but you are not prepared to make a commitment to this effect," the chairman said.

"I don't think we can," Caldwell responded, "because there are so many things in the future that could happen if we had to produce shows that would build an audience. . . . I could go on and do a soft-shoe dance for two hours, [but] nobody would look at me." He then argued that the BBG had never told him that he had to enshrine ten hours a week in the affiliation agreement.

"You are offering nothing but the fact that if you have sold programs and if the station is prepared to take them, then you will have some kind of operation," Stewart complained.

That's exactly what Caldwell was saying: in this regard, the network was a one-way street. The stations were bound to set aside the time, but he was under no obligation to fill it. Nor was he keen to make further promises to the BBG, which he made clear in the form of a rather unsubtle threat: "I would wish that the board not add any conditions to the granting of this network's licence, because if you do, it most likely will not start this [autumn]."

Carlyle Allison didn't like being threatened. "Mr. Caldwell, if your application stood or fell on this point, would you rather have it fall?" he demanded.

"Oh, that is a nasty one!" Caldwell replied. "After all this work, [I would naturally] want to say no, but honestly I hope that the board is not going to bring about a private network in Canada and then regulate it so that it cannot function. This is a private, profit-making network — this is one of the things we are to do, to make money — *not* to bring the symphony to the people of Canada. That is the CBC's function and we pay plenty for it. . . . If you are going to put extra regulations onto the private network so that we cannot operate with freedom I am afraid we might as well not accept it, because we will just lose . . . a million and a half or three million and then go out of business."

Bernard Goulet, another broadcast governor, was the next to wade into the fray. "I fail to see why you are so reluctant [to accept] a minimum of ten hours," he told Caldwell coolly.

Caldwell shot back that he didn't appreciate the imposition of "new regulations," other than those that "have already been published." This was both a tactical error and an error in fact. Andrew Stewart immediately read into the record his announcement of the previous December, which gave Caldwell permission to form a network, provided that he met certain conditions, including a minimum reserve time of not less than ten hours per week in the affiliation agreements.

Still Caldwell wouldn't bend. He began splitting hairs, arguing that the board had put a different interpretation on the word "reserve" than he had. Seeing that this was getting him nowhere, he then refused to guarantee even five hours of programming a week and launched into the following verbatim example of what the BBG had to listen to day in and day out:

"I sincerely hope, though, that we could deal on the network on the rules as laid down — now I must add, as we see them, which doesn't seem right because it seems that we have misinterpreted the word 'reserve.' But as we point out in our brief — and it apparently didn't come to anybody's attention then that we felt this was reserve time periods which we could fill as required — not that they were guaranteed because of the costs involved. We would like to think that we could move ahead on this with the rules and regulations as we know them now. If we are not doing it right, then change it." With that, Caldwell had the good sense to sit down.

Having weathered this opaque reasoning from his protégé, Andrew Stewart was in no mood to tolerate more of the same from Big John. Bassett, guarding against the possibility that Caldwell's application would be turned down, was applying for a thirty-day, three-city temporary network licence so as to broadcast his football games.

Stewart grilled Bassett, asking him when he'd acquired the rights to the games, whether the deal had the approval of the Baton Aldred Rogers board, whether he'd had conversations with the "football people" before he submitted the bid, and what if anything he'd told them about the extent of the coverage he could provide.

"Mr. Bassett, you did apparently represent to the football people you could deliver Ottawa and Montreal audiences as well as Toronto," Stewart observed.

"Well," Big John admitted, "I didn't say I could deliver it by a temporary network. I said I would apply to the board for this network and attempt to get it. The point . . . is that [the CFL] are not really to be blamed . . . in any way. This was my responsibility. I was prepared to gamble that amount of money, to gamble first that I could produce the product in these areas and secondly that I would be able to find advertisers who would think it worthwhile."

Stewart sighed and repeated his question.

"I represented to them that there were independent stations that were non-CBC affiliates in those areas that were eager . . . to cooperate with me in presenting football to their audiences," Bassett maintained.

Next, Stewart asked how Bassett had planned to deliver live football in four stations simultaneously. Bassett said he had been informed that it could be done.

"By what facilities?" Stewart asked.

"By telephone line — is that not what I was told?" Bassett replied.

"You mean by microwave," Stewart said. "I wish to pursue [this]. Was it by telephone line or by Bell microwave?"

"You will have to answer that," Bassett told Eddie Goodman — a wise move, since no one can deliver television signals over a telephone line, but Bassett didn't realize it.

"Well, I don't know what conversation Mr. Bassett had," Goodman said. "All I know is that when I came into the picture we discussed Bell microwave." Goodman then proceeded to handle all of Stewart's questions about the microwave and Spence Caldwell's option agreement with Bell. "I have proved again this afternoon, as I have on so many occasions, how little I really know about broadcasting," Bassett conceded.

"Mr. Goodman," Stewart continued, "I am under the impression . . . that at the time Mr. Bassett had his conversation with the football people, and even at the time that he submitted his bid, that he had not . . . discovered whether he would be able to procure microwave facilities or not. And he certainly had no understanding with either Bell Telephone or Mr. Caldwell, who at that time had an option agreement between them, that it was possible under the terms of [that agreement] for [him] to get the microwave facilities."

Goodman admitted that he didn't know what Bassett knew when he went to the meeting.

"You are quite right, sir," Bassett told Stewart. "I was not at all sure how I was going to do this. There were many areas which had to be worked out, but I had to make an initial decision. . . . I could do nothing without the rights. I had to get the rights or not get into it at all, and there was a time element, so I decided to buy the rights and go from there."

Stewart seemed appalled by Bassett's apparent recklessness, especially after he confirmed that Bassett did not have a sponsor lined up before he bid $375,000 a year for the two years of broadcast rights.

"Did you feel it reasonable at this time that you could recover $375,000 if you covered only CFTO?" Stewart pressed.

"No, I did not," Bassett replied.

"Did you consider it reasonable that you could recover $375,000 if you were covering the three cities?"

"I was hopeful."

"Have you in fact been able to do this?"

"No, sir."

"I am finished," Stewart concluded.

"So am I," Bassett said.

Next on the agenda was Alphonse Ouimet, whose purpose was to argue against Big John's temporary licence, not to oppose Caldwell. Nonetheless, he couldn't suppress his glee at the disastrous performances both men had put on. Dripping sarcasm, Ouimet claimed to have come to the hearing ready to compliment Caldwell on his progress, and to take credit for nudging Bassett in Caldwell's direction. "I am sorry [that Mr. Caldwell] has had . . . a great deal of difficulty and that his application does not seem to include any commitment to deliver anything or any commitment on the part of his affiliates to take anything," Ouimet said. "I am sorry about that, because I thought perhaps the firm stand that the CBC had taken with respect to football had somehow facilitated the task of Mr. Caldwell in getting all the affiliates behind him. Apparently we haven't been firm enough, because this seems to be a fairly nebulous second network that we are talking about."

So far, the CBC president had been restrained, but when it came to his battle with Bassett over the football rights, he let loose. "I wish I could remain silent," he began, "because what I have to say is not pleasant. On the other hand, it is a question which has such serious implications for the future that I find it necessary to rise and protest against what I consider to be one of the strangest, most puzzling, and some might say most presumptuous actions in the history of Canadian broadcasting."

Ouimet then presented a lengthy catalogue of Bassett's sins before yielding the floor to Big John for his rebuttal. Bassett said that, although he had listened with great interest to Ouimet's remarks, it appeared to him that despite Ouimet's "repeated suggestion that he welcomed competition, . . . his actions [did] not lend a great deal of credence to that statement." Bassett continued, "It is my understanding that the policy behind the creation of the new independent stations . . . was that competition should be set up for the publicly owned corporation."

In his closing comments, Spence Caldwell went charging off in yet another direction. He ranted at the CBC's objection to the new private network's name. Apparently Ouimet had lobbied with the secretary of state and didn't want Caldwell to call his creation the Canadian Television Network. "We practically cannot call this anything except . . . the Second-Class Citizens Connected Stations," he cried. "Maybe we can't even use the word 'stations.' [We] can't use Trans-Canada, Dominion, All Canada, CNR, CPR. I don't suppose we can call it Canadian. We can't use the words 'television,' or 'network,' and yet the secretary of state says that [our] name must be representative of what [we're] going to do."

His final point was a familiar one. "In respect to the guarantee which we were discussing earlier on the ten hours — I sincerely hope that the board will grant us a licence to proceed, that you will watch over what we are trying to do, and if we do not do . . . what we say we can, . . . then I think in a year or eighteen months, you can bring us to task here and we would not have a leg to stand on. We do ask permission to operate this network under the rules and regulations as it was formed."

That evening, with ample cause, Spence Caldwell, John Bassett, and Eddie Goodman went out for a drink or two. The next morning, Bassett woke up in their shared suite with bright red eyes. "My God, Benbo," Bassett shouted at Goodman, "my eyes are pools of blood! Call up Andrew [Stewart] and tell him to send the licence over here!"

A week later, Caldwell in fact received permission to operate his network, subject to one important condition, but with more flexibility than he deserved. His network reserve time could not "normally be less than ten hours in any week, and . . . not average less than ten hours over any twelve-month period." (Since Bassett had arranged to have the football games carried on Caldwell's network if Caldwell's application succeeded, Big John's three-city network application was null and void; the games were indeed broadcast, beginning that August.)

All this solved one of John Bassett's problems, but he faced many others. At the top of his list was Joel Aldred. Like Art Jones in Vancouver, Aldred appeared to be squandering the shareholders' money. He had spent $4.5 million, two and a half times the budget, to build a massive station, crammed with the most expensive equipment available, not to mention colour transmitters that wouldn't be used for another six years. He'd also hired more than 400 staff members, more than any other television station in North America. All this, in Big John's view, "damn near bankrupted the company." This was not an exaggeration; the station lost more than a million dollars during its first seven months on the air.

Much of the trouble stemmed from Aldred's isolation from his Baton Aldred Rogers partners. "He worked alone, had hired his own team, and was hard to communicate with," says Ted Rogers, who recalls that when they "became concerned about cash, Aldred was hard to pin down. Two-thirty in the morning was the only time we could meet him. [We] went up to CFTO and expressed our concern." John Bassett became disturbed and attacked Aldred, charging that there were no controls over spending. "I'm a loyal person," Rogers says. "We had to defend Aldred, although we really didn't disagree with Bassett."

Still, the final responsibility for this financial mess rested with Bassett. He was, after all, both chairman and chief executive officer of Baton Aldred Rogers. His Telegram Corporation Ltd. (the Telegram trust) controlled the company. It was his decision to put CFTO's operation in Aldred's hands. If he was going to delegate that degree of responsibility, he should have kept better track of the costs. Then again, maybe Bassett should have thought twice about committing $750,000 for the rights to televise football games.

The first wave of layoffs hit in March 1961. They were preceded by the departure of the program director, Rai Purdy, who had clashed with Aldred over who was to blame for the huge program cost overruns. Purdy moved to Vancouver and formed his own production company, which later supplied the musical variety show *Westcoast* to Spence Caldwell's new network. "Purdy was terrific," says Eddie Goodman. "He's the one guy who got screwed in all of this."

About this time, Bassett informed Aldred, who was about to take some much-needed time off at his farm, that he planned to hire a station manager. There hadn't been one at CFTO before; Aldred had always been a one-man show. Soon, however, Aldred was tipped off that the manager, Bill Crampton, would report directly to Bassett, who himself had moved into Aldred's office space, so as to keep an eye on things. The high-flying president was clearly on his way out. "Bassett had 51 per cent [voting control], so he fired him," Ted Rogers remembers. "You can imagine the board meeting; he wanted to fire the lot. The company had to be refinanced."

Bassett had to find a new source of capital. He approached Thomson and Southam, but neither were willing to invest in the company if the

Telegram trust wasn't prepared to cede control. So in late July, Bassett struck an agreement with American Broadcasting-Paramount Theaters Incorporated, owner of the ABC television network. ABC would buy 25 per cent of Baton Aldred Rogers's common share equity and 18 per cent of the preferred voting shares for $300,000, as well as invest in $2 million of debentures. (Aldred had been looking for alternative financing as well. He'd gone to New York and learned that NBC television was prepared to invest in CFTO, if Aldred could persuade the Telegram trust to accept a stock trade from Aldred Rogers — in effect, to sell out to him.)

This seemed unlikely, so the idea went nowhere and served only to delay Aldred's inevitable departure. Ted Rogers remembers being called to a meeting at John Bassett's house at one-thirty in the morning. He and his stepfather, John Graham, the lawyer for Aldred Rogers Ltd., arrived early, to be informed by an agitated Bassett that "Aldred's out, he's gone." Apparently, the Aldred Rogers investment in Baton Aldred Rogers Broadcasting had to be cut from 34 per cent to around 10 per cent to help make room for ABC's 25 per cent. Bassett told Rogers that, if he wanted to stay, he'd have to settle for 5 rather than 17 per cent of the shares. Aldred could also keep 5 per cent, but the offer was good only until three o'clock the following afternoon. Otherwise, said Bassett, CFTO was doomed. Rogers wanted to stay in, so he and Graham tried to reach Aldred by phone. They finally tracked him down, quite drunk, in a Montreal hotel room. Graham tried to explain Bassett's proposed refinancing to him, but each time he paused to take a breath Aldred would shout, "Tell him to go to hell!"

Downstairs, a disingenuous Graham assured Bassett that Aldred had listened patiently and wanted to sleep on it. "He can sleep until three," Bassett barked. "[Allan] Beattie will be knocking on your door at three for the answer. You'd better get Aldred there!"

Aldred wasn't there, but he did phone Rogers the next day and agreed to the 5 per cent ultimatum. Soon, however, he changed his mind, telling Rogers that he wanted to be bought out. "I felt terrible," Rogers recalls. "I sometimes argued with him, but there had never been any hostility."

Lawyer Allan Beattie, who was quarterbacking the ABC investment, remembers how difficult it was to get Aldred to sign off on the buyout in July 1961. "We had a real long session on a Friday night," he says. The next day, he had to attend his brother-in-law's wedding. On Saturday, he met with Aldred at nine o'clock, but Aldred kept dragging his feet. "I'm leaving at eleven," Beattie warned him. "If you haven't signed by [then], the deal's off." Aldred signed.

"The only person who made money out of CFTO in its first year was

Aldred," Ted Rogers says. According to Bassett's biographer, Maggie Siggins, Aldred pocketed $200,000 on his shares.

Years later, Aldred's partners, including John Bassett, conceded that they'd made a mistake by splitting with him. "Aldred built an infrastructure that served . . . well over the decades," Ted Rogers says. "He was right, the rest of us were wrong. If he'd had a strong financial partner, it would have worked."

"There's no doubt he did some good," agrees Eddie Goodman. "In 1960, he built a station that is home to a network in the 1990s. He put in colour TV when it wasn't allowed. That was a smart move, although it cost us an incredible fortune."

"I'm still proud of the fact that the station exists," Joel Aldred says.

In early August 1961, Donald Coyle, the vice-president of the international division of ABC, came to a closed-door hearing in Toronto, at which the various parties asked the BBG to approve the restructuring of Baton Aldred Rogers Broadcasting. This included the transfer of 100 common shares from Aldred Rogers Ltd. (Joel Aldred and Ted Rogers) to Ted Rogers, and 240 common shares from Aldred Rogers Ltd. (Aldred and Rogers) and 12 common shares from Heathcourt Boulevard Investments Inc. (Eddie Goodman and Charles Dubin) to American Broadcasting-Paramount Theaters Inc. (ABC).

Andrew Stewart and Eugene Forsey strongly opposed the deal, but the majority of the board recommended approval. However, they gave any interested Canadian companies until September 25 to match ABC's offer.

Their concern was that once American capital entered the country by the back-door means of lending money to private television stations, it would open the floodgates. "This transaction is like an iceberg: what the public can see, the share transfer, is only a hidden fraction of the whole," Forsey wrote to the other governors. "Much the larger, and more dangerous, part lies hidden. If CFTO is losing money on an impressive scale, and if ABC is providing it with a substantial amount of loan capital, . . . then it must follow as night the day that ABC will have control. . . . Approval of this deal means turning over, to an American network, control of the largest private TV station in Canada, . . . the key station in the private network. . . . Pressure to let in the other American networks will become irresistible; and before we know where we are, the Americanization of Canadian private TV will be an accomplished fact."

The Liberal opposition in Ottawa objected to the deal as well. As a result, on September 28, the BBG reversed its original recommendation, even though no Canadian offer had been forthcoming. "How could you sons of bitches go back on yourselves?" Eddie Goodman remembers thinking.

This time around, the BBG stated flatly that it was "not prepared to recommend any transaction involving the financial participation of American networks in a Canadian station." A dissenting opinion was voiced by Edward Dunlop, George Hees's brother-in-law. He argued that the stock transfer was quite acceptable, since the Broadcasting Act allowed a maximum of 25 per cent of the voting stock in a Canadian television station to be held by a foreign interest. By refusing CFTO's access to this capital, the board would "impair the interests" of the station.

"The board has made its decision and that's all there is to it," John Bassett told the press. Yet CFTO was heading towards bankruptcy and desperately needed that $2 million-plus from ABC. How could he obtain it without transferring any of the station's equity? What if ABC bought a special kind of debenture instead of the 252 common shares? With these debentures, ABC would be entitled to a 25 per cent share of the profit and the debentures themselves would be as irrevocable and irredeemable as permanent stock. "The debentures were very similar to equity, except that [their holders] didn't have a vote," Allan Beattie explains. In addition, a debenture deal would not have to be reported to the Board of Broadcast Governors. (Later, ABC asked Baton to buy it out — which Baton, by that time in far better shape, was pleased to do.)

When the dust settled on this last-gasp refinancing, the renamed Baton Broadcasting Incorporated was still controlled by the Telegram trust. Joel Aldred was out and Sovereign Film, Foster Hewitt, Ted Rogers, and lawyers Eddie Goodman and Charles Dubin held the remaining equity. All these parties, along with ABC, were represented on the Baton board, and ABC's Donald Coyle even attended two CTV meetings.

At least the worst of the surgery was over at CFTO. Staff had been slashed by almost 40 per cent. Joel Aldred's team was gone. The new station manager, Bill Crampton, was a manager "who specialized in what we now call re-engineering," recalls Allan Beattie. "He went into CFTO in a very tough way and got the costs under control." Now it was up to Crampton; the sales manager, Ted Delaney; and the vice-president of programming, Murray Chercover, to make the station pay.

Delaney, a former sales manager with the Hamilton and Barrie CBC affiliates, was a short and stocky figure with thinning hair. Chercover was his complete physical opposite — tall and gaunt with a pencil-thin moustache and a deep, rich voice. He had joined the CBC as a coordinating television producer and was present at the launch of its Toronto television station in September 1952. Owing to an inattentive technician, the first image that viewers saw was the corporation's logo, upside down. Five CBC bosses stood behind Chercover that day as witnesses to the gaffe. Among them were Ernie Bushnell and Stu Griffiths. Chercover, who suffered from panic attacks before every show, never forgot this embarrassment. Later, the stress of directing a live production called *Space Command*, which featured none other than William Shatner, almost landed him in hospital. It was questionable whether Chercover would find CFTO a less migraine-inducing environment.

Also new to the CFTO staff was Harvey Kirck, who'd been hired to read the early evening newscast and direct the news operation. At this time, news broadcasts originated both from the Agincourt studios and from a CFTO desk at the *Telegram*. In his memoirs, Kirck remembered John Bassett calling him, "his voice booming through the receiver loud enough to be heard at the end of the newsroom." Bassett might sometimes suggest a story idea, but according to Kirck he never meddled with the news itself.

In all, CFTO had narrowly weathered the storm. "We lost a great deal of money," John Bassett remembers. "I was comforted, however, by the knowledge that when private broadcasting had started in the United Kingdom, a lot of people had got involved with high hopes and great optimism. And then they lost their nerve. They sold out to other people, who made an enormous success. I knew that if we went through the bad times, the good times could come."

Says Ted Rogers, "We survived and kept at it. And under John's leadership, we became the greatest television station in Canada." Fred Eaton agrees: "Toronto, as John has always said, is the most competitive of all television markets. In the early days, CFTO went right to the wall, which is when he stepped in, and in his inimitable style led the company out of almost certain disaster. And made it into a tremendously viable company."

Other new stations faced catastrophes as well; Toronto's was just the largest. CFCF in Montreal had to re-organize its financial structure. On opposite coasts, the Vancouver and Halifax stations both struggled on the verge of bankruptcy. Only the second stations in Calgary, Edmonton, Winnipeg, and Ottawa, which faced little or no competition from American signals, survived without having to engage in a change-your-partners refinancing dance. Winnipeg's Ralph Misener confessed that their station was like many others — it went through some rough times. "[But] we did not bring in new capital or partners; we did not change management or reduce our services. Instead we persevered."

All together, the eight affiliates suffered almost $5 million in losses during their first full year of operation. One of their mistakes was getting into a bidding race to see who was going to build the biggest studio in each community, Murray Chercover said. "We ended up with an extraordinary expenditure on hardware, with very little left for [programming]."

Ray Peters of CHAN recalled that they were having trouble meeting the Canadian content quota. He said, "All the grand promises had fallen by the wayside; the money simply wasn't there."

"For some of us, those early days were almost disastrous," says Finlay MacDonald. "We were producing parochial — I could use a stronger word, but parochial — programs. . . . I was going broke, trying to satisfy content requirements — which, because of unforeseen expenses and overly optimistic revenue forecasting, were to prove [very] costly." John Bassett was "one of [their] saviours" when it came to honouring MacDonald's content obligations: "CFTO . . . provided us in Halifax, without charge, a great number of productions, which helped give our schedule a more professional look. I will be forever mindful of its assistance." Big John would do the same for other regional stations also, even though they had to wait for the programming to be shipped by air, since the ITO didn't have a microwave contract. But even CFTO was hard pressed to come up with a sufficiency of all-Canadian productions. Its own grand promises of symphonies, operas, and indigenous dramas, made during its application for the Toronto licence, had fallen by the wayside too. For example, in 1962, only 17 per cent of its prime-time programming was truly Canadian.

The network as a whole was doing little better. Spence Caldwell's for-profit entity couldn't make one, losing close to $1 million during the first year on air. It remained unproven and a sponsor's second choice. National advertisers preferred buying time on the CBC, whose more than thirty-five English-language stations delivered a much larger audience than the 2.5 million households who tuned in to the eight stations. Caldwell was already fishing for ways the BBG could modify its regulations to help him out — such as setting back introduction of the 55 per cent Canadian content rule to the fall of 1962; allowing programs of "exceptional interest to Canadians" (for example, the World Series) to qualify as Canadian content; and making it easy for a privately owned CBC affiliate to leave the public corporation and join CTV.

But the BBG was bent on making life more difficult, at least for Big

John. In February 1962, at public hearings in Quebec City, it proposed new regulations that would require private television stations to disclose the full details of their loans to the board, along with an accounting of advances received, debentures issued, and various arrangements made for outside management services. All these measures were aimed at Bassett and his secret debenture deal with ABC. "Not surprisingly, the governors appeared to take the view that this arrangement, while perfectly legal, was simply an evasion of their ruling, producing exactly the result they had sought to avoid — participation of a U.S. network in Canadian television," stated an editorial in the *Globe and Mail*.

Andrew Stewart, in particular, seemed furious at being out-manoeuvred. Upon learning that ABC's Donald Coyle had twice attended CTV board meetings, he'd sent a letter to Coyle, with copies to Bassett and Caldwell, telling the ABC executive that his "participation in the determination of policies of any approved broadcasting organization in Canada could prejudice the status of the organization." These were ominous words, but both Bassett and Caldwell replied simply that Coyle had been invited to the meetings — then hoped the issue would blow over. (It didn't. Bassett turned up at the Montreal hearings and mounted a stirring defence of his station's right to seek funds wherever and whenever it chose — but to no avail. The regulations passed that April, cramping his fiscal style in years to come.)

The year 1962 was another tough one for CTV's affiliated stations, although they reduced their combined losses to slightly over $1 million. Finlay MacDonald's CJCH in Halifax had its own brush with bankruptcy. On October 31, its bank suddenly cut off its credit and the station could not meet its payroll. "When you cannot meet your program commitments, you face the level gaze of the [broadcasting authority]," MacDonald said. "When you fail to meet your capital commitments, you face the level gaze of your equipment supplier and the first-mortgage bond holders. Sometimes it is difficult to know which level gaze is the more formidable."

Halifax's white knights proved to be Spence Caldwell and Maclean Hunter Ltd. (who together bought 27.5 per cent of CJCH Ltd. in 1962). MacDonald remained a CTV director and vigorously represented a Maritime point of view for many more years.

By 1963, the tide had begun to turn, and more affiliates moved into the black, with a combined profit for the eight stations of more than

$1 million. By then, CHAN Vancouver had brought in a third financial backer, Selkirk Holdings Ltd., 30 per cent owned by Southam Company. This was also the year that Frank Griffiths, last seen attempting to gain a licence in 1960, found a back door into the private network.

Next to Toronto, the Vancouver-Victoria television market was the most competitive in Canada, striving against a similar flood of American broadcast signals that crossed the border from Bellingham and Seattle, Washington. But the situation was quite different in one important respect. Only a third of the Buffalo stations' revenue came from Canadian advertisers, whereas almost all of the Bellingham station's did. So keen was KVOS to capture these dollars that it had moved its transmitter off-shore to one of the San Juan Islands, thus gaining unimpeded reach into Vancouver and Victoria. In response, the owner of CHEK, the CBC's Victoria affiliate, moved his transmitter to Saturna, one of the Gulf Islands, giving it greater coverage of Vancouver. In fact, CHEK was able to reach parts of Vancouver that CHAN could not.

Even so, CHEK was losing the ratings battle on all fronts and ran into financial difficulties. Frank Griffiths heard about the Victoria station's troubles and his Metropolitan Television made an offer to purchase it. This time it looked like a licence was in the bag for Griffiths, until a spoiler showed up at the public hearings. CHAN's president, Ray Peters, opposed Metropolitan's application on the grounds that, under Griffiths's ownership, CHEK would (a) become a Vancouver station and (b) air "wall-to-wall American strip programming." Peters argued that there wasn't enough room in Vancouver for five radio and three television stations, let alone KVOS in Bellingham, which siphoned off so many advertising dollars and was, by Peters's own admission, "knocking his ears off" when it came to ratings.

Peters's arguments worked, and Metropolitan's application was denied. Afterwards, Peters went around to CHEK and asked them if they'd like to sell to him, but the owners still had an option agreement with Griffiths.

Then Peters got another idea. Rather than launch a no-win war, why not merge the two stations? "Our signal at CHAN was poor," he recalls. "But we could compete with KVOS . . . by taking two weak stations and putting them together."

It was unlikely, though, that Peters could ever come to terms with Griffiths, who was angry at him for thwarting Metropolitan's application. Peters needed a go-between and therefore asked the BBG's Andrew Stewart to phone the respective players and make the proposal on his behalf.

"I still own the option," Griffiths insisted.

"Suppose . . . you come in as a Vantel shareholder," Peters replied.

"Okay," Griffiths said, "but I want to be the largest single shareholder."

At this time, Vantel had about two dozen shareholders, all of whom sat on the board, which made for crowded meetings. Foremost among them were Famous Players, Britain's Associated Television, and Selkirk Holdings, each of which held roughly 12 per cent. Griffiths's deal with Peters gave him close to 15 per cent. This granted his wish and made him the largest shareholder in the television operation whose ownership the BBG had denied him three years earlier.

At the June 24, 1963, meeting to hear arguments for and against the proposed merger, Frank Griffiths declared to the CHEK board that they were on the brink of receivership. There was only one way out. Metropolitan paid $700,000 for the station, assumed its debt, and merged CHEK with CHAN to form a new entity, the British Columbia Television Broadcasting System.

Ray Peters took over its operation. CHAN remained a CTV quasi-affiliate (although it still didn't sign an agreement with Spence Caldwell). CHEK remained a CBC affiliate, although the two stations cooperated on several joint productions as a cost-saving measure.

One happy by-product of this corporate union was a personal reunion. Heidi Sohnel, the young woman Peters had laid off two years earlier from CHAN, had meanwhile remained in Toronto with the CBC. One day, Peters found himself at the public broadcaster's offices for a no doubt boring meeting, and invited her to lunch. One thing led to another. Almost three years into their bi-coastal relationship (which was exacerbated by Sohnel's subsequent move to New York), Peters asked her to come back to Vancouver and marry him. The couple still jokes that she did so "to get even with him for firing her."

Not long after winning his network licence, Spence Caldwell found a new name for it: the CTV Television Network, or CTV. At the end of July 1961, he reached an agreement with Bell Telephone whereby CTV would lease its own live microwave circuits from the Trans-Canada Telephone System for seven years, at a total cost of $11 million in annual payments. Signing this contract would speed up the telephone companies' installation of additional microwave circuits from sea to sea, just as had been done in the Windsor–to–Quebec City corridor. At first, though, outside this area, CTV would use the existing national microwave system for two hours a day, when the CBC wasn't using it, to transmit programs to its affiliates to be taped for broadcast later. Over the years, CTV's annual rental payments would increase, as more and more capacity was added to the second national system.

That same July, CTV moved into new offices, taking a full floor of a new building that was still under construction on Charles Street East in Toronto. Caldwell boasted that it would be the "most modern network headquarters in the world." Every office contained a television monitor, but the CTV centre did not include a production facility of any description.

Ahead of its October 1 launch, CTV promoted itself to advertisers as "The Big City Network" — a "free enterprise" network that would provide service only in the country's "major population areas" and stress entertainment over information. Few programs, apart from "royal visits, or something like that" would go unsponsored — or so Caldwell hoped. "Any program is a better program, if it is sponsored," he pronounced.

And what he needed, right off the bat, were better, more saleable programs. That fall, CTV provided its affiliates with only twelve. Seven were foreign, most of which were American, such as *The Andy Griffiths Show*. Of the five Canadian programs, three were game shows — *Showdown* from Montreal, *20 Questions* from Winnipeg (a reworked British quiz show), and *Take a Chance* from Toronto (Roy Ward Dixon's radio quiz show adapted to television). The remaining two were musical variety outings — *Cross-Canada Barn Dance* and *Westcoast* from Vancouver. The latter was the most expensive and the best of the five. Naturally, it was also the first to be cancelled, after only a single fall season. Viewers were not impressed. They began referring to CTV as "the Quiz Show Network" and turned elsewhere.

"Spence wanted to produce everything at the cheapest possible cost," Finlay MacDonald remembers. "John Bassett, Lloyd Moffat, and I soldiered on in that money-grubbing network that CTV started out to be. Its structure did not serve the purposes expected by the BBG, nor the affiliates." Indeed, Caldwell was distributing only eight hours a week of taped network programming during the first fall season, two hours less than the BBG's requirement, but Andrew Stewart and his fellow broadcast governors had to give Caldwell a grace period. They saw themselves as protectors of the fledgling network, which had been formed with their active encouragement despite indifference or downright opposition from the individual stations. Stewart went so far as to appear in a film that was aired to introduce CTV as an important step in communications and another tie binding Canada together.

As network programming expanded to fourteen hours a week in early 1962, a fifteen-minute national newscast called *CTV National News*, was added to the line-up. It was broadcast nightly at 10:30 p.m. from facilities at CJOH in Ottawa and was co-anchored by the veteran newspapermen Charles Lynch and Peter Stursberg. But both appeared ill at ease, and the newscast soon died from lack of viewers. One of CTV's few critically acclaimed successes in the early years was the advertiser-sponsored *Telepoll*, an independently produced public-affairs program that began airing on Sunday afternoons that winter. Each week a sample group of 1,000 people in the network's eight cities used electronic polls to answer questions about current events posed by the editors of *Saturday Night* magazine from a CFTO studio.

The other mainstay of CTV's schedule in its first two seasons was John Bassett's Eastern Conference football games. In 1961, because the second microwave system hadn't yet been installed outside of Ontario and Quebec, Bassett sold his rights to the Grey Cup game to various sponsors. They, in turn, asked the CBC to broadcast the game. Then Bassett turned around and petitioned the BBG to instruct the CBC to let CTV's Toronto, Ottawa, and Montreal affiliates pick up the CBC feed. The BBG denied his request. The following year, Bassett, who still owned the Eastern Conference rights, and CTV, which now owned the Western Conference rights, got exclusive rights to broadcast the Grey Cup game also. This time they asked the CBC to allow its affiliates to carry CTV's feed. The trouble was that this feed came complete with commercials from CTV's sponsors, British American Oil, Nabob, and Labatt. Now it was the CBC's turn to refuse. Bassett then offered to provide the feed with or without the ads, but Spence Caldwell was having none of this. He claimed that Bassett had acted unilaterally on behalf of CFTO and insisted that, if the CBC wanted to tap in to the feed, they'd have to carry it advertisements and all.

Fearful that Canadians would be deprived of the game, the BBG intervened, ordering the CBC to carry CTV's commercials. The public broadcaster promptly refused to comply, arguing that the BBG was exceeding its authority, and that the CBC had no intention of allowing CTV to "use the national broadcasting service as a sales tool." The issue threatened to wind up in Parliament, but time was running out. A few weeks before the Cup, the CBC offered a compromise: it would make "courtesy announcements" mentioning CTV's advertisers. The Diefenbaker government backed this proposal, to which Caldwell agreed. In a fitting anti-climax to all these murky machinations, the game itself was cut short. This was the year that the Cup was held in Toronto's Exhibition Stadium, and fog rolled in from Lake Ontario, making it impossible for the teams to see their hands in front of their faces.

☆

John Bassett and the cigar-chomping Spence Caldwell might have made a Faustian bargain to ensure that there'd be a private network, but they never overcame their personal differences. Caldwell told Maggie Siggins that Big John used to call him as often as three times a day and that many of these calls would end in arguments. "He was also very annoying at our board meetings because he was talking about things he didn't know much about. He'd ask a question and rather than me answering all the time, I'd get one of the guys, a good broadcaster like Jack Davidson of Winnipeg, to reply. Davidson, in his slow way, would start to answer when Bassett would turn to one of his five aides and start to yak, yak, yak. He'd talk to beat the band. The rest of us could hardly hear a word. I'd finally say to him, 'When you ask a question, for Christ's sake, listen to the answer.'"

Actually, it's a wonder that Bassett found time to make himself such a trial to Caldwell. He had a great deal more on his plate. During the 1962 federal election, for example, he ran as a Tory candidate in the predominantly lower-income and ethnically patchwork-quilt riding of Spadina. Baton's present-day chief executive, Ivan Fecan, remembers Big John's regal passage through the Kensington Market area, where the young Fecan lived with his mother and grandmother. But Bassett's timing was off. When he accepted the nomination, the Tories dominated Metro Toronto, but the country's love affair with Dief the Chief was waning. Bassett didn't help matters by campaigning one night in his Rolls-Royce. On June 18, he was soundly defeated. Afterwards, Finlay MacDonald asked him how this could have happened, considering that CFTO and most particularly the *Telegram* had vociferously supported any number of worthy causes, including improved race relations and religious tolerance. "Use your goddamned head," Bassett told him. "Nobody likes crusading publishers. They don't go for this horseshit anymore."

In late October, Bassett and MacDonald watched President Kennedy's final television address during the Cuban missile crisis in the den of Bassett's mid-town Toronto home. "You were gung-ho about Kennedy's speech, and after hearing it you were convinced the Russians would blink," MacDonald wrote to his friend thirty-five years later. "I was scared shitless, but after all, you were the liberator of Amsterdam . . . , while I was a mere subaltern."

A month before the crisis, on September 24, *CTV National News* (produced, as before, at CJOH Ottawa) had returned to CTV's now twenty-two-hours-a-week schedule in the more traditional 11 p.m. slot. It featured two new co-anchor teams. The most popular was the achingly young and dapper Peter Jennings — the former host of *Saturday Date*, a CJOH teen dance-party show, who'd later become the star of *ABC News*. Jennings was paired with the somewhat more experienced Baden "Buzz" Langton. Unfortunately, CJOH's bargain-basement technical facilities made the newscast look amateurish.

Even worse, the network hadn't as yet budgeted for a "reverse microwave" feed, which would have enabled the affiliates coast to coast to transmit programming as well as receiving it. As a result, the understaffed and cash-strapped stations were forced to ship their local news films to Ottawa by air. These were so often delayed or lost that items from outside central Canada rarely made it into the newscast, even a day late, and *CTV National News* came off looking cheap and parochial compared to the CBC. Even so, this time around, the program would survive.

It had plenty to report. Egged on by John Bassett, George Hees led a revolt against Prime Minister Diefenbaker over the issue of nuclear disarmament, defeating the government in the House. The election was set for early April 1963. This time it was Finlay MacDonald who bravely ran as a Tory candidate, in Nova Scotia. "I did it on impulse," MacDonald remembers. "It was pure ego." He and many other Tories were wiped out, amid an atmosphere of nuclear jitters and anti-Americanism spurred by the missile crisis, and the Liberals swept back into power under Lester Pearson.

Seven months later, one of the twentieth century's seminal events shocked the world. On November 22, when John F. Kennedy was shot, Harvey Kirck raced to Agincourt and on no notice anchored CTV's coverage of the assassination. Peter Jennings reported on location from Dallas, and the Ottawa newsroom provided archival material, but the story was told from Toronto, where CFTO carried the CBS network feed. In a series of broadcasts aired under panic conditions, CTV was able to hold its own, presenting a reasonable cross-section of Canadian views and reactions coast to coast.

A few days later, Kirck received his third offer from *CTV National News* to become one of its regular co-anchors. This time he accepted. He didn't want to go to Ottawa, but he was sure that it wouldn't be long before the newscast moved to CFTO. At the close of his December 3, 1963, debut, Kirck picked up his pipe and stuck it in his mouth. This became a personal trademark during his early years on the air. Not long after his arrival, the format of co-anchor teams had to change when Peter Jennings and Buzz Langton both headed south to U.S. networks, and Kirck became the chief anchor of *CTV National News*.

4

The Cooperative — 1964–68

By 1964, Spence Caldwell's network was starting to fall apart, for a wide variety of reasons. The most successful commercial networks worldwide were those that owned or partially owned money-making affiliated stations in major markets. This was the case in the United States, where a network could own up to five different affiliates. Profits from these stations flowed directly into the network's coffers. But CTV did not fit this pattern. It owned no stations; it owned no production centre. In fact, it owned very little. It delivered its programming via leased microwave circuits over 4,000 miles and through six different time zones, which cost it an arm and a leg. It was trying to recover all its costs by attempting to convince some measurable portion of only 15 million English-speaking people (one-tenth the size of a U.S. network's potential audience) to watch what it had to offer. It was not doing well with cooking shows and quiz games — which, as Ray Peters remarks, "were unsuccessful with the audience and therefore with advertisers. And advertisers are the motor that makes it work." In short, Peters and his fellow station owners decided that they didn't need a network to do what they could do more efficiently and perhaps more profitably on their own.

On the one hand, the affiliates knew that they had to air better quality Canadian programs, so as to meet their content requirements. On the other, these programs did not generate the revenues needed to turn a profit for Caldwell's Bay Street shareholders, because viewers wanted to watch American shows. While the network could come up with improved Canadian programming, it didn't want to, because there was no money in it. An uneasy stalemate resulted, as everybody waited for the next shoe to drop.

By this time, the CTV affiliates had reactivated their earlier non-profit cooperative, the Independent Television Organization. It had lain dormant for a year or two as they threw their efforts into and behind CTV. Now that the network was perceived as a losing proposition, the re-emergence of the ITO, with Ottawa's Ernie Bushnell as president, marked the beginning of the end for Spence Caldwell.

The ITO had been active on two fronts. First, it produced its own Canadian programming, which was passed around among the affiliate members. CTV had nothing to do with any of these programs, which included *University of the Air*, a half-hour adult education series to which colleges in several different provinces contributed; *Canadian Talent Showcase*, to which Toronto, Montreal, Ottawa, and Winnipeg contributed in the first season; *Platform*, an Ottawa public affairs program featuring the news of the week in the House of Commons (the precursor of *Question Period*); five half-hours weekly of children's preschool programming, to which all the stations contributed; and *After Four*, a magazine show targeted at teenagers and produced at CFTO by Johnny F. Bassett, Big John's eldest son.

Far more troublesome for Spence Caldwell was the ITO's renewed shared purchase of American programs. Murray Chercover, who chaired the cooperative's programming committee, would soon be buying more American shows than CTV did, competing against the network in the one area it looked to for profits. In fact, the ITO was for all intents and purposes operating like a network, except that it had no microwave contract. The only programs Caldwell could offer that the ITO couldn't come up with on its own were a national newscast, live sports, and coverage of events such as federal elections.

Nor was Caldwell successful at selling network time to advertisers. He'd made it as "inexpensive as he could," but certain programs went unsponsored. Caldwell's deputy, Gordon Keeble, explains, "This put the first strain on the fabric of the affiliation, since the stations were understandably reluctant to see prime-time commercial availabilities going by unsold and without recompense from the network, so they wanted the time back. But the network, equally understandably, had to retain it in order to have something in its kitbag to sell."

This led to a confusing grab-bag of ad hoc agreements and trade-offs. For example, the stations compensated the network for unsold advertising time for CTV's broadcasts of the CFL games, as well as for their production and microwave distribution costs. CTV grabbed the advertising revenue from five out of seven national newscasts, leaving the stations to split the revenue from only two. These and other exceptions to the general rule were added to the affiliation agreement. "We kept patching the boat and kept on paddling, instead of following what . . . might perhaps have been the better course," Gordon Keeble admits, "and that [was] just to take the boat out of the water and rebuild it to accomplish the voyage that we all wanted."

When it came time to negotiate a new affiliation agreement in 1964, Spence Caldwell proposed one that incorporated all these many and varied special deals and left room for what he promised would be the production of quality Canadian programs. He also asked for more time in local schedules for network shows than the current 23 3/4 hours, and more advertising revenue than the 40 per cent the network currently retained. (This had risen over the years from its original 25 per cent, but Caldwell still wasn't making any money.) The affiliates refused him on both points, and the agreement that was eventually hammered out over a long series of acrimonious meetings (Finlay MacDonald remarks that "it's a wonder there wasn't loss of life") marked a crossroads for both parties.

Amazingly, since it was clear to everyone that Caldwell's grand experiment was heading for the rocks, CTV kept signing up new prospects. Three former CBC affiliates (Moose Jaw, Saskatchewan; Kitchener, Ontario; and St. John's, Newfoundland) came aboard one after the other, in time for the launch of CTV's second, third, and fourth fall seasons. But CTV's increased total of eleven affiliates was still less than one-quarter of the CBC's fifty English-language outlets, just as its coverage area was only 71 per cent of Canada's English-language population, compared to the CBC's 90 per cent.

And in fact, some of the affiliates — as opposed to the network as a whole — were doing well. All together, the original eight pulled in $4 million in profits in 1964. This rose to $6 million the following year and $8 million in 1966. But their success only drew further scrutiny from the BBG, which argued that the fat and healthy major-market stations could afford to subsidize an extension of network service into smaller, more remote centres.

The three new arrivals came aboard because the CBC had established its own stations in these cities. In 1963, Big John Bassett had personally persuaded the network to admit the Kitchener station, CKCO, which was half owned by the American-controlled Famous Players Corp. and one-quarter owned by the Rhodes scholar and phonograph inventor Carl Pollock, the president of Electrohome Ltd.

The St. John's station, CJON, belonged to none other than Geoff Stirling and Don Jamieson, last encountered at the second-station licence applications in 1960. They were close friends of Jack Pickersgill, an influential member of both the St. Laurent and Pearson cabinets. A decade earlier, they'd made use of this connection to beat out the CBC for the right to establish the city's first television outlet. Now that the CBC had obtained a licence, they had to find another network home.

That home, however, was far removed from Newfoundland. Jamieson's only complaint, when he later showed up at the BBG for a licence renewal hearing, was that CTV was dragging its heels when it came to linking CJON by microwave to the rest of the network. The CBC's station had taken over CJON's old hook-up, and CTV refused to pay Bell to install new circuits on the towers linking Halifax to St. John's, because the cost of doing so was far in excess of the revenue the station could produce for the network.

"We have to bring everything in either on film or videotape," Jamieson said. "If we run into bad . . . weather, we can find ourselves . . . without a single scheduled program for a given night. [But] the CTV service has been very useful to us. . . . First of all, of course, it is a source of revenue and also . . . gives us some Canadian content. But without the microwave, . . . we did not get any of the football games and therefore did not get that advantage in Canadian content." Nor did CJON receive *CTV National News*.

Jamieson was happier with the ITO, which provided a vital two and a half hours of programming a week at modest cost. He saw great potential in the cooperative and looked forward to more productions from CFTO, CJOH, and CFCF Montreal, as well as the Vancouver and Winnipeg stations. "I think the ITO has a good deal to recommend it," he said. "I believe the major contributions inevitably will have to come out of the larger centres, particularly Toronto and Montreal. I do not know what we [in Newfoundland] could [offer] in the way of variety or drama that would be of use all across the country, [but] we could probably do something in public affairs."

At its best, then, the ITO performed a very positive role, helping Jamieson and other smaller station owners over one hurdle after another.

On occasion, CJON borrowed equipment from both the Halifax and Ottawa stations to cover political conventions and special events such as an annual regatta. On the programming front, it received coverage of the Calgary Stampede from the Calgary station, *The MacPherson Report* from the Winnipeg station, and a number of news specials from the Ottawa station, all free of charge. When it needed additional Canadian children's programming, Ray Peters in Vancouver came to the rescue with a five-day-a-week show, again at no cost. Big John shipped along a number of CFTO productions and forgot to send a bill. Without this friendly support, CJON would have found it difficult to survive.

This turn of events no doubt galled Don Jamieson, who'd grown accustomed to getting what he wanted. He had advised the Liberals on their broadcasting policy during the 1963 election campaign, when Lester Pearson came into power. Thanks to Jamieson's input, the Pearson government did not disband the Tory-created Board of Broadcast Governors, as was expected. Instead, in keeping with the fine old Canadian tradition of patronage, the Liberals simply replaced the Tory loyalists on the board with loyalists of their own.

Upon assuming office, Jack Pickersgill, Pearson's secretary of state responsible for the CBC, asked Jamieson, then president of the Canadian Association of Broadcasters, to serve on a three-man committee whose mandate it was to formulate new directions in broadcasting. There, Jamieson immediately butted heads with the CBC's president, Alphonse Ouimet, and the BBG's chairman, Andrew Stewart, who'd survived the Liberal purge of the board, although his days were numbered. The "Troika," as the three men became known, could not reach agreement, in part because Jamieson held stern views. He thought that both the CBC and private broadcasters should be subject to the same degree of regulation and control. On bad days, he considered the public corporation to be a "potential threat to our free society." These and other dicta filled Andrew Stewart with foreboding and unease.

Upset by the Troika's lack of progress, Pearson decided it was time to bring back an old favourite — Robert Fowler, a prominent Liberal lawyer who'd headed up a royal commission on broadcasting in 1955–57. The Fowler Commission had submitted its findings to the St. Laurent Liberals shortly before John Diefenbaker was elected. To no one's surprise, the Diefenbaker government implemented very few of its recommendations.

Now, almost a decade later, Fowler got his revenge. The report from the Advisory Committee on Broadcasting 1964–65 (also known as Fowler II) was an all-encompassing indictment of everything Diefenbaker's

Tories had done. Fowler went so far as to float the idea of a return to a single authority that would both regulate the entire broadcasting industry and operate the CBC. He saved his greatest ire, however, for the private stations, who'd flourished under the protection of the previous government.

Above all, Fowler didn't want the ITO stations to get their hands on CTV. He faulted them, not Spence Caldwell, for being obsessed with profits and deliberately starving the network of funds. In his view, their "commercial power" had enabled them "to negotiate agreements which give little hope of financial success for the network itself. The essential trouble is that the affiliates do not want CTV to be a success. The station operators admit, quite frankly, that CTV is a private company organized to make money, and that most of the investment in it is held by people not in the broadcasting business. If there are to be any profits from private broadcasting, the stations want the profits themselves and are unwilling to let outsiders make money out of it."

Fowler then opened up his thesaurus and inveighed against what he saw as a "private hassle," a "jealous concern," an "unsavoury feud," and a "petty and silly attitude." All these, he believed, had to "be brought to an end — by voluntary action preferably, by compulsion if necessary." He felt that a private television network was "necessary" as well. But in the public interest (a concept that, according to him, had evaded the independent station owners) he suggested a number of ways "to overcome the difficulty." Among these was a forced merger of the ITO and CTV. If that didn't work, and CTV collapsed, Fowler thought it could be reconstituted as a non-profit trust, to be operated either by a separate board or by the new improved broadcasting regulator. In effect, he seemed to be veering towards the creation of a second CBC.

Thoroughly spooked by these proposals, the CTV brain trust retreated to Spence Caldwell's farm northwest of Toronto and spent two non-stop days and nights discussing Fowler II. A few weeks later, at a CTV board meeting held on the network's fourth anniversary, a defeated Caldwell tendered his resignation. Gordon Keeble, his long-time associate, succeeded him as president. "I think I've done a pretty good job," Caldwell said. "Now it's time to let these young punks take it and run. I've got a farm in Caledon East, a summer home at Sturgeon Point, and a thirty-foot Chris Craft at the [Royal Canadian Yacht Club] I used only once this May. [I'm going] to live a little. I've got an [investment portfolio] to look after." Those investments included his 37 per cent stake in CTV. (Caldwell indeed retired to his farm; eighteen years later he died in a car accident.)

With CTV teetering on the edge of bankruptcy, Caldwell had realized that the only way the network could survive would be if it owned at least one station in a lucrative major market. This would provide a steady cash flow to fund its operations. To this end, he'd lined up a consortium of publishing moguls (including Maclean Hunter and various Southam and Sifton interests), with a view to taking over Bushnell Television, the owner of CJOH Ottawa. But the offer wasn't rich enough for Bushnell's blood and went nowhere, leaving Caldwell without a leg to stand on.

Thus time had run out for both Caldwell and the network. If nothing was done, CTV's capital deficit would be more than $1 million by September and its cash deficit would be roughly half of that. In other words, the network company was insolvent. Something had to be done at once if the network was going to survive. The stations were not prepared to put any more money into a company they did not control. They were prepared, however, to take it over.

On January 4, 1966, the eleven ITO stations announced that they had agreed in principle to do exactly that, and — if they succeeded — to run the network as a cooperative. One of the prime movers of this scheme was Ernie Bushnell, the ITO's president. Bill McGregor, the general manager of CKCO Kitchener, described him as "the guide trying to lead everybody through this, identifying the stumbling blocks. He was a little short guy, quite stocky, with salt-and-pepper hair. . . . He gave the impression he was a tough infighter, that he had been to the wars."

The so-called Group of Eleven met formally at Toronto's Park Plaza Hotel the following day, to ratify their agreement and come up with a formula that would be acceptable to CTV's shareholders. They were prepared to return the $1 million-plus put in by Caldwell's original investors. A quarter of that sum would be in cash, and the rest in bonds to be retired in five years' time. The owners had retained Eddie Goodman and instructed him to draft the offer and present it to Gordon Keeble within twenty-four hours. Keeble duly tabled the offer before CTV's board. Caldwell and the other forty-five non-station shareholders accepted. The next step was to ask the BBG to schedule a special session, stressing the need for immediate action. Given the onrush of events, the BBG concurred, and the hearing was slated for February 23.

A week prior to this date, most of the Group of Eleven converged on the Holiday Inn in Winnipeg. Ray Peters flew back from Los Angeles, where he'd been negotiating co-production deals, and arrived in the middle of a snowstorm wearing his west coast raincoat. "I turned several shades of blue, and only thawed out last year," he says. Although CHAN had never signed up for Spence Caldwell's network, Peters was prepared to listen. Now, his station would become a shareholder in the new regime.

Like the ITO, the new improved CTV Television Network would be a cooperative, wholly owned by the member stations with no outside partners or investors. Each of the eleven stations could nominate one director to the board, and each would have one vote, as would the newly elected president. Each would share in the network's capital and operating expenses on the basis of its audience size and ability to pay. Under this formula, CFTO would make by far the largest contribution, assuming 25 per cent of the liabilities, but Big John would have only a single vote, just like everybody else. "Bassett had to give up a lot. He went a long, long way," Eddie Goodman says.

But Bassett didn't go all the way to the Winnipeg meeting. He, Eddie Goodman, and Goodman's junior counsel, Lionel Schipper, were at the airport when their flight was delayed for two hours. Bassett told Goodman he could have his proxy for the meeting. "Get the damn thing settled, Benbo," he said, and strode away. "Well," Schipper joked, "that's 25 per cent of the problem solved."

Bill McGregor did attend and recalls a scrap between CFTO and CFCF Montreal over which would function as the "flagship station." There was no question that Toronto commanded the largest audience, but Dick Misener of Canadian Marconi was confident that his long-established company was stronger. Also, as McGregor reminds us, the population of Canada's two biggest cities was "a damn sight closer together then." But in the end, the meeting didn't turn into a coronation, and there was no "king," real or titular, because enough of the affiliates insisted that the network be a democracy. "There was a need to have Toronto, Montreal, and Vancouver; without any one of them, the thing would be limping," McGregor says. Beyond that, the participants seemed to be taking one man, one vote seriously. So, by default, it was decided that Winnipeg's Ralph Misener would chair the new network.

Everyone at the conference was aware that everything they hoped to do had been expressly forbidden by Fowler II — but everyone thought they could bring the BBG around to their point of view. They began to thrash out the necessary details. Their proposed affiliation agreement committed them to sixty hours weekly of network programming, up from the previous twenty-four, which was on par with the CBC's national service. "There would be no more cooking or game shows, no more of that mindless kind of programming," Ray Peters says. How would they pay for it? The new shareholders' and affiliates' agreement called for the original 25-75 revenue-sharing scheme, with only 25 per cent going to the network. Still, the affiliates were convinced that 25 per cent would be enough — because, unlike Spence Caldwell's CTV network, their version had only to break even, not turn a profit.

On February 23, the eleven station owners appeared in the Dominion Bureau of Statistics Building, on the outskirts of Ottawa, to seek BBG approval of their plans. "It was the middle of winter," Ray Peters says. "We took cabs out to Siberia."

Eddie Goodman led the presentation, while Ernie Bushnell spoke on behalf of the affiliates and Gordon Keeble carried the ball for what remained of Spence Caldwell's CTV. Goodman had decided to keep Big John out of the limelight, but not out of the transcript. Newfoundland Broadcasting's Don Jamieson, while referring to his "selfish objective" to get St. John's connected with the network by microwave, alleged that he was "going to get simultaneous delivery out of the network, even if takes every cent that John Bassett has."

Murray Chercover described the revised network's proposed broadcast schedule and ran a sample tape. In the first year, he said, network programming would jump from almost twenty-four to about sixty hours a week. Chercover had budgeted $8.5 million for this, of which $4.5 million was committed to Canadian programming. Distribution costs, including microwave links, would almost double to $2.3 million. In addition to existing programs, which included CFTO's *Country Hall* and CFCF's *Insight*, an interview show hosted by the ex-CCF MP Douglas Fisher, Chercover unveiled *Bright and Early* (a precursor of *Canada AM*) and *Mr. & Mrs.*, yet another game show. So much for Ray Peters's vow not to offer any more of the latter. "We make no apology for these popular daytime features," Chercover told the board. "We take pride that these programs are produced by . . . and for Canadians, and over the years have demonstrated a popularity superior to their counterparts imported from the United States by the CBC."

Beyond one or two minor interventions from the usual suspects, the only real threat to the ITO's proposal was a rival application from Ken Soble and Maurice Strong, the president of Power Corp., who wanted to start all over again with yet another totally different private network. Goodman made short work of this. After they'd had their say, he rose and noted that he clearly remembered when CTV made its original network bid. "When I heard the resonant cadences of Mr. Soble roll out, I shut my eyes," he said. "And really, I might have been back listening to Spence

Caldwell give his presentation to the board in 1960." The board had no wish to open up a fresh can of worms. So — although Fowler II had counselled against this very course — the BBG took less than two weeks to give the Group of Eleven the go-ahead to buy the CTV network on March 4, 1966. There was one important caveat, which would come back to haunt them in later years. The board stated that multiple ownership would not be permitted. That is, nobody could control more than one CTV affiliate.

The newly appointed vice-chairman of the board, Pierre Juneau, later called these pivotal hearings a "very soul-searching and dramatic moment in broadcasting. There was a great amount of doubt expressed through public opinion in the country as to whether such an arrangement would work." Even Big John was forced to admit that, in backing away from the fears expressed in Fowler II, "the BBG showed a lot of guts." Now it was up to the affiliates to justify the notion that CTV could indeed work on a cooperative basis.

They started off with good intentions and a willingness to convene at the drop of a hat. At first, the board of directors seemed to meet once or twice a month. If it wasn't the board, then it was the programming, sales, engineering, or finance committees. "There was a flurry of meetings," Finlay MacDonald recalls. "We were eleven prima donnas with twenty-seven things on the agenda. What a rattle that was!"

But this was necessary, because CTV had to rush plans through for its 1966–67 season, when the network expected to begin broadcasting in colour. To mark the occasion, it commissioned a new tri-colour network logo, with the "C" superimposed on a red circle, the "T" on a blue square, and the "V" on a green inverted triangle — the one that endures today. Unfortunately, the cost of colour conversion and other expenses turned out to be higher than the hopeful estimates presented to the BBG. The affiliates were forced to adjust their formula. They agreed to pay for program production and purchase, as well as for microwave and videotape distribution out of gross revenues, before giving the network and stations their 25-75 split.

As well, there was a bit of juggling in the boardroom, as Maclean Hunter, which had sold its shares in Spence Caldwell's network, became a new CTV shareholder by purchasing a 75 per cent interest in CFCN, the Calgary affiliate. In return, Caldwell himself and Finlay MacDonald bought Maclean Hunter's smaller interest in the Halifax station. This brought Don Campbell, Maclean Hunter's vice-president of broadcasting, onto the board, where he would later be elected chairman.

Looking back, Ray Peters calls that particular group an "interesting board. They weren't pussycats." Put another way (as did Harvey Kirck, in his memoirs), "CTV's growing up would be long and painful."

At this point, Murray Chercover left CFTO to become the network's executive vice-president. In Chercover, CTV had found a programmer who understood numbers. "Murray was a visionary," MacDonald says. "[He] could take his dream and cost-account it. He was originally a producer and could criticize a script." Chercover moved quickly to develop co-production projects with American and British companies, because he felt that Canadian viewers were becoming more sophisticated after years of exposure to the best foreign programs. Just because the Canadian market was smaller, they could not "expect Canadians to respond to less desirable entertainment programs with lower standards of production, scripting, direction, or performance," he said. In his view, the experience garnered by participating in co-productions would help CTV raise its standards across the board and would lead to more polished and appealing all-Canadian content. Bassett wholeheartedly agreed with this position. The more co-production under the Agincourt roof, the better for him.

But CTV itself remained relatively a shoestring operation. For example, the programming staff (about half a dozen people) were armed with much less than one-tenth of the CBC's programming budget. Under the new affiliation agreement, the network had to buy or produce about fifty hours of programming a week, half of which was reserved as network sales time. In addition, it provided special events such as CFL and NFL games, along with coverage of federal elections, political leadership conventions, and other major news events as they occurred. All this brought the average annual CTV network service up to sixty hours weekly, roughly equivalent to the CBC's service and roughly half of a given station's total airtime.

Two-thirds of these programs would appear for the first time in colour. At Bassett's urging, the BBG had finally set September 1 as the date when colour broadcasting could begin, to which the CBC had agreed. Thanks to Joel Aldred's far-sighted policies, CFTO was the only studio in Canada with colour cameras ready to go — so Big John shrewdly jumped the gun and convinced the board to allow him to "test" his equipment. The "tests" went on for three months, while the CBC gnashed its teeth. On September 1, CTV waved goodbye to black and white with an hour-long special that included appearances by the BBG's chairman Andrew Stewart and Judy LaMarsh, the secretary of state. Still, the station had to buy nine more cameras as well as a new mobile unit for football and hockey games. The bill came to $2 million. Similar expenses would be faced by the other affiliates as they too fell into line.

Meanwhile, the new guard had also decided to cease production of *CTV National News* at CJOH Ottawa on a contract basis. Instead, a "central editorial unit" was built under the Agincourt roof, staffed by network employees. This, as Harvey Kirck wrote in his memoirs, "brought sighs of relief in the newsroom, the loudest from me."

The first newscast from the new Toronto facilities was broadcast in colour, except for a couple of items from the regions, and proved a great success. Nevertheless, the move to Toronto raised some controversy when CTV's new head of news and public affairs, Peter Reilly, publicly accused Big John of interfering in the news division. But the charges didn't stick and Reilly had to resign. "I'd been in control of the daily operations for some time," Kirck wrote, "and I'd never heard a word about our telecasts from John Bassett."

Bassett later said that if he'd tried to interfere, CTV wouldn't have been able to get responsible, capable journalists to work for the network. "They'd simply have said, 'Go to hell, I'm not going to work on a public affairs show if I've got to come in every Monday morning and get a memo from you as to what we're going to say,'" Bassett explained.

The news staff might not have heard anything from John Bassett, but CTV's directors did. "If he didn't like what was on last night, he'd rant and rave with that big, booming voice," remembers Ray Peters. "I'd wait until he got tired and then I'd say, 'Look John, that's a management decision.'"

But Bassett's tirades rarely went past the boardroom door. He understood, even if it had to be pointed out to him time and time again, that programming decisions had to be made by network management. The directors had a say — in his case, a particularly loud one — but they had to draw a line. "This was decided years ago, [when] we first came together to form the cooperative," Bassett said later. "Any other system would simply be chaotic. [In] the field of public affairs, one man would want to have the Liberal leader on all the time. Another might want to have the Tory leader. . . . With that gang, [the NDP leader] would never get on at all. . . . So responsibility was turned over to network management — and this applies to entertainment shows as well."

Another of Chercover's programming moves was to suggest that the network develop an hour-long public affairs program — a prototype for all the American news-magazine shows that would follow, like *60 Minutes*,

20/20, Prime Time Live, and *Dateline*. This involved "considerable expense," and Chercover thought he'd be "drawn and quartered by the board." But he pressed on, and *W5* (standing for who, what, why, where, and when) was born — a "very big gamble for a neophyte co-op network, [immediately] after the great *Seven Days* debacle."

This Hour Has Seven Days, an even more ground-breaking program, had been cancelled by the CBC brass in the winter of 1966 and it was unclear whether the corporation would have a replacement public affairs entry for the ten o'clock Sunday night time slot. *W5* went on the air (at that same time) ten weeks before the CBC launched another public affairs program of its own in the same time slot. Television critics, members of Parliament, and everybody else who wanted to see both shows complained long and loud. "I don't give a damn," said Chercover. "Why doesn't the CBC move [its show]? We were there first." Maybe — but, at the behest of the BBG, CTV rescheduled *W5* to nine o'clock, opposite the CBC's airing of *Bonanza*, which Chercover grumbled was "like cutting your throat." He wanted to air his own American hit show in peak viewing hours to compete with the Cartwrights: Ben (played by Canadian Lorne Greene), Hoss, and Little Joe. Even after CBC moved *Bonanza* to another night, replacing it with Canadian dramatic, variety, and other specials, Chercover was determined to push *W5* back to ten o'clock. "We were on Sunday night and that's where we belong, at ten o'clock, and we're going back there and let the CBC do what they wish to do." He pointed out, with some justification, that no outcry arose when both the CTV's and CBC's national newscasts were broadcast at eleven o'clock. People made their choices.

In fact, *CTV National News* commanded a respectable audience of 340,000 homes in 1966–67, and the network's average audience for all six of its prime-time Canadian programs was higher, at 469,000 homes.

For 1967–68, Chercover introduced four new Canadian shows, three of which were half-hour public affairs programs: *Question Period, Crossfire*, and *Canada: 101*. The fourth was *The Pig & Whistle*, a variety show featuring the Carlton Show Band and dancers who performed vivacious hornpipes, jigs, and reels in an oak-beamed pub (actually, papier mâché) constructed at CFTO. A Toronto critic complained that it made the CBC's *Don Messer's Jubilee* "look good," but conceded that it would quite probably prosper, even if it was "strictly amateur night at the pub." He was correct. CTV's average audience for Canadian shows grew to 512,000 homes that season, principally because of *The Pig & Whistle*'s phenomenal success. Still, CTV's average audience for its American programming was much higher, growing from 646,000 homes in 1966–67 to 691,000 homes in 1967–68, led by such hits as *I Dream of Jeannie*, *Bewitched*, *Ironside*, *Star Trek*, and *The Jackie Gleason Show*. Thus — in a foretaste of what was to come — CTV's average Canadian prime-time program delivered only three-quarters of the audience of the average U.S. offering.

☆

Meanwhile, back in the boardroom, CTV's soon-to-be-legendary squabbles were picking up steam. All of the parties involved remember these days with a mix of nostalgia and stark horror. In Finlay MacDonald's eloquent words, "[The] interrelationship of CTV affiliates was an exercise . . . characterized by goodwill, by compromise, by common hope, by cooperation and, from time to time, by obscenity and invective."

Big John was in the thick of it, of course. He enjoyed oral combat, but not with Ray Peters, whose high-minded and somewhat self-righteous persona rubbed Bassett the wrong way. In sum, they brought out the worst in each other. The script was familiar: Bassett would get agitated and profane, whereupon Peters would give him a "hard, stony look" and lecture him like an ill-disciplined child. This, Peters notes, went on for years: "On many occasions I was the leader of the opposition, so if anyone was going to get it, it would have been me."

CTV folklore has the two protagonists storming out of the room every forty-five seconds, but on close inspection, it seems that far more often, Big John bounced up and down in his seat but never quite managed to make an exit. Once, however, in the midst of a particularly thunder-and-lightning tirade, he slammed his papers on the table and disappeared. The other directors sat in stunned silence until someone asked, "What do we do now?" Someone else suggested that an emissary be sent to retrieve him. This bold plan was put into effect, and the envoy ran into Bassett on his way back down the hall. "That feels better," Bassett said, his satisfaction evident at having answered nature's call.

"He threatened all of us, several times," Ray Peters says. "But John [wasn't] unreasonable, just volatile. If you could sit him down and [talk quietly], tell him he was factually incorrect and lay out the facts, he'd come around."

Besides, Peters claims his biggest battles with Big John weren't personal. Bassett was forever lobbying to get more work for CFTO, even though Toronto enjoyed a virtual monopoly on the network's production of Canadian programming. Peters and the other directors — especially Stu Griffiths, the general manager of Ottawa's CJOH — quite naturally wanted a fair slice of the pie. "Stu was another arch-enemy of Bassett's," says Finlay MacDonald. By this time, Ernie Bushnell had sold most of his shares to his protégé and CJOH was Griffiths's station in everything but name. He went so far as to have the station carpenter build him a forty-foot yacht in a shed behind the production centre, a structure that soon became known as Marine Studio 3.

High drama erupted in early 1968, when the board kicked Gordon Keeble upstairs to the position of chairman and chief executive of the network. Murray Chercover, regarded by many as "a Bassett man," took over the presidency at the age of thirty-eight. Within a year or two, Chercover was chief executive and Keeble was out. Finlay MacDonald remembers that Big John himself dismissed Keeble in "a wild shouting match," yelling, "Depart! In the name of God, go!"

Ray Peters (who remembers Keeble as "a dedicated guy" and was sorry to see him leave) disagrees. Keeble's firing was "unfriendly and a major, major decision," but that decision wasn't Bassett's alone and would have required the backing of a majority of the board.

In subsequent boardroom mill-arounds, Chercover (who'd worked as CFTO's vice-president of programming, and still had a proprietary interest in many Toronto productions) would wind up acting as referee. Finlay MacDonald describes him as a long-suffering godsend: "'Let's do such-and-such,' Bassett would say, and we'd all shudder. [But Murray] had great managerial style. . . . He never lost his temper. . . . When he had problems with Bassett, he would just shake his head sadly. He can never be adequately thanked for handling Bassett."

All that having been said, the CTV Television Network would arguably not have amounted to much if not for Big John's overweening ambition, his willingness to take risks and the financial backing that CFTO provided to fund new network ventures.

And, despite all the tall tales about bitter infighting, CTV's directors occasionally stopped screaming at one another long enough to enjoy each other's company — notably at their annual Grey Cup weekend meetings. There were other memorable gatherings as well. Ray Peters describes arriving halfway through a board meeting held at Don Jamieson's fishing lodge in Newfoundland. Peters was delayed in Toronto, so he didn't travel with the group and had to hire a float plane when he arrived in St. John's. "I was used to [small planes] in B.C.," recalls Peters, "but this guy went right up on top of the clouds, spotted a little opening no bigger than that, popped through the hole, spun around, passed over the harbour and landed." The pilot then turned to his shaken passenger and in his thick Newfie accent said, "That's what we call cutting the cards with Jesus."

"That's when broadcasting was fun," Peters says. "We really had a lot of fun, but then it got serious."

Finlay MacDonald agrees about the joys of those early years. "I'll never forget them," he says. "[We had] a whacking amount of fun. We'd party, those of us who drank more than the rest of us." Bassett, MacDonald, and Jamieson made a happy trio. All three men were loaded with charm and the gift of the gab. (But their professional association was short-lived. The forty-five-year-old proprietor of CJON left broadcasting for Liberal politics later in 1966, where, unlike his two friends, he was elected to Parliament. Over the next decade or so, Jamieson held numerous Cabinet posts in successive Trudeau governments, including secretary of state for External Affairs. When he was appointed High Commissioner to the United Kingdom and Northern Ireland in 1982, Jamieson worked his magic on Queen Elizabeth, winning the rare sound of her regal laughter. Then, four years later, he died of a heart attack.)

During these early CTV years, Big John Bassett fell in love with Isabel Crawford (née Macdonald). A minor obstacle was that both of them were married — John to his wife, Moira, and Isabel to a friend of Bassett's eldest son, Johnny F. She was a beautiful Hitchcockian blonde school-teacher, just twenty-four years old when she was introduced to the forty-eight-year-old Big John in the summer of 1964, during a visit to the Bassett family's summer house in North Hatley, Quebec. At first, Isabel proved immune to the loud media mogul's domineering charm. Then he hired her as a reporter at the *Telegram*, and she got to know him better. Their love affair began soon after.

Since Isabel was an accomplished equestrian, Bassett went out and bought a new horse, as well as new breeches, boots, and riding hat. The animal soon rebelled, and Big John was thrown, breaking his leg and opening up fresh opportunities for high drama. One day, Bassett limped into a CTV directors meeting on crutches, while his chauffeur trailed behind, carrying a cushion. "Put the goddamn thing down there," Bassett ordered. He then settled himself into his chair, propped his shattered leg on the cushion, and launched into a thrilling account of what had happened. Halfway through, he stopped and smiled wickedly. "I felt a hell of a lot better when I shot the fucking horse!" he bellowed. This was an unfulfilled wish — but Big John had learned his lesson. Years later, when Isabel went on a group cycling tour of France, he followed at a safe distance in the comfort of a chauffeured car.

Eventually, love prevailed. John Fraser, then a cub reporter at the *Telegram* (where Big John was referred to by his staff as "Lord Bassett of Front"), witnessed the romantic scene when Isabel found out that she'd been named in the *Globe and Mail* that morning as co-respondent in Mrs. John Bassett's divorce proceedings. From the back of the newsroom strode Big John. "Isabel!" he shouted. A teary Isabel stood up so he could see her. "I'm here, John," she said. He put his arms around her and they walked back to his office together, as the entire news staff broke into spontaneous applause.

To escape the outrage of Toronto society, Isabel left the country and taught school in Kingston, Jamaica, for a term. Many people (including Johnny F., Douglas, and David Bassett and the four Eaton brothers) were upset by the May-December union, but John David and Signy Eaton supported their friend throughout his social shunning. Then, in 1967, after both divorces had been finalized, Big John married Isabel in a quiet ceremony performed by a rabbi.

They didn't stay out of the limelight for long, though. Brian Mulroney recalls seeing the newlyweds in September 1967 at the Tory leadership convention in Toronto. "I have in my mind's eye a picture of John and Isabel at the Royal York Hotel," he says. "I knew them very little then . . . , but I spotted them down the hall. While I've seen them hundreds of times since . . . , the image has stayed with me of two tanned, attractive, intelligent, gregarious people. John was at the very top of his form. . . . CFTO was going strong. He had the *Telegram*. He had the Argonauts. He was kind of like the toast of Toronto."

Nor could Big John restrain himself from responding to the ostracism. As recounted by the columnist Allan Fotheringham, Finlay MacDonald remembers being with Bassett in a Toronto nightclub shortly after his marriage to Isabel. Six straight-laced socialites entered the room. Big John, knowing that they thought of him as the veritable devil, stood up and shouted, "Ya, ya, ya!" at them, chasing them out of the club.

But these same socialites soon clamoured to spend time with the once scandalous couple, when Bassett's friends Bobby and Ethel Kennedy came to spend a weekend with the newlyweds in their new Rosedale home. The Bassetts hosted a dinner and dance in the Kennedys' honour at the Royal York Hotel and took Bobby to Maple Leafs and Argonauts games. A year later, when Senator Kennedy was assassinated, Big John acted as honorary pallbearer at the funeral.

5

The CRTC
versus CTV — 1968–77

One of the more unlikely friendships of our time developed between Big John Bassett and Pierre Juneau, the new chairman of the Canadian Radio-television Commission (CRTC), a new and marginally different regulatory agency established by Lester Pearson's Liberal government in early 1968.

A Jesuit-trained Montrealer, Juneau had co-founded the avant-garde *Cité libre* magazine with Pierre Trudeau and spent seventeen years with the National Film Board, where he rose to become head of French-language production. Judy LaMarsh, the secretary of state responsible for cultural affairs, had appointed him to the Board of Broadcast Governors as vice-chairman and as natural heir to Andrew Stewart.

Apart from Stewart, the Pearson government had succeeded in stacking the BBG with Liberal loyalists. Nonetheless, it was still perceived as the protector of private broadcasting interests, particularly of the CTV Television Network. The growing prosperity of CTV's big-city affiliates had spurred demands from various quarters that their profits be ploughed back into the broadcasting system. This concern was part of a growing economic and cultural nationalism, kick-started by Expo 67, which fostered renewed criticism of the wholesale Americanization of Canadian television screens.

To make a clean break from the broadcasting legacy of the Diefenbaker administration, the Liberals therefore disbanded the BBG and created the CRTC, appointing Juneau as chairman. It would be his mandate to uphold Canadian culture and to crack down on anyone — including the CTV station owners — who failed to toe the line.

Yet Juneau had already formed friendships with two of them: Big John and Stu Griffiths of CJOH Ottawa. Griffiths had in fact been Judy LaMarsh's candidate for president of the CBC until her 1966–67 plot to oust Alphonse Ouimet fizzled, much to Griffiths's bitter disappointment. Griffiths got to know Juneau when he served on the BBG vice-chairman's eleven-member committee on broadcasting, which reported just days before Andrew Stewart resigned and the CRTC was formed. Griffiths was also friendly with the new CRTC vice-chairman, Harry Boyle, a former CBC program supervisor who, like Griffiths, had worked there under Ernie Bushnell. All three men therefore had a shared past in the public broadcasting sector.

Juneau's friendship with Big John was more surprising. They might have been expected to be oil and water. But as they got to know each other, they found common ground — often on the tennis court, where Bassett usually won. Juneau thought that Bassett was an interesting man, a Canadian patriot, and open to reasoned persuasion.

Juneau told Bassett that something had to be done about the lack of leadership in the private network. He said the directors were running it like a private club, that they were interested only in fun and games on Grey Cup weekends. To improve the decision-making process, Juneau insisted the CTV board establish an executive committee with regional representation that would meet more frequently under the chairmanship of an authoritative figure. Juneau thought Bassett might be able to do the job.

That was the easy part. In addition, Juneau wanted CTV to meet two CRTC-mandated objectives: extending its service to sparsely settled areas and producing "significant" Canadian content (Cancon) programs.

The first goal would be expensive to achieve. In most cases, extended coverage would add little to the network's revenue base, while boosting its operating costs. No government monies or subsidies were available to fund the extension, as had always been the case with the CBC. Rather, in order to comply, CTV would have to reach new arrangements with its affiliates.

The cooperative's first step in this direction was to bring in CKCW of Moncton, New Brunswick, as its twelfth affiliate in the fall of 1969. At the same time, Clifford Sifton's CKCK Regina signed up as a replacement for CHAB Moose Jaw, which had been purchased by the CBC.

Two years later, CKSO Sudbury and CFQC Saskatoon both cut their

ties with the public corporation, making a total of fourteen CTV affiliated stations.

As may be imagined, none of these stations was rolling in money.
That's why, on a voluntary basis that came to be known as the Robin
Hood principle, the larger, more profitable CTV stations ("the haves")
agreed to contribute more to the network's operation than the smaller
stations ("the have-nots"), especially those that could demonstrate real
hardship. At a November 1969 meeting, the CTV board had decided to
commission an independent study from the consulting firm of Woods
Gordon, a subsidiary of the network's auditor, Clarkson & Gordon. This
study examined each affiliate's financial resources and the network's
operations as a whole and came up with a useful formula.

Each station's ability-to-pay cut-off was pegged at $2 million in
annual revenue. Once this figure was forwarded to and confirmed by the
CRTC, three classes of CTV affiliates were established:

- Full affiliates (the "haves"), which took in more than $2 million. They
  shared proportionately in any network profit and anted up proportionately
  whenever the network failed to meet its budget target, according to yet
  another revenue- and cost-sharing formula developed by Woods Gordon.
- Affiliates (the "have-nots"), which failed to make $2 million a year. They
  received a guaranteed annual time payment for hours that they reserved
  for network programming, whether or not the time was sold to advertisers.
  They did not share in any network profit, nor bear any portion of losses.
- Supplementary affiliates, which were usually CBC-affiliated stations in
  remote areas that were licensed to set up second transmitters in order to
  provide CTV service as well. These so-called twinsticks received no guaranteed annual payment, had no shareholdings, and assumed no financial
  responsibility in the network. They did get the full CTV service, along
  with sales rights to nearly all the programs, at no cost. They were responsible only for the costs incurred in delivering that service within their
  licensed areas. An example of this sort of third-string affiliate was CHFO
  in Thunder Bay, which signed up in 1971.

That same year, at a special general shareholders' meeting, the eight
"have" stations — Vancouver, Calgary, Edmonton, Winnipeg, Kitchener,
Toronto, Ottawa, and Montreal — agreed to support the six "have-nots"
— Saskatoon, Regina, Sudbury, Moncton, Halifax, and St. John's — with
a total of $600,000 in guaranteed annual time payments. This cost was
split in accordance with the Woods Gordon formula, with CFTO
assuming the largest share at 28 per cent.

So far, so cost-intensive — but the "haves" saw trouble down the line. Ray Peters of CHAN had already spent $2 million to extend network service to Kamloops, Kelowna, Vernon, and Penticton — $1 million to build and operate rebroadcasting units and another $1 million for an in-province microwave contract. This was "infinitely more" than he had anticipated. He asked the CRTC for more time to do the same for Prince George, the Cariboo, and the Kootenays, noting that, for the moment, CHAN enjoyed the "dubious honour" of being in a position to pay up, but adding that even further coverage in British Columbia and elsewhere across the country would mean even greater expenditures and tax the resources of even the most profitable affiliates. (Peters was particularly hard pressed when it came to bouncing signals around the hinterlands. As CTV's only west-coast affiliate, CHAN was expected to blanket the entire province, despite the fact that mountains got in the way. Eventually, its owner, British Columbia Television, would install more than 100 rebroadcasting units, thus qualifying as one of the world's largest private transmission systems.)

A year later, in November 1972, the CTV stations signed a new combined shareholders' and affiliation agreement, as well as a supplementary affiliation pact. Under the former, the six "have-not" stations received an additional $25,000 a year in time payments and remained off the hook on costs until their annual revenue exceeded $2 million, at which point they'd be upgraded to full affiliate status. This seems to have worked. Two years later, four of the former "have-nots" (Saskatoon, Regina, Moncton, and Halifax) along with CJCB in Sydney, Nova Scotia (the latest addition to the CTV fold), had passed the $2-million cut-off, leaving only Sudbury and St. John's as poor relations. Now there were thirteen outlets paying their own way — and CTV's coverage was growing with each passing year. In 1966, network signals could be received by 75 per cent of Canada's English-speaking population. By 1970, this figure had grown to 79 per cent and reached 87 per cent in 1972 and 92 per cent in 1975.

The CRTC congratulated the network on its efforts, but Murray Chercover, CTV's president, sounded a note of caution. He felt that pushing coverage any further into uneconomic markets would be exponentially more expensive — and, because the funds would have to come out of the network's or the individual stations' general revenues, would "erode [their] financial capacity to maintain, and more important to improve, [their] programming."

☆

Pierre Juneau's second goal — better Cancon programming — had proved more difficult to attain, but that didn't slow him down. Less than two years into his mandate, Juneau pushed to hike up daily Canadian content requirements to 60 per cent from 55 per cent, sparking the Great Cancon Battle of 1970.

Most of the CTV affiliates were up in arms and looked for help to Don Jamieson, by this time the federal minister of transport. He thought that Canadians were entitled to prefer American television if they wanted to and doubted that there was enough Canadian talent to go around. For his part, Murray Chercover claimed that the additional 5 per cent would run the network into the ground, turning a $4-million profit into a $9-million loss. He accused the CRTC of being fixated on "tonnage" — that is, quantity as opposed to quality.

At public hearings in April 1970, the Canadian Association of Broadcasters, the private stations' lobby group, embarked on an unprecedented seven-hour filibuster. Its president, Bill McGregor of CKCO Kitchener, argued that, while the higher quota might succeed in forcing broadcasters to produce more Canadian shows, they'd be so wretched that no one would watch. Almost all the member stations shared this view and backed the filibuster. The exceptions were Big John Bassett and Ottawa's Stu Griffiths, both of whom resigned from the CAB in protest at its methods. In fact, Big John made his feelings plain by sending his telegram of resignation directly to the hearings. His stance (and Griffiths's) was that more Canadian programs — be they good, bad, or indifferent — could only mean more production work for CFTO and CJOH.

Juneau knew this and was counting on Bassett's and Griffiths's support. CFTO, in particular, was fat and healthy, having become the most-watched station in the Toronto market. Big John attributed this in part to popular acceptance of its Canadian programming — particularly news, sports, and light entertainment.

But there was a price attached. An independent financial study of CTV commissioned by the CRTC confirmed what a 1971 Woods Gordon study commissioned by the network had concluded: CTV needed American shows that it could sell to advertisers at a high enough margin to cover the losses racked up by its Canadian programming.

Numbers told the story. CTV's average audience for its Canadian programs in 1968–69 was 588,000 homes. Two seasons later this total had declined to 530,000 homes, but rose to 590,000 in 1971–72, largely because more people were tuning in to the national newscast. By contrast, CTV's average audience for its American programming was 721,000 homes in 1968–69, rising steadily to 881,000 homes in 1971–72.

In the five years since CTV's re-organization, an average Canadian prime-time program delivered only 60 per cent of the audience of the average American program.

This is why replacing a prime-time hour of American programming with Canadian fare cost the network more than $800,000 in advertising revenue. The average American show generated $860,000; the average Canadian entertainment show (even though it cost a mere $12,000 to $35,000 to produce) brought in only $30,000. If you combined entertainment with news and information programming, the average Canadian show actually lost $60,000 an hour. Clearly, the network's survival depended on the right balance of American and Canadian programming — a balancing act that became known as cross-subsidization.

In May 1972, Juneau retreated on his Cancon proposal. CTV's Canadian content requirement would rise to 60 per cent daily, but fall to 50 per cent from 6 p.m. to midnight (although the CBC's requirement would remain at 60 per cent both day and evening), and American co-productions would also count as Cancon. This kicked off a renewed struggle among the affiliates to see who'd provide new programs to fill the time available.

Chief among them was CJOH in Ottawa, where Stu Griffiths hoped to make the renamed Bushnell Communications one of the country's largest producers and exporters of programming. He enlarged his facilities in anticipation of getting the CRTC's approval for an aggressive expansion in television, radio, and cable (which, as will be described later, hit a stumbling block, leaving him with four studios — two of them capable of handling large-scale network productions — that sat idle much of the time).

CJOH and Carlton Productions in fact produced two shows (*Anything You Can Do* and *The Amazing Kreskin*) for sale to CTV. Griffiths soon discovered, though, that these programs cost substantially more than he could recoup by airing them in Canada alone. But this did not dissuade him from attempting to develop other properties. In late 1972, he was in discussion with the novelist Mordecai Richler about making a Canadian version of *All in the Family*, at a projected cost of $20,000 to $25,000 per half-hour episode.

This came to nothing, and no other affiliate succeeded in putting together a drama series, either. Instead, in 1972, CTV committed to a $1.5-million-plus American co-production called *Police Surgeon*, a half-hour drama that succeeded an earlier show from the same producers called *Simon Locke, M.D.* It was filmed primarily on location around Toronto, or at the independent Lakeshore Studios, and broadcast network-wide on Saturday nights at 7:30. A cluster of U.S. stations picked it up to air in that same time slot. It cost $75,000 an episode, and 80 per cent of that sum remained in Canada.

Meanwhile, CFTO's Agincourt complex kept growing. Since 1970, Baton had spent $2.1 million to expand its studio facilities and $1.4 million on new equipment. Bassett was fond of claiming that CFTO's in-house production company, Glen-Warren Productions, was the "best single production house in North America." It was certainly the second-largest, outranked only by NBC in Burbank, California. This comparison was on Big John's mind, because two-thirds of Baton's $7 million in production business for the 1971–72 season came from sources other than the CTV network. Most were American. "They came up here to use our facilities and take advantage of our trained personnel," Bassett said. For example, James Stewart and Helen Hayes travelled north to star in a television adaptation of *Harvey*, a Hallmark Hall of Fame movie. Another non-network client was Bassett's son Johnny F., who produced a feature-length hockey movie called *Face-Off*, through his new company, Agincourt Productions.

Still, a third (or $2.2 million) of Baton's production revenues represented billings to CTV, a third of which was for the use of CFTO's facilities for network news and public affairs programming. Bassett considered this "a significant figure" and joked to the CRTC that one of Baton's advantages was "the very psychological strength we have because, as you know, I dominate the network." He quickly added that he wished this were true, and that, if he tried to veto a program whose origin was not Toronto, he would be "thrown out of the [board] meeting." He knew this, he said, because he had tried in the past.

And so he did. Back in front of the CRTC, Big John wasn't shy about admitting his desire to dominate CTV's Canadian programming: "I make no apology that when we go out . . . with pilots and so on, in competition with other affiliates, I want it all." When one of the regulators asked him whether there was any danger that CTV would become a one-station network with regard to production, he answered readily, "I hope so."

He was getting there. In 1971–72, CFTO contributed the variety shows *Rollin'* and *Half the George Kirby Comedy Hour* (the latter a CTV/American co-production, pre-sold to thirty-three stations on three U.S. networks); *The Ian Tyson Show*; *The Trouble with Tracy* (a five-days-a-week sitcom); a low-rent version of *Front Page Challenge* called *Headline Hunters*; and *The Waterville Gang*, a children's series about puppets who lived beneath the sea and preached ecology.

Although Big John wanted everything he could lay his hands on when it came to CTV's Canadian production, he did acknowledge the virtue of spreading things around. "The only winner in all of this is the network," he told the CRTC. "You have Vancouver and Ottawa . . . and Toronto, and we have already been served notice that Montreal is planning on increased activity in this field. [When] I say I want it all, that is as the head of a production company. But the fact is that it is of great benefit to the network to have three or four or five strong affiliates all competing strenuously for production business. [The] network is the beneficiary . . . , because it is the stations . . . who put up their own money, [gather] together ideas, and . . . bring pilots to the network committee and fight like anything to win."

Big John was correct in noting Vancouver's desire to do exactly that. British Columbia Television had spent $1.5 million upgrading CHAN's studios and equipment. "With this infusion of capital," Ray Peters told the CRTC, "I can assure you that our physical potential in program production is equal to any production centre in the country, despite what Mr. Bassett says."

Peters points out that his efforts to counter Baton's domination of the CTV network was supported by British Columbia Television's ownership. "I was reflecting company policy," he says. "The big friction between [us and the Baton group] was not due to personalities. My concept of the network did not sit well with Big John and Baton. Their stated objective was to have all of the network's production originate [from] CFTO. I thought that production should originate from all across the country. . . . That's where the friction started and it became very serious. It went far beyond a fight between John Bassett and myself."

But Bassett had very little tolerance for whining from any point of the compass. When one of the CRTC commissioners from western Canada, Gertrude Laing, started talking about a sense of regional alienation, he gave her short shrift. "Are you suggesting that the [CTV board] should approve and air entertainment programs of inferior quality only because they are made in the west?" he barked. "I would not necessarily agree that we were serving national unity, the people of the west or the Canadian public . . . by airing programs, if they were indeed inferior, simply because they were produced in one area."

This position had its merits, but everyone knew that Big John could be a terrible snob when it came to life outside his private stamping ground. "Until the west gets more population, I don't care how much goddamn oil they discover in Alberta," he later told Peter C. Newman. "Toronto and not Calgary is going to be the place where you do the deals, just like it's New York and not Houston where you go for the really big business.

It's all a matter of geography. You get out to western Canada, for Christ's sake — you know, Vancouver and those places, and you're away from the action. *This* is where it's at." As for the television industry, Bassett couldn't understand why any English-speaking Canadian actor, writer, director, or producer would choose to live outside Toronto.

Ray Peters conceded Big John's point that the largest source of potential talent was Toronto, but argued that Vancouver wasn't far behind. Speaking at the network's licence renewal hearings in 1972, he told the CRTC, "We have gone from no network shows produced in Vancouver two years ago to now five and a half hours." These included a game show called *What's the Good Word?* and the self-explanatory *Kareen's Yoga*, as well as a $2-million theatrical children's drama, *Story Theatre*, which aired contemporary adaptations of fables and fairy tales, and a musical offering, *The Paul Horn Show*, which was about to debut the following spring. "It is our own target to try to have about ten hours of programming on the network [by the fall of '73]," he said. "I am hoping that John Bassett has left the room."

Similar plans were in the works at CFCF Montreal (which provided a made-in-Canada version of the American game show *Beat the Clock* and the innovative children's program, *Puppet People*), and Kitchener's CKCO, which contributed *Romper Room*, another kid's diversion. As well, all the affiliates were expected to forward items to CTV's news and public affairs offerings, and to *University of the Air*, *Sports Beat*, and *Wide World of Sports*. (The latter began in 1964 as a ninety-minute series on Saturday afternoons, using an hour's worth of items picked up from *ABC's Wide World of Sports* and thirty minutes of home-grown clips from events such as the Canadian Figure Skating Championships and the Canadian Grand Prix. When Johnny Esaw joined CTV in 1966 as a sports consultant, he became its executive producer, continuing to do play-by-play for NHL hockey and CFL football.) With few other exceptions, though, CFTO ruled the programming roost.

When CTV's president Murray Chercover rose to speak at the 1972 licence renewal hearings, he expressed great satisfaction with *Police Surgeon*'s popularity with both Canadian and American viewers. Big John seconded that motion. He thought that *Police Surgeon* had shown "that we can compete in the field of drama, with a continuing production which is competitive and for a mass audience." In fact, he thought that CTV "could be doing three or four dramas of that kind which would be viable because of their production standards and could be saleable on the world market."

Pierre Juneau, however, was unimpressed by *Police Surgeon* and still less by CTV's plethora of variety and game shows. They did not tell Canadian stories or hold up a mirror to the Canadian identity. Where, he wondered, were the meaningful drama series the network had promised? "Programs like *Police Surgeon* . . . are straight entertainment, mass-appeal programs," he stated. The CRTC wanted to know when it would see programs with "more relevance to the country. When is CTV going to come up with series . . . like *Jake and the Kid* and *La Famille Plouffe*, programs . . . where a large number of [Canadians] can recognize themselves?" (Comedy series, by the way, fell into the CRTC's drama category. Drama was defined as filmed or taped entertainment of various sorts. Mini-series and made-for-TV movies qualified, as did situation comedies, but satire and sketch comedy did not. Nor did children's programming, although shows aimed at young adults and families did.) Representative programming would come eventually, but Juneau would see little of it while he occupied the chairman's post. He left the CRTC in mid-1975 (to be replaced by Harry Boyle) for the promised position of Minister of Communications in the Trudeau government. But, like Big John Bassett's before him, Juneau's Parliament Hill dream was dashed when he lost to the Conservative candidate, forcing him to bide his time until he was appointed president of the CBC.

At least, Juneau remained in place long enough to see CTV's answer to *La Famille Plouffe* — the smash sitcom *Excuse My French*, a weekly comedy series from CFCF Montreal's Champlain Productions that debuted in the 1974-75 season. It employed both French- and English-speaking performers. At the height of its popularity, 800,000 Canadian homes tuned in every Thursday night at 7:30. A rival sitcom on CBC in this same time period commanded less than a third that viewership.

This success pleased Murray Chercover, who had meanwhile delegated most of his programming authority. The hands-on decision makers were now Arthur Weinthal (who, as vice-president of entertainment programming, was in charge of all Canadian production except for news and sports), and Philip "Pip" Wedge, responsible as vice-president of programming for purchasing enough popular American shows to pay the freight for the Canadian ones.

Weinthal, a Montreal-born former advertising man, had a tough time developing new entertainment properties. If they were overtly Canadian, they had to be dirt cheap, so that costs could be amortized over CTV's tiny network of fifteen affiliates (only thirteen of which — the full affiliates — were paying their way). If the shows were expensive, they couldn't address Canadian themes or show Canadian locales, so that CTV could recover some of their costs by selling them to American distributors. Viewers in the States had no wish to watch obviously Canadian shows, but Canadian viewers had a voracious appetite for obviously American ones. So Weinthal chose to play it relatively safe. On the one hand, he commissioned more variety shows, usually fronted by American stars, which meant that the shows could be sold into the States. These American co-productions were shot at Big John's studio complex. But Weinthal, to his credit, had also given the green light to the wholly Canadian *Excuse My French*. Part of his job involved cutting through the clamour from the various regional affiliates, all of whom tried, in the course of CTV's nightmarish program committee meetings, to put their concepts forward, leaving Weinthal to pick the ones that worked best.

Pip Wedge, an expatriate Brit (and a more compact version of his friend Sean Connery) had a hard job too, but at least it involved more congenial and luxurious surroundings. As Murray Chercover had done before him, he would take flight each May to the Beverly Hills Hotel in Los Angeles to attend advance screenings of the American networks' fall schedules. His competition at these gatherings was representatives from the CBC, Hamilton's CHCH (which became an independent station in 1961), and Global (a southern Ontario regional network first licensed in 1972). Once the screenings finished, American distributors for the Hollywood studios, which supplied the programs to the American networks, would put the product up for grabs. Then the real wheeling and dealing began, since most of the shows were sold as part of a package, with potential hits and failures tied together. Throughout the 1970s, the CBC, armed with a fat public-funded chequebook, usually went home with whatever it wanted, while CTV got the rejects and the other buyers fought over what was left. But sometimes Wedge got lucky, locking onto an unlikely hit the CBC had overlooked, such as *Rowan and Martin's Laugh-in*.

By the time that CTV's next licence renewal hearing rolled around in November 1975, *Excuse My French* was the only truly Canadian "drama" on the network's schedule. Worse yet, it wasn't going to be renewed, even though it had achieved the third highest ratings of any Canadian program CTV aired that winter. The reason, as usual, was that it cost more money (about $850,000 a season) than it generated, forcing Champlain Productions, CFCF's in-house production company, to swallow the loss. Given this shortfall, and the fact that some of its actors and writers were about to head for Hollywood, Champlain Productions decided to pull the plug.

"No Canadian programming is paying its way," pronounced Chercover, back on his familiar soapbox in front of the CRTC's new chairman, Harry Boyle. Chercover went on to stress the need for cross-subsidization of marginally popular Canadian shows by American crowd-pleasers. "Canadian prime time represents over 52 per cent of [the network's] total program costs, but less than 24 per cent of the revenue," he said. By contrast, foreign (that is, overwhelmingly American) prime-time shows accounted for just over 12 per cent of total program expenditures, but generated 50 per cent of the revenue."

The CRTC digested this unwelcome fact of life and duly renewed CTV's licence in the summer of 1976. It praised the network for airing *Excuse My French*, a "drama with Canadian themes, concerns, and locales," but said it expected to see more money committed to Canadian fare. It also wanted to see *Excuse My French* replaced in the fall schedule, preferably with a show from someplace other than Baton's Glen-Warren Productions studio, which was churning out nearly half of all CTV's Canadian programs. "The Commission remains concerned that entertainment programs are not being supplied to the network by more member stations," the decision read. "The Commission remains convinced that Canadian creativity is not confined to one or two major cities."

It wasn't — but the imbalance wouldn't be addressed for quite a while. Arthur Weinthal had just conceived of a way to transfer the huge audience for the network's international skating competitions to a production called *Stars on Ice*, taped not on a rink, but inside CFTO's Studio 6. One of the show's producers was Debbie Wilkes, a former Olympic silver medallist. She auditioned 270 skaters for the show's chorus line, which had to navigate a 40-by-60-foot ice surface. In its inaugural 1976–77 season, *Stars on Ice* consistently drew more than two million viewers, making it the network's most successful weekly entertainment series so far. As an added bonus, it proved equally successful abroad and was sold to thirty-seven other countries.

Ironically, Big John Bassett had always disliked figure skating, even though the Canadian championships ranked among CTV's most-watched programs. That didn't matter; the broadcast pre-empted his hallowed station time. "We don't want no fancy skating," he'd growl. "I can't understand why people like [it]." Luckily for Big John, he could and did exercise choice by tuning in to the competition — in this case, a feisty independent Toronto station. "Thank God," he cried, "*M*A*S*H* was on CITY!"

☆

In the mid-1970s, the Trudeau government and the Canadian Radio-television Telecommunications Commission (the newly expanded CRTC, still under the chairmanship of Harry Boyle) introduced two policies it hoped would enable CTV and other broadcasters to keep on producing money-losing home-grown dramas. Both were designed to repatriate Canadian advertising dollars from American border stations, particularly WUTV in Buffalo and KVOS in Bellingham, Washington.

First, a new federal tax regulation (Bill C-58) prohibited advertisers from deducting as a business expense the money they laid out buying time on these stations if the ads were aimed at Canadian audiences. Second, the CRTC ordered cable operators to replace an American border station's signal with a Canadian one, if the program in question was being aired on both channels at the same time. This meant, for example, that Vancouverites watching *The Six Million Dollar Man* on KVOS would see CHAN's commercials instead, just as they would have had they been tuned in to the CTV affiliate.

These developments were good news for CTV, which needed all the dollars it could get, because its Canadian entertainment programming — indeed, all its entertainment programming — was in the tank. During the winter of 1977, only two CTV shows made it to the top twenty most-watched list nationwide: *The Six Million Dollar Man* and *The Bionic Woman*. Both attracted more than three million viewers, but both were all too obviously American. *Stars on Ice*, *The Bobby Vinton Show*, *Headline Hunters*, and *Gran Old Country*, all from CFTO, commanded over one million viewers each, making the top fifty. *The David Steinberg Show* from Toronto and *Julie* from CFCF Montreal stumbled in at number seventy and number seventy-one respectively, with just under one million viewers each. In sum, its rivals were eating CTV alive.

At the end of that appalling season, CTV dropped the shortlived *David Steinberg Show* and the long-running *Pig & Whistle*, as well as *The Amazing Kreskin* from Ottawa and *Sports Beat* from Montreal. It also — of necessity — decided to purchase three fewer hours of American programming and handed this time back to the affiliates to fill as they saw fit.

CTV did so because it was having trouble buying anything at all and risked being priced out of the Hollywood bazaar. In May 1977, Pip Wedge found to his disgust that the going rates had jumped by 50 per cent. The once-discountable Global flexed its muscles, stealing back three Norman Lear shows from CTV — *The Jeffersons*, *One Day at a Time*, and *The Sandford Arms*, which Wedge himself had lured away from

Global the season before. This reversed the usual pattern, by which shows like *The Love Boat* and *Charlie's Angels* started out on Global or CHCH Hamilton, became hits, and graduated up to one of the national networks. So unsettled was Wedge that he obtained the rights to *Soap*, a new prime-time spoof of soap operas, only by paying a premium to the distributor not to shop the program around, especially to the CBC.

Of course, a smaller American schedule translated as less advertising revenue to cross-subsidize Canadian programming. CTV could therefore afford to add only one new "Canadian" weekly series, another American co-production called *Search and Rescue*, an anthology about animals who saved people. This was filmed in Kleinburg, north of Toronto, with a Canadian cast. At $105,000 an episode, it seemed pricey for a daytime series, but at least it had been pre-sold to the NBC network for fifty-two weeks.

For a change of pace, CTV also committed to a British/Canadian co-production — the final four episodes of *The Avengers*, a pop culture classic starring Patrick Macnee as the secret agent John Steed and introducing Joanna Lumley (later the over-sexed lush of *Absolutely Fabulous* fame) as his partner, Purdey. Suzette Couture, who will re-enter the story more than a decade later as a major television writer, played a supporting role. All four segments were filmed in Toronto in September 1977 and had plot lines involving such creatures as a colony of aquatic spies who lived beneath the surface of Lake Ontario.

In the realm of mini-series, CTV formed an association with Astral Communications and Lorimar in the United States to dramatize the book *A Man Called Intrepid*, whose author, the non-aquatic Canadian master spy William Stevenson, had based it loosely on the horrific fates that befell real-life agents under his command during World War II when they attempted to crack the German code. The six-hour co-production aired on CTV and the NBC network in 1979.

Despite the fact that co-productions spread the risk around, CTV still felt compelled to cut back its Canadian prime-time programming by another hour in its 1977–78 schedule, giving back this time to the affiliates, too. Thus the stations were responsible for coming up with enough programming to fill all of prime time on Wednesday evenings, as well as the ten o'clock slot on Fridays — all this just when Harry Boyle resigned from the CRTC in the middle of his term at the insistence of the Trudeau cabinet. His replacement, Dr. Pierre Camu, an old school chum of Pierre Juneau's from Montreal, would not prove to be so sympathetic to the CTV network and its affiliates.

6

All the News
That's Fit to Air — 1972–77

The CTV network, second in so many ways to the CBC, in fact pioneered early morning national television. On September 11, 1972, it launched *Canada AM*, a ninety-minute news, lifestyle, and entertainment program. "When I was a young man I used to watch Dave Garroway's NBC *Today* show out of the Rockefeller Center in New York," Ray Peters says. "I became a great fan. Later, I kept telling Murray Chercover [that we had] to put together a news and current affairs show to compete with the American morning shows."

Years earlier, CTV had tried one. It was called *Bright and Early* — but, like the first stab at *CTV National News*, it was premature and quickly disappeared. Ray Peters did not give up. Instead, he kept pitching a revised concept to CTV's executive committee. Peters wanted the show to originate from Vancouver, but Bassett wouldn't bite unless it came out of CFTO. In the end, the committee agreed that Big John could have it, but only if it travelled "several weeks each season," and Murray Chercover was put in charge of getting it under way.

Chercover and Tom Gould, his vice-president of news and information programming, supervised the show's three months of preproduction. Gould, in turn, hired his former CBC colleague Don Cameron, a tough-talking war reporter and twenty-year news veteran, to both revitalize *W5* and handle the birth of the new program. They began to look at possible formats, aided by the show's first producer, Craig Oliver, whom they wooed away from the CBC's *The National*.

From the CBC perspective, according to Oliver, *CTV National News* was "a joke," and the entire network seemed "incredibly bush league." CBC would routinely beat it on stories by "a couple of days," because CTV continued to drag its heels on paying for the reverse microwave link. Most affiliates outside the Toronto-Ottawa-Montreal triangle were still shipping their news items by air, "handing an onion bag to the pilot or stewardess, and begging them to 'please take this to Toronto.'" When the length of the flight was combined with the time differences out west, it usually meant that film arrived long after the cut-off for the 11 p.m. (EST) national newscast with Harvey Kirck. This prehistoric arrangement would be slow to change — but at least *Canada AM* would provide an opportunity to use that material the next morning, while it was still relatively topical and fresh.

Don Cameron's picks as *Canada AM*'s co-hosts were the experienced Percy Saltzman (oddly enough, the first person ever to appear on CBC's Toronto station in 1952) and the twenty-six-year-old Carole Taylor, who'd worked for the Bassetts on the "After Four" teen section at the *Telegram* and on *After Four*, *Toronto Today*, *Topic*, and *The Carole Taylor Show* at CFTO. "She was a young girl when she first came [to us]," Big John said. "She'd won a Miss Toronto Beauty title, and my son [Johnny F.] hired her about twenty minutes later." Taylor remembers that *After Four* was Johnny F.'s "baby," first as a teen paper and then as a nationally syndicated program, on which she interviewed the likes of Gordon Lightfoot. "My ties were with Baton," she says. "I grew up on TV with them."

In advance of the launch, CTV sent Saltzman and Taylor on a publicity tour of all the affiliates' cities, so that they would become familiar to local audiences as "Canadian" rather than "Toronto" personalities ("for whatever evil implication that seems to have," Murray Chercover said).

From the start, *Canada AM* used its reverse microwave connection within the Toronto-Ottawa-Montreal triangle to do as many live interviews in these cities as was "warranted," and the show would travel to at least three centres for a week at a time during its first season.

Carole Taylor proved to be an effective and engaging host, at a time when women in television were still a novelty. It will, for example, come as no surprise that she was paid half Saltzman's salary. "We hired Percy to be the name, to give credibility to the show," said Craig Oliver. "We hired Carole because she was beautiful. But people turned off Percy. He was irascible in the morning, a grump. Carole was intelligent, as well as beautiful. They stayed for her."

But Taylor herself didn't stay long. She was married and a new mother. The extra-early-morning wake-up calls proved too punishing a schedule. This led to her oft-quoted cry for help: "Who do I have to sleep with to get off this show?" Actually, except for the hours, she considers *Canada AM* "my favourite show." But she left in 1973 and made a smooth transition, becoming the first woman to host *W5*, and was replaced on the breakfast show by Helen Hutchinson, who remained in the co-host chair for five years.

"I joined the show in 1973 when *Canada AM* was still an infant, just a few months old," Hutchinson recalled for the program's twenty-fifth anniversary. "In those days we didn't even know if it was going to grow up to be one [or] two years old. We didn't plan very far in advance, but you have to remember that we were pioneers in those days. Canada did not have morning television until we came along; we were inventing it as we went."

"Until *Canada AM*, CTV news was on the air only twenty minutes a day, like *Brigadoon*," explains Craig Oliver, who after a year of producing the morning program was promoted to CTV's assistant director of news and current affairs. "The viewers didn't see us at any other time." (But this higher profile may very well have been sought for less than noble purposes. According to former CTV news executives, *Canada AM* was created so that CTV could continue to meet its daily Canadian content quota of 60 per cent after it added a new afternoon American soap opera to its schedule. The soap, owned and supplied by Procter and Gamble, would make more money for the network than *Canada AM* lost. Which it proceeded to do, along with all CTV's other news and information programming. On average, this program category ran $150,000 an hour in the red.)

News and public affairs shows like *CTV National News*, *W5*, *Question Period*, and *Canada AM* may have lost money, but they helped forge an identity for the network — and, with the exception of *Question Period*, which originated from CJOH in Ottawa, they helped keep Big John's studios humming. The network maintained news bureaus in Ottawa, Montreal, and Vancouver, and a central assignment editor kept in contact with each of the affiliates, to track breaking stories in all the regions. CTV wanted as many live items in its national newscast as possible — but these rarely originated outside the Toronto-Ottawa-Montreal triangle, because Big John balked at the exorbitant cost of reverse microwave.

The vast majority of the time, network programming flowed west and east from Toronto, except for special events like football games.

Big John might claim that CTV's record when it came to airing regional sports events, news, and public affairs programs was "comparatively speaking, . . . far in advance of the CBC," but nobody else agreed with him. The issue of regional alienation would boil to the surface at the next round of CRTC hearings, which convened in November 1972 to consider the renewal of CTV's network licence.

Two months after the launch of *Canada AM*, a proud group of CTV executives appeared before Pierre Juneau and Co. Things went well at first. They rightfully boasted of a precedent-setting breakfast news show that had been well received by viewers everywhere. It came as a shock, then, when the commissioners turned on CTV's news service for its lack of topical items from the west and warned the network to do something about it.

"I think the commission would agree that *Canada AM* is a remarkable improvement," Juneau allowed. "*W5* is a clean, simple, and effective program that seems to be improving all the time." Then the hard questioning began.

Commissioner Armand Cormier wanted to know whether CTV could link all its affiliates full- or part-time by reverse microwave if it wanted to. Murray Chercover admitted that it could, and that this was the daily norm in the Toronto-Ottawa-Montreal triangle. Elsewhere, a reverse-feed capability was available, but was used only as warranted and at the network's discretion.

Vice-chairman Harry Boyle wondered whether cost was the prohibitive factor. Chercover agreed and outlined the problem. CTV's initial contract with Bell had established a priority rate for one-way transmission — that is, from Toronto. Transmissions from the regions back to headquarters were billed at double that rate. At the moment, Chercover said, CTV was spending roughly $2.5 million on the microwave — about 20 per cent of the network's annual budget. To keep the affiliates in constant touch would cost as much as $7 million, which he termed "ridiculous." For example, to link Toronto and Moncton on a per-occasion basis would run the network between $1,800 and $2,000 an hour. He added that he hoped to renegotiate the contract to bring the affiliates in on the action at reasonable cost, but that this was in the future.

Next in line were the affiliates, each with its tale of isolation and woe. Pierre Juneau kicked off by suggesting to Dick Rice and Bruce Alloway of Edmonton's CFRN that he "didn't very often see, on national public affairs shows, important, interesting, and dramatic elements coming from Alberta." Did they perchance feel the same? Alloway agreed and added that the problem was nationwide, because he didn't see enough of what was happening in Newfoundland.

Ted Chapman, the general manager of Calgary's CFCN, said that he had supplied a good quantity of material to *CTV National News*, but that he could send more only if CTV would pay for the reverse microwave link. Boyle wondered how he forwarded his input at the moment, and Chapman replied, "Air Canada."

Boyle was dismayed and started to get testy on Chapman's behalf. "We talk about the high degree of sophistication in Canada — and this is not a condemnation of CTV or you — it is a condemnation of the system. And yet we have to depend on Air Canada in order to make a principal television network operate, . . . because of the prohibitive cost of microwave. . . . If I were in your position, [that] would be a bloody irritation."

Chapman agreed and said that it was "most frustrating" to be sitting on a story the network wanted but wouldn't pay to have transmitted except by commercial airline flight. Next, the two men began to discuss Air Canada's Alberta-to-Toronto schedule and the deadlines involved in sending an item for inclusion in the 11 p.m. *CTV National News*. From Calgary, Chapman had only one option: unless the tape went out by eleven in the morning, it couldn't be used. Another flight left at four in the afternoon — but, given the time-zone difference, any shipment it carried would arrive at the network's broadcast headquarters too late.

Boyle wanted to be very clear on this point. "For the last time," he said, "your deadline is the morning. Calgary can burn down in the middle of the day and you would have to hire a special plane or else motivate the [microwave] circuits?"

"I'm sorry. This makes me rather annoyed," Chapman said.

"Us too," interposed Juneau.

By the time the commissioners talked with the representatives of Regina's CKCK, they were steaming. "In effect," Harry Boyle summarized, "you are not going to get . . . material onto *Canada AM* or *CTV News* unless it is an emergency situation" that would justify the cost of the microwave link. Pierre Juneau went further in his ire. "It is a bit sickening to hear and read . . . all that jazz about the fantastic progress of technology," he complained. "We still have not found solutions to problems of [this] kind." It all came down to time, distance, and a willingness to spend money. Blair Nelson of Saskatoon's CFQC ruefully noted that — although he was about to produce five half-hour programs for *University of the Air*, and had contributed several items to *Canada AM* and *Sports Beat* — it was inherently difficult to fly anything or anybody from his home city to Toronto. (At least the Maritime affiliates enjoyed an extra hour's grace, because the time difference worked in their favour, enabling them to get proportionately more items onto the national newscast.)

Stu Griffiths of Ottawa's CJOH-TV had a somewhat different take on things. For him, the universe revolved around the nation's capital, and he still resented the national newscast's move to CFTO. "About 60 per cent of every day's news stories originate [in] or relate to Ottawa," he said. By contrast, there were many days that Toronto failed to generate a story of coast-to-coast interest or importance.

Nor did Griffiths have much sympathy for the western affiliates, who he thought had been lax in proposing story ideas. "I know it is disheartening to break your neck and send the material . . . and have it turned down for reasons that you don't agree with," he said. "We forward a fair number of ideas ourselves, [but] I am satisfied that if they are [rejected it is because] of valid reasons . . . , rather than out of hand." Of course, it was far simpler for CJOH to send its stories in. Both it and Montreal's CFCF had the reverse microwave, which assured them direct access at certain times throughout the day — an arrangement that worked out to about $75 an hour. But, as Griffiths added, "you have to commit for seven days a week, 365 days a year" — a commitment CTV had no intention of making when it came to other, smaller affiliates east and west.

At least, not until the CRTC prodded it into action. In January 1973, the network's licence was renewed, but with a caution attached. "The provision of topical and relevant material from all parts of the country is basic in maintaining the national characteristic of information programs," the CRTC stated. Despite the cost of reverse microwave transmission, it considered airline delivery of tapes and filed items to be "unacceptable" and pledged that it would "work to achieve more satisfactory arrangements between common [microwave] carriers and the network so that member stations are consistently able to contribute national and regional material of immediate interest to network news and public affairs programs." This pledge, by the way, was not fulfilled. The CRTC would never facilitate subsidies, easements, or grants, and all the costs attendant on microwave — just like the costs of extending service to far-flung regions — would continue to be shouldered by the network alone.

Of course, one school of thought maintained that the network could afford to do so. "CTV's owners were pirates," Craig Oliver says bluntly.

"They were [taking] 25 per cent to 30 per cent [of the network's] profits and not putting any money into the news." According to Oliver, the CRTC said, "We're looking at your profits. What are you going to do about the news service?" The answer was: not much, in the early days. Most of the nightly newscast was made up of slightly edited items provided by NBC — ironically so, since the studio shots for the 1976 movie classic *Network*, a wickedly funny indictment of the American television news media, were filmed at CTV's news facility at CFTO.

☆

Over the next few years, the CTV news division got a little more money to open new bureaus in Edmonton and Winnipeg to cover the prairies, the Northwest Territories, and the Yukon, and in Halifax to cover the Maritimes. Most important, the network bit the bullet and anted up for reverse microwave feeds from all its affiliates. The transformation was sudden and dramatic. In the three months immediately following the 1972 licence renewal hearing, stations outside the Toronto-Ottawa-Montreal triangle shipped thirty-three news stories to network headquarters by air. Two years later, in the same three-month period, these stations shipped only 12 stories out of 105. The other ninety-three were transmitted by reverse microwave and broadcast while they were still topical and relevant.

Despite these improvements, *CTV National News's* lack of money and manpower kept coming back to haunt it. A notorious example was the federal election night debacle of 1974. An hour into live coverage, a computer failure hung Harvey Kirck and Ottawa bureau chief Bruce Phillips out to dry. The results from Toronto polling stations failed to materialize, and all the numbers on the display board behind them froze. Craig Oliver scurried to feed them whatever he could glean from the CBC or radio stations, but (in Kirck's words) "we signed off an hour earlier than we'd planned, out of sheer embarrassment."

Kirck described the CTV news team as exhausted from trying to match the goliath CBC each and every night. Mistakes were becoming more and more frequent, making them look "sloppy on the air." On March 6, 1975, the night that a national magazine had assigned two writers to watch the CBC and CTV newscasts as they were broadcast, CTV lost its link to Ottawa. Kirck apologized on air, as producers shuffled the story line-up. Technicians tried to sort out the mess while the crew searched frantically for material to replace the six minutes of Ottawa content that had gone into the void. They ripped wire copy off teletype machines and crawled on all fours — out of view of the camera, but not of the magazine journalist — to slip fill-in items to Kirck. The nightmare over, he signed off with the words, "I'm Harvey Kirck — I think."

At the same time that these snafus were plaguing Kirck and his co-workers, the national newscast's ratings started to slip. The network owners, though, felt confident enough to withstand CRTC scrutiny at their November 1975 licence renewal hearing, believing that they'd met the commission's demand for more regional stories at eleven o'clock.

And qualified praise was forthcoming. The CRTC applauded the network for increasing the number of news items from outside the Toronto-Ottawa-Montreal triangle, for establishing more news bureaus in the regions, and for funding reverse microwave links. It singled out *W5*, *Question Period*, *Canada AM*, and *Maclear* as "valuable" programs, reserving special mention for *Maclear*, which struck the commissioners as "lean and efficient, with the major proportion of its budget directed to production." That budget was by comparison a bargain. It cost the network $1.5 million a season for *W5*, $1.25 million for *Canada AM*, and a mere $620,000 for *Maclear*. In this instance, high quality came at reasonable cost. According to Craig Oliver, Michael Maclear was "one of the great foreign correspondents. . . . Don Cameron hired him to give the network credibility." While at the CBC, Maclear had bagged important interviews with numerous world leaders and represented a real catch for CTV. His acquisition encouraged Big John to boast that "in the field of . . . information programming . . . , we have never skimped." Even so, the CRTC complained that *Maclear* was the only non-entertainment Canadian program shown during CTV's peak viewing hours in prime time, when 90 per cent of the network's programs were American.

In 1976, Big John's wife, Isabel, a feminist author and guest lecturer at York University, became a co-host of *W5*, the network's showcase public affairs program. She replaced Carole Taylor, who wanted to live in the same city as her second husband-to-be, Art Phillips, a former mayor of Vancouver. In her three years as co-host, Taylor had reported from nearly every part of Canada and travelled on assignment to cover everything from floods in Honduras and the revolution in Chile to the Yom Kippur War.

Taylor, now chair of the Canada Ports Corp., recounts what it was like being the first female Canadian journalist ever sent to a battle zone. "Get your passport, you're off to Israel," she was told. "CTV is the beneficiary if you're killed." This knowledge offered scant comfort when she was filmed diving for cover during an air raid. Her story in hand, she then faced the problem of getting it back home. "I had to beg [one of the U.S. correspondents] to use his satellite time," she says. "He took pity on the poor Canadian, and let us tag on at the end." So much for Big John's claim that CTV never skimped. "Canadian television was done on such a low budget," Taylor says.

Still, she was sad to leave *W5*, as were the Bassetts at her departure. Johnny F. set up an interview at Vancouver's CHAN and recommended that they snap her up. Taylor said Ray Peters interviewed her, but declined to hire her, because "I had 'Bassett' stamped on my forehead." Although CFTO's and CHAN's jockeying for position at CTV was well known, she was devastated: "It never occurred to me that I might not get a job because of my Toronto-Bassett connections."

Ray Peters remembers the interview, but claims that his decision had nothing to do with Taylor's CFTO/Bassett baggage. "We had several meetings with her," he said. "We were very interested, but she'd priced herself out of the market. She was used to doing network programs, [with] fourteen stations paying her salary. She couldn't expect to get the same amount from [us]. I was anxious to have her on the news hour, but we couldn't agree on price." As a result, Taylor ended up with CBC Vancouver, hosting their *Pacific Report*.

Taylor's Toronto stigma, real or imagined, wasn't the only point at issue between Big John and Ray Peters, who later clashed over CHAN's apparent lack of interest in the election of the Parti Québécois in November 1976. Finlay MacDonald remembers Bassett telling the other CTV owners how important it was that they pre-empt their regular programming to cover the Quebec results live. "Peters hit the roof," MacDonald says, and Bassett gave him a "great lecture" on national unity and the need for bilingualism.

Again, Peters remembers things differently. Because of the three-hour time difference, he claims that most of the network's coverage came through during Vancouver's early evening news hours from 5 to 7 p.m. "We carried 70 per cent to 80 per cent live, and the rest in highlights," Peters says. "The situation was misrepresented by Murray Chercover and Tom Gould," CTV's news director, who shared Big John's views on the matter.

"BCTV didn't think it was important enough," responds Craig Oliver. "We had to struggle with them to carry federal elections. During leadership conventions they dropped out early." Oliver says he likes Ray Peters personally, but admired John Bassett for his "sense of country, however distorted." According to Oliver, the news division was well aware that the two men did not get on. "Ray versus Old Man Bassett," he says, "was a really personal antipathy, deep, and legendary. There were endless feuds."

Nine months earlier, though, Big John had managed to antagonize most of the CTV board and management team by choosing to appear on CBC as a commentator at the Tory convention in Ottawa, where Joe Clark was elected leader in a bitter contest with Brian Mulroney. "I think [Mulroney] lost the convention this afternoon at a time when he could have won it," Big John pontificated. "His task . . . was to show the delegates that his lack of experience in the House of Commons didn't matter, that he could excite the people of Canada and win a general election. He couldn't even excite a crowd of Conservatives who were dying to be excited — who wanted to get up and cheer. I think he blew it."

"If you don't think CTV was mad, you're crazy," Eddie Goodman says. In fact, Goodman himself had passed on the request from Tim Kotcheff, the CBC's executive producer of news specials. Big John was unbowed. "Those bastards at CTV never ask me, so why shouldn't I?" he retorted. In Ottawa, Big John and Isabel shared a hotel suite with the Goodmans. The morning after the convention, Bassett was watching CTV's post-mortem coverage when Jack Horner, another of the failed leadership candidates, told Fraser Kelly that the main reason he'd lost to Joe Clark was because of attacks by that "prince of the media, John Bassett, that you work for and by prince I mean p-r-i-c-k." Bassett arose and shouted at Goodman, "We're going to sue CTV!" The ridiculousness of the situation instantly cured Goodman's hangover. He told Bassett that they weren't going to sue anybody. Eventually, though, Goodman requested and received an apology from Big John's repentant CTV cohorts.

In 1976, sagging ratings at the flagship *CTV National News* finally motivated the network to spend more money on its news division. CBC had turned a once-close race into a rout, and *The National* was attracting 50 per cent more viewers each night. "The next big event was Lloyd Robertson," recounts Craig Oliver. "The numbers were slipping badly and Harvey [Kirck] was getting pretty tired."

That summer, construction began on a new set in CFTO's Studio 2. Don Cameron told Kirck to get some sharper clothes to match and sent him out on his first-ever cross-country promotional tour. Partway through, Kirck was recalled to Toronto and learned that Lloyd Robertson would be sitting beside him at the anchor desk.

Tom Gould and his deputy, Don Cameron ("a madcap, greatly flawed, but brilliant producer," according to Craig Oliver), had decided that Robertson was just what they needed to get back into the ratings game. Cameron called him to arrange a lunch, but Robertson kept putting it off. In late August, Cameron called again and suggested that Tom Gould join them. The threesome finally got together the day after Labour Day at Gould's house, where Robertson was offered a contract worth $85,000 a year for five years, almost double what he'd been making at the CBC. As an added incentive, he was given the opportunity to report as well as read the news.

This was what Robertson had long desired, but he was pigeon-holed as an announcer. He'd started his career during high school as a part-timer at radio station CJCS in his hometown of Stratford, Ontario. After graduation, he was hired full-time, reading the news and hosting a musical request show. From there he worked at several private radio stations in southwestern Ontario before landing his first announcing job in television at the CBC's Winnipeg station, and made it to *The National* in Toronto in 1962.

Even then, he emanated star quality. In 1976, he'd successfully hosted the Montreal Summer Olympics and wanted to do more special assignment coverage. The year before, however, he'd touched off a nationwide wildcat walkout of CBC reporters, who objected to his reporting of Britain's entry into the European common market. Under the CBC's stringent union rules, announcers were not allowed to do reporting jobs. The attitude was "It doesn't matter what it says — you read it." Robertson couldn't change so much as a comma in his script, which seemed to him a dead end. He could stick it out until retirement, reciting what was put in front of him in mellifluous tones, or he could make a move while he was in his prime and show what he believed he could do. "Lloyd didn't want to be on the slag heap of former CBC announcers," Craig Oliver says.

At the tripartite lunch, Robertson told Gould and Cameron that he'd come onside only if Harvey Kirck agreed to remain as a co-anchor. He also insisted that Kirck's salary be raised. The CBC, learning of this meeting, fought to keep Robertson. Knowlton Nash, then CBC's director of news and current affairs, put together a counter-proposal and tried to get it approved by the public network's headquarters. In response, CTV upped its offer to a ten-year contract. Under it, Robertson would be paid $85,000 in the first year, rising to $100,000 over five years. The final half-decade was open to negotiation. When Robertson and his advisers finally met with Nash, Robertson (who had mixed feelings about the move, given his loyalty to the CBC) revealed that he'd tried to make peace with several key union representatives earlier that day, but that they'd threatened to make his attempts at reporting a test case. This — and the fact that the CBC's offer didn't come close to CTV's — aided Robertson in making up his mind.

Nash decided to pre-empt CTV's thunder, announcing Robertson's defection (and his replacement by Peter Kent) at the press launch of CBC's fall season. In an aside to a colleague Nash whispered, "Lloyd's now a million-dollar baby in a five-and-ten-cent store." He was overheard, and to his chagrin the remark wound up splashed across front pages nationwide.

Back at CTV, Harvey Kirck claimed to be happy with the new arrangement. In his memoirs he described the difference between him and his new co-anchor: "Lloyd neat and trim, rather serious and perfectly poised behind the desk; me, the rumpled one, slouching, sartorially less than elegant." Kirck thought that they made an effective pairing. Robertson had a "smooth, serious, more formal delivery," while he liked to "tell" the story, in a conversational way.

Despite the duo's complementary strengths, CTV didn't see the huge ratings boost it had expected. During the winter of 1977, *The National* attracted 1.3 million viewers a night as opposed to 1.1 million for *CTV National News*. But that didn't deter the private network from poaching Tim Kotcheff, Robertson's former executive producer, at year's end. The hyperactive Bulgarian with the cheap suits moved in as CTV's executive producer of news and current affairs, taking charge as no one had done before. The newsroom was expanded and renovated, more domestic and two foreign bureaus (Washington and London) were added, and Kotcheff found a way to get the affiliates to cooperate with CTV news headquarters. Formerly, the affiliates refused to do anything for headquarters, says Craig Oliver. "They saw no reason for the network to have domestic bureaus. [They'd say,] 'What do you need reporters here for?'" He means that member stations resented the fact that CTV would parachute in its own personnel to staff the bureau, then bill their salaries as a network expense. According to the local mindset, a local reporter could do the job equally well and forward the fruits of his or her labours by reverse microwave.

But Kotcheff persisted, organizing the Daily News Service, a closed-circuit microwave hook-up that linked all the affiliate newsrooms with Toronto once a day. Member stations could use it to access reports compiled by CTV news staffers or by other affiliates elsewhere to use in their local newscasts. Their growing dependence on this service gave Kotcheff the clout he needed to put together a real news network. "Stealing the two strongest people [Robertson and Kotcheff] at CBC put us back in competition," Craig Oliver says, "although CTV was still pretty cheap."

Next in line for a CTV raiding party was the Global Television network. In 1977, CTV recruited Global's anchorman Peter Trueman, himself a CBC alumnus, to host a new biweekly public affairs program called *CTV Reports*, a magazine-style assessment of recent events that replaced both *W5* and *Maclear* in their regular time slots. As its producer, Mike Maclear got the money for satellite feeds that Carole Taylor had begged for. He also lined up an impressive array of back-up hosts, including CTV's former Ottawa bureau chief Bruce Phillips and Barbara Amiel, the future Mrs. Conrad Black. Maclear himself also participated on air. Despite the assembled talent, however, the show was a bust. By the end of 1977, Trueman was back at Global, complaining that Maclear had been so involved with the scripts that he was putting "words in my mouth," and before long, *W5* (though not *Maclear*) returned to the line-up.

Meanwhile, Isabel Bassett had left the network after one season on *W5* to become co-host of *Hourlong*, a new current-affairs program on her husband's station, CFTO. "I have no illusions it's what helped me get this job," she told the *Toronto Star*. "I've tried to live with it and accept it. But having influence simply because I'm Mrs. John W. Bassett still bothers me."

Big John, who often worked at home, also took part in this interview session, conducted amid the noisy chaos generated by his and Isabel's adopted daughters, Avery and Sarah, and their son, Matthew. "I think it's a lot of bull to think I overshadow her," he said. "If anything, I'm the highly paid, glorified babysitter who lives in her shadow. Isabel's face is far better known than mine — and a hell of a sight prettier. Beautiful. Sexy. Smart. That's my Isabel. Along with a hang-up or two, which is maybe understandable when you figure I'm old enough to be her father. Yet we've got a terrific marriage going." As for the question of undue influence, he roared with sudden laughter. "Baby," he cried, "if you don't help your wife or friends to get a job, who else do you help? Sure as hell you don't help your damn enemies."

7

These Little Affiliates
Went to Market — 1968–77

As the CTV Television Network extended its reach into the most remote corners of Canada, wrangled with the CRTC over the lack of distinctively Canadian drama in its schedule, and reluctantly spent more money on its national news and information service, some of its key affiliates set about building television empires of their own.

Open season was declared on CTV's member stations in late 1969, when the CRTC made an important policy change that allowed one affiliate to purchase another. Each case would be judged on its individual merits, wiping out the blanket refusal (the long-held position of the old Board of Broadcast Governors) that was meant to prevent control of the network being seized by one of the wealthier stations.

Stuart Griffiths of Ottawa's Bushnell Communications and Big John Bassett were equally keen to consolidate their power by owning a second outlet. At first, they eyed the same prize, Montreal's CFCF, then the network's second-largest station.

Griffiths was first off the mark, making a play for CFCF a year before the CRTC's policy reversal. He publicly dismissed rumours that his ambition put him in direct conflict with Big John, noting that the press had portrayed Bushnell's hope to increase its size as a struggle between the two personalities, himself and John Bassett. "It isn't that," he said. "I respect John Bassett for the fact that he's made a positive contribution to the network and I don't think John Bassett has used his position up to this time in any way dangerous to the network operation."

It was an eloquent tribute, but the press was right. Bassett and Griffiths were on their best behaviour in front of the CRTC, but behind closed doors, they fought. "I really don't compete with CFTO except in the boardroom," a supercilious Griffiths later said, "and I'm really quite content to have John Bassett be number one in terms of brawn . . . as long as he's not insisting on the same prerogative in terms of brains."

Stu Griffiths's ambition went beyond mere ownership of a second affiliate. He wanted to assemble a media conglomerate, combining television, radio, and cable, which would produce high-quality Canadian programs that could compete with the best coming in from the United States and Britain. He considered cable to be the key ingredient in the mix, because it would provide him with a regular monthly cash flow.

Bushnell Television had got into cable early on. In partnership with Famous Players and others, it had won cable rights for half the city of Ottawa. Its next move came shortly before it went public, when Ernie Bushnell discovered that Lord Thomson wanted to get out of the broadcasting business in Canada. Bushnell learned of this desire when he wrote to Thomson, asking for a donation to an Ottawa charity. Thomson declined, but wrote in a postcript, "I hear your company is going public. We have been thinking along the same lines. Maybe you would consider a merger. Let me hear from you."

Bushnell replied, "If you're ever again in this country and you wish to dispose of those down-at-heel radio and TV stations of yours, give me a call."

Thomson did so, meeting with Bushnell and Griffiths in Toronto. Griffiths then took charge of the negotiations to purchase three television stations, six radio stations, and a cable company from Thomson. All were relatively minor holdings in eastern Ontario; none was a CTV affiliate. Thomson was pleased at the prospect of getting them off his hands, and an agreement to this effect was reached in the fall of 1968.

At this same time, however, Griffiths had bigger fish to fry. He commenced negotiations to acquire Canadian Marconi's broadcasting assets: CFCF itself, and two Montreal radio stations, CFCF and CFQR. English Electric Co., Canadian Marconi's British parent, scoffed at Griffiths's first offer of $18 million, so he went ahead and made a second offer of $22.7 million without bringing it before the Bushnell board. This high-handed action caused one director to resign in protest.

Stu Griffiths's wheeling and dealing accelerated in 1969, the year he succeeded Ernie Bushnell as president of the renamed Bushnell Communications. Bushnell remained as chairman, but played a less active role. Griffiths's package of purchases-in-the-making kept getting larger and larger, until his proposed acquisitions (all of which were subject to CRTC approval) consisted of four television stations, twelve radio stations, and sixteen cable systems, stretching from Quebec to British Columbia. The total cost of Griffiths's shopping basket was $80 million, an immense sum at the time.

The scope of Griffiths's ambitions alarmed Pierre Juneau and Harry Boyle, his friends at the CRTC. They wondered if their favourite broadcaster was going "hog wild" over expansion, but the commission kept putting off public hearings into these acquisitions until it looked as if Griffiths had stopped doing deals and they could hear all Bushnell's applications as a single package.

Three hundred people packed the International Ballroom in Ottawa's Skyline Hotel on June 16, 1970, to learn how Griffiths would sell his grand vision to the CRTC.

"We believe that if there are to be large broadcasting units in Canada, such units should take the form of public companies whose securities are widely held by Canadians, thus offering the maximum participation to Canadians in their broadcasting systems and enabling companies to have ready access to the Canadian money markets for the funds they require to develop their activities," he said. "We further believe that such units should be integrated, combining, where possible, television, radio, and cable."

The CRTC went most of the way with him, but not far enough. In its decision, announced three weeks later, it approved all of Griffiths's television and radio purchases, thus legitimizing Bushnell's common ownership of both CTV's Ottawa and Montreal affiliates. Unfortunately for Griffiths, the commission would not permit him to close the deals he'd made regarding cable television systems. In his mind, cable was the coming thing, the vital factor. Without it, stocking up on stations did him little good; it was like having a car without an engine. His financial arrangements started to unravel and his grandiose plans went down in flames. At the beginning of 1971, Bushnell Communications forfeited its almost $1-million deposit on the Thomson stations and the $4 million it had put down for Marconi's broadcasting interests. One newspaper headlined its coverage of the end of Stu Griffiths's dream with the words: "Bushnell the Un-Empire."

☆

Allan Waters was the next would-be media mogul to attempt to capitalize on the synergy of common ownership of CTV's affiliates. He was the president and chief executive of CHUM Ltd., based in Toronto, which owned numerous radio and television outlets coast to coast. None was a CTV member station — but that changed in 1971, when CHUM acquired the controlling interest in CJCH Ltd., which owned the network's Halifax affiliate, CJCH.

Next Waters formed a new company, CFCF Ltd., to be owned 80 per cent by CHUM and 20 per cent by Canadian Marconi. Its purpose was to buy the same package that Griffiths had attempted to get his hands on — CFCF Montreal and Marconi's two radio stations in that city.

Again, the CRTC balked at bigness and cross-ownership. In late 1971, it approved the common ownership of CJCH and CFCF — but on the conditions that CFCF Ltd. sell the Montreal radio stations and that CHUM sell its long-standing interest in the Barrie, Ontario, television station CKVR, a CBC affiliate. "These divestitures are considered necessary by the commission in view of the increasing involvement of CHUM Ltd. in the CTV network and the importance of its radio broadcasting interests," the ruling stated.

Waters reconsidered. He didn't want to sell his stake in CKVR, and he dearly wished to buy the Montreal radio stations, so CHUM announced in early 1972 that it would not proceed with the scheme.

Instead, Waters decided to confine his expansion within the CTV network to Atlantic Canada. CHUM had already acquired CJCB (a CBC affiliate in Sydney, Nova Scotia) in 1969. A year later, CHUM, as stated, joined up with the former radio announcer Fred Sherratt and several other private investors to buy CJCH Halifax. Then CJCH Ltd. bought CKCW Moncton (which had been with CTV for several years) and CJCB Sydney joined the private network, too. This made for a total of three CTV affiliates under CJCH Ltd.'s control. Accordingly, in 1972, it launched the Atlantic Television Network (ATV) as an integrated system, complete with new equipment and new studios in Halifax. Finlay MacDonald, who'd left the broadcasting business for backroom Tory politics, was appointed to the CJCH Ltd. board, and Allan Waters and Fred Sherratt both wound up in the CTV boardroom, but with only a single vote to show for their trio of stations.

☆

In order to finance their own expansion in television and radio, the Bassetts and the Eatons decided to take Baton Broadcasting public in 1971. First, however, they had to get Ted Rogers to buy them out of Rogers Cable Company. Otherwise, they knew that the CRTC would come down on them like a ton of bricks, just as it had squelched Stu Griffiths.

It had been five years since Rogers had persuaded Baton to go into the cable business with him. At first, Big John hadn't been interested. Then, in 1966, Rogers filed licence patents with the Department of Transport and paid a $400,000 deposit to Bell Canada, which would wire up the areas he proposed to serve. At this same time, Bassett discovered that CKVR Barrie, co-owned by Liberal supporters Allan Waters, Geoff Stirling, and Ralph Snelgrove, planned to move its television transmitter to Toronto, which would have disrupted CFTO's signal. Cable offered a way around this problem, and Big John began to look more kindly on Rogers's proposition. (By 1967, the idea of making CKVR Toronto's third television station was a dead issue, despite several different licence applications and intense lobbying on the part of the co-owners' Liberal friends in Ottawa.)

Ted Rogers didn't have the money to pay Bell to wire all his cable areas, so he was still open to a Baton investment. Big John may have seen the light when it came to cable's advantages, but he couldn't resist being his usual over-aggressive self. "You're a director of Baton," he told Rogers, "and you signed an agreement that you wouldn't go into television within fifty miles of downtown Toronto. Cable is television, so you'll hold the cable licences and contracts in trust for us at Baton. If you don't agree, I'll get you!"

So it was that Rogers's investors met with the Baton group at Rogers's house. "I hope we can work this out," Big John said. "Ted, I've always thought of you as a son." One of Rogers's directors whispered, "Yeah, like a son of a bitch." Everyone laughed and Rogers stood up to reply. "In many respects, I've thought of you as another father," he told Bassett. "Okay. I'll put all the licences and Bell contracts . . . into a company. We'll split it fifty-fifty, but you'll put up two-thirds [of the money]. I'll put up one-third. I'll run it, but you'll put in your own chief financial officer." Rogers knew that this would appeal to Bassett, who liked to control his investments through a CFO, as he had attempted but failed to do while Joel Aldred was overspending on CFTO in the early days.

Bassett agreed to Rogers's terms and picked Gordon Ashworth as CFO of Rogers Cable Company. It grew to become Toronto's largest cable operator, but at one point Rogers thought he'd blown it, by bidding on some new cable sites with a cheque that Ashworth hadn't co-signed. "I'd broken the rules," says Rogers, "so I wrote a personal cheque and went down to see Bassett." Big John took the cheque, ripped it up, and gave Rogers a hug, shouting. "You're my boy!"

Everything was going well until the CRTC told Rogers and Baton to divest themselves of their interests in each other. The commission said it would not renew Rogers's cable licences unless he sold his shares in Baton and Baton agreed to get rid of its half-interest in Rogers Cable Company. "I was dumbfounded," Rogers remembers — as well he might have been; all the bank guarantees had Baton in for two-thirds of the debt.

An agitated Rogers went to see Bassett, who did his best to reassure him. "You've done a good job," Big John said. "You and Loretta [Rogers's wife] are good people. We will sell to a strong institution."

Rogers had another idea. He proposed that they get the assets valued. Then he would sell his Baton shares to Baton, and Baton would sell him its shares in Rogers Cable Company. One side of the deal was done immediately, but Rogers had a hard time raising the $2.5 million he needed. He paid Baton with a note due in eighteen months.

This arrangement, however, was interrupted by Baton's decision to go public, which it couldn't do with the note outstanding. To get a three-month extension, Rogers had to appear before the Bassett-Eaton trustees and sign away his right to insist on a valuation of the assets. "You know," Rogers told them, "we've done well together and you've honoured the obligation." Tears flowed as the trustees applauded this sentiment.

Rogers had until July 15, 1971, to raise the money, but he could manage only part of it. The day before the three-month deadline he called Dick Thomson, president of the Toronto-Dominion Bank, to say he wasn't going to make it. Thomson then phoned Gordon Osler, a special situations investor. Osler wanted a 15 per cent interest in and an option on an additional 10 per cent of Rogers Cable. Rogers and his wife had to take out a second mortgage on their home, and Loretta herself had to sign a bank guarantee. At ten minutes to midnight, they bolted down the necessary paperwork at the Toronto-Dominion Centre.

Rogers had an appointment with Bassett early the next day. He brought a bottle of champagne and a book inscribed "Presentation to J. W. H. Bassett." All its pages were entirely blank, and the certified cheque that cleared Rogers's note was tucked between the last page and the back cover. When Rogers entered the room, he took his keys out and placed them beside the book.

"No more presentations, Ted, it's over," said Bassett brusquely, misunderstanding the gesture. Rogers persuaded Bassett to open the book.

"There's nothing here!" Bassett roared, as he kept flipping the pages. At the back of the room, Bassett's son "Dougie" was holding the champagne. The cork blew just as Big John reached the last page. "Jesus Christ, what?" Bassett exploded. It was an emotional moment. "I was out of Baton and he was out of Rogers Cable," Rogers says. They all embraced and drank to the end of their long association.

The summer of 1971 loomed large for Big John for another reason, the death of his debt-swamped newspaper, the *Telegram*. Bassett had been trying to negotiate a wage freeze with three different unions, but they wouldn't accept the fact that the paper was in trouble. He took the extraordinary step of opening up its books to the unions' own auditors, who verified what he'd been saying, but the union leadership refused to make concessions. Feelings ran high on both sides, and the presses were sabotaged. As the unions' strike-vote deadline loomed in September, it didn't help matters that Bassett's name was splashed all over the news because of the sale of the Bassett-Eaton trust's interest in Maple Leaf Gardens for $5.8 million — a $5-million profit — and the purchase of the rest of the Toronto Argonauts football team, for $2.3 million.

Two weeks later, the Toronto Newspaper Guild voted to strike. This triggered Bassett's sale of the *Telegram*'s subscription list to the *Toronto Daily Star* for $10 million. On Saturday, September 18, a statement appeared on the *Telegram*'s front page. "The decision has been taken to cease publication of the Toronto *Telegram*," Bassett wrote. "It goes without saying it is the saddest decision I have ever made in my life in war or in peace." He then outlined the paper's losses, promised that the money from the sale of "certain assets" would be used to "liquidate the paper's commitments," and closed with the following apology: "I'm sorry I couldn't do better."

Many years later, Bassett told the author Jean Sonmor that he couldn't remember the last night of the *Telegram*. "It's somewhere deep in my unconscious," he said. "It's one of the most painful things in my life. [It] — and, much worse of course, the death of my son Johnny." At the time, Johnny F. was the only member of the Bassett and Eaton families who'd voted against shutting the paper down. Even Fred Eaton, who'd worked on the *Telegram*'s crime beat in the summer of 1959, wanted to take the cash and run. There was lots of cash to run with. Together, the *Telegram*'s subscription list and the building, now home to the *Globe and Mail*, were sold for $19 million, all of which went into the Telegram trust.

Whatever sadness was involved, the *Telegram*'s demise made Baton Broadcasting Inc., the owner of CFTO, Glen-Warren Productions, and the Toronto Argonauts, a more attractive public share offering. In early

November 1971, Baton entered into an underwriting agreement to sell $5.7 million of common shares, and the much-coveted offering closed a month later.

Big John, as president and chairman of the public company, still did not own shares, but his management contract rose to $125,000 a year. Johnny F., a vice-president, joined him on the board, and Fred Eaton represented his family. Eaton recalls feeling "very junior" alongside people such as Charlie Burns of the investment dealer Burns Bros., one of the underwriters of the public offering, who used to rush away from meetings "saying things like, 'I've got to leave now. I'm going to invest $1 million in the stock market,' or some other unbelievable sum." In any case, Baton itself turned out to be a great investment. Over the course of a year, its stock price doubled and the shares were split, two for one.

Nursing his disappointment back in Ottawa over "Bushnell the Un-Empire," Stu Griffiths was unprepared when Bushnell Communications itself became a takeover target in late 1971. Out of the west rode Frank Griffiths (to repeat, no relation to Stu), first encountered at the second-station licence hearings in Vancouver. He had since done well, continuing as a managing partner at Thorne & Riddell and forming (in 1966) the Western Broadcasting Company Ltd., which held his family's radio and television interests. The publicly traded company's most significant investment was in the British Columbia Television Broadcasting System, which owned both CTV's Vancouver affiliate CHAN and the CBC's Victoria affiliate CHEK. As CHAN's largest single shareholder, Griffiths looked eastward with envy and longing. Like his Ottawa namesake, he wondered why Big John should have a virtual monopoly on network production and was determined to establish a base for himself in Ontario.

By late 1971, two of British Columbia Television's major backers had sold out of the company. Famous Players was the first to jump ship, because it was primarily interested in cable. Associated Television (ITV) followed suit, glad to see the last of a boardroom that the minority investor Peter Paul Saunders describes as rife with dissension. This left Griffiths's Western Broadcasting in for about 39 per cent of the voting shares, Selkirk Holdings (largely owned by Southam) with about 32 per cent, and Canadian Cable Systems with about 11 per cent, followed by a number of individuals such as Saunders.

Willard Estey, a lawyer and a director of both British Columbia Television and Bushnell Communications, described the situation as follows: "We have three large corporate shareholders who are all very jealous of their position, and the company operates very effectively with that neat balance. Mr. Peters [Ray Peters, British Columbia Television's president] seems to persevere without paying much attention to any of us, which is probably the reason it works at all, and we all sit there resenting it, but it is so successful we can't say very much."

Frank Griffiths's first opportunity for expansion appeared when a friend announced that he was unhappy with his investment in Bushnell Communications. Griffiths snapped up these shares and bided his time. On learning of this transaction, Britain's Granada Television offered to sell him their 19 per cent interest as well. Granada's chairman, Lord Bertstein, was "extremely disenchanted" with Stu Griffiths's failure to assemble his "un-empire" and his insistence on pressing ahead with cost-intensive productions. Bertstein had "publicly aired his unfavourable views of the Bushnell management," and was delighted when Western bought him out.

As a result of these purchases, Western owned 27 per cent of Bushnell Communications in early 1972 and showed every sign of going for more. But Bushnell's president, Stu Griffiths, had no intention of letting an interloper seize his station. He lobbied hard with Pierre Juneau and Harry Boyle to prevent Western from taking over the company.

Juneau sent a telegram to Western, warning Frank Griffiths that his purchase of Granada's shares — and any further purchases he might make in the public market — would be "subject to the prior approval of the commission" if, in the CRTC's opinion, they were "likely to affect control of broadcasting companies." Juneau went on to touch upon the issue of "undue concentration of ownership or lack of local ownership" and ended by stating that the commission would "not feel bound to accept fait accompli situations."

Frank Griffiths didn't see what all the fuss was about. His lawyers had told him that he didn't need CRTC approval to buy shares in the holding company (Bushnell Communications), if he didn't buy shares in the licensee company (Ottawa-Cornwall Broadcasting). Only the latter course of action would result in a change of "control" at CJOH itself. Griffiths communicated this view to Juneau and signed off by adding: "I am so advised."

On February 29, Stu Griffiths attempted to calm Bushnell's employees, assuring them that Frank Griffiths had passed the word that Western's policy was not "to make staff changes when they associate with another company by purchase, as they have in our case."

The next day, the CRTC sent telegrams to all concerned, informing them of a public inquiry to determine whether there'd been a change of control at Bushnell.

A few days later, Frank Griffiths flew to Ottawa and met with Bushnell's management team. According to Stu Griffiths, Frank remarked that Western's current shareholding would, "under normal circumstances, entitle its holder to representation on the board."

Meanwhile, despite Juneau's cautionary telegram, Western was still in the public market, buying blocks of Bushnell shares from the United Venture Fund, the Investors Group, and North American Life. All (unlike the earlier purchase of Granada's holdings) were paid for with Western Broadcasting shares. These buys gave Western a 46 per cent stake in Bushnell Communications, which alarmed Stu Griffiths and Ernie Bushnell, who saw Western moving rapidly towards effective control. They'd made no attempt to block the repatriation of Granada's shares, but they refused to permit registration of the latest purchases, which they were entitled to do, under the terms of their original incorporation.

All these activities set the stage for the CRTC's inquiry, which kicked off in Ottawa in mid-April of 1972. Ray Peters, who'd been kept in the dark by Frank Griffiths about the ever-mounting share purchases, believed that Griffiths had made a mistake in trying to bypass the commission, no matter what his lawyers had advised. Now Griffiths was about to compound his error.

He began by launching into a brisk description of how public markets worked — a concept he felt the commissioners had failed to grasp. He then defended his purchases on the grounds that (unlike most Canadian broadcasting companies) Bushnell had never had a strong control group. In his view, it had failed to prosper because management was answerable to so broad a range of shareholders that there'd been no one in charge. He suggested that, rather than signalling a "change" of control, the consolidation of share ownership in Western's hands "had created a condition under which control will take place where none exists at the moment."

"Frank was not a particularly good communicator with government regulators," says Peter Paul Saunders. "He was inclined to lecture the people he was applying to. It was not lack of ability. It was lack of humility."

Asked about potential conflicts within CTV if his deals were approved, Griffiths cited recent precedent. "We have an interest, although not a controlling one, in British Columbia Television Broadcasting System Limited and now in Bushnell Communications Ltd., both of which are

CTV network affiliates," he said. "We do not find this position hard to reconcile, because it is precisely the position that was contemplated when the commission was prepared to recognize the purchase by Bushnell of the Marconi Television properties [that is, CFCF] in Montreal. This would have given Bushnell 100 per cent ownership in two CTV network-affiliated stations." In Griffiths's estimation, it didn't matter that this deal had fallen apart; the CRTC had been ready to accept it and ought now to get off his back.

Nor did he retreat from his demand for unfettered access to public markets when the time was ripe: "If we are going to have a public stock market, and if we are going to get public companies in the industry, and if the industry is going to maintain its growth in quality, it will require public companies to do it. If we are going to have these, then we must [have] some modus operandi that makes it possible to maintain a public market, so that if any of us feel unhappy with the management of a group in which we have an investment, we can sell, or if we . . . see good management somewhere, we can buy. I recognize full well your point, but I also recognize the counterpoint — that with public companies one must have some transferability."

With that, the inquiry wound down. A few weeks later, seeing which way the wind was blowing, a founding group of Bushnell Communications' local shareholders contacted Frank Griffiths and asked if Western would buy their 10 per cent interest. This would increase its total holdings to 56 per cent — control by anyone's standards — which made the purchase contract subject to CRTC approval and necessitated a full-blown acquisition hearing.

Big John Bassett had also been eyeing CFCF at the same time that his CTV colleagues were making their moves, but he didn't think the commission would allow him to own both of CTV's largest affiliates. Instead, he looked westward, to Saskatchewan.

Actually, Saskatchewan came looking for him. CFQC Saskatoon, a former CBC affiliate, had joined CTV in the fall of 1971, when the public corporation had established its own outlet in that city. Scarcely had Blair Nelson, CFQC's vice-president, settled into his director's chair than he approached Big John about the possibility of a buyout.

The Murphy family of Saskatoon had been in broadcasting for nearly half a century, but the four children of the pioneering A. A. "Pappy" Murphy were not active in the business, which included a radio station with the same call letters. Instead, everything was run by Pappy's sons-in-law (Nelson and Vern Dallin).

"We paid $4 million because there were four siblings," says Fred Eaton. "Big John asked, 'What do you want?' and they said, 'We want a million dollars each.' The family wanted to walk away."

Big John had no hesitation in making the deal, but how was he going to fly this one past the commission? For years, he'd been arguing the other side of the case. In a brief to Senator Keith Davey's 1969 Senate Report on the Mass Media, in umpteen *Telegram* editorials, and in previous appearances before the CRTC, Bassett had deplored the "uncontrolled growth, particularly of newspaper chains, because I believe that within a decade or two, most of the daily newspapers in Canada will be owned by not more than . . . three companies, unless a means is found to halt this trend."

Since all this was on the record, Bassett couldn't disavow his previous statements. "I again publicly express my support of the efforts of this commission to halt the development [of chain ownership] in electronic communications," he told the CRTC at their mid-May hearings into his Saskatoon purchase, held at Ottawa's Skyline Hotel. Then he mustered a couple of arguments as to why Baton's acquisition should be considered the exception to the rule.

First, despite the CRTC's view that local management was best, nobody in Saskatchewan had submitted a competing bid. Bassett said that Blair Nelson would remain in place as president of the new operation. Joining him and a local chief financial officer on the board would be Big John himself (as chairman), Fred Eaton (whose name was on a downtown department store), and Eddie Goodman — "that distinguished lawyer, great tennis player, skier and athlete, who spends most of his time encased in plaster for one reason or another."

Bassett's second argument was that Baton's superior resources would provide the capital and expertise that CFQC needed to extend CTV's signals throughout the northern part of the province (by means of rebroadcasting units) and supply "better and more varied" service throughout that "vast geographical area." His purchase was therefore "the consolidation of the strength of a smaller element with a greater element," and nothing to fret about.

Bassett said he'd got the message that the CRTC wanted Baton to know its limitations within the CTV network. "Too big is too big," he said. "If I was here having successfully negotiated the purchase of, let's say, CFCF Montreal — I mean, if I had done it — and they had been willing to sell and I could have afforded it — . . . I wouldn't have paid any money down and I wouldn't have made any deal without the permission of the CRTC. I think that two affiliates, one in Montreal and one in Toronto, is too big. I think the commission would think that was too big. There is no question, because Montreal is a viable situation on its own. They are not a Saskatoon."

Besides, Bassett felt that, on close inspection, Baton paled by comparison with other electronic media companies, which he took pleasure in naming. "I think we look so big because we are in Toronto," he said. "What about Frank Griffiths and CHAN? . . . I think that Western, with [virtually] the whole of British Columbia . . . , are probably bigger than we are. I would think that CHUM is bigger than we are, overall."

Bassett also claimed that Baton was a lot smaller than the Southam Company (because of its one-third interest in Selkirk Holdings), not to mention the whole of Maclean Hunter. "We have no cable holdings," he said. "I am always glad of the opportunity of stressing that before the commission." (By this, he referred to the CRTC-ordered sale of Baton's investment in Rogers Cable.)

"You are pleased?" asked Harry Boyle, the hearing's chairman.

"No, I am not pleased," Bassett said. "But my wounds are well healed now. The scabs have now gone into scars."

Another commissioner expressed concern that if the trend to consolidation continued unabated, Canada might end up with only three or four broadcasting companies.

Eddie Goodman disagreed with this assessment. "It is clear that there are going to be at least ten or twelve important companies outside of cable, and at least that number again in cable," he said. (Surveying today's broadcasting scene, what's clear is that the commissioner was a better prognosticator than Goodman.)

Other than exchanges such as these — and a strange incident during which a CRTC member from New Brunswick chided Bassett for "flipping a leg over his chair and passing remarks to his legal counsel" — everything went Baton's way. (Besides, that was Big John's style. Fred Eaton says that a typical board meeting found the directors sprawled around the room, while Bassett "threw his feet up on the desk and told us what was happening." Informality didn't imply a lack of authority, and Big John ran the business "with a very firm hand.") In any case, on June 8, 1972, Baton's takeover of CFQC was approved by the commission — six days after the public announcement of Western's effective takeover of Bushnell Communications and CJOH.

So Big John got his station, but little else. Blair Nelson continued to attend CTV board meetings and to participate in discussions regarding programming, general policy, and finance, but he no longer had a vote, because network by-laws allowed for only one vote in the event of dual ownership. "The big mistake we made," Fred Eaton says reflectively, "was that when we bought Saskatoon we didn't take their vote. We should have got two votes. That would have settled it." As things stood, Baton had spent $4 million, settled nothing, and moved no closer to control of CTV.

Despite the strategic error, though, Fred Eaton has fond memories of the prairie city. He, Big John, and other members of the Baton team trooped west later that summer to accept the keys to the station. Bassett told a wondering reporter that it was his first and last visit, nobody asked Eaton to say a word, and Foster Hewitt, the man Saskatonians had come out in droves to see, got to do most of the interviews.

The entire country stopped whatever it was doing to watch CTV's broadcasts of the September 1972 Canada-Russia Hockey Series with Hewitt doing the play-by-play. His protégé, CTV's sports director Johnny Esaw, had shocked the CBC by scooping up the rights for $1 million, paid to the now-infamous promoter Alan Eagleson. Later Esaw made a deal with the public broadcaster to split coverage of the games, which meant that the CBC carried the final, climactic contest, as twelve and a half million Canadians thrilled to Paul Henderson's winning goal with thirty-four seconds remaining on the clock.

Ernie Bushnell remembered watching one of the *Summit on Ice* games with Western Broadcasting's Frank Griffiths at a Bushnell Communications board meeting in Ottawa. The directors had met in hopes of reaching some sort of resolution about Western's effective takeover, but little progress was made. "We had a screen in front of us," Bushnell said, "and I must say that at times the discussion became rather difficult to follow."

A few weeks later, Frank Griffiths was back in Ottawa for the CRTC's public hearing into his proposed acquisition of Bushnell Communications. He began by claiming that control of CJOH would be a first for Western, because it didn't control the British Columbia Television Broadcasting System, even though it was indisputably the largest single shareholder. Willard Estey agreed with this assessment. "They neither have legal nor de facto control," he said. "I can say that from personal experience in surviving their board meetings."

Nonetheless, Pierre Juneau and the other commissioners were still concerned about the effects of concentration of ownership on CTV's Vancouver and Ottawa affiliates. One member asked whether Griffiths foresaw that CHAN and CJOH would compete for the right to do the same kind of programs for the network.

Griffiths very patiently pointed out that all of CTV's member stations had been doing this for years. If CHAN and CJOH wound up in direct competition for the right to produce a program, so be it. Western would only own a piece (albeit the largest piece) of each outlet, which was healthier, in his view, than the situation the CRTC had just approved — Baton's 100 per cent ownership of CFTO and CFQC.

Juneau questioned Griffiths's parallel, citing vast differences in the "production possibilities" of Ottawa and Saskatoon. Griffiths agreed, but said he was "led to believe that CFTO was currently the dominant force within CTV." CHAN wasn't, so the commission's fears on this score could be allayed, at least for the moment.

Next, Juneau reiterated the commission's concern about local involvement in CTV's member stations. He was implying that since Griffiths was a Vancouverite, he wasn't the ideal owner of the CJOH. Griffiths replied he hoped to establish a second residence in Ottawa, but he wasn't leaving the coast. He saw CHAN evolving into "a very wide-ranging production facility," which would use local equipment to provide programs for "the national marketplace" — in other words, a west-coast CFTO. This involved the creation of a new production entity, with an initial budget of $1 million, that would somehow develop new programs by combining the resources of CHAN and CJOH. Frank Griffiths's plan was to put Stu Griffiths in charge of it, thus ousting Stu from his presidency of Bushnell Communications.

Ernie Bushnell was determined not to help Frank Griffiths attempt to take over the company that bore his name. "I personally and a large proportion of our shareholders, many of them local citizens and employees of our company, strongly prefer to be left in a position of guiding and directing our own destiny," he said. "We have in the past tried to extend our size and abilities. [If] we remain masters of our own house, we shall try again in the future. . . . We may want to join forces with other broadcasters to achieve this — but if we do so, it will be our choice, obviously subject to the approval of this commission."

Stu Griffiths also used the hearing as a forum to publicly reject Frank Griffiths's takeover bid, despite the $1-million production sweetener. "Rather than be faced with a fait accompli which may have some virtues and some disadvantages," he said, "we would rather be in a position . . . if we wished to join forces . . . to choose our partners rather than to be chosen."

Five weeks later, the CRTC denied Western Broadcasting's application and instructed Frank Griffiths to sell all Western's shares in Bushnell as "rapidly as possible." CHAN and CJOH were two dominant stations, the decision said, and "in order to encourage a variety of voices and production centres in Canadian broadcasting it is desirable that some of the more dominant television stations in the CTV network be and remain independent of each other."

And that was that. Frank Griffiths never spoke before the commission again, leaving that pleasure to his senior executives.

☆

But Western (in the person of Ray Peters at British Columbia Television) wanted one more kick at the takeover can. If it owned a second B.C. affiliate, its influence at CTV's boardroom table would increase. Peters therefore hatched an interesting plan. "I convinced the CBC that they should have their own station in Victoria," he says. "Of course, I had an ulterior motive." After the CBC applied for a licence in 1973 and received approval in 1976, it began construction of a new owned-and-operated outlet in downtown Victoria, budgeted at $9 million. This was slated to open at the end of 1979, at which point CHEK would disaffiliate from the CBC and migrate to CTV.

Then the federal government ordered $71 million in cuts to the CBC's 1979–80 spending budget, and the half-completed building was boarded up. Peters remembers what happened. "The [chairman] of the CBC, in an effort to manipulate public opinion, [handed CHEK's] licence back to the CRTC, saying that the CBC could not afford to build the station. He thought [there'd] be a public outcry." There wasn't, and the building sat embarrassingly empty. From 1979 to 1982, Peters tried repeatedly to buy it as a new home for CHEK, but was rebuffed. Then Pierre Juneau, late of the CRTC, surfaced as the new chairman of the public broadcaster. "I went to see him," says Peters. "He wasn't even in his office yet." The two men struck a deal. British Columbia Television paid $3 million for both the station and a transmitter tower on Saturna Island. Because the building was incomplete, and much of its projected $9-million budget hadn't yet been spent on equipment, Peters figures he got the whole package for 20 cents on the dollar.

All of which put Western Broadcasting within sight of owning its second CTV affiliate. Not surprisingly, Big John Bassett got nervous. People were creeping up on him from all directions; CHUM already had three CTV stations in the Maritimes. So in early 1978, no longer satisfied with CFTO and CFQC, he set his covetous sights on CFCF Montreal.

Top: CFTO studios, circa 1960
(Courtesy of CTV Inc.)

Left: Spence Caldwell, founder
of the CTV network, in 1961
(*Toronto Star*/R. Innell)

Right: Joel Aldred, Big John Bassett
(centre), and Ted Rogers, in 1960
(*Toronto Telegram*/Frank Grant)

Top: The 1972 launch of *Canada AM*, featuring former beauty queen
Carole Taylor (Courtesy of CTV Inc.)
Left: *W5* team from the mid-1980s, including Harvey Kirck (second from
right) and Helen Hutchinson (Courtesy of CTV Inc.)
Right: News anchor Lloyd Robertson, the "brand name" of the network
(Courtesy of CTV Inc.)

Top: Doug Bassett and his father, Big John, in the 1980s
(*Globe and Mail*/John McNeill)

Left: Pallbearer Fred Eaton (front right) at the funeral of his "Uncle John" Bassett, in 1998
(*Toronto Star*/Rick Eglinton)

Right: Fred Eaton, the new president of Eaton's, in 1977
(*Toronto Star*/Boris Spremo)

Top left: Ray Peters, president of Western and WIC from 1977–89
(*Vancouver Sun*/Deni Eagland)

Top right: Doug Holtby, president of WIC from 1989–96
(*The Province*/Peter Hulbert)

Bottom: Emily Griffiths with her ailing husband, Frank, the founder of
WIC, in 1993 (*The Province*/Wayne Leidenfrost)

Top: John Cassaday, president of CTV from 1990–97 (*Financial Post*/Jeff Wasserman)
Left: Ivan Fecan, president of CTV from 1997 to present day
(*Globe and Mail*/Tibor Kolley)
Right: Murray Chercover, president of CTV from 1968–90 (*Toronto Star*/Keith Beaty)

Top left: Signature drama series *The Littlest Hobo*, 1979–85 (Courtesy of CTV Inc.)
Top right: Gemini-winning *Night Heat*, 1985–89 (Alliance Atlantis)
Bottom left: Gemini-winning *E.N.G.*, 1989–94 (Alliance Atlantis)
Bottom right: Gemini-winning *Due South*, 1994–99 (Alliance Atlantis/John Medland)

Top left: *Cold Squad*, a police drama set in Vancouver (Alliance Atlantis/Greg Corp)

Top right: *The City*, a social drama set in Toronto (Sarrazin Couture Productions Inc.)

Centre: The "new" CTV logo, circa 1998 (Courtesy of CTV Inc.)

Bottom: Doug Bassett (right) with heir apparent Ivan Fecan, in 1995 (*Financial Post*/Peter Redman)

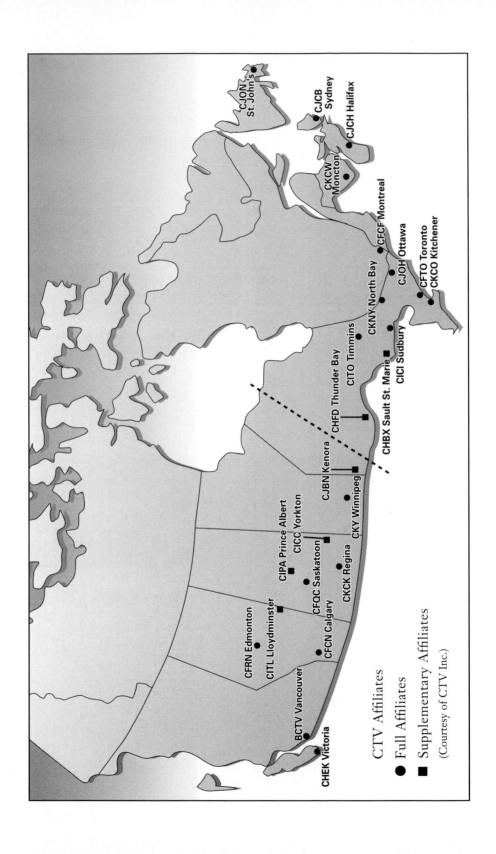

CTV Affiliates

● Full Affiliates

■ Supplementary Affiliates

(Courtesy of CTV Inc.)

CJON St. John's

CJCB Sydney

CJCH Halifax

CKCW Moncton

CFCF Montreal

CJOH Ottawa

CFTO Toronto

CKCO Kitchener

CKNY North Bay

CITO Timmins

CICI Sudbury

CHFD Thunder Bay

CHBX Sault St. Marie

CJBN Kenora

CKY Winnipeg

CIPA Prince Albert

CICC Yorkton

CKCK Regina

CFQC Saskatoon

CFRN Edmonton

CITL Lloydminster

CFCN Calgary

BCTV Vancouver

CHEK Victoria

8

The CRTC
versus Big John Bassett — 1978

After two strike-outs, and at age sixty-two, Big John Bassett finally got to live out his dream of election to the House of Commons: he played a federal Cabinet minister in a cameo for a critically acclaimed two-hour television drama about Quebec separation, produced by his own studios and broadcast early in 1978 by CFTO. Off-screen, his next major performance was scheduled for later that year before the newly retitled and reconfigured Canadian Radio-television Telecommunications Commission (which, thankfully, can still be referred to as the CRTC). Against a backdrop of political turmoil in Quebec and concerns about excessive media concentration coast to coast, he would attempt to convince the commission that it would be good for Quebec, Canada, CTV, and the entire broadcasting system if he, the quintessential Toronto broadcaster, took over CFCF Montreal, the network's second largest affiliate.

The CFCF saga, as recounted by John Bassett to the commission, went something like this. Back in the mists of time, CFCF radio was owned by a British company, and a special order-in-council was required to permit the Canadian Marconi Co. to be regarded as Canadian in order to expand into television in 1960. Nine years later, the situation was reversed when another order-in-council required Marconi to yield controlling ownership of its Canadian broadcasting interests. It tried to comply, but to no avail. For the next three years, Canadian Marconi was forever out on test drives, but prospective buyers kept returning it to the lot.

"All this took time," Bassett said, "and was obviously most upsetting to [those] who were charged with the operations of the [radio and television stations], with a resultant loss of morale and energy." An exact description — especially since the problem wasn't a lack of interest on the part of prospective purchasers. Rather, it was a question of getting a sale that would stick.

At one point, CJOH Ottawa had proposed a novel solution. Stu Griffiths (possibly to get Big John's goat) suggested that CTV itself buy CFCF and make the Montreal affiliate its new flagship station by moving the network headquarters and program operations from Toronto. Bassett's reaction can be imagined. "We didn't get any support for our suggestions, so we decided to have a go ourselves," said Griffiths — which he then proceeded to do, with results we know.

After Griffiths's schemes disintegrated, Allan Waters withdrew from his own prospective purchase, and Big John decided to snap up Saskatoon instead, Canadian Marconi rightly felt it had exhausted the possibilities within the CTV cooperative, so began to look elsewhere for a buyer. As a result, it ended up smack dab in the middle of Montreal's feuding Bronfman cousins.

On St. Patrick's Day 1972, Canadian Marconi accepted an $18-million offer from Multiple Access, a public company controlled by the sons and daughters of Sam Bronfman, which dealt in computer and communications services. By so doing, Canadian Marconi spurned a competing offer from Canadian Arena, a company controlled by the less powerful sons and daughter of Allan Bronfman, Sam's younger brother; Canadian Arena owned the Montreal Forum and the Montreal Canadiens hockey franchise.

Cut high into the side of a rock face in affluent Westmount, two mansions were once occupied by Sam and Allan Bronfman. The brothers were so close that they tore down the house between them to create a private playground for their seven children, complete with pool, hockey rink, and baseball diamond. The four boys — Sam's sons Edgar and Charles, and Allan's sons Edward and Peter — all expected to assume positions in the family's liquor empire. But as the Seagram Co. grew to become North America's top distiller, so did their sibling rivalry. First, Sam passed a resolution barring Allan's sons from working at Seagram, then forced them to sell their Seagram stock at a discount to their cousins. "The price was a lousy price, but we had to accept it. I think my father was quite humiliated, and sometimes took his frustrations out on us," Edward later told an interviewer. He and Peter never seemed to recover from these traumatic events.

The cousins' rancour became public knowledge after Edward and Peter's Canadian Arena lost out in the bidding for Canadian Marconi's broadcasting assets. The Edper Bronfmans then chose to intervene against Multiple Access at a CRTC hearing in Kingston, Ontario. At least, rather than duking it out in person, each side relied on its own battery of lawyers and accountants.

"I would be unhappy to feel that this is in any way a family matter in which there might be any indication of any difference of opinion between us," Multiple Access's lawyer Philip Vineberg said disingenuously. That was before Canadian Arena's representatives started levelling their accusations. They claimed that his clients had no broadcasting expertise and wanted only to offset Multiple Access's losses against a profitable company, then use the tax allowances to keep those profits. Afterwards, Vineberg adopted a different tone. "It only goes to show that when you have kind of a marriage you cannot [expect a testimonial] from a rejected suitor," he said. "It is apparent that Canadian Arena has taken the reaction of Canadian Marconi rather bitterly. [This is] a bitterness in which I would not like to share."

He then proceeded to rub salt in Canadian Arena's wounds by citing Edward and Peter's earlier failed attempt to take over Great-West Life Insurance (which had devastated numerous other shareholders when Great-West's stock price suddenly collapsed), but failed to mention that it was his clients' father, Sam Bronfman, who had sabotaged his nephews' effort.

Seeing the Bronfmans taking shots at each other through their lawyers was controversial enough. On top of this, the tone of the hearing — which concerned, lest we forget, the fate of an English-language station in Montreal — was highly politicized from the start. Before chairman Pierre Juneau could say a word, he was challenged by a member of the audience, who shouted that the only people who had anything to say about the matter at hand were a million anglophone Quebeckers, and that to shift the deliberations to Kingston was a disgrace.

At another point, Canadian Arena's lawyer Yvon Courtoy provided one of the hearing's lighter moments when he revealed that "Baton Broadcasting, of which John Bassett is president," was a minority shareholder in Canadian Arena.

"Canadian Arena presently has seven directors," the lawyer intoned. "Six . . . are residents of Montreal. [Mr. Bassett] has a long-time affinity . . . with the province of Quebec, but presently resides in Toronto."

"Does Mr. Bassett have any plans to change his residence?" asked Juneau.

"Mr. Chairman, I do not propose to reply for him. I doubt it, but I can assure you if he did he would be outvoted," Courtoy replied smoothly.

"But not outspoken," quipped Juneau, and laughter briefly filled the room.

Bassett's participation in Canadian Arena wasn't a big issue at the hearing, but CFTO's dominant position within the network kept bubbling to the surface. Bassett later argued that it was during CFCF's years of chronic instability, while Canadian Marconi was being shopped around, that "the CTV network was finding its feet, expanding its operations, and CFTO and its production arm in Toronto were developing and progressing aggressively to achieve the number one position in that very competitive market."

Multiple Access president John McCutcheon said that he was determined to challenge that position. "With the large and vital group of writing and performing talent that exists in Montreal, there seems to me to be no good reason why Toronto productions should continue to dominate CTV Canadian programming," he said. "Given approval of these applications, we will set about vigorously to expand program development and, over a period of several years, to gain a fair share of both CTV network and independent programming."

Once the commission decided to approve the transfer of Canadian Marconi's licences to Multiple Access, it was up to McCutcheon, a former professor of engineering and department chairman at McGill University, to fulfil that promise. He had his work cut out for him, because Canadian Arena's lawyers had been partially correct: nobody at Multiple Access knew much about television.

McCutcheon would have to deal with CFCF's thoroughly demoralized staff, who'd put most of their development on hold for the last three years while the prospective buyers came and went. As a result, CFCF's in-house production was relatively minor in 1972, with annual sales well below $1 million, compared to CFTO's $7 million.

That spring, Don Martz, then head of the broadcasting division at

Canadian Marconi and CFCF's representative on the CTV board, had presented five pilots for consideration by the network. Only one program, *Puppet People*, was selected.

Martz, who became a director of Multiple Access, was renominated to the board, and McCutcheon regularly attended its meetings so as to learn the ropes. From the moment the takeover closed in the summer of 1972, the new team was hard at work, attempting to initiate co-production projects with both Canadian and American partners. They were aiming to get one series — drama, adventure, or variety — into production in Montreal by the following winter.

The first result of these efforts was the smash sitcom *Excuse My French*. Unfortunately, its cost far exceeded its revenue, and after two seasons, CFCF's Champlain Productions decided not to continue with it. By then, though, CFCF had become the second-largest producer of local and network programs within CTV. Other titles included variety shows like *John Allan Cameron* and *Julie* (starring Toronto's Julie Amato) and public affairs productions like *The Editors*.

Things slowed down over the next two years, however, and Montreal's share of CTV's production payments dropped from 28 per cent in 1975–76 to 20 per cent in 1976–77. "Looking ahead, we see it more difficult even to hold the share we have," John McCutcheon said, "let alone increase it."

By 1978, things had levelled off — at least for Champlain Productions, whose annual sales had grown to $4.5 million (up from $1 million at the time Multiple Access took over). CFCF had placed five shows on the network schedule, but only one (*Julie*) appeared in prime time. Virtually all of CTV's prime-time Canadian programs were produced by Toronto, and the Baton group received over half of the network production payments.

Despite his comments at the CRTC hearings, John McCutcheon had come to accept this situation. Although he thought that Baton's dominance might ebb and flow, he knew it wasn't going to go away, for all sorts of reasons. On balance, he felt that Montreal wasn't doing badly and took the very reasonable view that there had to be a dominant station somewhere. Experience had shown him that any organization needed a single authority in order to function well.

"The network is in Toronto; CFTO is in Toronto," he said. "So it is logical that the network . . . should operate its own programming such as the *National News* and other public affairs programs through the Toronto member station. . . . This is a very expensive industry and Canada is a relatively small country. [It's] obvious that we must use our resources efficiently, and I consider that the use of CFTO's facilities by the network is a . . . proper move."

One reason for McCutcheon's change of heart was the Bronfman siblings' decision to sell their controlling interest in Multiple Access and get out of broadcasting in Quebec, where the political climate was not to Charles Bronfman's taste. Indeed, he had become an outspoken opponent of the Parti Québécois, or — as he insisted on calling them — "those bastards."

Unfortunately for the Bronfmans, their previous efforts to expand elsewhere (notably an attempt to buy CTV's Sudbury affiliate CKSO) had been stymied by the CRTC, which wanted Multiple Access to prove itself by making a go of CFCF. Only then would further applications be considered.

The Bronfmans' disenchantment with *la belle province* soon became a hot topic around the CTV boardroom table. One day, Bassett asked John McCutcheon, who had risen to the post of chairman of CTV's powerful executive committee, if the rumours were true. McCutcheon confirmed that they were, and Bassett made it clear that he was interested.

From that point, matters moved with speed. McCutcheon turned up in Toronto with Philip Vineberg, Multiple Access's lawyer, and Big John alerted Eddie Goodman and sounded out Foster Hewitt and several other Baton directors. Big John was prepared when McCutcheon and Vineberg rang the bell of his Rosedale home at four o'clock in the afternoon.

"Well, is it for sale?" Bassett demanded, before they'd had a chance to settle into their chairs.

"Yes, it is," they replied.

"Well, that's fine. What's the price?"

They named a number in the vicinity of $10 million.

"You've got a deal," Bassett barked.

In typical Big John style, the negotiations had taken only ten minutes, although he did call a special board meeting so that any Baton directors who were against the purchase could voice their opinions. "I'm going to tell you, he didn't leave us too much room for objection. But he certainly wanted everybody to know and was open to being told [otherwise]," Goodman said. Fortunately, the board shared Bassett's enthusiasm, and the agreement was drawn up and approved. Next came the hard sell, at the public hearing, which Big John wanted to slam through as soon as possible, because a new season loomed.

☆

A month later, on April 13, 1978, Big John Bassett sailed into the Hotel Le Meridien in Montreal to argue his case before the CRTC. He opened with a few remarks in French, saying he would do his best to answer questions in that language after the presentation, and asking in advance that the commission excuse his mistakes.

Much had changed since the snowy St. Patrick's Day in 1960 when he'd dazzled the old Board of Broadcast Governors with his verbal pyrotechnics and walked away with the original licence for CFTO. Among these changes was the political bent of the broadcasting authority. John Diefenbaker was a distant memory, and the Liberals had ruled since 1963. Under Pierre Juneau and Harry Boyle, the CRTC had earned a reputation for a certain chumminess with private broadcasters, even Tory ones. But the Trudeau government's appointment of Dr. Pierre Camu as chairman signalled a change at the commission — one that did not necessarily bode well for Big John. Camu, the former president of the Canadian Association of Broadcasters, was initially thought to be equally friendly to private interests. In fact, he'd accepted the post so as to be in a position to respond to the threat of Quebec separation, and the board was packed, in Doug Bassett's words, with "big Grits." One of them was Ron Irwin, later a member of Jean Chrétien's cabinet and still later, Canadian ambassador to Ireland.

The message from Irwin et al. was clear: if anyone was going to control private television in Canada, it would be a fellow big Grit, not a big Tory like John Bassett. And if anyone was going to own Montreal's largest English-language television station, it would be a true Quebecker, not an Ontarian. It didn't matter one whit that Bassett had grown up in the province, nor that he was fluently bilingual. The first of the Parti Québécois's never-ending referendums was still two years in the future, but the landscape of the city was already changing. English Montreal was in decline, and French Montreal very much on the rise. The wind was blowing against Big John, and he would have a very hard sell indeed.

With typical overconfidence, he decided to enlist no help from anyone. Eddie Goodman and Foster Hewitt were along for the ride, as well as four senior Baton vice-presidents, all in their thirties and forties. Among them was Douglas, "on whose shoulders," Big John noted, "the company's future will largely rest." Others were present, but not accounted for; this was the John Bassett show.

"The commission knows that I am not a particularly modest person," Bassett said, "but it is my belief that the team of broadcasters who have built CFTO and its production arm over the past eighteen years know as much about broadcasting as anyone in this country." Of the nine original second-station licencees, only he, Foster Hewitt, and Eddie Goodman were still actively engaged in broadcasting, he argued. "Finlay MacDonald has left Halifax; Marconi has left Montreal; Ralph Misener has left Winnipeg; Art Jones has left Vancouver; but we remain!" Such experienced ownership as Baton's would bring stability to CFCF, Bassett stressed.

He then addressed head-on the issue that would divide the commission.

"At this point I should like to deal a little more fully with the opinion I have seen expressed that approval of this application will create too great a concentration of ownership in the media and also that it will create too dominant a position for me within the CTV network. As to the first suggestion, I would point out . . . that Baton Broadcasting owns nothing in the field of communications in Montreal, or indeed in the Province of Quebec. As to the second . . . , I am sure . . . that there is no member past, present or future of the CRTC who hasn't heard for years the old statement that 'Bassett dominates the network.' [This] may be particularly galling to people like Allan Waters or Ray Peters . . . , but let me point out seriously that at the CTV network directors have only one vote, irrespective of ownership of more than one affiliate."

The proposed common ownership of CTV's Toronto and Montreal affiliates had come up for discussion at an executive committee meeting, Bassett said. CTV's president Murray Chercover had sent out a letter to all its directors, soliciting their opinions about Baton's proposed takeover of Multiple Access. Chercover had wanted to know if he should intervene against Baton's application on behalf of the network, but had heard no objections, not even from CHAN in Vancouver. Allan Waters and Geoff Stirling both expressed their verbal support. Kitchener's CKCO and Ottawa's CJOH, now part of Standard Broadcasting, had written letters in favour of the transfer of control.

A commissioner asked Bassett why there weren't more than two letters. "I think it's odd that I got the two," Bassett replied, to general laughter. "CTV may be a cooperative, but we don't go around publicly, and not very often privately, patting each other on the back and saying [things like], 'John, old boy, go and grab Montreal. I'm all for you.'"

He emphasized that approval of his application would not change anything at CTV, except improve the programming capabilities of the two affiliates, and promised to shift a number of productions from Toronto to Montreal. "Big deal," CFCF's Don Martz later told *Broadcaster* magazine. "That was a smokescreen. What would we get — the game shows? I don't think that would have done anybody a great deal of good."

And this was the crux of the matter: the idea that Baton would control two of the biggest production facilities in the country and that Big John would become the "Louis B. Mayer of Canada." If Glen-Warren Productions and Champlain Productions merged, Baton would account for almost three-quarters, in dollar terms, of all the network's production, and Baton's coverage area would be extended to almost a third of English-speaking Canada.

A commissioner asked at what stage Big John would think too much control of CTV resided in one person. If, for example, he bought all the affiliates, one by one? "Not if I was operating it," said Bassett, adding that he meant it sincerely. "I think I could operate the network a lot better than it's being operated. No question."

Ron Irwin, another commissioner, was not a believer. He criticized Big John for producing American programs and American-style Canadian programs, implying that Baton had been co-opted into the American system and thus constituted a threat to Canadian culture.

"Do you want me to answer, or do you want to bully me, or what are you trying to do?" Bassett demanded. "Because I don't bully very easily. Do you want to be factual?"

"I doubt if I can bully you," Irwin replied.

"Yeah, well, I doubt it too. But do you want to be factual?" Bassett pressed.

Big John had lost his composure. He did have an argument as to why doing such a high volume of American business was good for a Canadian broadcaster. He said it was important to raise the standard of domestic programming so that Canadian stations could compete for the attention of Canadian viewers, who spent 75 per cent of their viewing time watching American shows.

He added how much he loved to beat the Americans at their own game. "I tell you quite frankly that, [at my time of life], to make some more money to enhance my prestige, whatever it may or may not be, . . . is of absolutely no interest to me at all. . . . I've got a lovely house in the country. I've got a beautiful wife and a beautiful family, and those are my top priorities. But I love programming. I love to go down to America and take business away from Los Angeles and have them come up here and show them what we can do in Canada. And we've done it! We've done it successfully time and time and time again."

All this was true, and Big John continued to reel off all Glen-Warren's high-water marks: the Hallmark Hall of Fame movies, the evangelist Billy Graham's crusades, and numerous specials such as *The Nutcracker Suite* for the CBS network. Profits from these productions had helped to defray the losses from the Baton group's Canadian productions.

"*Separation* cost us $600,000," Bassett said. "We won't ever recover that. We have sold it to our colleagues in the network [for two-thirds of the cost], but we won't get it all back. We never got anything back on *Henry V*, [which cost $180,000], and on a lot of other shows." And so on, down this by now familiar road.

It wasn't enough to sway the commission. For one thing, Big John had made a tactical error in mounting his argument solo. "Perhaps he should [have] let his colleagues speak," says his son Doug. "It should have been more of a team presentation," Fred Eaton agrees. "Ted Rogers told Douglas [as much]. But I didn't think I or Douglas should speak." So Eaton sat silent in the audience, representing Baton's controlling family. For another, the CRTC felt that Big John wasn't bringing enough to the party, outlining sufficient tangible benefits if the deal went through. "I was at the hearing," CHUM's Fred Sherratt says. "They kept prodding Baton to put more on the table."

And Big John had to fight a more recent memory — his "too big is too big" mantra of six years earlier, when he'd gained control of CFQC by pointing out that Saskatoon wasn't Montreal. But that was then, and this was now. Right now, Montreal was a political hot potato. Nobody's takeover bid was going to be waved through without a struggle.

Still, the CRTC faced an internal battle, and took its sweet time reaching a decision, throwing Big John's plans for his fall schedule into doubt while he paced the floor. Six months later, in October 1978, the commission made its ruling — a close vote, with an unprecedented dissenting opinion attached. (Doug Bassett recalls that the decision was five-to-four against — because not all the commissioners had taken part in the hearing.) The dissent noted that neither the network nor any individual affiliate had opposed Big John's plan and thought it important for Canadian broadcasters to achieve "critical mass," so as to afford to produce "high standard" prime-time popular programs to compete against the "reality of massive Americanization of the Canadian broadcasting system." But the majority ruled, and the majority believed that the "improvements to Canadian television programming suggested by Baton were essentially presented in general rather than specific terms and that it was not concretely demonstrated by Baton how combined control of CFTO and CFCF would improve the level and quality of Canadian programming."

Today Fred Eaton says the decision demonstrated that "the CRTC, like most government bodies, is usually a step behind. It's very hard to see what's happening in the industry if you're not in it. . . . It was stupid, if you ask me. I know Big John would have seen to it that Montreal regained its prominence as a centre of [English-language] production. In my mind, it was crazy. Look at what's happened to that great city!"

"We were very upset, and the vendors were very upset as well," says Doug Bassett. "But life goes on."

Nine months later, by the way, in July 1979, the commissioners gave their blessing to the next applicant to appear before them — the Quebec broadcaster Jean Pouliot, who'd meanwhile gained control of Multiple Access. Pouliot had started his broadcasting career as an executive engineer with Famous Players, then returned to his home province and rose to become president of Télévision de Québec, the licensee of CKMI, an English-language CBC affiliate in Quebec City. At his hearing, he personally guaranteed that CFCF would continue to perform its role for Montreal's anglophone community. In its decision, the CRTC stated that Pouliot had "alleviated" concerns about concentration of ownership and control within the Canadian broadcasting system raised by Baton's earlier application.

Big John was terribly disappointed by the outcome, but life did go on, and he did win on an unexpected front. As part and parcel of the Montreal hearing, CHUM was given the go-ahead to buy Multiple Access's interest in CITY, Moses Znaimer's independent Toronto television station.

"After we got control of CITY," CHUM's Fred Sherratt explains, "we went to a CTV directors' meeting where our friends from the west suggested that this was a serious problem, that we at CHUM had a conflict of interest." Big John rose in his place at the table. "We're the Toronto affiliate," he said. "When we think there's a problem, we'll let you know." From that point on, Baton had CHUM's marker, and two decades later its support would prove crucial in Baton's ultimately successful takeover of the network.

Yet in the fall of 1978, despite all Big John's manoeuvring, he seemed to be no closer to exercising control of CTV than he'd been in 1961. During those years it had grown to embrace fifteen fully affiliated stations and four supplementary affiliates, as well as 218 rebroadcast transmitters. Its annual budget was $70 million; it sent its signals via 7,900 miles of microwave. It was in every sense and by anyone's definition a mammoth enterprise, but still it operated as a cooperative. Baton — although the owner of two affiliates, including the flagship CFTO — was allowed only one voting director on the twelve-member board. The time was ripe for change — but perhaps it was also time for Big John to pass the torch to the next generation.

Two

The Next Generation

9

The CRTC
versus CTV — 1978–85

As CTV launched its eighteenth fall season in 1978, the CRTC set its sights on the abysmal lack of Canadian drama on viewers' screens. It believed that matters had reached such a pass that before too long, every Canadian network — including the CBC — would be airing almost nothing except American or American-influenced entertainment. It had conducted a survey that found that when news, public affairs, and sports were taken out of the equation, 90 per cent of CTV's broadcast schedule consisted of U.S. imports. The remaining 10 per cent was composed mainly of cheap game shows like *Headline Hunters*, relatively inexpensive variety programs like *The Bobby Vinton Show*, *Gran Ol Country*, *Julie*, and *Stars on Ice*, and CTV's latest offerings, *Patsy Gallant* and *Circus*.

Patsy Gallant, hosted by the Québécois disco diva at CFTO, wasn't much of a departure from the norm, but *Circus* was something else again. It featured lions and tigers, elephants, trapeze artists, and two young performers dubbed "the Donnie and Marie Osmond of Canada." A big-top set was constructed in CFTO's Studio 6, under the personal supervision of Arthur Weinthal, CTV's vice-president of entertainment programming. He took a great deal of interest in the show, spending hours with the animals and their trainers. His aim was to make a "high-energy" program that would appeal to audiences on both sides of the border, and had pre-sold twenty-four episodes to American distributors on the basis of a one-hour special broadcast earlier that year.

The other surprise made-in-Canada winner, new to CTV that fall, aired no animal acts, only human ones. *Live It Up,* hosted by Alan Edmonds, Jack McGaw, and Mary Lou Finlay, was part journalism, part consumer affairs, and part witty narrative. But even it looked south for subject matter: the inaugural episode involved a visit to New York's Studio 54 disco.

All three shows performed well in the ratings, but none was the stuff of the CRTC's dreams. CTV's prime time continued to be dominated by the likes of *The Bionic Woman, Soap, Taxi,* and *The Carol Burnett Show* (which CTV's vice-president of programming, Pip Wedge, had picked up after the CBC dropped it from its schedule in favour of another American offering). There wasn't a regular weekly Canadian drama series, great or otherwise, airing in prime time. In fact, there hadn't been one since *Excuse My French* was cancelled three seasons earlier. Clearly, the network had been dragging its heels and could expect a rough ride from the regulatory authority.

The first affiliate to come under newly intensive fire was CHAN Vancouver. Its contributions to the network's schedule — the *Oscar Peterson Show, Rolf Harris, Oompaps,* and the *Alan Hamel Show* — included nothing resembling drama. This did not trouble Ray Peters, who defended his station at its licence renewal hearing in October 1978. He laid some of the blame at the CRTC's own door, for compelling him to install rebroadcast facilities in unprofitable areas. Extending CHAN's coverage to 100 per cent of the province had cost his company millions of dollars that it could never hope to recoup from the small communities it now served. If not for this enormous outlay, he said, he could have "put substantially more into network productions." Indeed, Peters thought that he merited the CRTC's thanks and that CTV as a whole should be congratulated for reaching 93.6 per cent of English-speaking Canada.

The commission wasn't in the mood for pats on the back. Roy Faibish, a recently appointed member (and a former executive at CJOH Ottawa), suggested that the network be required to open up its books, so that Canadians could know how much money stations like CHAN were making. The private network already kept the CRTC fully informed as to its finances, but Faibish also wanted obedience of the commission's rulings. Failing that, he wanted to start yanking broadcast licences.

☆

While the forces of Cancon mounted their assault on the wholesale Americanization of Canadian prime-time schedules, CTV's board of directors, chaired by Bill McGregor from CKCO Kitchener, spent seven weeks working with network management to prepare for the network's licence renewal hearing in February 1979. Then, out of nowhere, the Council of Canadian Filmmakers launched a pre-emptive strike by taking its case directly to the media in advance of the public sessions.

"CTV has been playing a shell game for years," the council's chairman, Kirwan Cox, informed the *Globe and Mail*. "The station owners deliberately keep the network impoverished in order to increase their own earnings. This strategy reduces the money available for Canadian programming." Then, according to Cox, the network could turn around and plead poverty when its program shortcomings were pointed out. The brief also accused CTV of inflating its overall program expenditures and cited figures to prove it. The *Globe* carried the filmmakers' brief in its entirety, sparking further editorial comment in the *Toronto Star*, which took the network to task in no uncertain terms.

Thanks to this publicity blitz, the CTV contingent (led by president Murray Chercover, board chairman Bill McGregor, and Ray Peters, newly elected chairman of the executive committee) was under no illusion as to what the fight would be about during the three days of public hearings in front of Dr. Pierre Camu and his CRTC cohorts. The battle was joined in the Salle des Nations, Auberge de la Chaudière, a hotel in the block-square complex of red-brick office towers on the Hull side of the Ottawa River, where the CRTC had recently been relocated.

Ever the showman, Chercover led off by emphasizing CTV's accomplishments at home and the recognition it had received abroad. First, he noted that, of the network's 300 employees, roughly 200 were involved with programming. He then proceeded to laud *CTV National News*, which had doubled its audience (to 829,000) over the previous ten years. "It is now the dominant national newscast," he said. "Lloyd Robertson, working with Harvey [Kirck] as co-anchorman, has become a Canadian institution. . . . When it comes to news and information programming, [Canadians] spend twice as much time watching CTV as they spend watching CBC."

CTV had also built a strong presence in sports. In addition to professional football and hockey, and Johnny Esaw's popular *Wide World of Sports*, the network had pioneered coverage of competitions such as the Canadian Figure Skating Championships and Skate Canada, and had proven itself at the 1976 Winter Olympics in Austria, leading the World Association of Broadcasters to invite it to coordinate coverage of the 1980 Winter Olympics in Lake Placid.

Chercover took pride in *Stars on Ice*, too, as "another example of a highly successful, original concept that is quite able to compete with the best television anyone else has to offer." He crowed that *Circus* had drawn larger audiences than some of the "CBC's most heavily touted [and] publicly financed Canadian properties, such as *René Simard, King of Kensington, Tommy Hunter*, and so on."

In sum, Chercover couldn't have been more thrilled with the acceptance of CTV's programming in Canada, the United States, and overseas. Worldwide sales had earned the network an extra $5 million in pocket money over the past three years. The 156-episode nature series *Untamed World*, perhaps CTV's best-known export, was seen in forty-nine different countries. *Stars on Ice* was being watched in thirty-seven nations other than Canada; the *Primitive Man* series, in twenty-two; the *Human Journey* series in more than a dozen; and the latest offering, *Circus*, in eleven.

As he tried to stress how well received CTV's current weekly service of sixty-six hours and fifty minutes of programming had become, Chercover explained the difference between CTV and the CBC: his network was "upbeat, not heavy, energetic." People wanted to watch what it had to offer. Bill McGregor agreed and added that the network had "more than made up for" any shortfall in drama per se with specials and mini-series such as the upcoming *A Man Called Intrepid*, not to mention the new co-produced weekly series, *Search and Rescue*.

But endless foreign co-productions and variety specials churned out with an eye to American sales (and no Canadian character to speak of) weren't good enough for the Council of Canadian Filmmakers. It slammed the network for the general "deterioration" of its Canadian programming, especially the lack of an original drama in two of the three years since its last licence hearing.

Then followed a burst of gloomy statistics from the filmmakers. The network's drama assignments for Canadian actors, they claimed, had dropped to 333 from 3,129 three years earlier. In fact, Canadian programming in the 8 p.m. to 10 p.m. time slot had dropped to half an hour a week in 1978 from two hours a week in 1976. The council alleged that CTV fulfilled its daily 60 per cent Canadian content requirement only by scheduling "cheap" game shows like *Definition* and information shows like the "commendable" *Canada AM* during the day, along with news in the evening. Peak viewing hours were given over almost exclusively to

American programs, which could usually be purchased for about 10 per cent of their production cost. In closing, the filmmakers recommended that CTV be granted only a two-year extension of its licence and put on notice that it would have to meet a number of conditions.

Chercover was incensed by this intervention and called its overriding tone "derogatory." He was particularly unhappy that the commission hadn't allowed him to respond to the filmmakers at once, but in the general rebuttal, by which time most of the journalists covering the hearings had scurried off to write their (to his mind) biased stories. "They've heard all the slams, all the aggressive and argumentative questions [that were] thrown at us," he fulminated. "We've been reported as 'crawling on our belly . . . like reptiles.' [The] bottom line is, we haven't . . . come here in a begging posture, we haven't come here pleading and apologizing. There is no apology!"

Chercover then revealed that one of the people who'd figured prominently in the filmmakers' brief had had two projects rejected by the network and could scarcely be expected to offer a balanced view. He was also furious that the brief had included confidential financial information, presumably obtained by underhanded means.

The only criticism of the network that Chercover would even partially acknowledge was its lack of an overtly Canadian drama series in its current schedule — or, as he put it, the lack of "that category of program which addresses itself to the Canadian identity with respect to Canadian place names, licence plates, and money and so on." With that exception, he argued, CTV generally offered a "better schedule, a better package of programming" than the CBC.

For his part, Ray Peters described the brief as "loaded with errors. . . . It is just incorrect." He noted cantankerously that he was attacking it "because [he was] known to be a very bad-tempered person." One of the filmmakers' errors, he pointed out, was their statement that the network retained only "25 per cent of each net dollar it earns," so that it couldn't make sufficient profit to spend on quality Canadian programs. Peters said that, on the contrary, all programming costs, distribution costs, agency commissions and so forth were charged against the net advertising dollars before they were distributed in the 75-25 split, according to the shareholders' agreement. Since all these expenses were taken off the top, about 70 per cent of what he called the "net margin" went to the network, and the stations received only 30 per cent.

Concerned that the CRTC's primary objective would now be to force the affiliates to fund more Canadian programming, Moffat's Ron Mitchell suggested that his Winnipeg station (which had been running a negative cash flow) and other similarly hard-pressed outlets be relieved of obligations such as extension of network service. "It sounds rather simple to talk about changing the formula and increasing the amount of money the network [must] spend on [Canadian drama] programming," Mitchell said. "[But] in the case of our company and [Ray] Peters's company, we are contributing money every year to keep the local service going in smaller communities." This was the number one priority set by the CRTC itself, before it started harping on the need for drama at any cost.

Murray Chercover agreed and went on to say that, if anybody was starving the network, it was the CRTC itself. He blamed the commission for bowing to political pressures and allowing cable television to penetrate even the most far-flung corners of the country, so that every household had access to American network shows. In his words, "No other broadcast system in the world so easily facilitates foreign domination of its domestic airwaves. No other broadcast system in the world is structured in such a way as to make it almost impossible to project long-term stability."

Bill McGregor chimed in, warning that the commission should think twice about imposing more regulations on Canadian content. As he had predicted when Pierre Juneau had pushed to raise Cancon to 60 per cent, the commission might get quantity but it wouldn't get quality. "For you to go beyond that figure in any more arbitrary and control-minded manner suggests to me that you're taking the exact wrong approach," he said. "You're following . . . the same line as was followed in the original concept of Canadian content. You're looking at it [as if] you have to have a pile of coal and you've got to shovel a ton."

This point was not lost on Pierre Camu. He too wondered, when it came to CTV's production, whether the commission would do better to "value quantity or quality." The question was asked again the following month, when the CRTC was slated to confront all the Toronto-area stations (including Global, CITY, CHCH Hamilton, the CBC's CBLT, CFTO, and CKCO Kitchener) about the long-delayed fulfilment of their Cancon obligations.

By the time these hearings got under way at Toronto's Park Plaza Hotel in March 1979, Camu had gone on the record to an attentive press with his concerns about the absence of Canadian content in prime time. "The Toronto area is the key to English-language television in Canada," he said. "It's where the industry leaders are. If we cannot obtain from them a little more creativity in contribution, in a more Canadian feel to the service, then where can we look for it?"

Commissioner Roy Faibish didn't know, but he was willing to find out. He cautioned Bill McGregor that holding a broadcasting licence was a privilege, not a right, and that "it's only a matter of time until other parties come along and say, 'Look, that guy's . . . had the licence for a quarter of a century. [He's] recovered his investment and made a little profit. I can do better than he can . . . , and I want a chance. [I'm] prepared to take less profit and whatever the consequences are, and do more.'"

Faibish got even more exercised when Global's representative took his turn in front of the commission. "You guys certainly know how to get the blood of a mild-mannered man like myself boiling," he said, "and it's boiling at the moment. [I] say to you that you place your network licence in jeopardy, . . . given the fact that the essence of the Global Network was to be an alternative." This was quite true. The CRTC had licensed Global as a regional Ontario network in mid-1972 on the condition that half of its Canadian programming would be provided by independent Canadian producers. After a shaky start, this plan degenerated into dismal failure. Then, when Global's new owners rescued it from bankruptcy, it filled its prime time with American shows like everyone else.

By the time Doug Bassett arose to defend CFTO's record in Canadian programming, the rhetoric had toned down a notch, but the commissioners raised similar concerns. This was a rough baptism for Doug, who'd just assumed the presidency of Baton — it was the first public hearing in twenty years where Big John hadn't been front and centre to speak on the station's behalf.

But Doug acquitted himself well. He began by mentioning *Hourlong*, a CFTO-produced program that was "close to his heart," because it was co-hosted by his stepmother, Isabel. Then he cited the thirteen-season-old children's show *Uncle Bobby*. While neither program was on the network schedule, CFTO provided both to some of its fellow affiliates free of charge. For example, *Uncle Bobby* had been seen in Newfoundland for the past five years.

This succeeded in waking up a commissioner from the Rock. "Looking at CFTO," he said, "I see two big glamorous letters T-O in your call letters. . . . I had imagined CFTO to be somehow distinct — reflecting what Toronto is really about as a . . . cultural and economic milieu. . . . [Then I] look at your schedule of programming and discover that it looks very much like CJON [in] St. John's . . . , which takes me quite by surprise. . . . I am amazed to find *Romper Room* [on the Toronto schedule]. I assumed we got *Romper Room* in Newfoundland because there was very little else that CTV was prepared to offer us."

Poor CTV! On days like this, it couldn't please any of the people any of the time. No doubt fearful of testing further the commissioner's capacity for amazement and surprise, Doug Bassett contented himself with explaining that CKCO Kitchener produced *Romper Room* for the full network — and that CJON, like CFTO, was lucky to receive it.

He then sailed on to another list of CFTO's shows, including the seven-year-old game show *Headline Hunters*, hosted by Jim Perry, and a twelve-year-old fishing program called *The Red Fisher Show*, today parodied by the comedian Steve Smith in *The Red Green Show*. CFTO contributed variety series to the network as well, like *Patsy Gallant*, which Baton had undertaken to produce after applying to take over CFCF Montreal the previous April. Although it was more Canadian than earlier variety outings, the commissioners remained unimpressed. They believed that the very concept was inescapably American.

"It's difficult for me to say that such-and-such a show is [either] a Canadian or an American show," complained commissioner Jacques Hébert. "I have the impression that they are really American shows in their style and format. . . . To me, [the CBC's] *René Simard Show* is an American show that happens to utilize the talent and charm of a young French-Canadian artist who is playing the part of an American star." To the suggestion that Baton's Canadian variety shows ought to score points because they had Canadian artists as guests, and that *Stars on Ice* looked particularly home-grown, Hébert replied, "Well, the ice [helps] a little bit."

In general, though, Hébert couldn't understand why Canadian broadcasters weren't making dramas a priority, even in what he called their "lower forms" — that is, soap operas and sitcoms. "Are we forever to be making Hollywood [variety and game] shows in Canada, rather than truly Canadian shows [that reflect our] culture, if we have [a culture] at all? . . . Right now, . . . broadcasters are trying to obey the law, . . . but I wonder if they are really obeying the spirit of the regulation, because a lot of the so-called Canadian content is not Canadian at all in its soul. I would like [you to demonstrate] once and for all that Canadians would not be interested in seeing Canadian families and Canadian farmers and doctors, even lawyers, in fictional settings. I can't understand that."

Doug Bassett said that CFTO was making the effort, and on a larger scale than the so-called "lower forms." He referred to the two-hour movie *Separation* that the station had produced instead of a drama series in the previous season. So far, Baton had recouped a portion of *Separation*'s development cost by selling it to the CTV network and was currently distributing it in Australia and Britain, though not in the United States. "Perhaps we might sell it in the United States closer to the [Quebec] referendum," he suggested.

CFTO also had under contract or licence thirty-six other Canadian feature films, including CTV's co-productions *Why Shoot the Teacher?* and *Outrageous* and Johnny F. Bassett's *Paperback Hero*. They told demonstrably Canadian stories, even though they tended to be aired during the summer, when (as Bassett bluntly admitted) they didn't have to compete "with *One Flew Over the Cuckoo's Nest*" on an American channel.

More important, he told the commission that CFTO had committed to producing a twenty-six episode, half-hour drama series for the coming fall season, which he hoped would be picked up by the full network. For "competitive reasons," Bassett claimed he couldn't say any more about the project (which turned out to be a revival of *The Littlest Hobo* and did in fact air nationwide that autumn).

Upon hearing this news, Pierre Camu asked Bassett if he had any more such items on the list. "We would have," Doug replied, "if [we'd] had a favourable ruling from Montreal" — that is, if Baton's takeover of CFCF had gone through. Even Camu had to admit that Doug's rejoinder was "fair enough."

In all, Doug was hitting his stride. When Jacques Hébert continued to disparage the quality of Canadian programming, Doug defended it with a sporting analogy. "You could perhaps relate [the strength of our station] to that of a football team," he said. "A good Canadian [team] has to have good Canadian talent in order to win. The Toronto Argonauts never had that . . . in the old days, and they obviously didn't have it when we were involved. . . . But that is the basic soundness of a Canadian team. We believe the basic soundness of a Canadian television station, such as [CFTO], is good Canadian quality programming that Canadians will watch. Canadians watch *Stars on Ice*, Canadians watch *Patsy Gallant*. Those ratings just don't come from American shows, as you well know. Canadians watch *Hourlong*. Canadians watch *Circus*. Canadians watch our news content [CFTO's local newscasts at 6:30 p.m. and 11:20 p.m. daily were number one in the Toronto market]. So I make no apologies about our programming. We have always tried to do more than everybody else."

Hébert wasn't convinced. He argued that if viewers in Dallas, Texas, were watching CFTO, they would not find themselves "in too much of a strange world all of a sudden. They would have *The Lucy Show* and

The Bionic Woman and *Carol Burnett.* . . . When they [saw] Patsy Gallant
they would say, 'Well, she's a little different, but the show is obviously
American.'" To turn this around, he foresaw the necessity of drastic
measures.

Roy Faibish agreed and warned Bassett that "quantum leaps forward"
were a fact of life in both physics and broadcasting. "I am saying [that] to
you not just because of the credibility of the commission, which is fundamental. [We] are at a turning point, and there must be some quantum
changes."

Eddie Goodman wasn't about to let that one pass. He stated that the
CRTC had to change its attitudes about media concentration if it wanted
changes on such a scale. "One of the things that those quantum leaps
require is a [policy] which favours opportunity through allowing size,"
he said. "This station believes that that policy is missing." Especially, he
might have added, after the commission's refusal to allow Baton to leap
in the direction of CFCF Montreal.

On August 3, the CRTC delivered a wake-up call to the network. It
complimented CTV on the high quality of its news, public affairs, and
sports programming, but failed to detect comparable results when it
came to "distinctive Canadian entertainment programming, particularly
in the field of drama."

Then, for the first time ever, it imposed a Canadian content quota for
a specific programming genre, making the renewal of CTV's licence conditional on its presentation of twenty-six hours (an average of half an
hour a week) of original Canadian drama in the 1980–81 season, rising to
thirty-nine hours (three-quarters of an hour a week) for the rest of its
five-year licence term.

Furthermore, it wanted these shows to appear in peak viewing hours,
after 8 p.m. At least half of the planning and development of the pilots had
to take place in Canada, and the shows had to feature explicitly Canadian
themes and unmistakably Canadian locations. Foreign co-productions
with all-purpose urban settings wouldn't qualify.

In addition, rather than allotting most of its production budget to
CFTO and CFCF, the network would have to let independent producers
in on the action. (The Council of Canadian Filmmakers had alleged that
independently produced Canadian programming had never exceeded
1 per cent of CTV's total Canadian schedule in the past six years.)
Finally, the commission stipulated that it wanted to see more shows that

"reflected the cultural life of Quebec to the rest of Canada," as well as more programs for children.

It was quite the shopping list, and it wouldn't come cheap, but the commission was clear as to who would foot the bill. Paying for all this brave new programming would "necessitate changes in the cost-sharing formula of the network, if not a complete change in the present cooperative financial structure." CTV was expected to "undertake without delay" a "fundamental review" of its most basic procedures and "report its progress in due course."

Enraged by this edict, the CTV owners vowed to fight the decision in the Federal Court of Appeal. They believed that the CRTC was overstepping its authority and infringing on the network's freedom of expression. They refused point blank to do more in the way of Canadian drama than to broadcast twenty-six episodes of *The Littlest Hobo* that fall season, and hired Eddie Goodman to argue their case in *CTV Television Network Ltd. v. Canada (C.R.T.C.)*. But not all the station owners were on side. "I don't remember whose brilliant idea it was to challenge the CRTC," Fred Sherratt says. "CHUM didn't think it was a great idea. But everything at CTV was usually done by consensus. There weren't many votes on things. Obviously, they'd decided [to] test the [commission]."

At least Ray Peters and Bill McGregor were of like minds on this issue. "The CRTC should not have been directing licencees of the CTV network to produce so many hours of drama," Peters says. "[A legislator] should not be in the programming business. . . . The commission said CTV wasn't doing enough in the way of Canadian drama. To a degree they were right, but we were doing all that we could at that time. We were spending more than we could take in; [the] stations were subsidizing the network. [So] we had to disagree with their decision. . . . How about the symphony, dance, poetry or other cultural objectives? Why single out drama?"

"We had no argument about [having to provide a certain] percentage of Canadian content," Bill McGregor adds. "But we were telling the commission, 'You don't have the power of censorship.' That was really the time we had to draw the line in the sand."

CTV also argued that it wasn't given adequate warning about the commission's unhappiness with its lack of Canadian drama programs. Although the CRTC had claimed that "much of the discussion at the February 1979 hearings dealt with this deficiency," the network alleged that the matter wasn't raised until the filmmakers' intervention.

Finally, CTV tried to get the commission's ruling thrown out on procedural grounds, noting that one of the commissioners who'd participated in the decision wasn't present at the public hearing. (This was true, and the CRTC now requires that anyone who takes part in a ruling has to have the grace to show up to hear the pros and cons.)

Meanwhile, as Goodman prepared his appeal, there'd been a change of power in Ottawa, with Joe Clark's Tories narrowly defeating the Trudeau Liberals in June 1979. The hapless Clark accomplished little before Trudeau's re-election the following February, but he did manage to get rid of the CRTC chairman. For years afterwards, Big John boasted that his pal Clark had "solved that particular problem" at his request.

Shortly after CTV announced that it would challenge the CRTC, Pierre Camu resigned, citing "an interesting job offer." After a six-week search, the Tories appointed John Meisel, a broadcasting neophyte and professor of political science at Queen's University in Kingston, Ontario — a decision reminiscent of the Diefenbaker government's original choice of Andrew Stewart to head the Board of Broadcast Governors.

A little more than a year later, at the end of 1980, CTV won a partial victory in court. The conditions pertaining to Canadian drama attached to its licence were set aside, thereby nullifying that licence and necessitating yet another hearing. Chief Justice A. L. Thurlow agreed that there'd been insufficient warning of the CRTC's intentions, adding that the film-makers' intervention hadn't recommended a minimum amount of Canadian drama. But Thurlow threw out the network's contention that the CRTC had no authority to impose such conditions. "We won half and lost half," Eddie Goodman remembers.

John Meisel gave notice that the CRTC would have to appeal the ruling, because of its procedural implications. If it stood, the CRTC would have to have two hearings for each licence renewal — one to determine the facts and another to give the applicant a chance to respond to the proposed conditions of its licence.

Meisel also took the Great Cancon Debate directly to the nation's couch potatoes. In 1981, he held informal public meetings in eleven cities. In its written submission, BCTV wrote, "If Canadians want to watch *Dallas* and [can] receive *Dallas*, [they] have the unquestioned right to watch *Dallas*." This example was chosen for a reason: *Dallas* aired on the CBC.

In its brief, CTV criticized "elitists who believe that they know better than the Canadian public" and who suspect that "there is something negative about mass popularity of television programs."

Unfortunately for the network, John Meisel proved to be no more populist than his Liberal-appointed predecessors. In the spring of 1981, he told the Canadian Association of Broadcasters, "There is a lot of programming that does not lift spirits, move hearts, enchant eyes. There is a great deal that is dreary, mindless, and repetitive." He said original Canadian drama and children's programs were "lamentably underrepresented." BCTV's Don Smith, then association chairman, called Meisel's sentiment only "slightly elitist" but argued that most viewers would not care to watch the sort of programs the CRTC chief preferred.

In May, CTV aired a mini-series even a "slightly elitist" person might have enjoyed, called *Escape from Iran: The Canadian Caper*. It dramatized the rescue of six Americans held hostage in that country in 1979, with the CTV building on Charles Street in Toronto doubling for Teheran's Canadian embassy. The network paid a $250,000 licence fee to broadcast this series. The independent producer turned around and sold it to the CBS network for $2.2 million.

In the late spring of 1981, the CRTC held licence renewal hearings for all the Toronto-area stations. Seven months later, they too received the customary reprimands. As it had earlier cautioned the network, the commission said they'd done reasonably well with news and public affairs programming, but had failed to develop and invest in original Canadian dramas and children's shows. Although it attached no specific content quotas, the CRTC cut the term of everybody's licence to three years from the usual five. As well, CFCF Montreal's licence was contingent on the station establishing a $1-million fund to develop programming with specific Quebec references.

Meanwhile, Eddie Goodman and his junior, Kathy Robinson, were getting ready to present CTV's case against the CRTC to the Supreme Court of Canada, following the commission's earlier appeal. Goodman was hopeful that CTV would prevail, in part because Willard Estey would be on the bench. Prior to this appointment, Estey had acted as a lawyer for the Canadian Association of Broadcasters and sat on the boards of British Columbia Television and Bushnell Communications. He was familiar with the industry and might have been expected to prove receptive to Goodman's contention that the 1968 Broadcasting Act (besides being "badly written") had not empowered the CRTC to give directions (other than generally applicable regulations or conditions of licence) concerning specific programs or program categories.

Things didn't go their way. "We got clobbered by [Chief Justice] Bora Laskin," Goodman recalls. "At the beginning of the case, the clerk [announced that] Justice Estey [wouldn't] be sitting [that day]. I turned to

Kathy and said, 'We've just lost the case.' Bora was very ill at this time and he was so nasty to Kathy; [he wouldn't listen]. This was her first case and he was impossible. He died shortly thereafter."

In their unanimous decision announced in April 1982, Laskin and six other justices threw out the Federal Court of Appeal's ruling: the CRTC did not have to give applicants advance warning about any conditions it planned to impose on their licences. "It cannot be said that CTV was being misled," Laskin noted in his judgement. "Conditions had been attached before, although not relating to content, and CTV was well aware of this power of the CRTC when reviewing licences."

The chief justice reminded the network that it was also well aware of the commission's dissatisfaction with "its performance in respect of Canadian drama." After all, CTV had already promised "improvement in that respect" in earlier applications. In sum, the high court ruled that the CRTC's 1979 decision, including the network's conditional licence renewal, "should be restored."

A disappointed Eddie Goodman felt vindicated in 1985 by law professor Hudson Janisch's analysis of the Supreme Court's ruling in the *University of Toronto Law Journal*. Janisch questioned whether the court was justified in the way the CTV challenge was "impatiently dismissed out of hand" in view of the "unquestioned" promise of the Broadcasting Act of "the right to freedom of expression and the right of persons to receive programs." Others agreed. In 1995, WIC Western International Communications's in-house lawyer Jonathan Festinger wrote in the *U.B.C. Law Review* that the Charter of Rights and Freedoms would make the Supreme Court's decision untenable today. The CRTC's demand that a "percentage of a specified kind of programming be supplied would be considered an infringement on CTV's freedom of expression," he wrote. "While a simple percentage-based Canadian content requirement would likely pass constitutional muster, most other forms of content control probably would not."

At the time, though, rival media took pleasure in CTV's comeuppance. One example will suffice. The *Toronto Star* argued in an editorial that Canadian broadcasters "have a greater role to play than merely acting as middlemen between American producers, writers, and performers on the one hand, and the Canadian viewing public on the other. It is precisely the CRTC's function to ensure that Canadians are given more of a choice in prime-time programming than opting either for *Barney Miller* with Canadian Tire ads, or *Barney Miller* with ads for the Erie County Savings Bank [of Buffalo, New York]."

☆

All this having been said and done, life went on much as before. In Bill McGregor's words, "Everyone walked away." The CRTC chose not to employ the big stick the Supreme Court had handed it. Instead, the commission issued CTV a series of temporary licence extensions, giving the network time to amend its cost-sharing formula so that it could afford to develop new Canadian dramas.

It had nowhere to go but up. In 1982, CTV's best-known Canadian performer was London, the German shepherd star of *The Littlest Hobo*, a made-in-Toronto series stripped of north-of-the-border references. Even the money the human characters used was American. Only eighteen to twenty episodes were planned for the 1982–83 season, as opposed to the twenty-six episodes that were aired three years earlier when the CRTC first flexed its muscles. This would leave the network thirty hours short of the prime-time drama requirement laid down before the court cases got under way.

As for the rest of its programming, nearly all the Canadian series introduced to CTV's evening schedule since 1979 had been low-rent game and variety productions: *Whatever Turns You On*, a showcase for young performers hosted by *Laugh-In*'s Ruth Buzzi and Ottawa's Les Lye; *Bizarre*, a "skitcom" starring the impressionist and comedian John Buyner; *Honky Tonk*, a country music series starring Ronnie Hawkins; *Thrill of a Lifetime*, a sort-of-game show where contestants got the chance to fulfil their dreams of acting in a movie or being reunited with a loved one, co-hosted by the future *Knots Landing* star Teri Austin; and *Claim to Fame*, in which two celebrity panels competed to see how good they were at lying. Only *Lorne Greene's New Wilderness*, hosted by *Bonanza*'s Pa Cartwright, now a committed conservationist, was a little bit different, more in the mould of *Untamed World* than anything that smacked of prizes or pop stars.

Of course, the studies and position papers just kept on coming. In 1982, the Federal Cultural Policy Review Committee, co-chaired by Louis Applebaum and the former CRTC commissioner Jacques Hébert, called on private broadcasters to make larger contributions to new Canadian programming, but provided no practical remedy. A year later, the CRTC's own *Policy Statement on Canadian Content in Television* bemoaned the fact that Canadian dramatic productions were "virtually non-existent" in the schedules of private English-language stations — then recommended a 35 per cent peak-time Cancon requirement.

Amazingly, given all these maple-leaf statements and arbitrary (not to mention unattainable) goals, the Trudeau government began to address the underlying economic challenge of producing programs for the Canadian market that could compete with the $500,000-per-episode budgets of American prime-time offerings. In 1983, the feds allocated $35 million to Telefilm Canada, in order to create the Canadian Broadcast Development Fund, paid for in part by an excise tax on cable subscriptions. Suddenly it was possible to get money into the system in ways that both benefited producers and enabled broadcasters to satisfy their licence requirements. (This money went directly to an independent production house, not the station or network that committed to a given project. That commitment had to exist; the money started flowing upon payment of a licence fee that gave the broadcaster the right to air the project — but not the rights to the project. In effect, the broadcaster simply rented an airing. Ownership remained with the producer, who derived all the benefits of any future sales.)

CTV's Arthur Weinthal, meanwhile, had given the green light to a dozen episodes of a new sitcom called *Snow Job* from CFCF Montreal's Champlain Productions for early 1983. Jean Pouliot's son, Adrien, later said that his station had paid $175,000 to its subsidiary to develop the pilot "because it was slated for CTV." Set in a ski lodge in the Laurentian Mountains, it focused on the antics of the guests and staff, among them a sarcastic manager, an egotistical chef, and a sex-obsessed ski instructor. Although distinctively Canadian in its locale, the series never connected with viewers as *Excuse My French* had. Some people found it sophomoric and formula-ridden, contributing to the view that CTV stood for cheap, trashy, and vulgar.

In its 1983–84 schedule, the network gave no indication that it would commission projects from independent producers in order to take advantage of the new Broadcast Fund. New that fall were *Just Kidding*, whose hosts interviewed children on a variety of topics, and the weekday afternoon talk-variety program, *The Don Harron Show*, out of Vancouver. Returning Canadian series included *Circus* (with a new ringmaster, the bilingual pop star Pierre Lalonde); *Live It Up*, *The Littlest Hobo*, *Bizarre*, *Thrill of a Lifetime*, *Lorne Greene's New Wilderness*, and *Snow Job* (for which CTV had requested extensive revisions, forcing CFCF to invest a further $200,000 in a second pilot).

At the end of 1983, CTV (already under fire for catering to the lowest common denominator) earned the dubious distinction of being named the most bloodthirsty of thirty networks around the globe in a study conducted by the U.S.-based National Coalition on Television Violence. Its prime-time schedule was termed a "ghetto of combat police shows," all except one of which had, of course, been imported from the States. This echoed a previous warning from the CRTC, but — besides being a case of the pot calling the kettle black — the study was somewhat flawed. The researcher had viewed all of CFTO's prime-time schedule rather than restricting his study to the network's one or two hours a night of imported American cop shows; Doug Bassett was not amused.

By this time, though, tension between CTV and its regulator had eased, with the Trudeau government's appointment of a new CRTC chairman in October 1983. John Meisel returned to his academic pursuits, and André Bureau, a former satellite-television executive from the private sector, appeared in his stead. One of his first actions was to repeal the recommended 35 per cent peak-time Cancon requirement before its implementation. He also hinted that the commission might reduce Cancon quotas if program quality improved.

CTV's schedule for the 1984–85 season presented no major changes, but *Circus*, *The Littlest Hobo*, *Snow Job*, and *The Don Harron Show* would not return. Torrents of petitions flooded the network from *The Littlest Hobo*'s roughly one million viewers, begging "Don't take our dog away." After six seasons, however, the series would go into repeats despite the grief-stricken letters.

No one petitioned to bring back *Snow Job*. Its third and final season had cost CFCF $264,000 for yet another pilot, just to persuade CTV to renew it. One of its writers, though, must have learned something about the craft of comedy writing, because he went on to work for *Cheers*, part of CTV's Thursday night simulcast of NBC's award-winning sitcom line-up that also included *The Cosby Show*, *Family Ties*, and *Night Court*. Pip Wedge had also ensured that the network held the broadcast rights to several one-hour American dramas such as *The A-Team*, *Magnum P.I.*, *Miami Vice*, and *Knight Rider*, along with two new action series, *Spencer: For Hire* and *MacGyver*. Midway through the 1985–86 season, CTV claimed the top three most-watched shows in English Canada: *The Cosby Show*, *Family Ties*, and *Miami Vice*.

And for the first time, CTV could also boast of its own made-in-Toronto American network action series, *Night Heat*. Originally commissioned by CBS to run in a late-night time slot, the gritty drama about detectives in a large though unidentified city was created by Sonny Grosso, the Bronx policeman who made the $32-million drug bust immortalized in *The French Connection*. Since CBS wouldn't pay top dollar for an 11:30 show, Grosso and his partner came north in search of high production values and lower costs. Murray Chercover recommended Alliance Entertainment as the Canadian co-producer, and

Telefilm's Broadcast Fund kicked in roughly one-third of the $500,000-an-episode cost. The initial thirteen instalments debuted on CBS in February 1985 and drew as many as five million viewers a night, knocking off Johnny Carson's *The Tonight Show* in key U.S. markets. Buoyed by this success, CTV brought an additional twenty-six episodes onstream that fall. In mid-season, the network would also air *The Campbells*, an ambitious (though less expensive, at $150,000 an episode) twenty-four-part, half-hour family drama series that dealt with the life of a widowed Scottish doctor and his children in 1830s Ontario — a "loudly stamped made-in-Canada show," co-produced with Settler Films, Scottish Television, and the Family Channel in the United States.

Also new to the CTV schedule in 1985–86 was *Lifetime*, an afternoon magazine show hosted by Peter Ferniak in Toronto, which (to Ray Peters's annoyance) replaced *The Don Harron Show* from Vancouver. CJOH Ottawa contributed *You Can't Do That on Television*, a weekly comedy show performed by kids, including a young Alanis Morissette. From Toronto's Glen-Warren Productions came the latest half-hour sitcom, *Check It Out!*, featuring Don Adams, from the 1960s secret agent sitcom *Get Smart*, as the cynical supermarket manager who believes he's surrounded by a good-for-nothing staff. It had been pre-sold to the USA Network and the Comedy Factory, another specialty channel.

CTV also planned two six-hour Canadian-made mini-series, the $12-million *Louisiana* and the $8-million *Blood of Others*, starring Jody Foster. Both took advantage of Telefilm money, as did *Peter Ustinov's Russia*, a six-hour limited series scheduled for January and February 1986. (Mini-series are normally broadcast in two-hour blocks on consecutive nights; limited series are usually aired in the same time slot over a period of weeks.)

No wonder Canada's "most private powerful broadcaster" invited journalists to the CTV boardroom in early June of 1985 to deliver a lecture about the "lack of recognition CTV gets" and the "totally inaccurate reports" of its poor involvement in Canadian production. Cutting the lights, Murray Chercover showed them a video montage of CTV's Canadian hits: *Live It Up, The Littlest Hobo, Bizarre, Thrill of a Lifetime, Lorne Greene's New Wilderness, Night Heat*, CFL and NHL games, *W5*, and *Canada AM*. "I cannot understand," he said, "why Canadians are not proud of what we achieve."

10

The Bassetts and the Eatons
Want CTV for Their Own — 1979–86

In many ways, Doug Bassett seemed ill-suited to following in the footsteps of a famous father and a glamorous older brother. For one thing, he didn't crackle with the same energy and force. More a cost-conscious businessman at heart than someone with a passion for the media, he was probably happiest when he had worked in advertising sales and developed a retail-flyer business, at a time when Johnny F. was assumed to be heir apparent to the Baton throne.

Unlike his golden, athletic brothers, the dark-haired Doug was more his mother's son, in both looks and personality. That's not to say Dougie — as his friends called him — wasn't a good athlete. For example, he was a member of the Bishop's College School bantam hockey team when it won the Eastern Townships championships. But he simply didn't compare with Johnny F., who played tennis for the Davis Cup team, cricket for Canada, and hockey for the Toronto Marlboroughs. At age fifteen, Johnny F. had been signed by the Maple Leafs, until Big John made Conn Smythe tear up the contract. Later, Johnny F. was offered a goalie scholarship to Yale, which he turned down, against his father's advice. "I was a B athlete," Doug says. "Johnny and David were both super As."

During the summers of the 1950s at the family's North Hatley estate, the noise from the fiercely competitive tennis matches between Big John and Johnny F. reverberated for miles. While Johnny F. and David were off on the junior tennis circuit, Doug worked at the *Sherbrooke Record*, starting off as a fourteen-year-old gofer in the press room. At first, he looked down his nose at sweeping the floors, until his bosses threatened to call in Big John — at which Doug gritted his teeth and grabbed a broom.

Otherwise, Doug's privileged upbringing was a fact of life, especially after the family moved to Toronto in 1952. Big John's three sons lived practically next door to the four Eaton boys, John Craig, Fred, Thor, and George, in Forest Hill. Their immediate futures were inextricably linked through the Telegram trust. "We were all very close, like brothers," Johnny F. told the *Toronto Star*. Soon, Doug followed John Craig and Fred Eaton and his older brother to Upper Canada College, before he and Fred headed east to the University of New Brunswick, where they roomed together. "We never got the feeling from our confrères that Torontonians were good and dynamic and strong. We were all 'Hogtowners,'" Bassett said of his Maritime experiences. This was a rather unproductive period, and Doug did not shine scholastically. Rather, he spent most of his time drinking hard liquor and generally messing up his life. In the summer of 1960, he and Fred travelled Europe in a red VW Beetle. Eaton tried to drag his friend to the foremost art museums, but Doug, by his own admission, would rather have been partying in the Crazy Horse Saloon and "getting laid." He had no stomach for further studies and returned to Toronto in 1961, where Big John got him a job as a salesman at the *Telegram*. He briefly considered becoming an Anglican minister, but decided not to, as it would have required a university degree.

After a frank discussion with his father only months after starting at the *Telegram*, Doug decided to try to make it on his own in Vancouver. When he had trouble landing the job he wanted at James Lovick Advertising, Big John had to make a call on his behalf. Oddly, one of the agency's clients would prove to be Bassett's future nemesis at CTV. "I met Ray Peters in 1962," Doug recalls. "He used to come in and sell airtime [for CHAN]. He had a reputation as very aggressive, very bright, and absolutely committed to [the city]."

Doug also worked briefly as an executive assistant to the Conservative provincial premier W. A. C. ("Wacky") Bennett, until Big John summoned him back to Toronto in 1963 to join the *Telegram*'s circulation department. By this time, Johnny F., who'd started at the paper as a sports reporter, was now vice-president, with a second-floor office next to their father's. Dougie, by contrast, laboured under the chartered accountant Joe Garwood on the first floor. Garwood was unimpressed by the twenty-three-year-old scion's attempts to shirk the work, marking it down to a kind of post-adolescent rebellion. "I was a bit of a playboy," Bassett now admits. (But sowing wild oats lost much of its appeal after his parents divorced a few years later over his father's love affair with Isabel. "It was one of those things," he told an interviewer in 1979, with great sadness. He was and remains utterly devoted to his mother.)

By 1968, the paths Doug Bassett would take were clearly marked out. By then, he'd gone through all the *Telegram*'s departments, with the exception of editorial, where Isabel, Johnny F., and Fred Eaton had all worked as reporters. He'd also grown up a bit, so Joe Garwood suggested to Big John that he test Doug, now twenty-eight years old, in a senior position at Baton's Inland Publishing Co. Ltd.

This was also the year that Doug caught the "pretty blonde" he'd been chasing. His marriage to Susan Temple that fall "changed his whole life positively," and he asked his father to promote him to vice-president as well. Not wholly convinced of Doug's newfound maturity, Big John started him out as Inland's general manager, in charge of three small newspapers located in Newmarket, Oakville, and Stouffville, Ontario.

"[Inland] wasn't a money earner, and no one could seem to make it work," Bassett remembers. "I had a new wife and a new outlook. Susan was only twenty years old and I wanted to impress her, so I applied myself." He got used to working from seven in the morning until seven at night, and to running his own show in suburbia, out of the shadow of Big John and Johnny F.

Slowly but surely, Doug and his trusty desk-top calculator expanded Inland into areas such as retail flyers and advertising inserts, going head to head with the rival Torstar subsidiary Metrospan Printing and Publishing Ltd. To make sales, he liked to use the family name, pointing out that a Honderich wasn't making house calls, but a Bassett was. Partway through the more than ten years of his watch, Inland moved its head office to Mississauga. There it built a new press and snapped up a dozen more papers, making it an attractive buy for Metrospan in 1981. "It became so big and so profitable," recalls its proud former president and CEO, who rightly garnered most of the credit for the turnaround.

Meanwhile, a restless Johnny F., whose biggest weakness was that he was easily bored, had gone charging off in search of novel challenges. He'd loved the newspaper business, because it touched on politics and sports, business and entertainment. He'd loved the television business too, because it allowed him to take creative ideas and see them through to completion within a year or two. "Big John really didn't know a lot of people at the station," recalls Tony Parsons, a former CFTO news anchor. "[Johnny] was more hands on." From creating the teenage television show *After Four*, Johnny F. went on to become a pioneer in the still nascent Canadian film industry, producing two hockey movies, *Face-Off* and *Paperback Hero*. But he always looked beyond whatever he was doing, to the next big venture that would engage his imagination.

Just before the *Telegram* folded in 1971, Johnny F. teamed up with John Craig Eaton and other young Toronto establishment jocks to buy the Toronto Northmen football team and the Toronto Toros hockey team. When the Bassett-Eaton trust decided it didn't want to be involved in the risky business of professional sports franchises anymore, Johnny F. resigned as president of CFTO and followed his acquisitions to the United States, where the Northmen became the Memphis Southmen of the World Football League, and the Toros were renamed the Birmingham Bulls of the World Hockey Association. In 1976, after both leagues went broke and Johnny F. was forced to sell his house on Toronto's Bridle Path, he sold his interest in the trust for $5 million. Later that year, he underwent his first cancer operation.

Although Big John had warned Johnny F. to get out of "damned sports," he'd never actually forced his grown-up sons to do anything against their will. But with Johnny F. absent in the United States, Big John had begun to look to Doug more and more often. First, Doug replaced his older brother on the Baton board in 1974, while he was still at Inland Publishing. "I guess I'm the invisible Bassett," he told *Marketing Magazine* three years later, when he was made vice-president and managing director of Baton. At that point, he moved into a new office at CFTO, which he decorated with photographs of his wife and their three beautiful young daughters, and of every prime minister since John Diefenbaker. Somewhat of an obsessive-compulsive, the eighteen-Matinee-cigarettes-a-day Bassett also had his own personal washroom installed. Five years later, at the age of thirty-nine, he succeeded his father (who remained as chairman) as Baton's president.

Even so, Doug was the last of his peers to take over the operation of a family business. In 1972, Galen Weston, then thirty-two, had returned from England to run the Loblaw's grocery store chain for George Weston Ltd. Four years later, at that same tender age, Conrad Black, who'd grown up in Forest Hill with the Bassett and Eaton boys, assumed the helm of the Argus Corp. and put Doug Bassett and Fred Eaton on its board.

And in May 1977, Fred himself, a month away from turning thirty-nine, became chairman, president, and chief executive of Eaton's and promoted his thirty-two-year-old brother George to second-in-command. Like their antecedents, they weren't averse to the trappings of success. Fred, for example, owned two Rolls-Royces, a 1962 model for winter and a 1950 model for balmy days. He also built an architecturally acclaimed $300,000 summer retreat on a seven-acre island in Georgian Bay. But the exquisitely mannered merchant prince, with boyish good looks and a brilliant, big-toothed smile, also worked hard to make his family empire grow.

These next-generation owners were "at their offices every single day from eight-thirty until five-thirty," Doug Bassett told *Executive* magazine in 1983. "We were given a trust, to build on what we've been given and not to think we're something we're not. . . . We all work and we work hard. . . . [Eaton] and Black and Weston — there are no owner-managers better than those three."

A sort of upper-class parochialism hovered around this tight Toronto circle — but one Montrealer who cracked the clique for a time was Brian Mulroney, then president of Iron Ore Co. "I really got to know Douglas in the late 1970s," the former prime minister remembers. "[He], Conrad Black, Galen Weston, and I were all on the [Canadian Imperial Bank of Commerce board]. We sat together and the other directors referred to us as 'the kiddies corner.'"

Fred Eaton, for his part, sat on the Toronto-Dominion Bank board. "We were all of the same vintage. We would meet every month for lunch," says Mulroney, who remained on the CIBC board until he became leader of the federal Progressive Conservatives in mid-1983.

Doug Bassett harboured his own political aspirations. He was asked to run as a federal Tory candidate on at least three separate occasions and later wished he could have been one of the seven guys in competition with Mulroney for the party leadership. "I'd love to be active in federal politics," he told *Executive* magazine. "That's where the action is, working with people who think and believe the way you do."

Their mutual interest in federal politics helped forge a strong friendship between the privileged Bassett and the aspiring Baie Comeau boy. "I've always enjoyed Douglas's explosive nature, except for his *revulsion* for profanity," Mulroney jokes. "There is nothing diffident about Douglas!" But many people disliked Doug for the same reasons that Mulroney professed to enjoy his company. He could be foul-mouthed and arrogant, sometimes reverting to his Bassett-brat habits. Yet he was also exceedingly loyal to his family and friends, especially the Eaton brothers.

Fred Eaton, as his family's representative on Baton's board, remained particularly close. "He was in the background, but we spoke on a daily basis," Doug says. "He's a brilliant businessman and intellectual, a man who knows art and music. He had a complete background on Baton. It was his watch."

As well as relying on his contemporaries, the young Baton president looked to Big John for sage counsel. "Perhaps the senior Messrs. Eaton, Weston and Black made business decisions themselves without seeking further information or advice. I'll make a decision, but before I do so I'll talk to the executives here and to my old man," Doug told *Executive* magazine. "My father didn't have a chance to talk to his old man on a continuing basis. Fred Eaton doesn't. Galen Weston doesn't. I guess I'm the only one who has a father to use as a resource." (In fact, Big John, Doug, and Fred Eaton teamed up in 1979 with Conrad Black in an attempt to take over FP Publications, the owner of the *Globe and Mail* and several other newspapers, but lost out to Ken Thomson of Thomson Corp., in part because of Big John's dark reputation as the man who killed the *Telegram*.)

Big John remained Baton's representative on the CTV board of directors, although he'd handed over the operational reins to his son and Joe Garwood. This transfer of power was manifested in the network's programming decisions. One of Doug Bassett's proudest accomplishments during his early years as president and CEO was the long-running family drama *The Littlest Hobo*, which cost a whopping $20 million to produce over the span of six seasons. Initially, it was budgeted at $60,000 per half-hour episode. Later that figure rose to $165,000. It eventually made money, Bassett said, because it was one of Canada's top international television sales successes, marketed to sixty-two countries. It also provided him with a family pet named Network, the son of London, *Hobo*'s German shepherd star.

Glen-Warren Productions' *The Littlest Hobo* and *Thrill of Lifetime*, a series that most Canadians thought was American in origin, both commanded audiences of more than one million viewers nationwide. This was the sort of Cancon that people wanted to see. "I appreciate that these aren't the type of programs that you think the CRTC wants us to do," Bassett told *Executive* magazine. "But we are meeting the requirements and we do more than we're required to under the regulations. We invest a lot of money in Canadian production."

☆

In early 1984, within a year of that statement, Doug Bassett went from being an owner-manager to little more than the Eaton family's hired hand at Baton Broadcasting, when he and his younger brother David sold the four Eaton brothers the roughly 20 per cent of the Telegram trust that they didn't already own. Doug approached Fred Eaton and made the offer. "They were more than fair," he says. "They were generous. They literally said, 'Name your price.' I worked out a price for the cash and shares [which was all the private, closed-end company contained at this point], put a control premium on it and rounded it up and they said, 'Sure.' I don't know any family as classy as Mrs. Eaton and her four sons." Doug and David received $15 million apiece. At least, Doug Bassett was a *rich* hired hand.

Over the next few years, the Eatons gradually consolidated their power at Baton. As young men, the four brothers had been their "uncle" John Bassett's largely silent partners — but now John Craig, Fred, Thor, and George were middle-aged. The "boys" had their own ideas and the ability to implement them. Through Eaton's of Canada (a private company owned equally by the four except for roughly 17 per cent held in trust for their mother, Signy), they owned all of Telegram Corp., which in turn had majority control (a 51.6 per cent stake) of Baton. No other individual shareholder held more than 10 per cent, and the Bassetts were completely out of the picture, although many people continued to believe otherwise.

George Eaton, then forty years old and the executive vice-president of Eaton's of Canada, joined his brother Fred on Baton's board in 1984. Fred remembers that Big John had been keen to have George play a part much earlier, and quotes a papal expression in Latin that Big John used, signifying that seeing George appointed to the board was "in Big John's heart." But it had taken a while before there was a vacancy for the youngest Eaton brother. He had been a bit of a rebel, although not in the usual Eaton mode. He was no playboy, nor did he drink. Instead, he wore shoulder-length hair and smoked marijuana. In 1965, he had enrolled at British Columbia's Simon Fraser University, then a hotbed of radical social activism, but dropped out after only one semester. He suffered from a mild form of dyslexia, so studying never came easily.

After a brief episode as a stockbroker, the rich kid who had inherited a hand-me-down Karmann-Ghia from his brother Fred spent his early twenties racing cars. Aggressive and determined, he talked his way onto the British Racing Motors Formula One team to become the first full-time Canadian Formula One driver, but the company was underfunded and Eaton's car a dud. Worried that he'd be killed on the European circuit, George returned to the States, where he spent large sums of money trying to build an all-Canadian Indy-class race car, only to abandon the project. In total, his six-year racing career cost him $2 million. George also dabbled in the entertainment-booking business, in partnership with his brother Thor. Finally, in the mid-1970s, he joined the family firm, trading in his Ferrari for a Buick and married life in the Toronto establishment. But he never lost his edge. The smoother, more polished Fred provided the link to other CEOs and acted as corporate spokesman for their extremely private family, while the abrasive, more combative George wielded power in the background.

Both Fred and George were in complete agreement that it was long past time for Baton to seize control of CTV. In other words, their enthusiasm had come to match that of the elder Bassett. "Big John was always of the opinion that [the cooperative] would never work," Fred Eaton says. Bassett wasn't shy about saying he wanted to "control the damn thing." Now the majority owners would set out to make that goal a reality.

Fortunately for the Eatons and Doug Bassett, the prevailing mood of the CRTC had changed since Big John's failure to buy CFCF Montreal. The regulator's new laissez-faire chairman André Bureau, who came from a business background, believed that size mattered in Canadian broadcasting, because smaller players risked being overwhelmed by competition from cable, pay TV, and satellite-transmitted signals. He thought it would take the financial clout of larger broadcasting units to improve Canadian programming so as to attract viewers.

The political landscape had changed as well. As of September 1984, there was a new Tory prime minister: Doug Bassett and Fred Eaton's corporate crony Brian Mulroney, who'd been elected with the biggest majority in Canadian history. "Douglas was a great help [during the election campaign]," Mulroney recalls. "We'd meet quite regularly; we'd go to their house for dinner. The Bassett family were all very supportive." The new occupant of 24 Sussex Drive was quick to repay favours owed, and the kiddies' corner of the CIBC board reunited as Doug and Susan Bassett, Conrad and Shirley Black, and Galen and Hilary Weston, as well as the four Eaton brothers and their spouses, enjoyed sumptuous black-tie gatherings at the prime minister's residence.

A year later, at Baton's annual meeting in December 1985, Big John Bassett, who'd been awarded the Order of Canada a few weeks earlier, announced that he was stepping down as chairman at the age of seventy. But he would remain as a director and chairman of the executive committee, as well as Baton's representative on the CTV board.

Big John was succeeded by the Eaton brothers' *consigliere* and long-time family lawyer Allan Beattie, the vice-chairman of Eaton's of Canada and a former trustee of the Telegram trust. He'd also been a family trustee of John David Eaton's will and worked for Big John on ABC's investment in Baton in the early 1960s, even though Bassett's main lawyer was Eddie Goodman. Not long after Doug Bassett became president of Baton Broadcasting, however, he gave Beattie's law firm, Osler, Hoskin & Harcourt, all of Baton's corporate legal work, while Goodman's firm continued to act on its behalf at licence renewal and acquisition hearings.

Beattie did not leave his Osler, Hoskin & Harcourt partnership until a year after he became Baton's chairman, at which point he moved into the same downtown Toronto office space that the Eaton brothers occupied. Beattie is quite candid about his role at Baton: "I was fundamentally there representing the Eaton family," he says. Fred Eaton explains that his proximity to Beattie helped him stay abreast of Baton's corporate concerns. "As a director, I was kept aware of whatever was going on," Eaton says. "But I could also consult Allan Beattie. My office is right next door to [his]. It's a fact of geography."

In fact, arranging that Beattie be appointed Baton's chairman was another subtle move by the Eatons to consolidate their control. This end was also served by the presence high in Baton's ranks of Joe Garwood, the president of Telegram Corp. "Mr. Garwood has been working for the Telegram Corp. and/or Baton [since] before I was around," says Doug Bassett, who worked so closely with Garwood that CTV's directors dubbed them "The Bobbsey Twins." Bassett too was as loyal an executive as the Eatons could wish for. "I think this arrangement is terrific," Bassett told the *Toronto Star* in 1984, referring to the consolidation of the Eatons' ownership of Baton. "As to how it will affect me, my job is to be president and CEO of Baton, where I expect to be until the age of sixty-five."

Debt-free and eager to expand its holdings within the network, Baton embarked on a six-year acquisition binge, which kicked off circa Christmas 1985. Fittingly enough, its first efforts were aimed at Saskatchewan. It had been fourteen years since Big John had bought CFQC Saskatoon for $4 million from the Murphy family. Now Doug Bassett and Joe Garwood were busily negotiating to buy four more outlets up and down the province, for a total of $61.5 million.

Both deals were worked out over the course of a month. First was the purchase, from Ron Skinner of Yorkton Television, of a CBC affiliate in that small city, in addition to twinstick CTV/CBC stations there and in Prince Albert. After an exploratory meeting, the Baton board gave Joe Garwood a "top level that we would be prepared to pay," Bassett explained. Garwood then undertook the tough assignment of flying to Hawaii, where Skinner had a condominium, to meet with him. The two men spent a week playing golf, while their wives bonded. "It was very pleasant weather," Garwood later recalled. "I think it rained [once] when we were on the golf course."

By Sunday morning nothing had been finalized, and Garwood's flight home was scheduled for the following day. The two wives urged their husbands to settle. And so they did, for $16.5 million — a price slightly higher than Garwood had been authorized to go. "There was no formula as to so much cost per thousand or times earnings or assets or what have you," Bassett said. "It was just a completely negotiated deal between Mr. Garwood and Mr. Skinner." Pleased with his success, Garwood caught the plane, and the pending acquisition was announced on December 18.

Meanwhile, a second deal had been quietly coming together. Ever since 1981, Big John and Doug Bassett had been talking with Fred and Paul Hill of Harvard Developments about some kind of joint arrangement between CFQC Saskatoon and CKCK Regina, which the Hills had purchased from Clifford Sifton. For a time, each wanted to buy the other, but to no avail. By December 1985, however, the Hills had changed their minds and met with Doug and other Baton representatives in Toronto. The negotiations dragged on until three o'clock on Christmas Eve day, because there was a gap to close. At first, Baton argued that it wouldn't pay more for CKCK than it had for Ron Skinner's three stations put together, and (in Doug's words) "it went from there." Where it wound up was at $45 million for 90 per cent of the Regina station — a price that struck many observers as out of line, and marked the beginning of Baton's pattern of rampant overspending. CHUM's Fred Sherratt noted that "five million would have been a good buy," adding that Baton, at this time, "was not well run." That may be, but CKCK was — and was cited by the CRTC as one of the most profitable stations in the land. "We did this deal on a handshake, and it is a lot of money to shake hands on," Paul Hill said. "The people at Baton did not come out to assess the situation for some time afterwards." Nonetheless, this purchase also became public knowledge on December 30.

It seems curious that Baton would be so eager to commit (as John Pollock of Electrohome put it) "huge dollars" in a province populated by fewer than a million people — even if by doing so, it gained a virtual monopoly on private television transmission. Besides, that monopoly was in doubt. Shortly before Baton's deals were finalized, Izzy Asper (the former leader of Manitoba's Liberal party and owner of Saskwest Television Inc.) had succeeded in persuading the CRTC to grant him licences for two more outlets in Regina and Saskatoon. Ron Skinner and the Hills had protested that the market was too small to support more competition and had appealed the decision to the Mulroney cabinet, which ordered the CRTC to take another look. A rehearing had been scheduled for early 1986, and the federal Liberals were of course mounting charges of partisan meddling. These were the controversies that set the tone for the separate hearing into Baton's purchases, which convened in Saskatoon that April.

Doug Bassett recalls feeling a trifle intimidated by the process. "I had done a licence renewal hearing, but [never an] acquisition," he says. "I made sure we showed the team to the commission. I had a fantastic chairman in Allan Beattie. Joe Garwood was there. Kathy Robinson was the legal counsel." These assembled talents had another important task: "They controlled me. I can be excitable," confesses Bassett, grinning and waving his arms to demonstrate just how far out of control he can go.

His handlers may have written the opening script, but the Q&A spotlighted Doug Bassett in an unabashedly one-man show, broadcast live on cable television throughout the province. Baton's director Blair Nelson introduced him as a "director of a number of prominent Canadian corporations, a governor of the National Ballet of Canada, a trustee of the Lester B. Pearson College of the Pacific and the Hospital for Sick Children of Toronto, and a director and vice-president of the Olympic Trust of Canada." He added that Bassett had been "recently presented with the prestigious humanitarian award by the Canadian Council of Christians and Jews for his contribution in the field of human rights."

Doug began by extolling the merits of "large economic units" — a theme that he'd return to again and again over the next six years of Baton's buying spree. "Common ownership of all four Saskatchewan stations permits the establishment of an innovative marketing approach," he said, adding almost as an afterthought that it also meant "much better programming."

Baton had also learned a lesson from its failed takeover of CFCF Montreal. This time it put enough on the table to allay the commission's fears, including a $16-million Saskatchewan drama fund, a new bi-directional microwave, and upgrades to the studios and production facilities.

Doug submitted another argument as well: "Baton's philosophy of strong local management." He pointed out that CFQC had not become a "glittering, glitzy, arrogant business because Baton Broadcasting [owns] it. I know they [now] have better equipment; I know they are paying their people more; I know they have more people working for them than they did; I know they also have a union where they did not before. . . . I think the people of Saskatchewan and the people working for [CFQC] and the Canadian broadcast system have benefited because Baton received approval to buy that operation from the Murphy family."

As far as the perils of concentrated ownership, Bassett found it "very difficult to say, 'Big is bad.' . . . Out west, probably since Confederation, big has been bad because of the eastern robber barons from Montreal — not from Toronto! . . . [But] you will see Galen Weston building a 200,000-square-foot food store in Edmonton to compete against the West Edmonton Mall. You see the Eaton brothers investing millions of dollars in Eaton Centres [across the] country. . . . If you are big, you get bigger." It was as simple and inevitable as that.

Questioned about how Baton's purchases would affect the CTV network, Bassett replied that they wouldn't, because each owner still had only one vote. Asked whether there was any nervousness among the other affiliates about Baton's expansion, he admitted that there might be, but that there were lots of checks and balances — among them, the fact that the network was "run by Murray Chercover" and was "subject to the board of directors and the executive committee." In sum, there was absolutely no cause for alarm (although there were improvements that could be made), and Doug closed by voicing his "delight" at the prospect of appearing before the commission on some future occasion with reference to another CTV affiliate or to the network itself, "because that is my hope one day."

While Baton waited for the commission's verdict, it was hit hard by the death of the much-loved Johnny F. Bassett, who lost his fight with cancer at the age of forty-seven on May 14, 1986. Since cashing out of the Telegram trust, he had been active in the United States with projects including a Florida real estate development, and had continued to dabble in film. He'd produced *Sneakers*, co-starring his teenage daughter Carling, then Canada's top-ranked female junior tennis player, and had lived to see her become the first Canadian to make it to the quarter finals at Wimbledon — an event witnessed also by her proud grandfather Big John.

Six weeks later, on July 4, the CRTC approved Baton's latest Saskatchewan acquisitions, satisfied that ownership by a "well-financed, experienced and committed broadcaster" would result in "significant benefits which clearly . . . outweighed any concerns." Now Baton had three full affiliates and two supplementary affiliates, but still only one vote. How could it control the network with a single vote? It couldn't — which is why, that fall, a frustrated Baton (led by Doug Bassett, Joe Garwood, and Big John himself) privately approached the other ten CTV shareholders about buying their shares in the network.

11

The CRTC
versus CTV — 1986–87

On the eve of its twenty-fifth anniversary, CTV was as difficult to govern as the country it spanned. The parallels were really quite exact. As one might expect of a central government, CTV's president, Murray Chercover, had surrounded himself with a bureaucracy composed of 400 people to provide a sixty-five-hours-a-week service. CTV's management, however, had to answer to sixteen different affiliates, each of which supplied a representative to the board. Only eleven, who spoke on behalf of the network's shareholders, were entitled to vote, but most decisions were made by consensus, with everyone participating in the rancorous discussions. "People have referred to my function as that of walking a tightwire down the centre of the boardroom table," Chercover said. "The question [is]: who is on which side of it, and which pit am I going to fall into?" He carefully walked that tightwire through this squabbling bunch of prima donna "premiers," with the haves and the have-nots contributing their equal say on a myriad of issues, from the significant to the petty. "Our major battles are frequently over [some] of the silliest things you could possibly imagine," said Bill McGregor of CKCO Kitchener. Doug Bassett echoed this opinion, saying that the board should not be discussing "what colour tie Lloyd Robertson is wearing." The board, in his view, should discuss and set policy. "Then you let management go and run the operation."

But no such luck — which had led Bassett and Fred Eaton to con-
clude that the current cooperative arrangement paralyzed CTV's
decision-making, at a time when the industry was moving at hyper-
speed. Bassett believed that CTV needed a single authority to function
efficiently, and that that single authority should be Baton's own management, not CTV's. Hence his attempt (actually the latest of several
overtures) to buy up the other stations' shares. According to Ray Peters,
it was rejected because a Baton-dominated network wouldn't have permitted sufficient representation from all parts of the country. Everyone
knew that the cooperative was inefficient and unwieldy, but at least it
allowed input from coast to coast, and nobody (with the exception of
Baton) was prepared to see the show run by Toronto.

And so the board meetings continued to resemble parliamentary
Question Period on a very bad day. Yet another study conducted by
Woods Gordon criticized the affiliates for poking their noses into issue
after issue that didn't concern them. The trouble was that sixteen directors meant sixteen points of view, not to mention whatever opinions
the second row of affiliate executives might voice as they jostled for space
in a hot, stuffy, and very crowded room. One former director told
Edward Greenspon of the *Globe and Mail* that most meetings were distinguished by "a spirit of weeping, obscenity, screaming, yelling, and
practically having fist fights." CFCF's Jean Pouliot actually stopped
attending them altogether after his doctor advised him that they were
bad for his health.

For the time being, then, Baton's takeover attempts were put on hold,
although individual discussions continued between the stations about
whether they ought to sell their shares. "Baton was always in a position to
buy," Ray Peters recalls. And, whenever he was asked about his plans for
the network, Doug Bassett would reply, "I want to own it."

In some ways, the CRTC itself had kick-started Baton's long-held ambition to control CTV seven years earlier, by advising the network to
re-examine its financial structure (or at least its revenue- and cost-sharing
formula), with the goal of committing more resources to Canadian drama
programming.

In 1980, Jean Pouliot had headed up the first restructuring committee
that tried to do something about the cooperative arrangement. He failed.
After the Supreme Court upheld the CRTC's authority to impose
Canadian drama conditions in 1982, and the commission had granted

CTV a number of temporary licence extensions, a second committee took another stab at the problem, with similar results.

Now, D-Day neared and CTV's financial structure remained unchanged, despite yet another "objective outside" study of the network's woes undertaken by the ever-present Woods Gordon. Just as the consultants were preparing to submit their findings in the fall of 1986, the owner-affiliates were dealt another blow. The Report of the Task Force on Broadcasting Policy, otherwise known as the Caplan-Sauvageau report, was released. It had any number of things to say, as well it might have, because it cost the taxpayers $3 million. Gerald Caplan, its co-chairman, went on record with his belief that CTV's ownership structure had to change and that "the CRTC must dictate that change," because it wasn't in the interests of the affiliates to surrender any of their power. He accused the affiliates of taking $100 million of CTV's $127 million in annual revenue, starving the network of the money it needed to produce Canadian drama. Not surprisingly, CTV said that Caplan had got his numbers backwards — that the $100 million was spent on programming and other network expenses, not taken by the affiliates at all, and so on for many a fun-filled week.

Woods Gordon, for its part, made several more or less useful recommendations. First, it suggested that CTV cut down on its plethora of committee meetings, which ate up an average of thirty hours weekly. It also felt that the board should be authorized to make financing decisions without having to consult with each of the affiliates each and every time and that, in special cases, when a quick decision was imperative, the board should be empowered to delegate this authority to its executive committee.

CTV's revenue and cost-sharing formula would be changed as well. The total cost of the network's operations, including any special projects such as the Olympic Games, would be charged against total revenues, and the stations would get whatever was left over, divided up according to audience share. If the network lost money, they'd have to make good the shortfall. This replaced the traditional ad hoc system whereby affiliates were hit, usually late in the fiscal year, with a special assessment whenever the network ran short. (The revised system was approved by both the board and the shareholders and was fully introduced two years later.)

Meanwhile, though, CTV was fast approaching its day of reckoning: its first full network licence renewal hearing since 1979, when it was ordered to produce more children's programming and was blasted for the lack of Canadian drama in its prime-time schedule. What had it done in the seven years since that decision?

Children's programming in 1986–87 included the twentieth season of *Romper Room and Friends* from Kitchener, *Paul Hann & Friends* from Edmonton, *Let's Go* from Winnipeg, and Ottawa's *You Can't Do That on Television*. Slated for 1987–88 were a new show called *Extra! Extra!* from Montreal's Champlain Productions (which concerned six young journalists, who at one point got a real-life interview with Prime Minister Brian Mulroney) and *Cinderella*, a two-hour Christmas special from Vancouver starring the ballerina Karen Kain.

Canadian drama was not so bright a picture, particularly in peak viewing hours. Indeed, there was really only one show to brag about, the half-hour weekly family series, *The Campbells*, which aired before eight o'clock, as did *Lorne Greene's New Wilderness*, *Live It Up*, *Thrill of a Lifetime*, *Check It Out!*, and Glen-Warren Productions' latest crowd-pleaser, *Pet Peeves*, which dealt with viewers' gripes by turning them into comedy sketches. In prime time, CTV's only "Canadian" drama series was the venerable *Night Heat*, which continued to disguise street signs, currency, licence plates, and anything else that might discommode viewers in search of an all-purpose metropolis.

Otherwise, CTV pinned its hopes on thirty-four hours a year of Canadian movies, mini-series, and limited series including *Sword of Gideon*, Alliance Entertainment's dramatization of *Vengeance*, George Jonas's Canadian best-seller about a secret Israeli anti-terrorist team.

Seven years earlier, the CRTC had encouraged the network to rely more heavily on independent producers to meet its new drama requirements. CTV had done so, but only after government subsidies made these co-productions more attractive and cost-effective than developing programs with its affiliates. Since the creation of the Canadian Broadcast Program Development Fund in mid-1983, CTV had been associated with projects involving more than $30 million of Telefilm money and total production budgets of some $107 million. In the 1985–86 season, during which the network aired a mere 1.5 hours a week of Canadian drama in prime time, independents such as Alliance had received more than three-quarters of the sums CTV paid for all its Canadian programs, other than news and sports.

This, as Murray Chercover noted, "put the independent sector [in a more] viable position." It also left CTV's affiliates out in the cold, as Canadian production moved to a largely out-of-house function subsidized by taxpayers' money from a largely in-house function whereby a handful of broadcasters such as Baton paid the full cost. Alliance, not Baton's Glen-Warren Productions, could expect to get the biggest slice of CTV's domestic production. "I created the CTV relationship for

Alliance," Murray Chercover says, and Bill McGregor agrees: "[Alliance's CEO] Robert Lantos is in the business because of Murray Chercover. Chercover set him up." Maybe — but Alliance became the country's biggest independent production company because Lantos himself played the Telefilm game better than anyone else.

For the moment, then, CTV had a problem. In its new licence period, the network proposed to air only two hours a week of Canadian drama in peak viewing hours, and it didn't have a showcase series of any description to roll out for the CRTC. At a board meeting held on October 20, 1986, the directors stared at the application they'd already filed with the commission and agreed that it was going to buy them nothing but grief.

The board therefore authorized the executive committee to improve the network's Canadian drama commitments, if management could find something suitable before the hearings began in about three weeks' time. Several projects were considered and rejected. Then, with only a week to go, Murray Chercover got a call from Robert Lantos, informing Chercover that the CBC had stalled on a drama series the company had developed. Loosely based on the family saga of the Montreal financier Paul Desmarais, *Mount Royal* would follow the lives of the fictional Valeur dynasty into the worlds of high finance, high fashion, politics, and journalism. Lantos stated that he was about to return his advance and get a release. Chevcover reacted quickly: "Fine, come on over." The CTV president was delighted. A fully developed project that precisely met his target objective had fallen into his lap, and he and Lantos quickly closed a deal. In one fell swoop, *Mount Royal* would raise CTV's prime-time Canadian drama commitment to 2.5 hours weekly during the 1987–88 season, and three hours weekly over the following four.

On the Sunday night before the renewal hearing was to begin, members of the executive committee — Ray Peters, Jean Pouliot, Randy Moffat, and Fred Sherratt (on behalf of an ill Allan Waters) — held an emergency meeting in an Ottawa hotel. Big John Bassett wasn't there. According to Ray Peters, "the [committee], working with management, took over the [licence] application" and unanimously agreed (with no input from Baton) that CTV should commit to three hours of drama programming in the upcoming season by signing on for *Mount Royal*. This, Peters noted, "caused a couple of programs to be dropped from the program schedule that [were] produced by Baton. [I] think that was a very good decision." The committee also agreed to spend $7.4 million to finance the first year of *Mount Royal*. Under the new revenue and cost-sharing formula, the affiliate stations would therefore receive $7.4 million less for their station time in 1987–88, yet this seemed essential if the CRTC was to be appeased.

☆

The next morning, November 17, CTV hauled out its big guns. The team gathered at the Hull Convention Centre, in a windowless and cheerless concrete bunker known as the Outaouais Room. At its far end the CRTC commissioners perched on an elevated dais. Below them and to their right were Murray Chercover, Bill McGregor, and Ray Peters. Seated on chairs in the audience were the other members of CTV's executive committee, including Big John Bassett, Standard Broadcasting's Allan Slaight, representing the Ottawa affiliate, Maclean Hunter's Ron Osborne representing Calgary, and Sunwapta's Bruce Alloway representing Edmonton. Together they were requesting a full five-year renewal of CTV's network licence, which was unfortunately by no means guaranteed.

André Bureau, the CRTC's chairman, was quick to set the tone in his opening remarks. "CTV's program schedule is available to almost 98 per cent of English-speaking households in Canada," he said. "The [network] and its affiliates retain 29 per cent of all viewing of English-language television and are thus number one in Canada. . . . The network's and [its] affiliates' share of total private-sector television revenues have risen to . . . 47 per cent, [and their share of total private-sector television profits] to 48 per cent. The success of the [network's] operations has enabled its affiliates to become some of the largest and most successful television stations in Canada. Six of [its] affiliates are among the ten most profitable stations in Canada."

In other words, the CRTC didn't want to listen to any more excuses. "Let us be clear," Bureau continued. "The commission expects to be convinced . . . of a true desire, clear plan and firm commitment to combine the substantial . . . resources of the entire network to enhance the quality of the Canadian portion of the network service. . . . Relations between the commission and the CTV network have not always lived up to their potential, but now that the Supreme Court has clarified the CRTC's authority we can more easily discuss the mission, role and specific forms of contribution that can be expected."

Murray Chercover was prepared for this, but had decided to play it coy, holding back his announcement regarding *Mount Royal* until mid-afternoon. Instead, he began by recapping CTV's record on other fronts.

Of the $300 million that the network had spent on Canadian programming in the seven years since its last licence renewal hearing, more than three-quarters had gone to its news, public affairs, and sports programming, with tangible results. The ratings for these categories were gratifyingly high, and things were going smoothly, despite the departure of Harvey Kirck as Lloyd Robertson's co-anchor on *CTV National News*. But Kirck remained as a commentator, and he — along with Lloyd Robertson, the weekend anchor Sandie Rinaldo, and CTV's Ottawa bureau chief Pamela Wallin — were in the audience to lend their support to the application.

Next, Bill McGregor strove to address the CRTC's claim that CTV lacked a distinctive Canadian character by citing examples of its public affairs programming. "*Question Period* clearly would not fail your test," he said. "*Canada AM* clearly passes the test." McGregor obviously wasn't on the same page as the commissioners. Later he wasn't even in the same volume, when he suggested that CTV's airing of Bell Telephone commercials also contributed to the Canadian identity.

The much more savvy Chercover bided his time. He knew exactly what the commission wanted, but he was prepared to let the CRTC take its usual shots. The next target was Arthur Weinthal, CTV's vice-president of entertainment programming, who had the unenviable task of defending "industrial" or "generic" drama series — shows that created plenty of jobs but were devoid of specific Canadian locations, themes, and concerns, which allowed them to be sold to the American market. Save for *The Campbells*, almost all of CTV's drama production fell into this category — including *Night Heat*, which had just been presented with a plaque signed by the premier of Ontario to honour the completion of its fiftieth instalment. "Anybody who knows Toronto will recognize Toronto on viewing any one of [those] fifty episodes," Weinthal claimed when the CRTC focused on the show's anonymous urban settings. He admitted that they did not specifically mention Toronto, but suggested that this was the norm. "We have to acknowledge and . . . be sympathetic to the demands of producing programs on an international basis," he said. "I don't think that there is anything unCanadian about *Night Heat*, certainly in terms of the response by law enforcement people that they consider it a fair and accurate reflection of big city police life." (A few weeks later, in fact, *Night Heat* was named the best dramatic series of 1985–86 at Canadian television's first annual Gemini Awards.)

Chercover supported Weinthal's contentions. His priority was a given program's popularity, not its essential Canadianness. In fact, he became a trifle contemptuous of the commission's view that using Canadian place names, licence plates, and money was critical to building a home-grown television-production industry. He pointed out that, of the $30 million spent on *Night Heat* so far, fully $26.4 million had stayed in Canadian hands. And Ray Peters backed him up: "Our big concern down the road is to make sure that we are . . . putting programs on the air that are going to deliver an audience," he said. (Several months later, however, a combative Peters went too far in his comments to Edward Greenspon of the *Globe and Mail*: "It doesn't matter to us whether the commission likes the programs or a task force likes the programs or members of Parliament like the programs. They may describe us as all being cultural peasants, but we must deliver programs to the public that they want to see.")

By mid-afternoon, the commissioners were getting chippy, so Chercover decided to play his trump card. "Hopefully," he said, "we will be able . . . to introduce a new project which we were not able to file [with our application] because it was not completed in terms of the relationships that were to be established."

"I am surprised that you did not mention it . . . this morning," Bureau interposed. "We are reviewing past performance, but we are eager to hear about your news."

Chercover was eager to convey it. He launched into a glowing description of *Mount Royal*, a "massive program undertaking" that would involve a two-hour launch episode during the present season, followed by a minimum of fifteen one-hour instalments the next year, and options for each successive year of a further eighteen to twenty-two. Chercover hoped that Telefilm would agree to invest in what was (as set up by Lantos, who'd been working on the package for the better part of seven years) essentially a Canada-France co-production.

André Bureau was dubious and couldn't refrain from pointing out that the CBC had very recently been laying claim to the exact same project.

"This one is contracted and committed," Chercover replied.

"We have heard the same kind of words a few weeks ago," said Bureau, and then relented: "Well, I am pleased to see that it will finally be done." He then spent a good deal of time questioning Bill McGregor and Ray Peters about the latest Woods Gordon study — particularly the new revenue and cost-sharing formula and changes to the network's operating structure that would allow for speedier decision-making. In fact, he wondered if these changes had led to the rapid acceptance of *Mount Royal* and asked when the project had come to the network's attention.

Peters confessed that everything had taken place in the previous twenty-four hours.

"That is what I thought," Bureau said. "There is a God somewhere. You were pretty quick on that decision. . . . How did it work?"

"The executive committee . . . received a report from our president," Peters replied. "We reviewed the project and the committee, which has the full authority of the board, made the decision [that we should] go with that project and [that] we should announce it here today."

With that, Peters retired from the stand. Only after the hearing adjourned for the afternoon did CTV actually sign the production contract for *Mount Royal*.

A few weeks later, on December 1, three CTV shareholders — Baton, CHUM, and Mid-Canada Communications (which owned the network's Sudbury, North Bay, and Timmins affiliates) — were back in action at yet another hearing in Ottawa. Each was seeking a licence to operate a brand new independent station in the nation's capital, which would of course be in direct competition with CJOH.

The Baton team of Doug Bassett, Allan Beattie, Joe Garwood, Ted Delaney, and Kathy Robinson promised to build a $20-million state-of-the-art station and production facility in the city and to provide millions of dollars in new Canadian programming, including a showcase series titled *The History of Canada*.

Asked about conflicts too many and varied to list, Bassett replied, "We believe that the ownership of network affiliates, as well as [of] an independent station, presents no inherent conflict. We take our network obligations seriously, and know, moreover, that any diminution of the strength of Canada's private network will also weaken Baton." Later, he said, "Well, we are certainly not going into this with the idea of destroying or even hurting any . . . of our friends in the business. . . . We are not out to rob or take away from what is in this area already."

Allan Slaight was absolutely beside himself. He'd acquired CJOH in 1985 by paying Conrad Black $177 million for Standard Broadcasting. This had proved to be a doubtful investment. Over the past two years, CJOH's operating profits had dropped by a stunning 57 per cent. There were already eight stations fighting it out for revenues in the Ottawa-Hull area — the same number as in the Toronto-Hamilton market, which was four times larger. Besides, as he told the commission, "the obvious conflicts that would rapidly emerge at [CTV] should Baton, CHUM, or even Mid-Canada be licensed are too bizarre to contemplate." He noted that several other CTV affiliates and private parties had "exhaustively researched and analyzed the market and determined firmly that there just wasn't room for another station."

Three months later, however, the CRTC in fact awarded Baton the new Ottawa licence. The decision resulted in a great deal of controversy, in part because Jim Robson, the commissioner who'd chaired the hearing (and had also chaired the hearing that saw Baton take over the four stations in Saskatchewan earlier that year), was found to have been offered a substantial consulting contract by Bassett et al.

So it was that a flurry of appeals came out of the woodwork. Slaight asked the Mulroney government to overturn the decision, as did Mid-Canada Communications. Another failed applicant, Global Television, joined the parade. For his part, Doug Bassett remarked that the disgruntled objectors were "snivelling around" and vowed to kick off a lobbying campaign of his own.

The upshot of all these efforts was that the Tory government passed an order-in-council, referring the matter back to the CRTC for re-examination and necessitating yet another hearing, which was scheduled for late August of 1987. Allan Slaight was pessimistic about its outcome. In his words, "the CRTC rarely changed its mind," and the odds of the original decision being overturned seemed remote at best.

☆

Be that as it may, the Ottawa debacle set off a civil war in the CTV boardroom, exacerbated by unexpected and doom-filled financial revelations. First was the fact that the network was $50 million in debt, thanks largely to payments for feature films that wouldn't be rebroadcast. Second was the executive committee's decision to spend an initial $7 million-plus on *Mount Royal*. Third, the board had learned in December 1986 of a $10-million shortfall in advertising revenue.

Allan Slaight, who was furious anyway because of Baton's encroachment on his turf, said that CJOH's special assessment had more than doubled during the previous two years, while payments received from the network had declined by almost a third. He foresaw that, in 1987–88, these payments would disappear. He and other affiliate owners were terrified by the prospect of tossing money into a bottomless pit.

In response, Big John Bassett and a number of other directors insisted that a tough new financial officer be hired. The man they picked was Duncan Morrison, a Canadian who'd earned a reputation for slashing and burning a Pittsburgh steel company until it turned around. Morrison signed on in March 1987 and ordered a $21-million write-down of the feature film inventory, paid for by the affiliates in yet another special assessment. Baton's share was $2.7 million after tax, and Standard Broadcasting anted up $1.2 million.

At the same time, CTV's executive committee came to grips with the shortfall in advertising revenue. During a particularly lively board meeting, Big John asked Chercover whether it was true that the head of network promotion had a staff of fourteen people.

"Twelve, maybe fourteen, something like that," Chercover said.

"Jeezuz Christ, Murray!" Bassett roared.

In fact, Big John had begun to turn against Chercover more than a decade earlier. Doug was no fan either. He believed that Chercover was a lax administrator who'd gone overboard on empire-building with a CTV staff that numbered 400 employees. But neither Bassett could oust Chercover by fiat. Any decision to remove him would have had to be put to a vote; it wasn't a matter of shouting "Go!", as Big John had done with Gordon Keeble in the early days.

Chercover, for his part, was fed up with having been on the receiving end of Big John's tirades for twenty-five years. He disliked Big John "because he argued and yelled," says Eddie Goodman, who'd acted for CTV in its contract negotiations with Chercover in the late 1970s. In Goodman's recollection, Chercover couldn't believe that they wouldn't pay him what he asked for. "[He] had a mammoth ego," Goodman grumbles. "He couldn't distinguish between himself and the network."

Perhaps that was because Chercover received (and took) the credit, at least in the outside world, for turning the Quiz Show Network into CTV, complete with a credible news department, *W5*, *Canada AM*, world-class sports coverage, and even the occasional Canadian drama series worth watching. Inside the CTV boardroom, his reputation was somewhat more problematic. Nonetheless, the Canadian Association of Broadcasters had awarded him its Gold Ribbon Distinguished Service Award in the autumn of 1986, and *Variety* magazine had lauded him as a "strong executive" and a "gifted salesman," whose road to the presidency of CTV was "paved with grease paint, not spread sheets."

But spread sheets were now the order of the day. To deal with the loss of advertising revenue, CTV's executive committee decided that the network "had to cut operating costs all across the board," Ray Peters recalls. He claims that it was left up to CTV's management to determine exactly where those cuts would fall.

On March 5, when the *Toronto Star* broke the story that Harvey Kirck and the former *Canada AM* and *W5* co-host Helen Hutchinson were among thirty network employees to be axed, CTV faced one of its worst-ever public relations crises.

The layoffs were poorly handled. Kirck claimed to have learned about his dismissal by reading the *Star*. Murray Chercover issued a statement calling the story "mere supposition" and retreated into a convenient illness. He then issued orders that talking to the press was a firing offence and spent the week denying that any firm decisions had been taken. Finally, in an internal all-staff memo dated March 18, he acknowledged the $10-million advertising shortfall and explained that 90 per cent of CTV's budget was locked up in programming and distribution contracts. Therefore the money would have to come out of network operations. "There will be no wholesale firings, and the network is not going to be gutted," he wrote.

The following day, Chercover flew to Ottawa and appeared before a House of Commons committee. He told its members that cutting 30 out of 400 jobs (17 of them from the news department) was nothing compared to recent firings at the CBC. He also assured the committee that the sail-trimming would not "diminish the quality of our service to the public."

In the realm of damage control, CTV's management tried to shift the blame for the layoffs onto the affiliates. "Budget woes blamed on tight-fisted stations" read the sub-heading on the *Star*'s scoop. "The stations are so cheap they wouldn't spend two bits for a box seat at the Second Coming," an unidentified management source later told *Maclean's* magazine. A similarly unidentified affiliate source chipped in with the opposing view: "The goddamned place is in trouble because the network has been spending too much money. They should have seen the storm clouds." Plainly, one or both of the Bassetts were having a fine old time in the deep background.

☆

And what, amid these many adventures, had become of the network's licence? On March 24, the CRTC renewed it for a full five years. André Bureau complimented CTV on "maintaining the high standards of its news and public-affairs programming," but warned that foreign bureaus in Washington, London, Jerusalem, and Beijing were to remain open, along with all of its domestic bureaus. The CRTC also wanted to see a news correspondent based in Newfoundland.

The decision went on to recognize CTV's participation in coverage of the 1988 Winter Olympics, which were about to take place in Calgary, and cited the high quality of the network's dramatic features, mini-series, and limited series such as *Peter Ustinov's Russia*, the work of Baton's Glen-Warren Productions. Still, the commissioners remained displeased with CTV's commitment to Canadian drama series. CTV had proposed spending $403 million on all of its Canadian programming over the next five years, 75 per cent more than the $230 million it had laid out from 1981 to 1986. This, according to the CRTC, wasn't enough. Now the commission ordered additional spending on Canadian drama in the final two years of the five-year licence period.

The CRTC commented on CTV's revised promise (based in part on the arrival of *Mount Royal*) to raise its broadcasting of Canadian drama in prime time from 1.5 hours in 1985–86 to two hours a week in 1986–87, 2.5 hours a week in 1987–88, and three hours a week for the next four years. The commission felt this fell "considerably short of the network's potential." Accordingly, the licence renewal was granted only on the condition that Canadian drama account for four hours a week in 1990–91 and 4.5 hours a week in 1991–92. Worse still, all but one hour a week in each of the five years would have to compete head-on in peak viewing hours with the most popular American shows.

"CTV's wrists slapped again — violently," proclaimed the *Toronto Star*. "Maybe we cried wolf before about not being able to afford more Canadian content," moaned Allan Slaight to that same newspaper after the CRTC's decision, "and we were naughty to do it, but this is not the time to hit us." Doug Bassett, for his part, told the *Star* that Slaight should quit "snivelling" and get on with the job.

During their long week of acrimonious meetings earlier that month over mounting debt, declining advertising revenue, and the CRTC's decision to award the new Ottawa licence to Baton, some of CTV's directors had become more amenable to the idea of overhauling the ownership structure. Several of the owner-affiliates who'd rejected Baton's takeover offer the previous year felt they could no longer afford to remain as shareholders if it meant carrying their proportionate share of the network's losses. Accordingly, Big John Bassett, Ray Peters, and Jean Pouliot formed a new committee whose mandate, in consultation with Woods Gordon, was to try to reduce the number of owners in the cooperative, perhaps to four or five regional players. Owner-affiliates who sold their shares would remain as affiliates of the reconstituted network, but instead of taking a slice of the revenues or bearing a portion of the losses, they'd simply be paid for their airtime. (Even though Pouliot had become ill from the stress of, in Bill McGregor's words, "trying to deal with Big John," McGregor had asked him to take part in this committee, which would have to be composed of heavyweights if its findings were going to be heeded. Unfortunately, the trio failed to come to an agreement.)

In May, CTV informed the affiliates that, based on its lower expectations for advertising revenue and increased spending demands on the part of the CRTC, the network projected a $100-million loss over the five years of the new licence, with $48 million of that loss occurring in the final season of 1991–92. It was decided that the restructuring committee would have to go back to the drawing board, setting as its priority a revised affiliation agreement to address the problems of the smaller stations, followed by a new ownership structure and a revised shareholders' agreement. In the meantime, however, some of the smaller owner-affiliates were so alarmed by the impending sea of red ink that they asked Baton to put together another proposal for taking over the network. At the same time, the seventy-one-year-old Big John Bassett announced that he was retiring from the CTV board. In a letter to the *Toronto Star*, posted from Florida, he stressed that he had "no intention of becoming involved in any more TV battles or discussions."

And what of the pivotal series gamble that had turned the tide in CTV's favour at the licence renewal hearings? Over at Telefilm Canada, prescient staffers had declined to invest in *Mount Royal*, fearing that it was a disaster in the making. Telefilm's new Mulroney-appointed chairman Jean Sirois overruled his underlings, and Robert Lantos got $5 million of government money for seventeen $1-million episodes. Thus, *Mount Royal* became the most expensive series produced in Canada to date. To make room for it in CTV's schedule at the beginning of 1988, two of Baton's network programs would have to bite the dust.

12

Ray Peters
versus Doug Bassett — 1987–88

Ray Peters's friends describe him as the consummate gentleman, but he declared war on Doug Bassett late in the spring of 1987. First, Peters stalked out of an eight-hour meeting with Bassett and Joe Garwood at the Vancouver Club. Bassett and Garwood had travelled west because they'd put together another deal whereby Baton would take control of CTV, supported by Fred Sherratt and the CHUM group. They'd already talked with several other CTV owners about selling their shares and had been told that they'd better start with British Columbia Television, since Peters was bound to oppose them.

Quite so. In the course of a heated discussion that started at lunch and continued on past dinner, Peters claims that an abusive Bassett refused to answer a series of questions that Peters put to him five or six times, such as "How are you going to run the network? What's your business proposal? What are your objectives?" When Bassett failed to respond, Peters says, with more than a trace of smugness, "I knew he had no plan." In mid-evening, the disgusted Peters walked out on the "name-calling" Bobbsey Twins and got ready for the worst.

"Broadcasting is no place for amateurs" was the Ray Peters mantra. He claims he didn't "see anyone within the Baton group with the talent to run the network." He was also tired of what he called Baton's "bully-boy tactics." "The friction started over production and it became very serious," he says. "Baton [had] been successful over the years in manipulating the program committee to vote for its programs, and frankly, that's how you get programs like *Thrill of a Lifetime* and *Pet Peeves* into the program schedule." Thus, Peters's fight was no longer with his fellow founding director Big John Bassett, who'd never participated in any of the sub-committees. Now Peters was taking aim at the group that sat behind Big John at the board meetings — Baton's chief of programming and sales Ted Delaney, Joe Garwood, and Doug Bassett.

"We were talking about selling seats in the gallery," Bill McGregor jokes. "People in the front row would be acting up for those in the back. People like Big John were losing touch with the day-to-day goings-on in their own plant. Ted Delaney used to be on the phone to John before a board meeting to pump him up. Sometimes John would come directly from CFTO's sales department and raise hell." McGregor adds that frequently Big John would come into the boardroom after someone at CFTO had "wound him up."

Thus many of the issues that arose between Ray Peters and Baton related not so much to Big John but to that "second row." There was also a generational problem. Young executives were crowding the sixty-year-old Peters on his home turf, where Frank Griffiths's eldest son, Frank Jr., was undercutting his authority. The forty-six-year-old Doug Bassett represented a similar threat at CTV — "and Douglas was much less open to reason than [his father]," says one former director. "If you argued with [the Old Man], he'd listen." Another director says, "Either you can take Douglas or you can't. He can be very pompous and arrogant and an absolute pain in the ass. Peters couldn't handle [him]."

Fred Sherratt of CHUM agrees: "Ray Peters didn't like Doug Bassett. He had liked and respected Big John. Neither Bassett was really a TV person. The difference was that Doug Bassett thought he was a broadcaster, while Big John never pretended to be one." In fact, Doug's office at CFTO contained no television screen. "I don't have time to watch TV," he told the *Toronto Star*.

"It was no secret that there was no love lost between Ray Peters and Doug Bassett," says John Pollock of Electrohome. "Ray was a father figure. Doug was unusually outspoken. . . . They'd have at each other with four-letter words. . . . It was apparent at CTV that the Bassetts and Eatons were interested in controlling [the network]. A lot of people were very supportive, like CHUM, but others were less than sanguine about them becoming the sole controlling shareholder. It was their attitude that put people off."

Doug Bassett remembers the Vancouver showdown differently. He believes it started out as a CTV board meeting, not a private one. The one thing the two men do agree on is that Peters walked out. Bassett pauses before continuing in a more restrained fashion than one would expect from the so-called Bully of Baton: "Ray Peters was a shooter. He always felt that the eastern bloc, headed by Toronto, was out to grab everything at the network. He was entitled to his opinion. There was keen competition. We did a lot of CTV work because we were in Toronto and CTV didn't own anything except its [licence]. We were an irritant to some of the directors from other parts of the country."

Later, Doug and Joe Garwood had another showdown with a CTV director, this time at Toronto's Four Seasons Hotel. "What the hell do the Eatons know about broadcasting?" this person demanded. Doug Bassett takes this sort of remark very personally. "If they knock the Eatons, they're knocking me!" he blusters, adding, "I felt like punching him out." (This was the sort of remark Ray Peters frequently made about the Eaton family. He says he anticipated that the Bassetts and the Eatons would someday want to control the network and claims that he was responsible for including the one-station, one-vote rule in the original network by-laws with this eventuality in mind.)

Meanwhile, faced with the unattractive prospect of Baton setting up a rival independent station in Ottawa, Allan Slaight wanted out of CJOH. Fortunately, while he was preparing for the second round of hearings into that application, he bumped into George Eaton at a function in Toronto. "Why don't we buy your station?" Eaton asked. Slaight was agreeable, a series of secret negotiations began, and the deal was announced on July 14.

Baton agreed to pay $85 million for CJOH and Carleton Productions, which (as usual) many said was too high a price. Slaight denied that CTV's financial problems had spurred the sale, but conceded that the idea of contributing money to the network over the next few years had been a factor in his decision. Mostly, though, he felt that CTV's woes "were not insurmountable." What he couldn't accept was "the option of having a very well-financed and well-managed independent coming into the market to compete against us."

Joe Garwood, Doug Bassett, and Allan Beattie, whom Slaight considers a "real gentleman," had negotiated the deal for Baton. Once the agreement was reached, Baton informed the CRTC that it was surrendering its still doubtful licence to operate the new Ottawa station. The

CRTC therefore cancelled the August 24 rehearing, but promptly scheduled another acquisition hearing for early 1988. "It was a big gamble," Doug Bassett recalls. "We gave up the . . . licence without knowing whether we'd get approval to take over CJOH."

Approval of the deal would give Baton ownership of CTV affiliates in the country's largest and fourth-largest markets. Baton was already the number one player in television in Canada, with about 11 per cent of total revenue. If the Ottawa purchase went through, its ranking in the radio and television industry would rise to number three from number six as measured by total revenue.

A flurry of stories during the summer and early fall of 1987 forecast Baton's takeover of the network, including an article in the "Report on Business" section of the *Globe and Mail*, which featured a photo of a smiling Big John and Doug Bassett and the headline: "Bassett's dream of getting CTV moves nearer reality." Doug later criticized this coverage when he appeared before the commission seeking permission to acquire CJOH. He took issue with the article's claim that "we are out to control 51 per cent of the network, [that we want] to own CTV. That is completely false. My father has said publicly for many, many, many years [that] he would like to be more involved with CTV, and he is entitled to his opinion. But the fact of the matter is [that] Baton's position now is . . . not having 51 per cent. Let's get a group of shareholders together and let's do a deal, but commensurate with the responsibility of the shareholding group."

Despite these comments, Doug in fact harboured ambitions of Baton's becoming CTV's single controlling shareholder. For a hired hand, he wasn't doing too badly. True, he owned only 120,800 shares of Baton, worth a piddling $1.6 million, compared to the Eaton family's 14.2 million shares, worth almost $200 million. But cashing out of the Telegram trust had bought him a house in Forest Hill, a few doors from Fred Eaton's mansion opposite Upper Canada College, and 200 acres on Lake Rosseau in Muskoka. He enjoyed a collection of twelve vintage mahogany boats, and an ultra-sleek cigarette boat christened *Pistoff* (so named because of his wife's reaction to its purchase). His social circle included luminaries such as the American congressman Joe Kennedy Jr. (the eldest son of Big John's friend, the late Bobby Kennedy), and he hosted the Duke and Duchess of York at his summer "cottage." Doug's life was good. Only one thing seemed necessary to complete it.

"Dougie is about to become something neither the Old Man nor anyone else in Canada has ever been before: a national network television mogul," wrote Rod McQueen in the October issue of *Toronto Life* magazine. This possibility scared CTV's news and public affairs department.

They feared that the younger Bassett would nickel-and-dime their already depleted and demoralized staff. The Old Man had spent lavishly on his news operations, sending his reporters as far afield as Moscow and South Africa, but those days were at risk of becoming a thing of the past. "Big John was never interested in detail," the calculator-wielding Doug Bassett told McQueen. "I am, because if you can control your costs, you can spend more. If your costs get out of line, it can kill ya. I'm chintzy because I don't like [employees] at the trough, going to Bucharest, Romania, to some goddamn film festival. . . . They're scared of their personal positions because some of them aren't hacking it — but nobody will make a decision to make the news better."

In September 1987, Doug Bassett took his father's seat at the CTV board-table. He was "the new boy," as he put it, sitting next to "pioneers in Canadian broadcasting" like Ray Peters, Bill McGregor, and the truant Jean Pouliot, who disobeyed his doctor's orders and returned to the meetings, accompanied by his son Adrien.

Doug Bassett thought he could do a better job than Big John. "There has been one enormous change at CTV [at] the board level," he said. "My father was a man . . . set in his own ways; a man who over his great [twenty-six-year] career made friends, caused some disagreements among his allies, and did not in all areas think primarily of CTV . . . when he was on [its] board."

The new boy started out with a bang, by presenting a radical restructuring proposal that would enable Baton to take control of the network, together with a new affiliation agreement. The former called for Baton representatives to form a majority of CTV's board (more than 50 per cent of any quorum) and to appoint the chairman, who would cast the deciding vote in the event of a tie.

But handing control of the network over to Doug Bassett was only one possible solution to CTV's ills, claimed Bill McGregor. "This isn't a simple thing," he said. "It isn't simply a matter of someone walking in with a bag full of money and making an offer."

Ray Peters recalls that Baton's application to buy CJOH set out "its plan to control [CTV] and [described] how its ownership of CJOH was a major component of that plan." This is what Peters objected to. "Dougie was making a run at trying to control the network," he says. "We didn't give a damn who owned CJOH, but we didn't want approval of that application to give tacit approval to Baton's takeover."

Baton might have been alone in its ambition to control the network, but not in the hope of occupying a bigger position within it. In the summer of 1987, for instance, rumours had been rife that after more than two decades of ownership, Dick Rice of Sunwapta Broadcasting was ready to sell CFRN Edmonton. Baton, Maclean Hunter, and CAP Communications (which owned CKCO Kitchener) all rose to the bait. Then, in September, Sunwapta accepted a $50-million offer from Electrohome, CAP's parent company. If the CRTC approved this deal, CAP would become the third largest player at CTV, behind Baton and WIC Western International Communications and just ahead of CFCF Inc.

Still, for many affiliates, a network role was becoming less and less attractive. In early November, Peters noted that it was "very gloomy out there in the real world." By this, he referred to CTV's costly new drama requirements and the likelihood of another slump in the advertising market. Bill McGregor chimed in with the news that, far from rolling in wealth, one CTV member was "in an operating loss position," and that the "bottom six" stations had a return on investment "of only 8 or 9 per cent."

At McGregor's urging, the larger owner-affiliates like Baton, CFCF, CAP Communications, and Maclean Hunter (the haves) had agreed to make life easier for the have-nots, by absorbing some of their funding obligations. This new revenue- and cost-sharing formula was part of a revised affiliation agreement filed with the CRTC at the end of November 1987. For example, Baton, as the owner of three affiliates, would receive as airtime payments almost 25 per cent of CTV's net revenue. This figure would rise to 33 per cent if Baton's takeover of CJOH Ottawa was approved. But Baton also agreed to pay more than 28 per cent of the network's costs (more than 37 per cent, if it gained control of the Ottawa station). By contrast, CHUM, the owner of three Atlantic affiliates, would get roughly 8 per cent of net revenue and be responsible for about 4 per cent of the costs.

This arrangement was thrashed out with Doug Bassett. "I honestly don't believe that my dad would have gone with Mr. McGregor and moved this motion," he said. (Yet Big John had made a similar concession in 1966, when CFTO agreed to shoulder 25 per cent of the network's costs, in return for only one vote out of twelve at the boardroom table.) Doug predicted that it would cost Baton an extra $1 million during the first fiscal year of the new agreement to "offset and help the smaller affiliates." It was even more of a "great expense" than it sounded, because the way things were going, it seemed unlikely there'd be any net profits for the owner-affiliates to share in the foreseeable future.

☆

At the beginning of 1988, the Peters-Bassett feud went public, when Peters, on behalf of BCTV, wrote a letter of intervention to the CRTC, arguing against Baton's purchase of CJOH. He stressed that this was not his normal practice, but that he was "convinced that this application has far-reaching consequences that go well beyond the Ottawa market," and would have a "potentially damaging effect" on the network as a whole.

Peters alleged that Baton had dominated CTV for many years, manipulating the network's programming decisions to suit its own selfish purposes. He included with his written intervention a copy of CTV's 1986–87 schedule, which he claimed demonstrated Baton's "involvement in no less than twenty-two out of twenty-nine weekly hours of CTV's Canadian programming." By contrast, the other affiliates combined contributed a scant four hours.

(Doug Bassett called this calculation a fallacy, because CTV, as well as all sorts of independent producers, often rented Glen-Warren Productions' facilities. "They pay us to use . . . our cameras; [they] turn on the lights and go," he said. "The same thing can be said for the news, for *Canada AM*." This position was to a degree defensible. *The Campbells* wasn't a Glen-Warren show. Neither was *Night Heat* nor *Mount Royal*. Baton used to dominate the network's Canadian production, but in recent years it had given up a lot of ground to independents such as Alliance.)

Peters pointed out, though, that in 1985–86, Baton had received $12 million from the network for "programming services." When that was added to CFTO's $3 million in airtime payments (and an additional $1.3 million that went to the Saskatchewan stations), Baton was raking in $16.3 million — five times more than any other affiliate.

Peters accordingly asked the CRTC to limit Baton's ownership and voting position in CTV to 25 per cent, proposing instead that four players — Baton, WIC Western International Communications, Kitchener's Electrohome, and Montreal's CFCF — share equally in a new company that would buy the network from its present affiliate owners.

In the face of this unwelcome provocation, Doug Bassett hit the roof. Asked by John Partridge of the *Globe and Mail* how he planned to respond to Peters's intervention, he brandished a copy of the speech he would deliver the next day at the public hearings into the CJOH takeover and "energetically raised the middle finger of his right hand."

☆

To everyone's surprise, Doug had managed to compose himself when the time came for him to address the commission, although his better manners probably owed more to the presence of his friend Fred Eaton on the panel behind him than to any desire on his part to placate the CRTC. "The reason I went was because Allan Beattie said it would be a good thing, if [only] to let them know there was a living, breathing Eaton, a human face," recalls Fred mildly. He took no part in the hearing, save to respond to one question from André Bureau about Baton's future plans.

"Of course we cannot tell in a regulated industry what the commission's policy is going to be," he said. "[But] I would say, as Douglas has, that Baton . . . would view each opportunity on its individual merits, too. I would not want to say that we were on an acquisition grab to get every TV station in Canada because that is not the case. And obviously we probably would not have as nice a letter from our bankers. . . . I do think that there may be further opportunities for Baton to expand, and I think that, as long as it is under the control of the CRTC, it is not going to do anything that is detrimental to this country. I say that as a person whose family has been in business in this country for 110 years. Our family are believers in Canada, and we are believers in Canadian television, and we are believers in this team that sits in front of you, because we think they do as good a quality job as is done in this country."

Doug Bassett's presentation rang familiar bells. He used the larger-economic-unit-equals-better-Canadian-programming equation and again made sure to put sufficient benefits on the table. He pledged to spend $14.7 million on CJOH's programming in 1988–89, anchored by a major new dramatic mini-series, *The History of Canada* (Baton's largest drama commitment since *The Littlest Hobo*), and a number of music specials featuring the Quebec singer Veronique Beliveau (whom Bassett said had been brought to his attention by his teenage daughters). Baton also promised to invest almost $5 million on capital improvements at CJOH and another $2.5 million at Carleton Productions. In all, the package totalled almost $43 million.

Inevitably, one of the commissioners raised the twin hobgoblins of western alienation and central Canadian control, but Doug was prepared. Attending university in the Maritimes, working briefly in Vancouver, and owning television stations in Saskatchewan had broadened his horizons, although he took a minute or so to get up to speed. He told the commission that he, his wife, and their three daughters spent holidays in the west "instead of going to Florida." Then he got on topic. "I don't know why western Canadians in the broadcasting business should be so anti-Kitchener or anti-Toronto or anti-Montreal," he said. "Opportunities arise. Somebody in Winnipeg [could have purchased the Regina] television station, but they didn't. . . . I don't make any apologies for what so-called Toronto people do."

He was warming to his subject. He then addressed Ray Peters's intervention, with a measure of respect that was hard to reconcile with his middle-finger-waving performance the previous day. "It's not a question of Mr. Peters not liking me or me not liking Mr. Peters," Bassett said. "He's a professional in the business, as [I] and my colleagues are. [We] are friends and we are colleagues and we have to continue to communicate."

He then denied his ambition to control the network. The only problem was that there was not equal representation at CTV, he argued. "But we believe there should be. We are not asking, [nor] is Mr. McGregor or . . . Mr. Peters or Mr. Pouliot, that one person should control CTV. Our position . . . is representation by population. That's all."

Later Bassett expanded on the point. If four people wanted to form a new company to own 100 per cent of CTV, the shareholdings "should be commensurate with responsibility," depending on how many stations each party owned. Whoever was "on the hook for more money . . . should have more votes."

Asked what had happened to the benefits of the cooperative's one-owner, one-vote formula, Joe Garwood replied that it had served its purpose for quite some time, but that times had changed, given recent losses and the prospect of more to come. Bassett agreed. "If [these] loss projections are correct," he said, "[some of the smaller affiliates] just can't afford to pick up the tab." He went on to say that most of the smaller affiliates didn't want to pay for CTV; they preferred to be just affiliates, not shareholders. Bassett said he didn't think that CTV was going to fall apart, but someone had to pay for its commitments. "It's time to change the structure of the network," he declared, "[and run it] as a company owned by a small group of shareholders," subject to the CRTC's approval. In his view, the will existed among affiliates both large and small to change the present shareholders' agreement, and he expected to see a new one "worked out by the end of August."

Bassett closed the first day of the hearings with a passionate plea. He said he wasn't alone in his commitment to a stronger CTV and a belief that the strength of Canadian television lay in Canadian programming. He said that this was the policy of Baton's board of directors and, more important, its majority shareholders. "You heard Mr. Eaton talk about how he believes in Canada and in Canadian television," Doug said. "So [this] is not a question of a one-shot Charlie coming in here to try to be the great saviour of [CTV] and be a nice guy with the commission. This is something which we have to do. . . . And damn it all, we are going to do it, because it is going to work and it has to be done."

The following day, it was Ray Peters's turn to speak. Strangely enough, it was he, not Doug Bassett, who managed to get André Bureau's back up. As Peters explained why the CRTC's approval of Baton's purchase of CJOH would result in Baton gaining effective control of the network, Bureau twice interrupted to warn him about his remarks.

"Bureau was furious," Peters says. "I knew him. I had hired him as president of Cancom [Canadian Satellite Communications] because WIC was [its] controlling shareholder." He realized that Bureau was getting "quite annoyed" when "he started to turn red from his neck up."

"Why is BCTV so strongly opposed to Baton taking control of CTV?" Peters wondered rhetorically. "We are convinced that such a development will undermine still further the national . . . character of the network. Already far too much production is concentrated in Toronto." He pointed out that the CBC also had its headquarters in Toronto and that Canada did not need another national broadcasting service controlled and operated from there.

"Baton . . . has dominated CTV for far too long," Peters declared. "We have simply stopped submitting pilots and script outlines to CTV. It is a futile exercise! It is a waste of our time and money. Each time we do, we get skated offside by the Baton machine, and our shows are not properly considered. . . . The network, bullied by Baton, has great difficulty encouraging the development of programs from [other] sources. . . . That attitude will continue to prevail as long as Baton is in a position to force its objectives on the network and the smaller affiliates."

He countered Baton's argument that it was only fair that it exercise control, given the large share of network costs it had to bear, and that it should have "board representation commensurate with that responsibility." This, he charged, ignored the fact that Baton received a share of network revenues that was "substantially greater than that of the other affiliates." (The CRTC failed to ask him how this argument held up if the network showed no profit after paying its costs.)

Then Peters made his pitch for encouraging regional representation. "We have asked the commission, if it intends to approve this application, to attach conditions that will restrict Baton's ownership and control of any future, restructured CTV to [not] more than 25 per cent, and to require more balanced production . . . between Baton and other CTV members. . . . We feel very strongly that, rather than have the network . . . taken over by Baton, four willing participants should each have 25 per cent.

And they are CFCF in Montreal, CKCO in Kitchener, Baton [in Toronto], and BCTV [in Vancouver]."

The Q&A followed, during which Peters reeled off a list of affiliates who wanted no further part of network ownership. CHUM, he said, owner of the Halifax, Moncton, and Sydney affiliates, and a strong supporter of Baton's takeover of the network for the past five years, had "indicated that they really do not want to continue as a shareholder." So, according to Peters, had Maclean Hunter, the owner of CFCN Calgary; Randy Moffat, who owned CKY Winnipeg; and Mid-Canada Communications, which owned stations in Sudbury, Timmins, and North Bay.

André Bureau cut him off before he could add Newfoundland to his list. "I am sorry to interrupt," he said, "but I think, in all fairness, you should speak on your behalf, and we should try to avoid referring to parties who are not part of this process here, particularly when you try to identify their feelings more than their official positions."

Thus chastened, Peters moved on to address principles. The key was regional representation. With four shareholders, CTV would have strong ownership based in Quebec, Ontario, and western Canada. He said he was disappointed that CHUM had indicated that they didn't want to remain a shareholder. If they could be persuaded to stay, the network would have a fifth voice, from the Maritimes, and all five parties could then retain a 20 per cent ownership, which he considered to be the perfect model.

He explained the difference between his ownership proposal and that of Baton. "Baton see their position as taking over the network and infusing additional capital that the network needs in order to carry on the operation. What I see is the four or five shareholders carrying out the same operations."

He strongly disagreed with Bassett's prediction that there would be a new shareholders' agreement by CTV's year end. "We don't have a hope in hell of reaching any kind of shareholders' agreement or any kind of restructuring agreement on the network," he argued, "unless there is a clear message that comes out of this hearing. The position of Baton over the years [at CTV board meetings] has been outrageous. If you approve this application without conditions, in my view, it will be out of control."

A while later, André Bureau interrupted for the second time. He was surprised that Ray Peters would ask the CRTC to intervene in negotiations regarding the network's "ownership structure." He was also "a little bit concerned about the kind of precedent it could create within the broadcasting system" if the commission started to become involved in discussions between parties before they came "officially" and "openly" before the commission.

Doug Bassett played up Bureau's concern in his rebuttal. "Mr. Peters suggested that the commission take the opportunity of our application to acquire [CJOH] to place specific terms and conditions on the restructuring of the CTV network," he said. "We disagree with this position. It is our position that approval of the application before you would not affect the ownership structure of CTV. Our vote would [simply] become one of ten, rather than one of the eleven that exist today."

13

The End of an Era — 1988–89

Less than a week after their headline-making public brawl, Doug Bassett was organizing a revolt to oust Ray Peters as chairman of CTV's executive committee. Then Peters pre-empted the coup by announcing his resignation at a meeting on February 1, 1988. "There was a groundswell and Doug Bassett was stirring the troops," Peters concedes, "but after ten years as chairman and eleven years as CEO of WIC [Western International Communications], I was making plans to head for the back nine of the Capilano Golf course. . . . The time was right for somebody else to take over."

If anybody had earned the right to putt around in peace, it was Peters. He'd been attending CTV board and committee meetings since 1966. As chairman of the executive committee, he'd had to fly to Toronto almost every week, often on short notice and usually on an overnight flight. He'd shower, shave, try to cope with whatever brand of hell was breaking loose that day, then rush to catch an early evening flight back west, arriving home at ten or eleven at night. Then he'd have to be at his desk the next morning. He claims to have worked twelve- and eighteen-hour days, often seven days a week, for thirty years.

Peters's successor as chairman was Maclean Hunter's president and CEO, Ron Osborne, who represented CFCN Calgary on the CTV board. The meeting at which Peters resigned marked Osborne's first day at the executive committee table. He believed that he was chosen for two reasons: he wasn't obviously aligned with either the Bassett or Peters camps, and, as a chartered accountant and the senior official of a major Toronto-based media company, with a reputation for being cost-conscious, he had the necessary financial skills to help steer the network through its current licence period.

Osborne was not wedded to the idea of CTV's twenty-two-year-old cooperative arrangement. In fact, he understood Doug Bassett's wish for representation by population. "I see no harm in some form of proportionality in voting rights," he told the *Financial Post*. "Not all the participants are in the same position as Baton, which has a much greater vested interest in the network." Later, he told Patricia Best of the *Financial Times of Canada*, "We're going from an entrepreneurial company to a professionally managed company. The era of the founders of CTV is over."

Eleven days after Osborne was elected chairman, CTV's directors gathered in chinook-warmed Calgary for a full board meeting during the day and an evening gala that preceded the opening of the Winter Olympics.

There they started working on new five-year financial projections, which looked a bit rosier than had been the case the previous May. "The network [is] back to a much more normal type of operation," Bill McGregor said. "As a result, [advertising] sales have improved. I don't suggest . . . that they're blooming, but [they've] improved considerably."

Next, ten of the eleven station owners signed or agreed to sign the new affiliation agreement. The holdout was Mid-Canada Communications, which refused to sign until its Timmins and North Bay stations were upgraded to affiliate status. When the other shareholders agreed to the change, the network's sixteen affiliates increased to eighteen. With that hurdle overcome, the talk turned to ownership restructuring. At least the discussions weren't as heated as they'd been two weeks earlier, when Ray Peters had opined that he didn't think CTV would ever resolve "the difficulties within [its] own boardroom."

The driving force behind the desire to make long-overdue ownership changes was the network's poor economic performance over the previous two years, said McGregor. This had led many of the smaller affiliates to say, "I don't know whether this is a club I can afford to remain in." Now, said McGregor, the situation had stabilized. Changes to the affiliation agreement, by which the bigger boys agreed to pay more of the network's operating costs, as well as changes to the committee structure, had resulted in "less pressure and less of a drive for a major change in the shareholding arrangement."

Nor was McGregor ready to ditch the one-owner, one-vote principle — even though the eleven owners were "eleven egocentric people who certainly made life difficult for one another." Rather, he argued for the status quo, despite its warts. "I would suggest [that] there is no difficulty in thinking that we could go on in the present cooperative arrangement . . . , and be [as] successful as we have been [for almost] twenty-five years," he said.

He conceded there had been disputes over production, but wouldn't comment directly on Ray Peters's accusation that Baton had manipulated the programming committee and grabbed the lion's share. Whatever points of contention had existed were waning now, he said, because "many of the programs that we do [are] handled by independent producers."

Certainly, the owner-affiliates had something to celebrate together in Calgary. CTV had won the right to host and broadcast the Winter Olympics domestically, with Lloyd Robertson, who'd covered seven Olympics for CTV and CBC, as one of the co-hosts. Over two and a half weeks, CTV aired almost 120 hours of "goal-to-goal, top-to-bottom" coverage, thanks in large part to the affiliates' state-of-the-art mobile units.

The Calgary Olympics marked the culmination of Johnny Esaw's association with the games as CTV's vice-president of sports. He and the network had come a long way. In 1964, when CTV had paid $5,000 for the Canadian broadcast rights to the Winter Olympics in Innsbruck, Austria, all of its footage was flown from Frankfurt to New York and on to Toronto so that highlights could be aired the following day. Ultimately, as CTV's capabilities increased, a deal was struck whereby it would cover all the Winter Games, beginning in 1976 when they were back in Innsbruck, while the CBC would cover the Summer Games, starting in Montreal that same year. This meant that the public network was stuck with the Moscow boycott of 1980, and CTV had the headaches of covering the Winter Games in Sarajevo four years later.

That had marked the end of the agreement. The CBC announced that it wanted the Calgary Olympics for itself. Both networks presented competing bids, but CTV came out the winner, having offered US$3.6 million. This entitled it to provide live-action coverage (as well as a daily highlight package) to all the international broadcasters that held rights to broadcast the games in their own countries. CTV didn't get rich as host broadcaster, but it did garner record advertising revenues (according to

Esaw, the network's sales department reported that the games were "the most lucrative product [they'd] ever sold"), record audiences, and generally positive reviews.

☆

Several days after the Games began, some of CTV's directors trooped north to the provincial capital, there to attend public hearings into CAP Communications' purchase of Sunwapta Broadcasting, the owner of CFRN Edmonton, for $50 million.

CAP's president was CTV's chairman, Bill McGregor, who began by inviting the commissioners to take a moment and head for Calgary, where they'd see the unfolding of "a world-class product." McGregor was legitimately delighted; nearly a decade later, he counted CTV's coverage of the Games among his proudest hours at the network helm.

In fact, these hearings were marked by a cordial and largely non-confrontational atmosphere. Dick Rice, the eighty-seven-year-old radio and television pioneer, described the lengthy history of his company and spoke of his "long friendship" with Carl Pollock of Electrohome, CAP's parent company, which was by this time under the "ownership of his son John." (The elder Pollock had died in 1978, and John, along with his sister, had inherited slightly less than three-quarters of Electrohome's voting shares.)

John recalls that he and his father had been talking with Rice about buying CFRN ever since the early 1970s. But the still vigorous Rice was not prepared to sell, and somehow, seventeen years sped by, during which time Maclean Hunter, another potential purchaser, backed off. Now that an agreement had been reached, CTV's fifth- and sixth-largest affiliates would share common ownership, making CAP the network's third-largest player, after Baton and WIC.

The usual questions regarding concentration of ownership and western alienation reared their heads, but McGregor and Pollock knew what they were doing. CAP scored points because it was based in Kitchener, not the despised Toronto; the two men pledged to establish an advisory committee in Edmonton, chock-a-block with community representatives; and Dick Rice himself agreed to chair the station's new board. In all, it was relatively smooth sailing — and the right move for John Pollock at this time. He foresaw further consolidations within the communications industry. If they came about, he said, the position of "smallest and weakest player" was "not a very desirable place to be."

☆

A few months later at CTV's headquarters, the management team wore long faces. The network's showcase Canadian drama series *Mount Royal* had proved to be a spectacular bust. Robert Lantos's personal fascination with wealth and power had not proved attractive to audiences. At its low point, *Mount Royal* drew a disastrous 330,000 viewers an episode. Advertisers revolted, as did CTV's shareholders, who'd put over $7 million on the line, with further commitments to follow.

During the post-mortem, it was recalled that when Lantos had first pitched *Mount Royal* to Arthur Weinthal at a breakfast meeting years earlier, Weinthal had burst out laughing when he heard how much the thing would cost. By the time Lantos got his first season on air, American mega-soaps such as *Dallas* and *Dynasty* were in decline. *Mount Royal* was a dinosaur, the last of its breed, and CTV would have to find another, less expensive way of filling its CRTC-mandated three hours a week of Cancon drama in the upcoming season.

Fortunately, *Night Heat*, which had picked up a second Gemini award for best dramatic series in 1986–87, as well as being voted the most popular Canadian show of 1987, would be back for another year, as would *The Campbells*. Down at the bottom of the creative barrel, CTV had unearthed yet another half-hour German shepherd outing called *Katts and Dog*, which concerned a rookie policeman who'd been assigned to work with a furry partner. When it went to American pay television, this series was titled *K-9 Cops*, which didn't make it any more successful. Then there was *My Secret Identity*, from Toronto's Sunrise Films (dealing with a teenager who possessed various supernatural powers and had to contend with an eccentric neighbour) and a mercifully short-lived series from Toronto's Producers Group International, about a high school principal who moonlighted as a professional wrestler.

CTV's slate of new Canadian mini-series sounded somewhat more promising. It included *Passion and Paradise* (the story of the 1943 murder of Sir Harry Oakes in his Bahamian retreat, from Toronto's Primedia which wound up being simulcast on ABC), and the six-hour *Coco Chanel*, which starred Geneviève Bujold as the legendary Paris fashion designer. It, like *Mount Royal*, was filmed in Montreal and Europe, courtesy of an international consortium of producers that included — wait for it — Alliance.

At the opposite end of the social spectrum, CTV had bought the upcoming season's number one American sitcom, *Roseanne*, featuring the rotund "domestic goddess" and her blue-collar family, including the most miserable teen ever played on the small screen, Darlene. Pip Wedge had also picked up the Candice Bergen hit *Murphy Brown* and five other shows that didn't last the season. As well, in the course of his ongoing rivalry with Global, he managed to snatch two of the Ontario network's American programs, *Head of the Class* and the Vietnam-era drama *China Beach*.

Five weeks after the close of the Calgary Olympics, the number of CTV shareholders was cut from eleven to nine. The CRTC's tough but fair chairman André Bureau decided in favour of Baton's purchase of CJOH Ottawa and CAP Communications/Electrohome's acquisition of CFRN Edmonton. This brought about a shift in the balance of power. Baton loomed even larger, now that it owned four affiliates and was entitled to one-third of the advertising revenue that the network distributed to its member stations. WIC was still number two, but CAP Communications/Electrohome had vaulted ahead of CFCF Inc. into third place, now that it owned both Edmonton and Kitchener.

Whatever their disparities in size, however, the nine owner-affiliates each had the same, single vote, just as before. Doug Bassett found this intolerable and continued his quest for representation by population. Whichever way you measured it, that would mean that Baton would have more than 25 per cent of the votes, a prospect many other shareholders dreaded. The result was another impasse, just as there'd been in 1980 when the first restructuring committee was formed. Bassett had predicted that there'd be a new shareholders' agreement signed, sealed, and delivered to the CRTC by the end of August 1988, but he'd failed to reckon with his opposition. He still had his allies — among them, CHUM's Allan Waters, who acknowledged that Ray Peters's idea of four or five strong regional shareholders would be an improvement on the cooperative arrangement, but remained convinced that it would be best to have Baton as the single controlling shareholder rather than "four big conflicting interests." But Bassett had his enemies too, primarily the intractable Peters, who told *Broadcaster* magazine that "Baton may be the biggest, but they're not the best. Others have more experience, look better on the air, and are just as deserving of a position of control."

By the summer of 1988, Peters had little more than a year left on the CTV board. He was going to have to take early retirement from WIC in order to pre-empt a coup, mounted by the company's ailing founder,

Frank Griffiths Sr., who wanted to replace his long-time chief executive with a younger man and fellow chartered accountant. "He approached me back in 1988," remembers Doug Holtby, then the forty-one-year-old pro-tégé of the rival media magnate Dr. Charles ("Doc") Allard in Edmonton, and a founding director of Canadian Satellite Communications.

Holtby's first involvement with Griffiths had been in 1985, when WIC assumed control of Cancom. "Frank joined the board," he says, "and I understood why he was so successful. He was very, very bright. He could look at an income statement, he could look at a balance sheet and he could tell you what was happening with the company."

Holtby, whom Griffiths hand-picked to run his growing media empire of nine radio stations, three television stations, and the controlling interest in Cancom, was only three years older than Griffiths's eldest son, Frank Jr., then WIC's vice-chairman. Many observers thought that Frank Jr. pushed his father to replace Ray Peters, perhaps in hopes of running the company himself. If so, Holtby's recruitment effectively thwarted his ambition. But in Peters's version of events, it was *he* who decided to leave WIC because *he* was fed up with Frank Jr., who assumed a bigger role when his father's cancer prohibited him from spending as much time in the office as usual.

Among other flashpoints, Frank Jr. insisted that WIC hire a relatively unqualified friend of his for a key executive position. Peters had already interviewed several top candidates and met with the board to report his findings, only to be told that the friend was a shoo-in. "There's no way," Peters replied. "We control the company," retorted Frank Jr., and the matter was settled, against Peters's better judgement.

That's when Peters decided to start packing his bags. "I left because of illness," he explains. "I was sick of them and they were sick of me. The whole Griffiths family is dysfunctional. None of them get along. . . . Arthur [the second son] was trying to head off on his own, but Frank Jr. and [his mother] Emily insisted . . . on making emotional decisions and second-guessing me."

Indeed, Emily had insisted that her husband employ Frank Jr. in the first place. He'd run through several insurance positions before he came to roost (complete with six-figure salary) as a WIC director in 1982, the year after the company was incorporated. Yet even she didn't wish him to succeed his father.

Emily herself had wanted a directorship and asked Peter Paul Saunders to intercede with her husband. The elder Griffiths had refused, telling Saunders that she wouldn't be a "constructive influence." Frank Sr. had enough trouble with Emily's kitchen-table management. She treated

WIC like her private fiefdom, believing that it wouldn't have been created without Ballard family money. "Emily was calling the shots from the background," Saunders says. "But her motives were not rational business motives. Those who crossed her were dealt with."

Another family friend agrees that Emily "came on pretty strongly. If she couldn't dominate someone, she was very much against them. She put a great deal of pressure on Frank. [It's] my understanding that [he] loved his sons, but [believed that] neither [of them could] run the company." Incidentally, Griffiths never seemed to consider his two daughters, Mary and Emily Jr., as potential successors.

Nor was Ray Peters the only casualty of the Griffiths family approach to management. In the early days of Western Broadcasting, CKNW New Westminster's general manager, Bill Hughes, had been Frank Griffiths's right-hand man. Indeed, Hughes got Griffiths into hockey.

In 1975, Hughes had encouraged Frank Sr. to buy the Vancouver Canucks hockey club. Griffiths agreed to do so when he was out of the country, and the deal was put together by long-distance phone calls. On his return, however, he had second thoughts, but Emily changed his mind back again. She'd dated a hockey player before meeting Frank, she was passionate about the game, and she was keen that Western Broadcasting make the $8.5-million investment in North West Sports Ltd., the hockey franchise's parent company.

Frank Griffiths's management philosophy (as long as he could fend off Emily and Frank Jr., who both wanted to have a bigger say in the running of the family business) was to find the right man, pay him well, and let him alone to run the company. Yet, only two years after the move into hockey, Griffiths had a falling out with Hughes for no apparent reason. At least Hughes had the comfort of some $7 million in pocket for his premature retirement.

Griffiths held similar views when it came to Western's board. Allen Lambert, a former chairman of the TD Bank and a Western director from 1978 to 1994, remembers that "Frank was an unusual man. . . . He'd been so successful and had such a grasp of the industry, but he ran the company in a very democratic way — as long as you accepted what he was recommending! [Others might make] a presentation, and Frank wouldn't show his hand. But you knew [the matter] wouldn't have been presented [at all] if he was not in favour."

When Ray Peters was appointed Western Broadcasting's president in 1977, its annual revenues were $17 million. It owned 46 per cent of British Columbia Television, which in turn owned CHAN Vancouver and CHEK Victoria (then a CBC affiliate); 33 per cent of Okanagan

Valley Television, which owned CBC's Kelowna affiliate CHBC; and seven radio stations located in New Westminster, Calgary, Winnipeg, and Hamilton.

By 1980, CHEK had switched to CTV, and British Columbia Television therefore owned two CTV affiliates. Two years later, Ray Peters persuaded Peter Paul Saunders and three other long-time British Columbia Television shareholders to exchange their voting shares in these stations for shares in Western Broadcasting, giving Western and the Griffiths family a controlling 59 per cent stake in British Columbia Television, ahead of Selkirk Communications.

By then, Frank Griffiths had decided it was time to tap the public markets again. The family bought out the rest of Western's shareholders, and in 1982 transferred all its television and radio assets (with the sole exception of North West Sports) to the newly incorporated Western International Communications (WIC). There were two classes of shares: voting A shares, owned entirely by Western, and non-voting B shares, which would be sold to the public. There was also a coat-tail provision, which would convert the non-voting shares to voting shares in the event of a change of control. This, according to Edmund King, then Western's investment banker at Wood Gundy, the lead underwriter for WIC's public offering, was put in place so that control would pass seamlessly to the next generation of Griffiths — not so that WIC could be sold profitably to a third party.

The public offering sold out in three days flat and raised $50 million. Peter Paul Saunders and his colleagues were quite happy to take the non-voting WIC shares, because of the coat-tail provision. "We were quite comfortable with the management, [particularly] Ray Peters," he says. "And we were friends with Frank Griffiths. We trusted each other."

By now, the Griffithses were so wealthy that the silver-haired, bespectacled patriarch could spend the late spring and summer months aboard his eighty-seven-foot mahogany launch *La Feline*, which came equipped with an office and a satellite dish. Here he could indulge his passion for fishing. In May and June, he and Emily headed north to Alaska; in July and August, they trolled the Strait of Georgia and made shorter excursions to April Point on Quadra Island. Winter weekends were spent in their cabin at the Whistler ski resort, and Christmas holidays in the family condo near Diamond Head in Hawaii. No wonder that Ray Peters rarely clapped eyes on Frank Griffiths more than a dozen times a year, and Frank Jr. could throw his weight around in his father's absence — a situation that was exacerbated when the elder Griffiths's health declined.

But Peters still had one last big deal to complete before he and his wife, Heidi, retired to the house they were building above the Glen Eagles

Golf Course, up the West Vancouver coast from the waterfront site where the Griffithses were building their own multimillion-dollar concrete-and-glass mansion. This very complex and very costly ($217.5 million) purchase from Maclean Hunter, which was announced at the end of 1988, saw WIC buy several of Selkirk Communications' broadcasting holdings: the 41 per cent of British Columbia Television and the 50 per cent of CHBC Kelowna that it didn't already own; two independent television stations in Calgary and Lethbridge, both with the call letters CFAC; and two Edmonton radio stations. Peters played a leading role in all these negotiations, and in 1989, he accompanied Frank Griffiths to Allarcom, Doc Allard's Edmonton broadcasting company, where another deal was hammered out whereby Doug Holtby was hired as his replacement at WIC.

Meanwhile, back in the CTV boardroom, another "original" was about to depart. On March 15, 1989, the network's bone-weary head honcho Murray Chercover announced his resignation. Twenty-four years had passed, and it was getting more and more difficult for him to "walk the tightwire" between CTV's eighteen directors. He may also have anticipated the "Mexican standoff" that was two years away.

There were also health problems to consider. A former CTV director says, "Murray smoked more than anyone you know. And in the latter years, he was a real hypochondriac. His briefcase [was full of] pills. Most of it was psychosomatic illness, but he did have . . . a heart problem, which was dealt with the year he left." It was Chercover's desire to quit the presidency as soon as the board could decide on his successor, although he agreed to act as a consultant, focusing on program development and production, until his retirement at age sixty-five.

One of his programming deputies, Arthur Weinthal, committed the network to air its first Great Canadian Drama Series in the upcoming 1989–90 season: the breakout Alliance production *E.N.G.*, set in a Toronto television newsroom and featuring the complicated relationships that beset a female producer (Sara Botsford) and the two men in her life (Art Hindle and Mark Humphries). There was no disputing the Canadianness of this show, an urban, multicultural Canadianness rarely seen on the small screen. Each of the initial twenty-four instalments cost more than $900,000 to produce, for a total of $19 million, of which CTV initially contributed a third. When financing ran out, even after Alliance involvement, Telefilm involvement, and CTV investment involvement,

Baton met the $150,000-an-episode shortfall and committed additional funds for the pilot as well.

CTV scheduled *E.N.G.* at 10 p.m. on Thursday nights, replacing *Night Heat*, and placing it in direct competition with top American drama series such as *L.A. Law* and *Knots Landing*. Despite the tough time slot, *E.N.G.* drew a respectable 800,000 viewers a week in its first season. On the occasion of his thirtieth anniversary with CTV, Weinthal confided that *E.N.G.* was his best-loved production. Giving it the green light may not have been his smartest business decision but, as he told *Playback* magazine, "it was a solid script from day one. It was all Canadian, about us. The subject matter was socially relevant, always entertaining. [Week] after week for five years, we turned out solid entertainment."

In what seemed an embarrassment of riches after decades of Cancon poverty, CTV also began broadcasting twenty-six instalments of a new half-hour Canadian drama series called *Bordertown* in the fall of 1989. A $13-million co-production from Alliance and Tele-Images of France, it was set in 1880s Alberta and concerned a frontier settlement where the border ran directly down Main Street. One side was patrolled by a naive, by-the-book, and typically Canadian North West Mounted Police corporal — the other by a rough, wise-ass, gun-toting, and typically American U.S. marshall. It was shot in Maple Ridge, a Vancouver suburb, and the crew dubbed the results a "Pacific Northwestern."

Another highlight of the network's fall schedule was the $51-million mini-series *The French Revolution*, which starred Jane Seymour and an international cast of hundreds. This all-over-the-map co-production featured equally international financing on the part of CTV, Alliance (surprise!), and a number of French, British, Italian, and German funding sources.

Under the by now shrinking category of new non-Alliance programming, CTV prepared to launch its own daily afternoon talk show, *Shirley*, hosted by Shirley Solomon in Toronto. Returning Canadian series included *The Campbells*, *Katts and Dog*, and *My Secret Identity*, all of which combined to make 1989–90 by far the network's most Cancon-filled season to date.

Yet, CTV faced a catch-22 situation. Profit margins on its American programming were eroding fast, as the cost of buying U.S. shows jumped by nearly 22 per cent in 1989. Meanwhile, advertising revenues generated by these programs fell by almost as much, so that the network had less money to subsidize its new money-losing Canadian drama series. Worse still, the network's CRTC-dictated drama commitments had nowhere to go but up — to four and then four and a half hours a week over the next two seasons.

So penny-wise had CTV become that, not long after Chercover announced his retirement, it was outbid by Global Television for the rights to simulcast *Cheers*, the network's second-most-watched program the previous season, when its price went through the roof. Bill McGregor says that losing *Cheers* was Baton's fault, not Pip Wedge's or Chercover's. For some odd reason, Baton's executives had vetoed taking up the sitcom's renewal option at a programming sub-committee meeting, thus ceding to Global the cornerstone of its future domination of the simulcast airwaves, and helping to ensure that CFTO would lose the Toronto-area ratings war to Global in 1989–90 for the first time ever.

In June 1989, Ray Peters summed up his position at the CRTC's hearings into Maclean Hunter's $600-million takeover of Selkirk Communications and the spin-off of $217.5 million of Selkirk's assets to WIC by stating that most television stations nationwide were controlled from either Toronto or Montreal. This, to his mind, was unacceptable. "CTV should not be controlled [by] the eastern part of the world," he said. Rather, "it should be controlled by a group of broadcasters and owners [from] across [all] the country, to reflect the country as a whole, and we feel very strongly about that."

At this same time, one of the dreaded eastern broadcasters, Doug Bassett, reached agreements in principle for Baton to buy three more CTV affiliates, one more supplementary affiliate, and another possible supplementary affiliate, all in northern Ontario. In short, Baton agreed to pay $57 million for control of Mid-Canada Communications, the owner of CTV/CBC twinstick stations in Sudbury, Timmins, and North Bay, and a CBC-affiliated station in Pembroke, which Baton wanted to bring into the CTV fold. Baton also agreed to pay $14 million to a separate company (Huron Broadcasting) for the CTV/CBC twinstick in Sault Ste. Marie. Once again, Baton was accused of overspending — notably by Electrohome's John Pollock, whose company, along with Moffat Communications, had also been in the running.

If these deals were approved by the CRTC, Baton would own seven of CTV's eighteen full affiliates, and eleven of its twenty-five stations. Thus, Baton's share of payments for affiliate airtime would rise to 35.8 per cent, compared to WIC's 16.1 per cent and CAP Communications/ Electrohome's 14.6 per cent. As well, CTV's shareholders would be reduced to eight from nine, with each holding an 11.1 per cent equity interest and a single vote.

The day after this announcement, CTV's owners convened for a board meeting. Doug Bassett asked that Baton's two supplementary affiliates in Saskatchewan be upgraded to full affiliate status, which would have given Baton control of nine out of CTV's by now twenty full affiliates. The board, urged by WIC, CAP Communications/Electrohome, and CFCF Montreal, promptly vetoed his request.

Three and a half months later, on September 28, the CRTC approved all of WIC's purchases from Maclean Hunter, except the radio stations. In one grand sweep, this delivered to WIC 100 per cent ownership of CHAN Vancouver, CHEK Victoria, CBC's Kelowna affiliate, and the independent Calgary station.

Three weeks later, on October 18, Bassett's nemesis retired from WIC at the age of sixty-three, with another two years left on his contract. "It was right on schedule," Peters recalls. "I had already resigned as chairman of CTV's executive committee, where there was someone else ready to take my place. I'd started to list; I was burnt out. WIC paid me for the remaining two years, because Frank Griffiths was concerned that I would go elsewhere." Others saw it differently. They say that Peters didn't want to retire and that he had a problem with succession. Doug Holtby claims that it was stipulated in his contract that he would succeed Peters as WIC's chief executive — but, according to Peter Paul Saunders, Peters wouldn't delegate authority, believing that no one else was capable of running the company. As a result, he was forced into premature retirement. Arthur Griffiths, Frank Sr.'s second son, took his place on the WIC board, and Holtby became a director of WIC the following year.

Whatever may or may not have been going on in the background, Peters gave a gracious hand-off to his successor at WIC's annual meeting on December 8, 1989. "For a long time, it has been my desire to recruit Doug Holtby to our company," he said. "I am very pleased that Doug joined as executive vice-president last spring, and succeeds me as president and CEO." Peters also reminded WIC's shareholders how the company had grown under his presidency, from $17 million in revenues in 1977 to over $200 million in projected revenues in the coming year.

In another matter of succession, CTV's directors were busily searching for Murray Chercover's replacement in the final months of 1989, amid rampant rumours that top Canadian broadcasters wouldn't touch the job no matter how high the salary, because they knew full well the nature of the network's financial problems, its onerous Cancon drama quotas, and the internal jockeying for power by its owner-affiliates, especially by the man who would be king, Doug Bassett — who, according to Bill McGregor, forced Chercover to leave early. "The Bassetts are good enough businessmen," he explains. "They were looking at a stalemate and it [was] time for Murray to go." In other words, Doug believed that CTV needed an experienced CEO at its helm to steer it through choppy economic waters, not an aging and ailing broadcaster.

Although CTV's advertising revenue had recovered somewhat during 1987–88 and the network earned $28.3 million, of which $22 million was available for distribution to the affiliates, those earnings dropped to $7.4 million in 1988–89. Of that, a scant $2 million was available for the affiliates to share. Even worse, the network was heading towards a huge loss of $2.3 million in 1989–90, as the recession gutted advertising budgets.

These woes were compounded by mounting fragmentation of the television market, brought about by the explosive and unforeseen growth of viewing options, which knocked CTV's share of the prime-time audience from a little less than one in every three viewers on its twenty-fifth anniversary in 1986 down to one in five viewers in 1990. Increasingly, people were switching to Global if they wanted to see American imports, and to specialty or pay channels if they wished to watch something halfway interesting.

Happily, "Father Television," as Murray Chercover was known, received the credit he deserved for creating a legacy of nearly a quarter-century of flawed but nonetheless popular programming at CTV. On November 20, 1989, the sixty-year-old executive was given a special citation at the 1989 International Emmy Awards gala in New York "in recognition of his extraordinary career." Two months later, his "hypochondria" proved to have substance when he checked into a Toronto hospital for a triple bypass operation.

14

New Kids on the Board — 1989–91

CTV went through another generational shift four days before Christmas 1989, when WIC's forty-two-year-old president and chief executive Doug Holtby took Ray Peters's seat at the boardroom table, as CTV's directors gathered to interview the thirty-six-year-old John Cassaday for the position of network president. On Christmas Eve, in a rare unanimous decision, they hired him.

A Hamilton native and the son of a food-industry executive, Cassaday had dropped out of an Honours Journalism program at the University of Western Ontario in the mid-1970s and taken a summer job with RJR-MacDonald. He stayed on as a special-events manager in Alberta, then rocketed up through the ranks of General Foods Inc. and Campbell Soup Company Ltd. while earning an MBA part-time at the University of Toronto. His innovative advertising and marketing solutions, such as a new gourmet frozen food line called Le Menu, helped bring about a reversal of fortune at Campbell's, where he was named president in 1987. He also took delight in cost-cutting measures, but even his executive staff layoffs were exuberantly packaged with the acronym WOW, which stood for War on Waste. In 1989 Cassaday and his family moved to England, to see whether he could work his magic on Campbell's sickly British subsidiary. But they'd barely unpacked when the executive search firm The Caldwell Partners called Cassaday on behalf of CTV to ask if he'd be interested in making a career switch to broadcasting. Tired of being pigeon-holed as a food executive, Cassaday decided to accept the challenge, knowing full well that CTV had major problems.

"He got out of the soup business and into the soup," says CHUM's Fred Sherratt. "John Cassaday did a wonderful job of mixing it. "

On his first day on the job in March 1990, the lanky, clean-cut Cassaday found himself in charge of "an organization with a great history and wonderful, dedicated people, but [one that was] struggling to adjust to a rapidly changing environment. We were in effect bankrupt at the time." Cassaday's recollection is correct. Revenues and ratings were crashing in tandem, and "the shareholders had to belly-up money," in sharp contrast to the halcyon days of the 1970s and 1980s, when the network was distributing $25 million to $30 million a year in airtime payments to its affiliates.

From the start, Cassaday focused on the advertising community, arranging two meetings a day with current and potential sponsors. By the summer, CTV had signed a $40-million four-year marketing partnership with Coca-Cola. He also set about re-energizing the aging CTV "brand" and revamping, rescheduling, and overhauling CTV "products" like *W5*, *Canada AM*, and *CTV National News*. Nicknamed "Soupy Sales" by rival broadcasters, Cassaday demonstrated his fondness for brand names with on-screen talent as well, recruiting high-profile personalities to join such established stars as Lloyd Robertson, Craig Oliver, and Pamela Wallin.

The veteran broadcaster Eric Malling, who for fourteen years had co-hosted *the fifth estate* at the CBC was hired to co-host *W5* that fall, just as Cassaday scheduled the public affairs show to run an hour earlier, at 7 p.m. on Sunday night, head to head with *60 Minutes*. The real reason for this change was to make way for *America's Funniest Home Videos*, but in a surprising twist, the renamed *W5 with Eric Malling* thrived in its new time slot, and ratings jumped almost 25 per cent.

At *Canada AM*, Cassaday ordered a new, more stylish set and picked the telegenic J. D. Roberts, a former CITY anchorman who'd been working in the States for the past seven years, to replace the well-informed but old-style interviewer Norm Perry. Ratings climbed by an immediate 16 per cent. At *CTV National News*, whose viewership had slumped alarmingly, another new set was constructed, which used a working newsroom as a backdrop to Lloyd Robertson's anchor desk. And in Ottawa, CTV's bureau chief Craig Oliver lobbied Cassaday for better studio space than its current "slum in the national press headquarters."

Oliver remembers that this was "the first thing I hit [him] with, when I went out to the airport to pick him up." Once again, Cassaday responded, investing in "a major league setting," overlooking Parliament Hill.

But how to pay for all this? Exactly as before. "No one's intellectual curiosity is satisfied by buying packages of American shows," Cassaday told *Toronto Life*. "But it's how we make our money. Those shows have to subsidize not only our news operation but also our Canadian drama. The challenge is to find the right balance so you can continue to do good stuff."

In fact, one of his first excursions on the job was a pilgrimage to the Beverly Hills Hotel with Pip Wedge to meet with American network executives. When the pair returned to Los Angeles for that May's screenings, CTV had to pass on more than thirty new U.S. series because of skyrocketing prices. (From 1986 to 1991, its American program costs climbed by 43 per cent, to $46.4 million.) Instead, Cassaday and Wedge stole *Knots Landing* and two minor hits from Hamilton's CHCH and confined themselves to buying only three new shows: the enduring *Law & Order*, and those twin favourites of the intellectually curious, *America's Funniest Home Videos* and *America's Funniest People*. They would prove to be by far Canada's most-watched entertainment shows during 1990–91, drawing nearly 2.5 million viewers a week.

Arthur Weinthal needed every advertising dollar CTV could extract from its *America's Funniest* double bill in order to support the network's quota of four hours a week of Canadian dramas. Back for another season were *E.N.G.*, *Bordertown*, *My Secret Identity*, and *Katts and Dog*. New to the schedule was *Neon Rider* from Atlantis Films and CHAN Vancouver, a weekly one-hour drama set on a ranch for troubled teenagers, with Winston Rekert as the resident social worker. Next were two sprawling mini-series: the four-hour *Young Catherine*, from Toronto's Primedia Productions and various British partners (it starred Julia Ormond, Vanessa Redgrave, and Christopher Plummer in a retelling of the story of Catherine the Great), and the equally epic *Berlin Lady*, a romantic thriller set in Europe before the two world wars. CTV also planned to revive the CBC's award-winning children's series, *Owl TV*, and couple it with a new science show, *Wonder Why?*

Bordertown and *My Secret Identity* had each drawn over a million viewers in 1989–90, but overall ratings were down a stunning 14 per cent, the main reason being "something like two hundred scheduling changes," Cassaday said. And the tinkering continued, although not to the same degree. *E.N.G.* moved to nine o'clock on Thursday nights, where it proved more popular, as a counter-programming alternative to *Cheers* and, later, *Seinfeld*, both simulcast on Global. (Counter-programming is the strategy of scheduling a program against the prevailing expectations for a particular time period.)

At the network's June show-and-tell, designed to induce advertisers to prepurchase commercial time on the fall shows, Cassaday staged a glitzy sales presentation at Toronto's Winter Garden Theatre, introducing the new schedule and the market-tested slogan "Tuned into You."

Later that month he went across the country from station to station, meeting people at the affiliate level. One station manager was pleasantly shocked, remarking that Murray Chercover had never come for a visit. Also on Cassaday's agenda was the development of a five-year plan, along with a long-delayed restructuring of the network's ownership. To this end, he formed his own executive team, recruiting his Campbell Soup alumnae and contemporaries Tom Peddie and Paul Robertson, and began to hold regular weekly meetings of CTV's new management committee. This comprised Peddie (as senior vice-president of operations and chief financial officer); Robertson (as senior vice-president of marketing); Arthur Weinthal (still vice-president of entertainment programming); Pip Wedge (still vice-president of programming); Tim Kotcheff (still vice-president of news); and Gary Maavara (the new vice-president of sports and corporate affairs, replacing Johnny Esaw, who retired in September 1990). "We meet every Tuesday morning [for four hours]," Cassaday said, "and the focus of these conversations is: 'How can we create the synergy we need?'"

Doug Bassett was on his way to becoming the elder statesman of the next-generation CTV, in age if not in style. After more than a decade as Baton's president and CEO, he was at the peak of his social standing in February 1990, when he persuaded Prime Minister Brian Mulroney and his wife, Mila, to attend Toronto's Brazilian Ball, an annual charity event renowned for its lavish setting and scantily clad dancers.

The ball brought out the city's rich and famous every time around, but the Mulroneys' participation was a real coup for that year's chairwoman, Susan Bassett. "Douglas's wife is just lovely, a marvellous woman," Mulroney says. "We had another commitment but Mila has a great affection for Susan and Douglas. 'Let's do their thing, let's move things around,' she said." According to the society chronicler Rosemary Sexton, Susan's efforts helped raise "$720,000, a figure still unmatched."

Mulroney remembers that as soon as he and Mila entered the ballroom, "Douglas was right there, a sergeant major dictating what we were going to be doing. . . . He took [charge] of the event and every five minutes he moved us along. 'Talk to these people, not to them. Dance with this person, not with her.' Finally, I told him, 'If we mix this up, I'll be on the dance floor with you!'"

That was Doug Bassett to a T — an obsessive-compulsive manager who sent memos instructing CFTO employees how to park their cars in the station lot and personally cleaned out ashtrays in the Niner Diner cafeteria. After a bitter twelve-week strike at the station two years before, staff who'd crossed the picket lines in school buses with blackened windows gave Bassett a Fisher-Price toy bus. Bassett put it on display in the station's lobby, where it remained until it was stolen one dark and stormy night. Bassett was furious at the theft, as only he could be.

But like his father before him, Doug could be a bona fide patriot. His showcase drama, the $5.2-million *Divided Loyalties*, a CTV blockbuster movie broadcast during the week of the Brazilian Ball, recreated an eighteenth-century saga of Six Nations native Canadians, British redcoats, American revolutionaries, and United Empire Loyalists, centring on the story of an educated Christian Mohawk who was betrayed and manipulated by the whites. The battle scenes alone cost a small fortune. Produced by CTV's former vice-president of news and information, Tom Gould, the project had been rejected for funding by Telefilm, whose officials didn't like the script and deemed the budget too high. Bassett could have stopped right there, even though the *History of Canada* series, of which *Divided Loyalties* was the first instalment, was part of the benefits package that Baton had put on the table around the time of its attempt to acquire CJOH Ottawa. Instead, he stood behind the project. He'd also commissioned a new dramatic treatment of the life of the World War I fighter pilot Billy Bishop, based on the book *Courage in the Early Morning*, written by an Eaton and Bassett family friend, Billy's grandson, Arthur Bishop.

Nonetheless, at the July 5 public hearings into Baton's $72-million takeover of Mid-Canada Communications' northern Ontario stations (which, if approved, would give Baton ownership of seven of CTV's eighteen affiliates), the CRTC was back on its customary hobby horse, wondering when Baton would be "big or strong enough" to develop prime-time drama or entertainment programming that could "compete with or displace" American shows.

Bassett not unnaturally replied that he was trying to do so already, with *Divided Loyalties*, *Courage in the Early Morning*, and musical entries headlining the Quebec chanteuse Veronique Beliveau.

"More by way of specials," replied Fernand Belisle, the CRTC's vice-chairman, "but what about ongoing, continuing series?"

Bassett handed off the question to Joe Garwood, who explained that in the past two years Baton had spent $4.8 million supporting CTV's prime-time Canadian drama programming: covering the financing shortfalls for *E.N.G.* and *Owl TV*, and picking up the slack on *Katts and Dog* when its tax shelter fell apart. (But there'd been a quid pro quo involved. For example, in exchange for its investment in *E.N.G.*, Baton had received that series' North American distribution rights, while Alliance held rights for the rest of the world. This represented a strategic shift away from Baton's former practice of simply renting its studio facilities to independent third parties, who then controlled the resulting programs absolutely.)

For its own group of owned and operated stations, as opposed to the network as a whole, Baton had developed two new shows in the past two years: *Sunday Edition* with Mike Duffy and the *Dini Petty Show*, a daytime talk show that in fact competed with *Shirley* on the full network. *Dini's* annual budget was $2.5 million, compared to the $500,000 it would have cost Baton to purchase the broadcast rights to a syndicated American talk show.

Next, Bassett retook the microphone, to fill in the blanks on a whopping $34-million benefits package that had been pledged to support the Mid-Canada acquisitions, including $6 million earmarked for a Canadian soap opera. This as yet untitled project would kick off with twenty-six weeks' worth of shows, which Bassett felt sure would be so well received that producers would "come out of the woodwork," clamouring for a chance to be involved with it and other exciting new projects. Already, he said, Baton had received fifteen different proposals at all hours of the day and night, some of them (according to Joe Garwood) outlined "literally on napkins."

In the midst of his Q&A session, Bassett took a moment to quietly celebrate the departures of Murray Chercover, Ray Peters, and his father from CTV. "[It] is a whole different world," he said. "There are a lot of new members on the board of directors; there is a new president and chief executive officer. A lot of the founding directors, . . . who had their own biases, are no longer active in the management of their television companies; therefore they are not on the board. . . . There is no question in my mind that . . . there seems to be a different will and a different modus operandi. . . . Unlike in the past, [the directors] are letting the managers manage the asset, and the shareholders are not trying to force the network to carry their own programming, or to reduce . . . or increase costs, or what have you. [CTV] is now being operated . . . as a business."

If Baton's applications were approved, he reiterated, CTV's current ten-member board, comprising the nine shareholders and president John Cassaday, would be reduced to nine voting members, including eight shareholders, each with an 11.1 per cent equity interest. Mid-Canada's nominee George Lund would no longer have a voting right, but he and other representatives of the Sudbury, Timmins, and North Bay affiliates would still attend meetings and participate at the board level, at the invitation of chairman Bill McGregor. Asked about the probable effect of Baton's purchases on the network, Bassett replied, "I don't believe [they] will have any negative impact. . . . Certainly Baton will not have any more control in the programming than our colleagues, Mr. Holtby, Mr. McGregor, Mr. Pouliot, or [whomever]. We have one vote, as they do."

☆

Within days Doug Bassett was singing a different tune about "Mr. Holtby." He publicly expressed concerns that WIC might be preparing to ditch CTV and forge its own network of independent stations that would compete with him and everybody else to buy Canadian broadcast rights to American programs. Bassett's fears were lent credence by the fact that in mid-July, Holtby (on behalf of WIC) had struck a deal with his former mentor, Dr. Charles Allard, to buy Allarcom Ltd., the broadcasting company he grew up in, for $157 million in cash and shares. If the deal was approved, WIC would have seven television stations: two CTV affiliates in British Columbia, one CBC affiliate there and another in Alberta, and three independents, also in Alberta. Thus, WIC would become the country's third-largest private English-language television operator, measured by viewing share, after Global and Baton.

Thirteen years earlier, Doc Allard, a former surgeon turned multi-millionaire real estate developer and corporate investor, had made the twenty-six-year-old Holtby controller of Allard's new Edmonton television station, CIVT. Holtby, a chartered accountant who looks disconcertingly like a football linebacker, enjoyed the energy of a place where all the staff were in their mid-twenties. Ten months after CITV went on the air, the station manager quit, and in a surprise move Allard promoted Holtby to fill his shoes. Holtby used to drive out to Allard's cattle ranch on weekends, so that he and Allard could walk and talk their plans.

CIVT ranked as one of the pioneers in Canadian television production. The station's first efforts were concert specials (which were successfully exported to sixty countries) and an investment in Anne Wheeler's feature film *Loyalties*. Its next big move came in 1979 when Allard and Holtby committed Allarcom money to provide financing and Edmonton production facilities to *SCTV*, a half-hour sketch series about an ersatz television network created by Toronto's Second City comedy troupe, which had aired on, but been cancelled by, Global.

Holtby and Andrew Alexander, the show's executive producer, tried to negotiate a licensing deal with the CBC, but the public network wanted them to insert another two minutes of "distinctively Canadian" material per episode. When Holtby and Alexander remarked to the writer-performer Dave Thomas that the CBC was being its usual ridiculous self, Thomas quipped, "What do you want us to do? Throw up a map of Canada and sit there wearing toques and parkas?" That's how the "Great White North" sketches originated, featuring the beer-addled, take-off-eh! characters Bob and Doug McKenzie. "Doug" was in fact christened in honour of Doug Holtby, who reacted to Thomas's suggestion with the deathless words, "Fine, as long as it doesn't cost very much, just do it."

Later, Holtby flew to Los Angeles with Alexander to pitch *SCTV* to Brandon Tartikoff at NBC, who picked up a ninety-minute version for the 1981–82 and 1982–83 seasons. "It was the first show outside of the continental U.S. to be bought by an American network," says Holtby, "and it was a great thing for Canadian culture with a small 'c.'" Along the way, it also won two Emmys, spurring the CBC to air a sixty-minute version of its own.

Holtby recalls that *SCTV* "opened doors" and was a "tremendous benefit for every producer in the country." After Allarcom invested in a new $7-million sound stage in 1987, other indigenous successes followed, such as a $2-million investment in Anne Wheeler's Genie-award-winning feature film *Bye Bye Blues*, which later attracted an audience of close to one million viewers on the CBC. This project was executive-produced by Tony Allard, one of Doc's six children, who took time off from his legal practice to become involved with the production side of the business. Once, he and Holtby flew to Vancouver for a meeting and wound up ("two friendly Alberta boys in the big city") with a cut-rate rental car. As they pulled out of the airport, Holtby spotted none other than Ray Peters, cruising along in his Mercedes convertible with the top down. Holtby, who'd met Peters through Cancom, amicably tooted the horn — but Peters, not recognizing them, "didn't even look back. [He] just raised one arm and gave us the finger!"

By 1988, when Frank Griffiths approached Holtby about coming to WIC to succeed Peters, he was ready to make a move, having begun to feel pressured by Doc Allard's son-in-law Harold Roozen, who saw himself playing a role in the family business. Upon moving into his new office at WIC's corporate headquarters in downtown Vancouver, a city where he'd lived until he was sixteen, Holtby was quick to adopt the style of a west-coast media mogul, buying a new Jaguar and a babe-olicious cigarette boat to speed around English Bay, while he waited for his wife and two daughters to join him from Edmonton.

At the beginning of the 1990s, WIC had achieved success in getting CTV to broadcast made–in–British Columbia drama series. Five years earlier, it had been a wasteland, but now, counting *Bordertown* and *Neon Rider*, Holtby conceded that the balance was 50/50 between east and west.

Holtby didn't see the same balance, though, when it came to CTV news. He was tired of information being filtered through one metropolis — of what was or wasn't nationally important being decided by editors in Toronto. He mentioned as an example the introduction of Sunday shopping in Ontario, which led *CTV National News* that night, despite the fact that it had been the norm in British Columbia for five years, and Alberta for ten.

WIC's BCTV had long fought for a national suppertime newscast that would originate in Vancouver and be anchored by Tony Parsons. In April 1990, it submitted four pilots to Tim Kotcheff, CTV's vice-president of news, and the network's board. Rumours swirled that CTV would agree to one of these proposals, perhaps splitting the anchor desk between Parsons and Lloyd Robertson, and shifting a portion of its network news production to the west coast.

Tony Parsons represented BCTV's answer to Lloyd Robertson. He'd been anchoring BCTV's suppertime newscast since 1975, a year before Robertson arrived at the network. Parsons had started off as a reporter for CFTO, working out of its old downtown bureau at the *Telegram*. Later, he was named anchor of CFTO's eleven o'clock *Night Beat News*, but in 1973, when he was refused a promotion to the six o'clock *World Beat News*, he headed west to CTV's Vancouver bureau. Ray Peters spotted him in the act of covering a dramatic hostage-taking situation at a British Columbia prison. Parsons had been working around the clock for three days, clad in jeans and denim jacket, but still managed to look charismatic and composed. "We have to have this guy," Peters told his news director, and Parsons was duly brought aboard. This was indicative of Peters's concern for BCTV's news operation. From the very beginning, he'd allocated a disproportionate amount of the station's budget to news, public affairs, and information programs, so that BCTV now had an impressive two-hour news block between 5 and 7 p.m. that was watched by one million people.

CanWest Global's Izzy Asper, another broadcaster who wrapped himself in the western flag, shared Doug Holtby's opinion of the Torontocentric national media, but his plan was to establish a national news centre in Winnipeg. This, to his mind, was vital if the eastern stranglehold was to be broken. "Watch television," he cried in 1990. "Watch how [the rest of] Canada views the west. Watch the irrelevance and the insignificance and the global colonization that is portrayed!"

To address these woes, the pyrotechnic Asper asked the CRTC to force WIC's independent Calgary and Lethbridge stations, along with Allarcom's independent Edmonton station, to affiliate with CanWest Global's five independent outlets (in Vancouver, Regina, Saskatoon, Winnipeg, and Toronto) to form a third national system. Once this bright scheme was accomplished, the stations would pool their dollars to create a "national quality news service," which might include a "national news broadcast" centred in western Canada so that the independents would have access to the same quality of news as the CBC and CTV; to acquire national rights to American entertainment programs; and to generate Canadian dramas, children's programs, documentaries, and other "under-represented sectors of the program schedule."

Thus it was Asper, the self-styled King of the Independents, and not Doug Bassett, the would-be King of CTV, who opposed WIC's purchase of Allarcom, stirring things up at the CRTC's November public hearings into that transaction. Asper began by outlining his greatest fear — that WIC would bid aggressively for the rights to American hit shows, driving up their prices and depriving him of the profit margins that cross-subsidized the few Canadian programs that appeared on his group of stations.

"Let's get our act together. This . . . country seems to have a death wish," the gravel-voiced Asper concluded. The CRTC remained unmoved and refused to interfere. If Asper wanted a third national system, one of the commissioners retorted, he should hammer out a deal, just as Doug Holtby had done.

In fact, Asper had tried to do exactly that, making an offer to buy the independent Calgary and Lethbridge stations from Maclean Hunter. So had Allarcom, but they'd both lost out to WIC. Now WIC was going to own the independent Edmonton station, too. That left Asper with a gaping hole in Alberta and doomed his long-stated ambition to own an unbroken string of stations in Canada's major urban markets. Asper was not at peace with this prospect. If there was going to be a western-based system that would challenge the dominance of eastern broadcasters, Asper wanted it to be CanWest Global, not a merged WIC and Allarcom.

After all, Asper had been talking to WIC's Frank Griffiths about merging their companies into a western powerhouse for the past eleven years, but these discussions invariably foundered on the issue of control. Asper was not an easy man to get along with. Aggressive, litigious, and relentless, he'd spent a lifetime in ferocious disputes, first as a tax lawyer, then in the political arena as leader of the Manitoba Liberal party, and finally as a private broadcaster. From a single television station based in a former Winnipeg supermarket, Asper and his fellow Winnipeggers Seymour Epstein and Paul Morton had teamed up with a future CTV shareholder (Toronto's Allan Slaight) to rescue Global Television from bankruptcy in April 1974, just three months after it went on the air. The new owners axed half the staff and replaced Global's expensive made-in-Canada programming with cheap American imports. Ontarians (the only viewers privileged to receive its signals at the time) took to calling it "The Love Boat Network." Financial calm, however, served only to exacerbate the personal conflict between Asper and Slaight, who invoked a buy-sell clause in the partnership agreement in late 1976. Within ten years, the three Winnipeggers were embroiled in a slugfest of their own, with Epstein and Morton suing Asper, and Asper filing a countersuit while accusing Morton of siphoning off Global funds to pay for his high-flying lifestyle.

During this five-year legal battle, Asper challenged the Mulroney government to keep licences for new stations in Regina and Saskatoon, had an angry falling out with his one-time CanWest partner Gerry Schwartz, and engaged in a second tortuous nine-year legal rout with Allarcom over control of CKVU Vancouver. Asper won that one.

He won the Global battle, too. A Manitoba court ordered Asper and his estranged partners to resolve their ownership deadlock by auctioning Global to the highest bidder in mid-December 1989. After an hour or so, Asper was the one left standing with a $382-million bid, paying $150 million for the equity he didn't already own.

Asper then set his sights on Calgary and Edmonton. He had no wish to venture outside large urban centres, because — as CTV had learned — extending service to remote areas was a money pit. Naturally, CTV charged Asper with wanting to skim the cream and skip the obligations. As John Cassaday had told *Maclean's* when CanWest emerged as the victor in the fight for Global, "If it's a network, let them play by network rules. Let them make the same commitment to Canadian content, to international news bureaus that we do. Let them get their signal into Split Lip, Manitoba, like we do."

Fortunately for Doug Holtby, the CRTC rejected Asper's warnings about WIC, approving the WIC-Allarcom transactions in February 1991. WIC assumed ownership of the independent Edmonton station, and Dr. Allard (along with his son Peter) joined the WIC board. But barely a year later, the doctor died of cancer, leaving an estate worth $140 million. "Doc Allard sent a plane up to Edmonton to bring me down to his place in Palm Springs," Holtby says. "That's when he told me he was ill. [He] was like a father to me; he called me his other son."

Asper, meanwhile, refused to give up on his third national system. In early 1991, Montreal's Pouliot family had been pressured by their bank to solicit bids for all or part of CFCF Inc., whose money-losing French-language Quatre Saisons network had brought the company to the brink of bankruptcy. Jean Pouliot arranged to meet with Asper in Florida in mid-March to discuss his rescue proposal, by which Asper would invest $65 million, and CFCF would become a twinstick operation, carrying both CTV's and Global's signals. (The deal fell apart in September because of an unfavourable tax ruling, and CFCF Inc. survived, after stringent cost-cutting.)

Around the same time that Asper and Pouliot were meeting in Florida, Maclean Hunter put CFCN Calgary up for sale at a price between $80 million and $100 million, a move that would take the media giant out of television altogether. Ron Osborne explained this development by noting that CTV had gone from a company where each owner had a single station, to one where two or three major players owned most of the affiliates, and that Maclean Hunter was therefore at a distinct disadvantage. CanWest Global was quick to express interest, along with Baton and Electrohome. "[Asper] was after [CFCN]," Doug Holtby says. "He was going to buy it and [then] swap it for WIC's independent Calgary station."

Holtby had ruled WIC out as a potential purchaser of CFCN, since WIC already owned the Calgary independent, and he'd just reached an agreement with Maclean Hunter to buy its independent in Hamilton. Besides, he had other duties on his plate. He had been asked the previous fall to chair CTV's new restructuring committee, in hopes of sorting out the network's ownership woes and arriving at a workable affiliation agreement. The board authorized him to appoint his own committee, but Holtby added only John Cassaday, his fellow new kid on the board. They hired Heather Reisman, a Toronto-based conflict specialist (who strangely enough was married to Izzy Asper's former partner Gerry Schwartz), but four months of regular meetings between her and CTV's eight shareholders made no headway, not even when it came to simple issues such as voting procedures. "[Reisman] had no success at all," Bill McGregor says. "[Everyone] was very polite, and she thought she was making great progress. [But] in the end — nothing." Electrohome's John Pollock agrees. "Heather is a capable girl," he says, "but she found us more than daunting." Or as Doug Bassett put it, "There was no will to go forward."

15

The Gang of Five
versus Doug Bassett — 1991–92

For the next two years, the press covered every twist and turn in the saga of the warring network owners. In the memorable words of Peter Kent, the future Global news anchor, "CTV is a cat-fighting co-op, the whipping boy of all the member groups that own it. CTV is like the former Yugoslavia." In fact, CTV was more like Canada itself, a fragile federation that would be lucky to survive its constitutional crisis and the threat of Baton's separation.

At an April 1991 dinner atop Toronto's Sutton Place Hotel, Baton's Doug Bassett made a buyout proposal to the seven other shareholders, but was rebuffed. His recollection is that he'd been asked to make the proposal, and that the other directors liked it, although some of them had said, "We want more money."

Bassett said that CHUM's Fred Sherratt had responded, "Well, we're on the right track now. We're just bickering about the price." CHUM usually supported Baton's attempts to control the network, but this was an especially inauspicious moment. WIC, Electrohome, and Moffat Communications wanted to remain as shareholders; CFCF Inc. and Maclean Hunter had both put their affiliates up for sale; and Newfoundland Broadcasting didn't really enter into the equation, since it had no financing responsibilities.

Bassett claimed that he'd told the group, "Look, it doesn't have to be Baton [that owns CTV]. [If] Mr. Pouliot or Mr. Moffat or anybody else [wants to buy it], give me the same deal as [I'm] giving you and we'll just be affiliates." He recalled that the other owners had responded, "No, we don't want to do that."

WIC's Doug Holtby, for one, hadn't been interested. "I don't know who invited Mr. Bassett to make his proposal," he said, "and I don't know of anybody who liked [it]."

"It wasn't a serious proposal, although Bassett thought it was," says Electrohome's Bill McGregor, who describes Baton's CEO as a "hail-fellow-well-met kind of guy," someone who shakes hands and pats people on the back but doesn't get around to talking to them. As for Fred Sherratt, he remembers the offer as being more like something that came off the back of a cigarette package. He thinks that Bassett was just testing the waters by "blue-skying" a vague scheme, even though Joe Garwood ran through some numbers after Bassett made his pitch.

Holtby agrees. "It was a non-offer," he says. "They'd pay up all the debt and take over CTV." (Holtby also says that WIC would have been willing to do the same, but it was unlikely that anyone would have let them.)

Be that as it may, Bassett was getting tired of trying but failing to arrive at some sort of clear-cut resolution. "[CTV's owners] have spent considerable time and effort over the last five years to develop a share-holders' agreement," he said. "This has proved to be a frustrating experience. The latest effort chaired by Mr. Holtby ended without reso-lution. As he reported . . . , 'I join others who have failed to resolve these network disputes.'"

Why was Bassett so upset? Perhaps because Baton's seven CTV affili-ates gave up advertising revenue on forty hours of network sales time each week for which Baton received no compensation. Up until the late 1980s, CTV had been making money, so much of this revenue had made its way back to Baton at year's end in the form of profit sharing. Now that CTV was in the red, Baton got zip for broadcasting programs (both Canadian and American) that it could have either produced or bought for itself. "We give [CTV] forty hours a week and get very little in return [except] credibility, because Lloyd Robertson and Sandie Rinaldo are on our [stations]," Bassett complained.

Even more galling was the fact that Baton's obligation to underwrite CTV, should the Canadian Imperial Bank of Commerce ever call the network's note, was three times its equity interest. But this responsibility wasn't reflected in Baton's voting power; it still had exactly the same say as Newfoundland Broadcasting. No wonder that Bassett despaired of ever finding a solution to the problem and vowed that, in any case, he'd made his final offer to buy CTV.

All in all, 1991 was not a banner year for Canadian broadcasters. CTV laid off twenty-three people that April and closed its news bureaus in Newfoundland and Manitoba as it headed for its second consecutive annual loss (a punishing $2.7 million in 1990–91). The following month, it informed the CRTC that it could not provide a new shareholders' agreement for consideration at its upcoming licence renewal hearings because it faced a number of uncertainties, including the possible sales of the Montreal and Calgary affiliates and (in a worst-case scenario) the possibility of Baton's departure. It also requested a measure of relief from the extra Cancon spending quotas imposed in 1987.

That May, a federal task force, co-chaired by Ray Peters, recommended that this request be granted, since CTV's conditions of licence were "not realistically achievable in today's economy." It also suggested a three-year moratorium on new broadcast and cable licences in order to preserve existing networks and stations.

CTV's president, John Cassaday, put on a happy face for the media buyers at the network's June preview of its fall schedule, held that year in a giant tent amid the neo-Gothic colleges of the University of Toronto. Jugglers, a Dixieland band, and the presence of numerous on-air personalities helped to camouflage the network's woes. New to CTV's schedule from Hollywood was the Tim Allen vehicle, *Home Improvement*, a perfect fit for middle Canada's network of choice. There was also a new Canadian-but-could-be-anyplace series called *Counterstrike*, a co-venture among CTV and Alliance Entertainment (a division of Alliance Communications), a French broadcaster and production company, and the USA Network. It starred Christopher Plummer as the wealthy benefactor of an elite anti-terrorist squad based in Paris. *Neon Rider* and *E.N.G.* would return, the latter with a little added sex and sizzle, since Cassaday had commissioned audience surveys to find out what kind of story lines appealed to viewers. *Bordertown* and *Katts and Dog* might return midway through the season, but *My Secret Identity* was gone, the victim of insufficient American syndication.

CTV hadn't scheduled enough Cancon drama to meet its raised quota of four hours a week in 1991–92, of which three and a half hours were supposed to be aired in peak viewing time. The reason was simple: it couldn't afford to do so. In its submission to the CRTC, the network had estimated that the cost (in lost ad revenue) of running only three hours a week had climbed to more than $15 million, and it flatly refused to lose even more.

☆

In early June, Doug Bassett reported the first quarterly loss in Baton's history. Meanwhile, he'd been lobbying Brian Mulroney for a patronage appointment as High Commissioner to the United Kingdom and Northern Ireland, but when Mulroney called from his porch at Harrington Lake in July, it was too late. "I offered [Douglas] a major diplomatic post," Mulroney recalls. "He turned it down. [It] would have been the culmination of his long interest in politics; he'd have been operating at a very high level. [But at that time,] he was very much involved in putting together acquisitions. Baton was working on a strategy for CTV . . . , so he said he couldn't accept it."

Indeed, Bassett couldn't take the London posting for several reasons. First was his health. He'd recently undergone surgery to remove cancerous skin cells, afflicted by the same disease that had claimed the life of his brother Johnny F.

Second was Baton's health. Its shares had stalled in the $5 to $9 range and would remain there for the next five years. What had once been a $200-million-plus investment for the Eaton family fell to the $70 million to $125 million range. Doug Bassett was nothing if not the Eatons' loyal servant. After all, he'd been working for them his whole life, and he'd have to work even harder to restore the value of their shares.

Third was the fact that Fred Eaton had recently made it clear that *he* wanted to be appointed High Commissioner, and it was he who moved on that fall, having resigned from all his executive positions and directorships, as well as every club that didn't admit women. ("[Fred] did an excellent job," Mulroney recalls. "I got that feedback from Her Majesty Queen Elizabeth and Margaret Thatcher. They were both taken with him, especially Her Majesty. Fred and [his wife] Nicky were her favourites.")

With Fred representing Canada abroad, his brother George was left as the only Eaton on Baton's board. By then, he'd accumulated his own set of toys, as well as an array of corporate titles. Fred had his cut-stone mansion in Forest Hill, his baronial farm in Caledon, his cottage in Georgian Bay, the obligatory pair of Rolls-Royces, and his yacht *Brave Wolfe*, but George wasn't exactly deprived, having built a 24,600-square-foot, $7-million, retreat (also in Caledon) that was half again as large as his Forest Hill home.

Like his older brother, George was keen to see Baton control CTV and approved Doug Bassett and Joe Garwood's pursuit of CFCN Calgary, until Maclean Hunter took it off the market after failing to receive a satisfactory bid.

Doug Bassett publicly expressed concern but did not cry foul to the CRTC when WIC expanded its empire in western Canada. It was a different matter, though, when WIC moved into Baton's backyard, making a deal to purchase CHCH, the independent Hamilton station. In a letter to the commission, he claimed that CTV's "viability" would be threatened if WIC controlled the Vancouver and Victoria affiliates, along with independent stations in Calgary, Lethbridge, Edmonton, and (if CHCH were sold) Hamilton-Toronto. If the latter deal went through, two-thirds of WIC's holdings would be in the independent sector.

Doug Holtby deplored Baton's hypocrisy. "It is not our intention to hurt CTV," he said. "[I] take exception to Baton suggesting that when we entered into an agreement to buy an independent in Edmonton, it was somehow a local issue, [but now], when we enter into a transaction to buy a station in the Toronto area, it is a CTV issue. That isn't the way this world works. . . . The world does not begin and end in Toronto."

At public hearings on July 10, Bassett said that Baton was different from WIC because, "when the opportunity arises, we buy television stations within the framework of CTV." He went on to explain that WIC, as part and parcel of snapping up independents wherever it could, "would be establishing the foundation of a national service directly competitive with CTV, [while maintaining an equity interest in the network]. It is more than reasonable to assume that the resulting conflicts cannot be worked out."

Baton and CanWest Global both expressed the fear that WIC would begin competing for the national rights to American shows, escalating the competition among Canadian buyers and jacking up prices. Holtby replied that, on the contrary, WIC would maintain the Hamilton station's newly adopted position of not doing so — except to protect the rights it already held against bids from other Canadian buyers.

CanWest Global then asked the CRTC to instruct WIC not to compete for national rights under any circumstances, but the commission refused to interfere in the marketplace. Bassett said that Baton would drop its opposition if WIC gave up its ownership stake in CTV, and its Vancouver and Victoria stations became mere affiliates, but Holtby wasn't interested. He stated that WIC (in slightly different guise) had been an original founder of CTV, that it wanted to remain in CTV, and that it had no intention of forming a competing network.

Fed up with CTV's never-ending ownership squabbles, the CRTC decided to see if it could move some of the pieces around. In mid-October, it approved WIC's purchase of CHCH Hamilton, but on the condition that WIC sell either CHAN Vancouver or CHEK Victoria. In all likelihood, Baton would be the buyer, making it CTV's dominant owner. WIC would then disaffiliate its sole remaining CTV station, form its own independent network, and do business as it pleased. But no such luck. "I find it impossible to believe we would comply," said Frank Griffiths, then recovering from a recent heart attack at his new waterfront home in West Vancouver. "It's nonsense." He had a point. Why should WIC give up a CTV affiliate that was contributing millions of dollars to its bottom line, in order to take over CHCH, an independent basket case that nobody else wanted? And so WIC surprised the commission by appealing its decision.

Meanwhile, John Cassaday, having struck out with Heather Reisman, had another trick up his sleeve. He hired Roger Fisher, a Harvard law professor and internationally renowned conflict resolution specialist, to see whether he could bring peace to the CTV board. Fisher had helped draft the Israel-Egypt Camp David Agreements and had successfully mediated between North and South Korea, between the African National Congress and the South African government, and between the various ethnic factions in the former Soviet Union. Surely he could persuade CTV's shareholders to find common ground.

The owners' first meeting with Fisher, which took place over the course of a three-day weekend in November 1991 at the Briars resort north of Toronto, went on late into the night. Fisher had told Doug Holtby to bring a supply of baseball hats to the retreat. There were four hats for each owner, bearing the titles "Director," "Shareholder," "Affiliate," and "Competitor." The idea was that each participant could put on whichever hat best signified his conflict of interest when he was speaking.

Holtby describes this weekend as "a hell of a lot of fun, a real ball." Others were not so enthusiastic; Doug Bassett still grouses about "that bloody hotel." "There were a lot of egos in the room," Gary Maavara says. "But whenever someone started to be a big man, Fisher would excuse himself and go off and call the president of the United States or something. You weren't going to one-up Roger Fisher."

After two more meetings in Montreal and Vancouver, the three-month process was set to culminate in a shareholders' auction, scheduled for the end of January 1992, in the ballroom of Toronto's Sutton Place Hotel. This would determine how much money, if any, each shareholder wished to kick in to the network and how many votes it would get in return, thereby putting an end to the debilitating one-owner, one-vote rule. The only non-participant was Doug Bassett, who stuck to his mantra that CTV needed a single controlling shareholder, preferably Baton.

Cassaday's team attempted to alleviate the tension at this climactic, five-hour bidding session with a burst of mixed sports imagery. First they erected a huge poster, reading "If we build it [presumably the new, improved network] they will come." Next, they left a Team Canada hockey sweater, along with yet another baseball cap emblazoned with the words "CTV Ownership Championships," on each of the eight share-owners' chairs. Roger Fisher donned a referee's uniform, and each participant received a baseball autographed by all his colleagues. Fred Sherratt still has his in his office.

After three rounds of blind ballots, WIC, CFCF, and Maclean Hunter had bid $6 million each for a 30 per cent ownership stake. Electrohome and Moffat were in for $1 million each, or 5 per cent, making a total investment on everyone's part of $20 million. These shareholders were immediately dubbed the Gang of Five. Baton, CHUM, and Newfoundland Broadcasting were out as owners, but opted to remain as network affiliates.

"Don't cry for Douglas Bassett, and don't cry for Baton," Bassett told the *Globe and Mail*, pointing out that the Gang of Five would have to come up with a package that was acceptable to Baton and its eleven full or supplementary affiliates.

Within weeks, Maclean Hunter's Ron Osborne was trying to do exactly that. He called on Bassett, suggesting that the ownership structure could be rejigged to include Baton as a 20 or 25 per cent shareholder, but Bassett wasn't going to play unless he could have most of the marbles. Nor was he swayed in this resolve when John Cassaday sent him a bumper sticker from CFCF's president, Adrien Pouliot (which reportedly read "My CTV Includes Baton" — a play on "My Canada Includes Quebec"), and a videotape on which various CTV personalities such as Lloyd Robertson urged him to reconsider his position. Instead, in March, Baton tabled an affiliation proposal of its own, but there was no face-to-face meeting between Bassett and Cassaday, whose relationship was strained by Doug's conviction that Cassaday was no longer on his side.

☆

Almost as soon as Baton was out as a CTV owner, it was back in, but not before one or two deals took place. Given the importance of the Toronto Blue Jays regular-season games to Baton, Bassett was upset that CTV hadn't concluded an agreement with the baseball club. (It did, however, retain broadcast rights to the league championships and the World Series.) With the season opener fast approaching, the Blue Jays terminated negotiations with CTV and gave the CBC three days in which to acquire the rights to sixty games, on the same terms that had been offered to CTV. Baton immediately arranged with Ivan Fecan, the head of the CBC's English-language network, to get these rights for five years at a cost of $60 million. Bassett offered twenty games to the CBC and thirty-five games to CTV at $200,000 each, but CTV's western affiliates refused to participate, in part because the time-zone difference meant that the showings typically interrupted their local supperhour newscasts. Bassett therefore undertook to air these games on his year-old Ontario Television Network (ONT), which comprised Baton's seven Ontario CTV affiliates and Electrohome's CKCO Kitchener. Baton boasted its biggest audience ever that September when almost seven million viewers watched the Toronto Blue Jays win the World Series on Baton's CTV affiliates. They lucked out with back-to-back World Series in 1992 and 1993, Bassett remembers.

Baton and CTV officials finally met face to face on March 17, 1992, at Baton's downtown Toronto head office, to discuss airtime payments for Baton's eleven affiliated stations. Three different market assessments, obtained independently by CTV, had placed a value on Baton's airtime of between $63 and $82.5 million a year, well beyond the network's means. Baton is said to have asked for $16 million a year, but even that was unacceptable to the network, which offered a scant $4 million.

Another three-hour meeting on April 9 also failed to reach a settlement with Baton, despite the presence by phone of Roger Fisher. This effectively killed the new shareholders' arrangement, and network ownership reverted to the original eight owners, not the Gang of Five. Shortly thereafter, Bassett called Ron Osborne, telling him that Baton wanted back in.

The official story was that Bassett had been biding his time, waiting for the Gang of Five to see the light and realize that their arrangement had been premature, because it hadn't thrashed out the terms of the affiliation agreement. Another explanation was that he'd been amazed that the Gang of Five would dare to continue without him. Misled by the bumper stickers and videocassettes, he'd simply overestimated Baton's importance to the network.

Sent back to square one, a disappointed John Cassaday said he could live with the cooperative in the short term, as long as the network got the $20 million in capital that had been pledged at the auction, so as to start paying off its long-term $40-million debt. Cassaday wasn't insisting on cash in the bag. The $20 million could be in the form of shareholder loans, or a new class of preferred or common shares, he said. Baton balked at picking up 35 per cent of the network's debt (as it would have been expected to do, under the old formula), arguing instead that it should be responsible for only 12.5 per cent, its voting stake. (CHUM and Newfoundland Broadcasting still wanted nothing to do with either shares or loans.)

☆

And there the matter rested, in momentary limbo. Then, on May 5, Baton broke a cardinal network rule by competing against CTV for the Canadian broadcast rights to five American shows — *Home Improvement*, *Murphy Brown*, *Knots Landing*, *Family Matters*, and *Dinosaurs* — which it planned to air on ONT. Having protested so vigorously against WIC's expansion into the independent sector because it might drive up the bidding at the Hollywood bazaar, Baton itself had now become the fourth-largest buyer of U.S. programming, after the CBC, CTV, and Global. Baton maintained that this was a pre-emptive strike against Global, not a bid to break up CTV, and attempted to calm things down by subcontracting its rights to other CTV affiliates in non-competing regions.

"Dougie's nuts," responded one industry insider. "He's got more money than brains." Then, a week later, Bassett handed his critics more ammunition, by reaching an agreement in principle to pay $29 million for two independent stations in London and Wingham, Ontario. These were owned by Martha Blackburn, a friend of both the Bassett and Eaton families. Next, Baton kicked Electrohome's CKCO Kitchener out of ONT, announcing that the Blackburn stations would take its place. Electrohome (and everyone else) grew concerned that ONT was becoming a network to rival CTV. After all, over the next two years, it proposed to increase its common programming from ten and a half to thirty-five hours a week, almost as much as CTV's forty hours a week of network sales time. Cast loose, and facing the prospect of becoming an orphan station, CKCO therefore arranged to share programming with WIC's independent Hamilton station, CHCH, forming an association known as Market One Television. All these adventures of course resulted in a new flurry of charges and countercharges. "Baton were bullies," Doug Holtby recalls. CHUM's Fred Sherratt is more specific. He says that Joe Garwood was running ONT, and it was he who wanted "to bail out of CTV. He created more animosity than anyone else."

Doug Bassett remembers things differently. By his telling, "ONT was a marketing vehicle to compete against Global because it had all of Ontario." He reiterates that Baton had no intention of quitting CTV. "It was a strategy," he says. "We would never have left. The [CRTC] wouldn't [have] allowed it. All our licences were subject to us being affiliates of CTV. It was not in my mind. It was not in Fred [Eaton's] mind, either."

Since Baton now owned the rights to several staples of CTV's programming, the network hosted the June preview of its 1992–93 season at CFTO. John Cassaday joked with the advertisers that with so many executives present from the owner-affiliates, "we've set up a little boxing ring in the back, and they're going to duke it out for ownership of the network." CTV was back on the bandwagon of Big Events: movie premieres; mini-series such as the upcoming *Return to Lonesome Dove*; the Academy Awards, the Grammys, and the Emmys; and the Summer Olympics in Barcelona. Obviously, Cassaday did not rate Canadian drama series as Big Events. *E.N.G.* and *Counterstrike* would return to the schedule, but there was nothing new in the pipeline (although Baton would soon unleash *Forever Knight*, whose hero was a vampire-turned-cop, for late-night broadcast on the CBS network).

By June, CTV had succeeded in reaching informal one-year pacts with all of its affiliates, even those owned by Baton. Doug Holtby had suggested that, rather than trying to get a unanimous, omnibus affiliation agreement, each shareholder negotiate its own separate deal for a specific annual payment. "Splitting the affiliation and shareholder agreements was one of the ways of trying to deal with the logjam," Bill McGregor recalls. To calculate fair payment for the stations' airtime, CTV went to third parties, but in each and every case, the figure the network put forward was "far below" the value arrived at by the arbitrator. "The affiliates agreed to have 'water in their wine' because of the value of continued involvement with the network," John Cassaday said.

Even though Cassaday was predicting a $5.3-million profit for the year ending August 31, two consecutive years of red ink had saddled the network with a $5-million deficit. The shareholders agreed that no profit would be distributed to the affiliates that year — and that, the following year, at least 25 per cent of any profits would be held in reserve by CTV to reduce its debt.

Accordingly, Baton, WIC, and several other owner-affiliates insisted that CTV's total network service be reduced to forty-two and a half hours from almost seventy hours weekly. CTV would still program forty hours of network sales time, but only two and a half hours of station sales time.

The larger station groups demanded this because they wanted to acquire their own programming, rather than have the network present it to them on a plate.

"They weren't warring about ownership," Gary Maavara contends. "They were warring about time." Fred Sherratt agrees. "The stations wanted as much time as they could get," he says.

Except for the smaller and more vulnerable stations. "Randy Moffat [of CKY Winnipeg] was . . . quite concerned about the drop in station sales time product," Holtby said. "It hurt him because he was in such a competitive market." Bassett was less sympathetic. He suggested that if Moffat needed programming above and beyond the forty hours of network sales time, he ought to "go down to L.A. with Pip Wedge and John Cassaday and say, 'You have clout. [I'd] like you to buy me the Manitoba rights to whatever the program is.'"

Next, having sorted out the new affiliation agreements, CTV's shareholders tackled the shareholders' agreement. Here the issues of who owned what and how much voting power came with it were much more emotional.

After a marathon meeting in late August, the shareholders in fact signed a pact giving them proportionate representation based on revenue share — but on an expanded board. Since Baton stations generated 35 per cent of the network's revenue, it would get three votes. WIC, Electrohome, and CFCF Inc. would each get two. A week later, Bassett changed his mind, fearing that under this arrangement, the Gang of Five would ride roughshod over Baton. His alternative — which would have worked in Baton's favour — tied voting power to the capital and loans a given shareholder supplied to the network.

In late September and early October, Bassett and Holtby got together in private to try to work out a solution. They decided that if Baton or WIC remained as shareholders, they would require guaranteed compensation for their airtime, whether or not the network made a profit. Under this plan, CTV would set aside at least half its budgeted operating profit (advertising revenues minus programming and distribution costs and CRTC licence fees) each year, beginning in 1993–94, to pay its twenty-five affiliates to carry its shows. Baton, as the owner of eleven of the twenty-five affiliates, would get 35 per cent of the guaranteed payments. Payments would be adjusted upward if CTV's performance exceeded its budget, but would not drop if the targeted profit wasn't reached. As well, there'd be a new recapitalization agreement, with each shareholder investing in debentures convertible into equity in the network, for a total investment of somewhere between $15 million and $20 million. All these measures, Bassett and Holtby believed, could be put to a vote at the annual meeting in November.

"I don't see why there [couldn't] be an agreement in principle," Bassett said at the time, "because all of the affiliation agreements . . . will have been signed by then, provided that we can [get hold of Geoff] Stirling. [Then we can] deal with the shareholders' agreement and an infusion of cash into the network, so that [it] can pay its bills to the affiliates, redeem the debentures and the preferred shares, and satisfy the bank's request to put down their loan. Then we are on to business."

Baton and WIC may have temporarily reconciled because both wanted to get their respective purchases of independent Ontario television stations approved by the CRTC, but two other CTV partners viewed Baton's impending acquisition of the Blackburn stations with alarm. Electrohome warned that Baton was trying to create an Ontario mininetwork that would compete with CTV, the CBC, and Global. For its part, CFCF Inc. asked the commission to impose specific requirements on Baton's proposed takeover that would prohibit it from separating from CTV.

Bassett tried to blunt Electrohome's protest at the October public hearings. He reminded the commission that Big John had been instrumental in bringing CKCO Kitchener into the network, and that Baton had provided financial support for many of the programs that it had broadcast over the decades, spending $15 million during the past five years alone to underwrite series such as *E.N.G.*, *Katts and Dog*, and *Owl TV*.

Electrohome didn't think it had any obligation to Baton. "We don't usually intervene in these proceedings," Bill McGregor said. "However, in this case, we had no choice, notwithstanding our [long] association with Baton, . . . Douglas Bassett, and his father." (McGregor admits that Big John made it possible for CKCO to join up, but says that they'd "paid that debt many times over.")

Next, McGregor argued that Baton's purchase of rights to the Blue Jays regular-season games, and to the five American series, would harm CTV in general and CKCO in particular. He thought that ONT should apply for a network licence, since half of the English-language population resided in Ontario. If Global had done what Baton did, he suggested, Bassett would have been the first to say, "It looks like a network, walks like a network, and quacks like a network." (Bassett contented himself with muttering a string of loud obscenities during Electrohome's intervention. "I irritated him a little," McGregor says, "and I kind of enjoyed doing it.")

When it came time for Baton's ten-minute rebuttal, Bassett went on and on and on. Among other things, he argued that ONT was not a network. Asked what a network might be, he famously snapped back that it was "a group of people quarrelling."

At the forty-minute mark, Fernand Belisle asked him how much longer he was going to be. "I am sorry, Mr. Chairman. This is quite emotional," Bassett said, and continued talking until they broke for lunch. Afterwards, he filed the rest of his rebuttal into the public record.

Earlier, Belisle had been nonplussed by Bassett's efforts to convince him that CTV's civil war was over, now that Baton and WIC were on speaking terms. Belisle noted that the CRTC had been trying to get the network to sort out its ownership woes for seven years, but that "so far, it [had] had no effect."

"That's because you had to deal with my father and Ray Peters," Bassett replied. All those ancient rancours, by his telling, were now in the distant past. "I am thankful that the board of directors are working together," he said. "There is not that animosity, there is not that jealousy, there [are] not those tangles . . . , the boardroom fights and whatever that you used to hear about, which were legendary in their time."

How, then, are we supposed to view Bassett's fight with Bill McGregor? McGregor says dryly, "There were many bad guys stopping Baton [from getting what it wanted]. It wasn't just WIC."

16

The End of the Cooperative — 1993

John Cassaday had expected to uncork champagne at CTV's annual meeting in late November 1992. Seven shareholders had already pledged to sign the new long-term shareholder, affiliation, and recapitalization agreements, which were set to close on January 27 the following year. There was just one snag. Geoff Stirling and his son Scott, who owned Newfoundland Broadcasting, wanted more time to study the implications of the as-yet-unsigned pacts — for example, the fact that the one-owner, one-vote rule would no longer exist, opening the door for any single shareholder to buy control of the network.

Like the other seven parties, Newfoundland Broadcasting held 100 common and 50,000 preferred network shares — a 12.5 per cent stake. In the past, whenever an owner had bought another affiliate, the shares attached to that station had been distributed equally to all the other owners, leaving voting power unchanged. From now on, though, anyone who purchased an affiliate would gain its shares also, with a resulting increase in voting power. "That changed the landscape," Baton's controlling shareholder Fred Eaton states, "and we got control of CTV."

But not immediately. Baton would have to buy many more affiliates over the next four and a half years in order to gain control, because changes to the agreement weren't retroactive, and Baton didn't get proportional representation for its existing seven affiliates and four supplementary affiliates. John Cassaday explains, "The shareholders' agreement provided the mechanism for a controlling shareholder to emerge." The only questions were: who would that shareholder be, and when would they be in a position to assume control? Once a controlling shareholder emerged, the agreement provided for the minority shareholders to sell their shares to that shareholder.

The new arrangement also did away with veto power. Some time ago, Cassaday had asked CTV's lawyers to verify what enabled each shareholder to veto, or to prevent action being taken on, various issues that came before the board. To their surprise, they couldn't find "any clear statement of that in the existing documentation. . . . It had never been written down." The need for unanimity on financial matters had always been a mere convention.

"In the past, as a co-op, we worked on the basis that what was good for one had to be good for all," Cassaday said. "So, in effect, while it was not a formal agreement, it was certainly an informal agreement that each shareholder had the right to vote. In this new structure, which [would operate] more like a business under the Canadian Business Corporations Act, . . . no one shareholder [had] the right to scuttle anything." Instead, such an action would always require approval of the majority. This thought was doubtless on the Stirlings' minds as well.

"I felt that the old structure was in effect paralysis," Cassaday said. "[Now we] have a structure in place that is going to allow the kinds of decisions to be made, that have to be made, to ensure the company is successful. What I couldn't live with, and what [CTV] couldn't live with, was unanimity, because unanimity just meant death." In other words, CTV would be transformed at last from a cooperative into a modern company, and Bill McGregor's beloved "Magna Carta," which had stood up for twenty-seven years, was about to head for the shredder.

According to Doug Bassett, the key to hammering out a new shareholders' deal had been the new system of minimum guaranteed annual payments for each affiliate's airtime, whether or not the network made money. "As affiliates we're no longer responsible for the [network's] profits and losses," he said. "We're suppliers."

The third part of the historic accord was a commitment on the part of network shareholders to buy $2 million each of convertible debentures, to be converted into roughly two million common shares. This would take place only when they'd had the chance to examine the CRTC's decision on CTV's upcoming licence renewal and decide whether they could live with its conditions. Cassaday termed this "an act of prudence on the part of a group of investors with scarce resources." (Eventually, the Stirlings decided not to invest in the debentures, opting instead to give up their shareholder status, but to retain their station's affiliation. According to Cassaday, this stance "was respected by all the members of the CTV shareholder group, and [was] in fact a decision that other shareholders had contemplated at one point in time.")

On January 27, 1993, a jubilant John Cassaday could finally crack the champagne at a formal signing ceremony in the CTV boardroom. All was momentarily quiet on the takeover front, the CRTC having meanwhile approved of Baton's acquisition of the Blackburn stations, and of WIC's purchase of CHCH Hamilton. As the *CTV National News* cameras rolled, seven shareholders inked all three agreements, each investing in the $2 million of convertible debentures, to be converted to a 14.3 per cent equity stake. This, Cassaday noted, provided an equity base for the first time in network history. Previously, CTV had been completely financed by debt. Now, it planned to use $6 million of the $14 million to pay down the bank debt, and the rest to pay off money owed to the affiliates.

The gathering's tone was so convivial that Doug Bassett and Doug Holtby were photographed laughing together. CFCF's Adrien Pouliot reminded the press that his father had chaired CTV's first restructuring committee in 1980. It had taken thirteen years of shouting, fighting, name-calling, swearing, rejected buyout offers, tentative deals, and lots and lots of baseball hats to get to this point.

John Cassaday called the whole process an emotional ride. The key, he said, had been to focus on issues, not personalities. The accord was not a perfect solution, he admitted. "That [probably] wasn't achievable. But we [made] a tremendous breakthrough. . . . There was a deep recognition of just how difficult it was to get everybody to come together. [Now] we have an ownership structure [that] will allow the network to operate effectively, clearly defining the roles and responsibilities of affiliates and shareholders."

Even CRTC chairman Keith Spicer paid tribute to Cassaday's efforts, citing his "vision and common sense and great diplomatic skills." Lloyd Robertson agreed and indulged in a triple metaphor: "The president and the executive group at CTV often had to possess the instincts of Machiavelli and the diplomatic skills of an Averell Harriman or Lester B. Pearson."

Cassaday said that his job had been to keep "eight brightly coloured balloons [the network's shareholders] in the air at one time and in the same space. Once those balloons started drifting apart, that would be the end of CTV."

"John Cassaday saved CTV," pronounced Doug Bassett. "He worked his butt off."

But victory had come at considerable cost. Two weeks later, the network gave pink slips to twenty-five people in the second of a wave of downsizings. In all, over 100 staffers — about 25 per cent of the total workforce — lost their jobs. In other cost-cutting moves, executive salaries were frozen for two years, and the network reduced the cost of its Canadian programming by pushing for lower licence fees and selling its equity investments in several series. (For example, Baton had assumed CTV's equity investment in *E.N.G.* during its fourth season on air.) All these measures were helping the network to turn around, assisted by a rising audience share. CTV captured 18.3 per cent of all Canadian viewing, both English and French, in 1992–93, as it doubled its earnings to $10.3 million.

John Cassaday tested the new shareholders' arrangement at the directors' meeting that May. He wanted the board to authorize CTV's applications for two specialty services (transmitted by satellite and available only through cable systems) that would provide headline news and regional sports. He suspected that CTV hadn't applied for a sports specialty channel six years earlier because it couldn't get the decision out of the boardroom, thanks to the built-in vetoes of the cooperative structure. This time around, Cassaday obtained unanimous approval, except from Doug Bassett, who abstained because Baton had a competing headline-news application on the boil in partnership with the CBC.

Bill McGregor thinks he knows why Bassett was competing against the network he wanted to own. "Doug lost the game during the negotiations for a new shareholders' agreement," he said. "He came out feeling [that] he was trapped in the same old co-op, since nobody was going to sell. He turned to the specialty field to try and make his mark."

A few weeks later, Cassaday took centre stage at the June preview of CTV's 1993 fall season, held this year at Toronto's McLaughlin Planetarium, whose domed ceiling provided a suitably impressive surface on which to project excerpts from Steve Bochco's new police serial, *NYPD Blue*. This was the network's Big Event for 1993–94, and much more exciting than a fifth season of *E.N.G.*, a third season of *Counterstrike*, and the debut of *Matrix*, a made-in-Canada series that featured a Mafia hitman-turned-crimefighter played by Nick Mancuso, which had already been shown and cancelled by the USA Network.

☆

Early that September, Cassaday and Tom Peddie flew to St. John's, Newfoundland, to persuade Geoff and Scott Stirling to sign off on their long-term affiliation agreement. The elder Stirling was by now even more eccentric than he'd been in the early days, and a multimillionaire to boot. Fred Sherratt recalls that he'd made a fortune by putting "half his profits into gold bullion, which he bought at US$39 an ounce." Stirling was also hard to reach, since he spent part of the year camped out in a castle in the middle of the Arizona desert.

His member station CJON was something of an oddity, too. It functioned more like a supplementary affiliate, contributing nothing in cash to CTV, even though it leaned heavily on the network to fill its broadcast week. Over the years, it had traditionally run short, and the Stirlings resorted to bringing in massive doses of American programming via satellite. As a result, they were often reprimanded by the CRTC, since (according to Bill McGregor) "their Canadian content was quite seriously offside."

The Stirlings were therefore none too happy to see CTV's network service fall to forty-two and a half hours a week from sixty-nine, and demanded more money for airtime payments. "It was outrageous," Doug Holtby says. "They were negotiating the best deal, but it was part of the [same old] problem at CTV. You can't have one shareholder who holds up the company." In the end, the Stirlings backed off and signed the agreement, but only on the condition that the network expand its signals to Labrador for the first time.

As CTV's overall service took a dive, so too did its expenditures on Canadian programming. Blue Jays baseball and CFL football were things of the past. As a cooperative, CTV had run the Blue Jays games on Wednesday nights, during affiliate sales time, not network sales time. Now, "we felt no inclination to go out and acquire programming to simply spend an additional $15.6 million," John Cassaday said. Nor had the network bid yet for the rights to the 1996 Summer Olympics in Atlanta or the 1998 Winter Olympics in Nagano, Japan.

"They are not built into our plan," Tom Peddie said, adding that the baseball playoffs, the Canadian Open golf tournament, and the figure skating championships were. He went on, "We have . . . an agreement with our affiliates to gain access to [their] airtime to present [these] programs." In a letter to the CRTC in May 1993, which he hoped would calm the waters at the upcoming licence renewal hearings, Cassaday explained why ceasing to carry the regular-season Blue Jays and CFL games had reduced CTV's expected outlay on Canadian programming by 53 per cent.

When it came time for the next Great Cancon Battle at the end of September 1993, John Cassaday's pitch was simple and direct, but hard for the CRTC to swallow: a seven-year licence with drastically reduced commitments to Canadian programming.

Cassaday began with a rhetorical question. "Have we lived up to the conditions of licence which we accepted in 1987?" he asked. "The answer [is] 'Yes.' We spent more than $400 million on Canadian pro gramming. It was a quantum leap forward, shock therapy, if you will — a commitment of courageous proportion, but we survived."

CTV had indeed spent $403 million on Canadian programs over the course of its previous five-year licence, but what about the additional spending on Canadian drama that the CRTC had ordered in the final two years of that period? The network had clearly failed to comply in 1991–92. It was supposed to schedule three and a half hours (of its total four and a half hours a week) of Canadian drama series in peak viewing hours. In fact, it had broadcast only three one-hour drama series (*E.N.G.*, *Neon Rider*, and *Counterstrike*) in this time period, amounting to a half-hour shortfall. In 1992–93 and 1993–94, it once again fell well below its commitment. Even worse, it proposed to be out of compliance in the future.

"We are prepared to commit to three hours [a week] of prime-time Canadian drama," Cassaday told the commission. This cut no ice with Gail Scott, a former host of *Canada AM* who'd come to roost on the commission. She rebuked Cassaday for committing to fewer Canadian programs in the year 2000 than it had aired in 1991. "I don't see any quantum leap forward," she said.

Cassaday replied that, even with its current three hours a week of Canadian drama series, CTV was doing as well as or better than its competitors. The CBC's English-language service, which Cassaday said he envied because of its "government appropriation," was producing only half an hour more. He added that Global, whose projected airtime revenue was $151 million in 1992–93, compared to CTV's $146 million, was scheduling three hours a week as well, but pointed out that Global had twenty-eight hours a week of prime time to program. CTV had twelve. Indeed, Cassaday would complain that being a network was a "drag on CTV's earnings potential," putting it at a disadvantage vis à vis Global, which could program significantly more low-cost, big-audience American hits and spend only 20 per cent of its revenue on Canadian programming, compared to CTV's 40 per cent.

Nor did Global have a national mandate for news and public affairs. "If you were to add the popular and expensive-to-produce *W5* to the three hours of drama that we are committed to, you would have four hours of premium-quality Canadian programming" in CTV's twelve prime-time network hours, Cassaday argued. "That is one-third of our total time." Another third was taken up by American series, and the final third by movies and specials, of which — by Cassaday's telling — at least thirty hours would be Canadian in the 1993–94 season. By combining all these elements, he contended that CTV had fulfilled "the magical fourth hour" in prime time.

These calculations failed to convince Gail Scott. "You're asking the commission to put Canadian entertainment in a ten-year freeze," she said.

Cassaday replied by quoting the balance sheet. To replace a prime-time American program with an hour of Canadian drama would result in "an approximately $5-million reduction in the network's profitability," he said. "And quite frankly, Commissioner Scott, that is a $5 million reduction that we just do not have." Later, Cassaday would add that if CTV had had "two years of lead time, we would have cancelled *E.N.G.* and replaced it with an hour and a half of less expensive programming. Unfortunately, that didn't seem like the right thing to do."

No kidding. But Cassaday had the temerity to keep harping on *E.N.G.*, the winner of more Gemini awards over its five-year run than any other Canadian series. Not only was it too expensive to make, it didn't draw big enough audiences in Cassaday's world. "We know that we can get an audience of about 1.2 million each week, if we have a program of the quality of *E.N.G.*," he said. "That is not enough. We need to be at the 1.5 [or] 1.6 million level to generate an acceptable return. So we know that doing as good as *E.N.G.* is not good enough." This despite *E.N.G.*'s proven success in holding its own against *Cheers* and *Seinfeld* in a hotly contested time slot.

The trouble was that *E.N.G.* did not square with Cassaday's concept of Big Events programming. New series and one-shot wonders generated cover stories in television guides. "We see Big Events as the differentiating factor," Cassaday said. "Big Events is not just sports. Big Events [are] mini-series like *Young Catherine* or *The French Revolution*. Big Events are the Canadian Country Music Awards or the Academy Awards. These are the programs that have the capability of attracting huge audiences . . . in excess of two million viewers." Cassaday's aim was that CTV would be known and seen as "the home of the Big Event." All else was secondary and to a degree expendable.

Gary Maavara, the network's vice-president of sports, agreed. He said that he had tried to focus *CTV Sports Presents* into a "Big Event live format." Skating, for example, featured three Big Events a year — the Canadian Championships, Sunlife Skate Canada, and the Durasoft Challenge. Other Big Events included the two Canadian Open tennis championships, the Canadian Open in golf, and the Big Event of the Year, the Winter Olympics in Lillehammer.

News also involved Big Events, such as the Meech Lake Accord, the nationwide referendum on the Charlottetown Accord, and the Gulf War. "As I look to the future, I see a CTV that has clearly branded itself," Cassaday said. "And while it still enjoys the benefit of having Lloyd Robertson as the cornerstone of its franchise, it will be recognized for its other personalities, and for its populist or story-telling approach."

Cassaday saw this approach as the real difference between CTV and the CBC. "We are much more 'Main Street' Canada," he said, "as opposed to 'university halls.' . . . We like to think that we can touch people with our storytelling. We are not trying to educate them."

Nonetheless, Cassaday emphasized, CTV's first commitment was to its news and public affairs service. "Whether you are in a big market like Toronto or a small market like Saskatoon . . . , you are going to have access to at least forty hours of consistently high-quality programming," he said. "You are going to have Lloyd Robertson at eleven every night; you are going to have . . . *W5* every Thursday night at ten. . . . *Canada AM* is another classic example . . . a cohesive force that brings Canadians together from coast to coast."

All that was well and good — but in keeping with what Cassaday called the "Let's Make a Deal" atmosphere of the public hearings (and the CRTC's ongoing "preoccupation" with Canadian drama), he was pre-pared to make an offer. Although CTV wouldn't commit to more than three hours a week of Canadian drama series over the course of its new licence, it was willing to come up with thirty hours a year of Canadian movies, mini-series, and limited series, five hours more than agreed to under its 1991–92 licence condition, because, he said, they were making money on Canadian movies. That would bring the network's total commitment to Canadian drama up to a weekly average of three hours and thirty-five minutes, only twenty minutes a week shy of the quota demanded under the terms of its current licence.

The CRTC was indeed prepared to make a deal — but not to give up on its time-honoured fixation. Cassaday's rants about the high cost of indigenous dramatic programming set alarm bells ringing, so the commission took steps to safeguard the future of quality Canadian-drama series such as *E.N.G.* In early February of 1994, it renewed CTV's network licence for five years, not the seven that Cassaday had requested.

CTV had proposed spending $15.2 million on Canadian dramatic programming in 1994–95, one-quarter less than it had spent in 1991–92. "[That] is one heck of a lot of money," John Cassaday had said at the hearing. "My math is not too good, but over seven years that is close to $80 or $90 million." (He was correct in describing himself as mathematically challenged; the total was in fact $105 million.)

The network's attempt to slice the licence fees it paid to independent producers, its decision to no longer make equity investments in independently produced programs, and its reduced inventories of Canadian feature films all conspired to result in reduced expenditures on entertainment programming. In defence of these measures, both Cassaday and Tom Peddie had used the example of the silicon chip. "One chip of memory ten years ago would have cost a million dollars," Peddie said. "Today it is ten bucks. That is 100,000 times cheaper, [but] with a better quality than you had [before]. All we are saying is that [it] is possible to do more quality with less."

Concerned by this and other analogies, the CRTC made it a condition of the network's licence that CTV spend $18 million (about $3 million more than it had proposed) on Canadian dramatic programming in 1994–95, and provided a formula to calculate the expenditures for the remaining four years of the licence term. In other areas, it proved more flexible. It accepted CTV's commitment to broadcast three hours a week of regularly scheduled Canadian-drama programming, but only for the first three years. In the final two years, this total would have to rise to three and a half hours weekly. These programs could be broadcast at any time between 8 and 11 p.m. on weeknights and between 7 and 11 p.m. on weekends, so that CTV could schedule a family drama series in the early evening on Sundays and have that count towards its Cancon quota.

Perhaps because the network had bragged about making money on its Canadian movies, mini-series, and limited series, the commission also stipulated that CTV air a minimum of forty-eight hours a year of these, eighteen hours a year more than had been proposed.

In sum, then, an abbreviated licence with tougher conditions wasn't what Cassaday had bargained for. His next challenge was to expand CTV into the headline news and regional sports specialty markets. Team CTV was still high from the Winter Olympics in Lillehammer, where 120 network personnel were on the ground to cover 150 hours of the Big Event of the Year, supplying a feed to countries such as New Zealand, Australia, Indonesia, and Iran. On the final morning of the games, CTV had, at its peak, a Canadian audience in excess of 5.5 million viewers.

Cassaday launched the headline news application in February 1994 with a mock warning to the commission: "[Eric] Malling advised me . . . that if we don't get the licence he is going to do an expose [of] the CRTC on *W5*." Keith Spicer remarked that he'd been "looking for somebody with integrity" to do exactly that. These pleasantries over with, Cassaday then boasted a little about Lillehammer, which provided an even better segue into CTV's application for a regional sports specialty licence.

Unfortunately for Cassaday, the CRTC wanted to know exactly who was in favour of the applications. He had called the board's vote unanimous, so the commissioners were displeased to learn that Doug Bassett had abstained, looking towards a news service of his own. This struck them as both suspicious and familiar. Despite the hoopla surrounding the new accord, it looked as if nothing much had changed — that, once again, CTV was dumping its internal problems on the commission's plate. Finally, the CRTC decided that CTV's owners weren't to be trusted, and neither specialty-service application was approved. "At this stage," says Fred Sherratt, the CRTC "wasn't going to give CTV a licence for anything."

Three

The Takeover

17

John Cassaday
versus Ivan Fecan — 1993–96

Doug Bassett's search for his own successor began in earnest when he phoned Ivan Fecan at eight-thirty in the morning on November 19, 1993, the day after Fecan announced his resignation as head of the CBC's English-language television network after six and a half years in the programming hot seat. By rising early, Bassett beat out WIC, CanWest Global, and several international broadcasters and studios to make the first offer to the forty-year-old Fecan. Three weeks later, Fecan agreed to switch channels to the Baton team and develop a new programming strategy for its station group. This was an obvious hole at Baton, its chairman Allan Beattie recalls. "We didn't have anyone with that kind of experience." Fecan's return to the private sector set the stage for a battle between him and CTV's forty-year-old president John Cassaday for the top job at what would become Baton/CTV.

About two years earlier, Doug and Susan Bassett had been introduced to Fecan and his wife, Sandra Faire, by the owner of Toronto's Paisley Shop antique store. "God, darling, he loves old English furniture just like we do," Bassett told Susan as they walked to their car. "He can't be all bad." (Fecan says that old English furniture was his WASP wife's interest. For him, it became an acquired taste, although the couple couldn't afford it when he was with the CBC.)

The two men talked again a few months later, when CTV decided not to pick up the broadcast rights to the Toronto Blue Jays games, and CBC received an exclusive three-day negotiation period. This was "a perfect example of the tension between CTV and Baton," Fecan explains. "It was the right decision for [the network], but not for [its largest affiliate]."

Bassett called Fecan, who asked him if he wanted the rights. "I sure do," Bassett replied. "Will you give me twenty-six games a year for Friday nights?" Fecan asked. "Yes, I will," Bassett said. "I won't exercise the option, then," Fecan responded.

That was the sum of their negotiations and the beginning of a beautiful friendship. "People can't believe Ivan would trust me like that," Bassett says. "I guess he'd heard I was a decent guy and that my word is my bond."

Fred Eaton, who would step down as High Commissioner to the United Kingdom and Northern Ireland in July 1994 and be re-appointed to the Baton board later that year, adds that, although "I didn't know Ivan then, I understand he was suitably impressed by Douglas, because [Douglas] could act very quickly."

"Do you know what I like about Douglas?" Fecan asked Rod McQueen in the *Financial Post*. "He's got the biggest balls of any broadcaster in Canada."

Bassett got to know Fecan better when he invited him and his wife to Baton's corporate box at SkyDome to watch the Jays. This was when Bassett introduced Fecan to George Eaton, who was devoting more of his time to the family's broadcasting interests and less to their department store chain.

"I kept asking Ivan to come work with me," Bassett says. Meanwhile, he kept telling George that "this guy Fecan is a real shooter." Finally, Bassett convinced Fecan to switch back to private broadcasting and talked the Eatons into coming up with a plum offer that included generous stock options.

They did the deal at George Eaton's 16,000-square-foot home on Dunvegan Road in Forest Hill, the one with the grand ballroom, hidden movie screen, fitness room, wine cellars, and top-floor apartments for the household staff. Bassett asked Fecan to join Baton as a senior group vice-president of broadcasting and a member of the Office of the President. He suggested that if all went well, Fecan would be chief executive officer someday and sweetened the package with a red Mercedes-Benz as a signing bonus. "Doug is a great closer," Fecan says. "He has a wonderful sense of the grand gesture." Fecan doesn't remember Bassett making any "firm promise" that Fecan would succeed him, though. "Doug was looking at other people as well," he says. "I still had to prove myself."

Ivan Fecan didn't have the privileged upbringing of a Doug Bassett or a George Eaton. His Russian Orthodox mother had fled the Soviet Union and ended up in Canada, where she married but soon divorced. Although trained as a doctor, she learned that her qualifications weren't recognized in her new home and had to resort to unskilled employment in a hospital in order to raise her only child — who, until the age of four, spoke only Russian and Ukrainian. They lived with Ivan's grandmother in a small house on the cusp of Toronto's Little Italy and Kensington Market neighbourhoods. Fecan went to public schools, not the all-male Upper Canada College, and learned from his mother's example that women were just as capable as men. Later, he married a strong, independent woman (the variety and film producer Sandra Faire, whom he met at the CBC) and was noted for welcoming female executives to his team.

Fecan's first glimpse of the glamorous world of the Bassetts occurred in high school, when he was a student representative for the "After Four" section of the *Telegram*. "Big John and Johnny F. were there," he says. "It was so exciting; it felt like the centre of everything."

In the early 1970s, Fecan studied fine arts at York University, dropping out before he got his degree to begin his meteoric rise through the Canadian broadcasting industry, from CBC Radio to CITY to CBC Toronto to head of variety programming at the public network by the age of thirty. Fecan was the corporation's youngest mid-level executive and set himself further apart with his elegantly long hair, a vintage Mercedes, a beautiful, working wife, and a renovated house in Cabbagetown.

Early on in his fifteen months in the variety department, Fecan signed Anne Murray to a deal involving a number of specials. Then, in 1985, while in Los Angeles, he was introduced to NBC's chairman and CEO Grant Tinker through Murray's American manager. Tinker suggested that Fecan meet with his own programming whiz, the thirty-five-year-old Brandon Tartikoff, at NBC's Burbank offices. Tartikoff, the youngest entertainment president in network history (he'd been appointed in 1980 at age thirty), would lead his team to their first-ever prime-time victory in 1985–86 — a remarkable turnaround, since three years earlier, NBC had been in the cellar. It would continue to dominate the ratings for the next five seasons in a row, with a powerhouse line-up of half-hour sitcoms (*The Cosby Show*, *Family Ties*, and *Cheers*) that marked the beginning of

NBC's "Must-See TV" on Thursday nights, as well as one-hour drama series such as *Hill Street Blues*, *St. Elsewhere*, and *Miami Vice*.

The two men spent several hours arguing about the theory and practice of television. Then Tartikoff asked Fecan to critique the pilot for a sketch variety show. Fecan screened the tape in the office of Tartikoff's deputy, Warren Littlefield, which annoyed Littlefield, who walked in and demanded, "Who the hell are you?" When it came time for Fecan's verdict, he told Tartikoff that the project was an "unmitigated piece of drek." Tartikoff told Fecan to get out of his office, because he'd just ordered six episodes. Besides, the series was produced by his best friend, Michael Nesmith, a former member of The Monkees.

The sketch variety show bombed. Three months later, back in Toronto, Fecan got a call at home. "It's Brandon," said Tartikoff. "Okay, you win. Do you wanna work here?" It was an offer Fecan couldn't refuse. And so, in mid-1985, at age thirty-one, he headed for Burbank, where all the television executives seemed young. "I went from being a baby at CBC to being the new boy but an old boy at NBC," Fecan laughs. "I had no idea that [a] four-and-a-half-hour flight would age me that much."

Tartikoff used Fecan to run interference between the network and independent late-night comedy and variety producers who either weren't on speaking terms with NBC's executives or were taking up too much of their time. Among other duties, Fecan shuttled back and forth to New York, trying to facilitate his fellow Canadian Lorne Michaels's return to *Saturday Night Live*, where Dick Ebersol, the interim producer (who'd attended Yale with Tartikoff), had his own cadre of loyalists.

Fecan also spent several miserable months in Philadelphia, trying to ignore the high-decibel rantings of Jay Leno's manager, Helen Kushnick, so that the network could develop comedy specials featuring the future late-night star. Only one made it to air and promptly bombed. After more than a year of commuting to these hand-holding assignments with some of the biggest egos in American television, one pleasant month of shepherding the production of two in-house movies-of-the-week in Vancouver, and some frustrating months of trying to develop in-house series at the network's NBC Productions, Fecan was ready to come back to Canada, where his wife had remained as a CBC variety producer. "Air Canada got very wealthy off of us," Sandra Faire recalls. Once her husband was no longer in power at the corporation, project opportunities started pouring in, and Faire "foolishly took every one that came along." That changed, though, with Fecan's return in mid-1987 as director of programming for the CBC's English-language network.

"Everybody in Canada thinks they could run the CBC," Fecan acknowledges. "I had a big mouth and a lot of opinions." He also had a mandate. In 1986, one hundred of the public broadcaster's best and brightest minds had developed a plan to Canadianize the English-language network's prime-time schedule. (The CBC defines prime time as 7 to 11 p.m.). The goal was to raise Canadian content from just over 75 per cent to 95 per cent by the early 1990s — a highly ambitious undertaking, given the Mulroney government's Draconian cuts to the CBC's budget. But Fecan took control of its implementation, shaping it to his own experiences and vision.

Fecan feels that his greatest contribution was importing an American-style development system that produced and continues to produce great Canadian entertainment programming. "I'm most proud of [that]," he says. "Out of that came all the shows." Before his return, in-house CBC producers were guaranteed a certain amount of airtime and the budgets to fill it. Fecan argued that development money belonged to the schedule and forced them to compete with independent producers in a meritoc-racy, where the best project won. He thus made enemies inside the corporation — especially those unions whose contracts stipulated that half of all production had to take place in-house. Fecan didn't care. The independents had access to Telefilm's Broadcast Fund, which he viewed as a good way of stretching the public broadcaster's cut-back resources.

Out of that development system came Sullivan Entertainment's *Road to Avonlea*, Salter Street Films' *Codco*, Lorne Michaels's *Kids in the Hall*, and the CBC's in-house mini-series *Love and Hate: The Story of Colin and JoAnn Thatcher*, produced by Bernie Zuckerman and written by Suzette Couture, about the former Saskatchewan cabinet minister convicted of the brutal murder of his ex-wife. Fecan's development team also pushed *Degrassi Junior High* into prime time and brought in new writers to transform the network's in-house drama series *Street Legal* from a politi-cally correct, poorly plotted drama to a sexy melodrama, later adding the manipulative vixen character Olivia, played by Cynthia Dale. As a result, the series attracted 1.2 million viewers a week in the spring of 1990.

There were, of course, a fair number of disappointments and embar-rassments — among them, a cottage-country sitcom that never got the bugs out. "Who can forget *Mosquito Lake*, as much as I'd like to?" Fecan quipped in October 1990. He was addressing the Canadian Association of Broadcasters' annual conference, where he participated in a panel discussion with his future rival and CTV's newly appointed president, John Cassaday.

At the conference, Fecan broke the ice by alluding to CTV's well-publicized capacity to self-destruct and seemed to be on the point of optioning the story. "Perhaps some people don't believe that sex, greed, lust, and betrayal ever happen in Canada," he said. "They've obviously never been to a licence renewal hearing. I was going to say they've never been to a CTV board meeting, but I'm not sure about the sex part."

Fecan then observed that when he'd returned from NBC, the public corporation had enjoyed a pretty good reputation in news, but a mediocre one in drama. Conventional wisdom had held that Canada couldn't compete with American productions. "Today," he claimed, "people say our dramas must be American because they are so popular." He argued that this stemmed from the fact that they were "relentlessly Canadian . . . with recognizable themes, recognizable institutions, recognizable places." Quality knew no borders. For example, Fecan had made a deal with Brandon Tartikoff to sell *Love and Hate: The Story of Colin and JoAnn Thatcher* to NBC (where it was a number one hit in July 1990, just as it had been in Canada the previous year, earning the CBC "a very tidy profit").

John Cassaday replied, "I can tell you that, as happy as they were at CBC about *Love and Hate*, we were as happy at CTV for them, because it was an indication to all of us that we had a chance to succeed in that big pond."

Fecan also talked about *E.N.G.* — the Great Canadian Drama That Got Away. That ball had started rolling when he'd met with its developer in 1987 in the bar of the Fantasyland Hotel in the West Edmonton Mall, and had been pitched on a movie-of-the-week pilot that could be developed into a one-hour series. A year later, CBC had a terrific movie and a great outline (or "series bible"), but the corporation was in one of its government-cutback crunches and could afford to bring only one new series onstream. It chose *Road to Avonlea*. The developer sold the package to Alliance Entertainment, which headed (almost inevitably) for CTV.

WIC's Doug Holtby clearly remembers the CAB conference. "It was interesting to see John Cassaday and Ivan Fecan talking," he recalls. "They basically said the same thing, but from different perspectives. [John] was looking [on] it from his marketing side, and the importance of having the best product you can to sell. [Ivan], of course, is from the production side, and he was saying, . . . we've got to create excellence."

Holtby claimed to be thrilled by the sea change in attitude towards Canadian programming. "My first experience . . . in television was watching American signals in Vancouver, where I was born," he said. "My generation . . . viewed Canadian programming with disdain." On the other hand, his daughters "love watching Canadian shows." He said they were excited when they learned that a show was produced in Toronto. To them, he said, "'Canadian' is not a bad word, because [now] we are doing things that are world quality." (They were certainly acceptable to Canadian audiences. The CBC's *Road to Avonlea* and *Street Legal* and CTV's *E.N.G.* and *Bordertown* routinely placed in the top thirty programs nationwide during the 1990–91 season.)

In September 1991, within a year of the broadcasters' conference, Ivan Fecan and Trina McQueen succeeded their retiring boss, Denis Harvey, as vice-president of the CBC's English-language television network, splitting the position in two: vice-president of arts and entertainment, and vice-president of news, current affairs, and Newsworld.

The prime-time highlight of the 1991–92 season proved to be the December broadcast of *Conspiracy of Silence*, a mini-series produced by Bernie Zuckerman and written by Suzette Couture, which explored the racist murder of a native woman in The Pas, Manitoba. It drew an audience of more than three million in Canada.

The following season, Fecan's team added Wayne Grisby and Barbara Samuels's aboriginal drama series, the Alliance-produced *North of 60*, to the line-up, as well as John N. Smith's *The Boys of St. Vincent*, a provocative and topical exposé of sexual abuse in a Catholic orphanage. A court injunction prevented the four-hour mini-series from being shown in Ontario and Quebec, but it still managed to draw two million viewers when it first aired in all the other provinces in December 1992. A year later, an average one million Canadians tuned in over two nights when it was rebroadcast right across the country. Another success was an in-house movie-of-the-week titled *Liar, Liar*, the story of a young Vancouver girl who, angry with her father, accuses him of sexual molestation. Written by Nancy Isaak, it aired in January 1993 and was subsequently sold to CBS.

But Fecan made mistakes as well. His detractors point to his role as one of the "unindicted co-conspirators" responsible for shifting the CBC's national newscast to nine o'clock in November 1992. One critic likened this move to the introduction of the New Coke. Actually, it was the brainchild of Gérard Veilleux, the CBC president, and executed by Tim Kotcheff, CTV's former vice-president of news, who'd defected to the public network that summer. Kotcheff killed *The National* and *The Journal*, blending them into the one-hour *Prime Time News*, co-anchored by Peter Mansbridge and Pamela Wallin, another CTV expatriate. Almost one-fifth of CBC's national news audience switched to CTV, and many never came back. *Prime Time News* averaged only 882,000 viewers in 1992–93, compared to 1.3 million for *CTV National News*. The repositioning fiasco helped to ensure CTV's domination of the news ratings throughout the 1990s, although Lloyd Robertson's popularity helped CTV retain its lead when *The National* returned.

At the beginning of 1993, Fecan took over Trina McQueen's turf, becoming vice-president of the English-language television network. Some believed that he'd engaged in political manoeuvring to oust his rival for the job. Fecan had come under increasing attack for hogging the spotlight and the controls at the CBC. For all those who hailed him as a creative messiah who'd led the CBC into the promised land of popular home-grown quality dramas, there were hordes who vilified him as a false prophet responsible for "the network's commercialization and Disneyfication."

To be sure, Fecan could botch things up, especially when it came to situation comedies and the ill-fated 1992–93 talk/variety show, *Friday Night! with Ralph Benmergui*. This was a bigger and costlier bomb than the sitcoms, because it was so heavily promoted. To add insult to injury, Fecan resurrected it for a second season, but the CBC killed it within days of his departure.

Still, in 1993–94, the last season to bear Fecan's imprint, the CBC launched two lasting hits: *Royal Canadian Air Farce* and Salter Street Films' *This Hour Has 22 Minutes*, created by Mary Walsh of Codco. After three sitcom flops in a row, Fecan's group had decided to concentrate on sketch comedy and political satire, for two reasons. A wealth of talent was waiting to be tapped, and a superior product could be provided for much lower budgets.

CBC's fall 1993 prime-time schedule boasted 91 per cent Canadian content. This was shy of the original target, but the shows themselves were richer and more diverse than could have been imagined several years before. True, audience share had plummeted to an all-time low during Fecan's regime, but CTV and the major American networks had experienced the same proportional decline.

And mavericks like Fecan attract fierce enemies. When he decided to quit the CBC in late 1993 (not long after Gérard Veilleux made his exit), critics accused him of leaving a job half-done. To them, Fecan was just one more rat deserting a sinking ship.

In truth, however, Fecan had indicated that he was ready to move on the previous year. He felt he risked becoming stale and needed to shake himself up creatively by trying something new. His duties demanded "110 per cent effort all the time," he wrote in his letter of resignation to the CBC's interim president Tony Manera. "I've done my best for every single second. And frankly, I've always believed that this job is finite. No one should program one place for too long. It's now time for someone else to take the helm." He refused to dwell on his mistakes, arguing correctly that there were plenty of people who'd happily do it for him. Why should he deprive them of their role in life?

"There was an awful lot of jealousy of Ivan," comments CHUM's Fred Sherratt, who's known Fecan since he was a news director at CITY. "Trying to change the CBC was like trying to turn the *Queen Elizabeth* around in a river. It was disastrous." Now that Fecan was coming to Baton, he had "the opportunity to prove the myth."

Fecan joined Baton just in time to witness the fate of the Baton-CBC application for a headline-news service in early 1994. "I was a potted plant at the hearing," he recalls. The CRTC didn't give Baton the nod, so it would have to try again in the next specialty-licence sweepstakes.

By this time, however, the Eatons were assessing Baton's progress or lack thereof. Since 1986, Doug Bassett and Joe Garwood had bought eighteen television stations in Saskatchewan and Ontario for a quarter of a billion dollars, but Baton wasn't much closer to owning CTV. According to Electrohome's John Pollock, "The Eatons were saying, 'Where's this thing going? Is it going anywhere?'"

Not only was Baton burdened with $170 million of debt, its stock price was wallowing below $7, making the Eatons' investment worth less than $100 million. As well, Baton's shares had paid no dividends for years. As Fecan puts it, the Eatons couldn't "survive the siege of Moscow" forever.

In early 1994 (about the time that the John Labatt Broadcast Group — the first of many such suitors — made an unsuccessful purchase offer), Baton hired McKinsey and Company, the blue-chip management consultants, to help it conduct an exhaustive strategic review. This resulted in a four-point plan:

1. Most important, take control of CTV, one of Canada's best television "trademarks."
2. Buy as many stations in as many major markets as possible, extending

Baton's reach from coast to coast, and build "brand equity" by means of a new Baton Broadcasting System (BBS) trademark in front of the local call letters, as a fallback position in case the takeover of CTV proved unsuccessful.

3. Diversify Baton's revenues through specialty channels, since subscription fees were becoming a larger source of cash than advertising.

4. Lobby to change Telefilm's funding rules (which prohibited broadcasters from owning the distribution rights to independent Canadian-made drama programs), so that Baton could participate in the rewards of Canadianizing its prime-time schedule.

Ivan Fecan played a role in the McKinsey study, as part of his initial roving assignment. "I was given the job title of senior vice-president of broadcasting, and a pretty nebulous mandate," he says. Basically, he "had a year or two to study the company."

That fall, the new tri-coloured BBS logo began to appear on viewers' screens across Ontario and Saskatchewan. To raise the profile of its new brand, Baton recruited Paul Robertson from CTV, as the new senior vice-president of marketing and a member of the Office of the President. He'd built a reputation for innovation at the network, going so far as to produce in-house infomercials for advertising clients.

Implementing Baton's strategic plan also required significant restructuring, such as the sale of Ottawa's Carleton Productions; the centralizing of each of the twenty stations' buying, billing, and purchasing operations; and the elimination of the executives involved in those functions at the station level. More than 250 full-time employees lost their jobs.

By contrast, at the beginning of 1995, Fecan was promoted to the post of executive vice-president and chief operating officer, thus improving the odds that he'd be Doug Bassett's chosen heir. The animosity that later developed between him and CTV's president, John Cassaday, probably had its roots in the fact that Fecan was now in line for the position that Cassaday coveted.

Meanwhile, Cassaday had expressed bitter disappointment at being refused the headline-news and regional sports specialty-channel licences. Three-quarters of the $200 million that CTV would spend on Canadian content in 1994–95 was budgeted for news, information, and sports. But how was he to expand the network's business if he couldn't capitalize on its core areas of expertise?

Cassaday also had the delicate problem of managing the succession at *CTV National News*. Lloyd Robertson announced in June 1994, that he'd be signing off when his latest two-year contract expired in 1996. This would allow Cassaday's golden-haired boy, Keith Morrison, to take over as chief news anchor. Apparently, Morrison had been considering offers from the American networks. "There was no way I could . . . let Keith slip back across the border," Robertson said.

Morrison, a former anchor on *CTV National News* and *The Journal*, had gone south in 1986 to work for NBC's Los Angeles affiliate until Cassaday repatriated him in 1992 to replace the departing J. D. Roberts, who'd gone to CBS in New York. A man with solid news credentials, Morrison was also good-looking, considerably younger (at age forty-seven) than the sixty-year-old Robertson, and rumoured to be a bit of a flake.

"In Canada, unlike the U.S., we haven't always gone for the pretty face," says CTV's Ottawa bureau chief, Craig Oliver. But Cassaday believed that attractive women (like the new *Canada AM* anchor Valerie Pringle, a CBC veteran who'd swapped networks with Pamela Wallin, taking her seat on the morning show halfway through the 1992–93 season) and handsome men appealed to viewers. In the 1990s, CTV became known as the home of Canadian beefcake, notably Roberts; Morrison; sports reporters Dan Matheson and Rod Black; Art Hindle and Mark Humphries of *E.N.G.*; and Paul Gross of *Due South*.

Unfortunately, Morrison blew his chance to take over the anchor desk. "[Keith] wanted to push up the date, and that got to Lloyd," Craig Oliver recalls. In fact, Canada's "most trusted journalist" was ambivalent about retiring. He'd enjoyed the past three years, during which CTV had clobbered the CBC in the news-rating race. Robertson was at the top of his game and didn't like being pressured by anyone. "Lloyd went to see Cassaday and it just began to unravel," recalls Knowlton Nash.

At a stormy ten-minute meeting in April 1995, Cassaday fired Morrison — coincidentally, just three days after the CBC canned Pamela Wallin as co-anchor of *Prime Time News*. Rumours spread that CTV's shareholders had insisted that Morrison be axed, but Doug Bassett denies it. "[Morrison] was a management decision," he says. "We didn't know; the board wasn't informed. After it happened, we sure wanted to know."

A year later, in May 1996, Lloyd Robertson was front and centre for CTV's second and successful try at a headline-news specialty service, this time in partnership with TVA, the French-Canadian private network. Robertson told the CRTC that the channel (CTV News 1) would enable CTV News "to provide much greater coverage to our country, its regions, and our people," and to "augment the high quality coverage already delivered by our national news people in Quebec." (By this time, in addition to Montreal and Quebec City, CTV operated national news bureaus in Vancouver, Edmonton, Toronto, Ottawa, and Halifax, along with foreign news bureaus in Washington, London, Beijing, Jerusalem, and Moscow.)

Robertson was accompanied by so many on-screen news personalities that the hearing's chairman, Fernand Belisle, joked that he could understand why Valerie Pringle was alone on *Canada AM* that morning. Cassaday, who led the presentation, told the commission that the twenty-four-hour service would complement *CTV News*. "The [CTV] brand is one of our most valuable assets," he said. He boasted that the network excelled in its coverage of news and sports, both of which were "very defensible from . . . foreign competition [because] they are live, [they] are indigenous, and we have a tremendous brand name competence associated with them. . . . We can compete with anyone."

The CRTC seemed prepared to support CTV in this round of specialty licences, because the network's shareholder disputes appeared to be in the past. Although WIC came forward with three competing applications for headline-news channels (including one from CTV's Vancouver affiliate, BCTV), they were for regional, not national, services.

While he awaited the CRTC's verdict, Cassaday signed Lloyd Robertson to a new three-year contract, expiring in mid-1999. He too was a valuable asset. Not only did *TV Guide* name "Uncle Lloyd" Canada's most trusted journalist for the ninth time in ten years, the Canadian Association of Broadcasters bestowed its Gold Ribbon of Distinguished Service Award on him for 1995–96. *CTV National News* continued to prosper in the ratings, averaging 1.3 million viewers nightly compared to 1.1 million for the first twenty minutes of *The National*. *Canada AM*'s ratings had spiked upwards as well, rising 19 per cent in 1995–96. Only *W5 with Eric Malling* had lost viewership that season.

W5 (Canada's longest-running public affairs show) had been on the verge of cancellation six years earlier, when the CBC's leading investigative journalist had switched networks to recharge it. In 1993, its best year ever, more than one and a half million viewers watched the retitled program's coverage of New Zealand's economic downfall, framed as a warning of Canada's perilous future. This segment sparked a nationwide debate about the national debt. Neo-conservatives embraced the piece, while the left-of-centre attacked it, most notably Linda McQuaig in her book, *Shooting the Hippo*. Malling went on to do hard-hitting pieces about the health-care system and the welfare mentality of the east coast fishery, but the show's frequent schedule changes and pre-emptions, coupled with a reaction on the part of viewers against Malling's irascible crusades, contributed to its decline in the ratings.

At the June launch of its 1996–97 season, CTV announced that the single-minded Malling would leave the program and embark on a series of documentary specials with the self-explanatory title *Mavericks*. *W5* without Eric Malling would be revamped into *W Five*, a less investigative and more celebrity-oriented news magazine hosted by a rotation of CTV news stars such as Lloyd Robertson, Sandie Rinaldo, Valerie Pringle, and Craig Oliver. (Sadly, Malling succumbed to depression and drink, and died at the age of fifty-two in September 1998.)

W5 with Eric Malling had left CFTO in mid-1994 for CTV's new open-concept surroundings in downtown Toronto. After thirty-three years in rented headquarters at 42 Charles Street, and having looked at twenty-nine different sites, the network had moved its executive offices and sales offices, edit suites, and tape transfer areas into custom-designed space on three floors of one of the Eaton Centre towers.

The plan was to accommodate two 5,000-square-foot studios, but one would be used as offices until the network gained its headline-news licence. CTV used the other for news reports, *W5 with Eric Malling*, and *CTV Sports Presents*. *CTV News* and *Canada AM* remained in Agincourt, because the network had a five-year, $3.8-million annual lease with Baton until the end of August 1995, although they were expected to move to the Eaton Centre when it expired. (Later, CTV reconsidered and renewed the Agincourt lease until the end of August 1997.)

At the time, Tom Peddie claimed that, even given the cost of the upgrades, the network was able to relocate for about the same price it had been paying at Charles Street, because the Toronto real estate market was in such a decline. John Cassaday's critics said that the splashy new headquarters were just another instance of his need to keep up with other CEOs, in line with CTV's new sponsorship of the CEO of the Year Awards and Cassaday's seat on the board of Canadian Airlines, but WIC's Doug Holtby disagrees, claiming that the network's staff supported the move. "[They'd] voted for building their own facility, for having their own environment," he says. In his view, Charles Street was run down, and the network was paying an "exorbitant amount of money to rent [from] Baton. Back in the 1960s, CTV should have built its own infrastructure."

☆

John Cassaday had promoted CTV as the home of Big Event sports since mid-1992, but the network couldn't offer much in 1994 after the Winter Olympics in Lillehammer ended, with one exception. CTV and Baton paid $2 million to co-option the rights to National Basketball Association (NBA) games — not small potatoes, but not the Olympics, either. The CTV/TVA consortium's US$16 million bid for the upcoming Atlanta Summer Games hadn't come close to matching the CBC's US$20.75 million. Something was wrong with this picture. How could the public network afford to spend so much? It had previously blown CTV "out of the park" with a US$10-million offer for the 1992 Winter Olympics in Albertville, France. CTV had bounced back with US$16.5 million for the 1992 Summer Games in Barcelona but wound up losing money on its coverage. So gun-shy was Cassaday that he'd tried to dump the rights to Lillehammer, but couldn't find a buyer, and was lucky to make a "very small profit."

Still, Cassaday had had enough of bidding wars. (His mood was not improved by the fact that CTV's first application for a money-making regional sports channel had meanwhile been turned down.) He accused the public network of squandering public funds. On June 27, 1994, CTV released a document titled "A Perspective on the CBC," commissioned by its vice-president of sports, Gary Maavara, and prepared by the consultants Harrison, Young, Pesonen, and Newell. It maintained that the CBC was losing up to $70 million a year on *Hockey Night in Canada* and other sports programming, and stood to lose as much as $11 million on the Atlanta games. The *Globe and Mail* used this study as the basis for a series of highly critical editorials, prompting Jim Byrd, the head of CBC's English network, to condemn "the amateurism of CTV's foray into gutter accounting." He contended CTV had based its calculations on inaccurate numbers. "Was it sour grapes over losing Atlanta?" he suggested.

"I don't have a hard-on for the CBC," John Cassaday informed the *Toronto Star*. Then he turned around and accused his rivals of "gobbling up everything that moves" in sports, which he identified as the second most popular Canadian program category.

By September, CTV had shifted Gary Maavara out of sports and back to his roots as vice-president of development, public affairs, and senior legal counsel; and Doug Beeforth, an Emmy award-winning former producer of American network sports, was named as his replacement.

In May 1995, CTV signed a three-year contract with the NBA to broadcast about thirty games, including some featuring the two newly launched Canadian franchises, the Toronto Raptors and the Vancouver Grizzlies (the latter owned by WIC's Griffiths family). This contract also covered the all-star game, six playoff games, and the finals. The CTV sportscaster Rod Black would act as host. Perhaps this constituted Big Event stuff, after all, and Cassaday predicted that basketball would become the dominant sport of the 1990s.

A month later, CTV lost the rights to broadcast the 1998 Winter Olympics in Nagano, Japan, when its US$14.5-million bid was edged out by the CBC's record-setting US$16 million after more than four hours of high-stakes negotiations. "That's the level we felt was affordable for us," Cassaday said. "We're very disappointed."

The following year, Cassaday, Gary Maavara, and Doug Beeforth were back in front of the CRTC, to pitch (this time successfully) both the regional sports specialty service and another channel that sounded like "Big Events Pay-Per-View." Its proposed programming consisted of both major sports contests and important gatherings such as the 1995 G7 economic conference in Halifax, for which CTV had been named host broadcaster.

Cassaday went back to his roots, when arguing that viewers would be willing to shell out for this kind of programming. "Ten years ago, I launched Le Menu dinners in Canada . . . at $5 to $7," he informed the commission. "The frame of reference at that time was Swanson TV dinners, [at] $2. We had to reframe [the value equation] in consumers' minds. . . . We had to get them to stop thinking about army food on a tin plate and start thinking about a new set of benefits — microwaveable, a dish that looked [like] real china, a unique combination of sauces and foods — and we succeeded in doing that."

Next, he recited a long list of goods and services costing between $5 and $10 that Canadians had wholeheartedly embraced — including a dozen Tim Hortons doughnuts, four Kellogg's Pop Tarts, six toothbrushes, a month of *TV Guide*, or a month of telephone options such as call answer and display.

"I guess you can take the guy out of the food business, but you [can't] take the food business out of the guy," the CRTC counsel joked.

"It has been my experience that it is always nice to have something to fall back on," Cassaday replied.

Just so — because running CTV wasn't getting any easier for the former food executive. Aggressive competition from the CBC had put Big Event sports programming out of fiscal reach, and aggressive competition from Izzy Asper's CanWest Global meant that American sitcoms and dramas were becoming more costly with each passing season. In the 1990s, Global reigned as the single largest acquirer of American network series on the planet, becoming the undisputed master of the simulcast game. As if that weren't bad enough, virtually every private broadcaster in the land (including CTV's own shareholders) was directly or indirectly involved in purchasing the national rights to American programs.

Baton had entered the fray in May 1993, when it purchased the national rights to five series for its ONT network (the forerunner of BBS), while WIC regularly bought British Columbia rights from Baton and Alberta rights from CanWest Global. In Ontario, WIC's independent CHCH Hamilton was part of Market One Television — a joint marketing and buying agreement between it and Electrohome's CKCO Kitchener.

CTV began to lose its simulcast dominance to Global in the spring of 1989, when it failed to renew its national rights to *Cheers* after the price went up. It made a similar mistake with *Seinfeld*, which it dropped after only one season. In May 1993, it tried to get its hands on *Frasier*, but was outbid by Global, which also nailed down national rights to *The X-Files*. At least CTV managed to pick up Steven Bochco's new police serial, *NYPD Blue*, for $75,000 an episode. This became a high-scoring staple of its 1993–94 season, but it was stolen away by Global the following year. CTV had offered $131,000 an episode to telecast the second season, but Asper's team countered with $135,000 an episode for a two-year period. (Just as the 1994 fall season began, CTV filed suit against *NYPD Blue*'s Hollywood producer, Twentieth Century Fox, and Fox's Canadian distributor, EPS Entertainment Service Ltd., seeking either aggravated, exemplary, and punitive damages or a restoration of the broadcast rights. The suit later fizzled out.)

To thwart Global's raiding parties, Baton and WIC had agreed to team up with the network in May 1994 to buy certain programming packages together — that is, to co-option the national broadcast rights. (Size mattered, and Global had more clout because it bought for its entire 126-hour schedule, whereas CTV bought for only forty hours of network sales time, of which a mere twelve were in prime time. Combining forces with its two largest affiliate chains would help even the contest.) "Both ourselves and Baton have a common interest with the network to ensure that it is strong," explained WIC's Doug Holtby, as he prepared to join Ivan Fecan, John Cassaday, Paul Robertson, and Arthur Weinthal for the annual May rush down to the Beverly Hills Hotel to compete for the best American pilots.

Essentially, there were now only two buyers for the Canadian market: Global and the CTV-Baton-WIC consortium. The latter managed to fly back from Los Angeles with the national rights to Steven Spielberg and Michael Crichton's *ER* (which soon became the top-rated drama in the United States), having passed on a more or less similar hospital series, *Chicago Hope*. But Global got that one, along with *Party of Five*, and added *Friends* to its simulcast roster of NBC's Thursday night hits for 1994–95. Each season, the gap seemed to widen between CTV and its independent arch-rival with the deep pockets.

Global's pockets were becoming so deep they appeared bottomless because it already owned the rights to the most popular American shows and had to turn advertisers away. Advertising buyers were spending up to 80 per cent of their prime-time entertainment budgets on Canada's top twenty programs, almost all of which were American, and most of which were running on Global. The advertising agencies' major clients were clamouring for placement in the top ten shows in the major Canadian markets. During the Spring Sweeps period of 1995, Global aired eight of the top ten programs in the Toronto-Hamilton market, compared to CTV's two, and five of the top ten shows in the Vancouver-Victoria market, compared to CTV's single hit.

In the second year of CTV-Baton-WIC's collaboration, the new consortium successfully renewed *ER* for two more seasons and picked up the special-effects-laden mini-series *Gulliver's Travels*, which Arthur Weinthal accurately predicted would be a blockbuster. For itself, Baton acquired the national rights to *The Drew Carey Show*, selling the British Columbia rights to WIC.

But CTV made little progress on the simulcast front. In the second half of the 1995–96 season, Global owned the rights to seven of the top ten shows in the Toronto-Hamilton area, led by *Seinfeld*, *The X-Files*, *Friends*, and the two other sitcoms in NBC's Must-See Thursday line-up. CTV had the rights to only two — *ER* and the long-lasting *America's Funniest Home Videos*.

At the start of that season, Baton had struck a strategic alliance with Electrohome, which Doug Bassett claimed would help CTV deliver stronger prime-time programming, because there'd be a larger group of stations over which CTV could amortize the cost of national rights. In fact, though, the pact sparked new competition between CTV's primary partners because it killed off Market One Television, making WIC's CHCH Hamilton an orphan in Ontario. WIC felt it necessary to up the ante. In May 1996, it bid against CTV, Baton-Electrohome, and Global for national rights to the top new American sitcom *Suddenly Susan*, which it simulcast on CHCH and some of its other stations in a prime-time slot, instead of picking up whatever CTV was providing.

CTV did manage to return from Los Angeles in preparation for the 1996–97 season with Michael J. Fox's new sitcom, *Spin City*, and the next big mini-series, *Odyssey*. But the network had to swap the rescheduled-for-Wednesdays drama series *Law & Order* for a new Baton acquisition, because it had agreed to leave all of Wednesday and Friday evenings clear for its affiliates to program. On its own, Baton purchased the national rights to *Melrose Place*, *Cosby*, and several other shows, only to be frustrated by WIC's rejection of *Cosby* for its British Columbia stations. In sum, the CTV-Baton-WIC collaborative agreement seemed to have come undone even before its expiry at the end of that year, and Global continued to skim the American cream, simulcasting nineteen of its twenty-six hours of weekly prime time in 1996–97.

John Cassaday used the profit margins from CTV's now diminished roster of American hits to cross-subsidize its Canadian news, sports, and entertainment programs. By the mid-1990s, news and public affairs shows were in the black, and sports broke even (partly because CTV had lost the broadcast rights to Blue Jays baseball, CFL football, and the Olympic Games). Canadian drama still lost money. In fact, after allocating sales, promotion, and administration costs, it lost twice as much proportionately as sports, and five times as much proportionately as news.

It also represented an enormous opportunity cost. At CTV's licence renewal hearing in 1993, Cassaday had told the CRTC that replacing an American hour of drama with Canadian drama in prime time cost the network approximately $5 million a year it didn't have. He was referring to a study conducted by Coopers & Lybrand, which found that the average American series generated $200,000 an hour in ad revenues for its Canadian broadcaster, who paid $80,000 an hour for the national rights — a positive margin of $120,000 an hour. By contrast, the average indigenous (that is, identifiably) Canadian drama series brought in approximately $125,000 an hour in ad revenues, but cost $200,000 an hour in licence fees, resulting in a $75,000 an hour loss. By airing it, a broadcaster would both incur the loss and forgo the profit, winding up $195,000 an hour to the bad. Multiplied out over the typical American series run of twenty-two to twenty-six episodes, that figure produced Cassaday's plus-or-minus $5 million annually.

All of which helps to explain why CTV cancelled *E.N.G.* in March

1994, causing Robert Lantos to publicly embarrass Cassaday at the Gemini Awards a few days later by offering him the statue for Best Dramatic Series that *E.N.G.* had just received. Then CTV axed most of its in-house development personnel, who'd no longer be needed if it proposed to meet its three-hours-a-week quota of Canadian prime-time drama series with cheaper industrial (all-purpose, sell-them-to-the-States) dramas, for which CTV's licence fee could go as low as 10 per cent. According to the Coopers & Lybrand study, the average Canadian industrial drama generated $120,000 an hour in ad revenues (slightly less than an indigenous show), but cost only $100,000 an hour in licence fees, resulting in a reduced loss of $20,000 an hour and a reduced opportunity cost of $100,000 an hour or approximately $2.5 million a year. This was Cassaday's excuse for favouring industrial dramas, which could be pre-sold to U.S. cable networks or syndicators, thus financing up to three-quarters of the production budget. That's why, in the course of a sales presentation to network advertisers in June 1994, he made the claim that CTV's schedule would no longer contain "American programs or Canadian programs — only quality, world-class TV."

Three new Canadian industrial dramas debuted that fall. First was *TekWar: The Series*, which replaced *E.N.G.* on Thursday nights at nine o'clock. Produced by Atlantis Films and made in Toronto, it was based on the science-fiction novels penned by William Shatner, *Star Trek*'s Captain Kirk. Twenty-four episodes costing $1.5 million each had been pre-sold to the USA Network. Next was *Lonesome Dove: The Series*, which continued the story of characters created by Larry McMurty. Its twenty-four episodes were also budgeted at $1.5 million each. It was produced by Telegenic, shot on location in and around Calgary, and had been widely sold for syndication in the States. In Canada, it would air on Saturday nights.

The third series, *Due South*, an action-comedy from Alliance Entertainment (a division of Alliance Communications) starred Paul Gross as the straight-arrow Canadian Mountie who's thrown together with a streetwise Chicago cop. It would be the first Canadian drama series ever to be simulcast back home from one of the Big Three American networks in a prime-time slot — Thursday nights at eight o'clock.

Due South was born in September 1992, when Robert Lantos and Jeff Sagansky (then the president of CBS) met in Toronto for lunch to talk about developing a Canadian/American television version of the Australian movie hit *Crocodile Dundee*. With Telefilm backing and the firm expressions of interest from CBS, Alliance produced a two-hour pilot the following summer.

CTV's vice-president of entertainment programming, Arthur Weinthal, liked its "self-deprecating humour," how it gently mocked both Canadian and American stereotypes, and hoped that the project would go forward. He was not an easy man to impress. Nicknamed "Dr. No" by one independent producer because CTV wouldn't buy his series until he had a deal with an American broadcaster, Weinthal refused to commit to more than the pilot and seven episodes of *Due South* until CBS came on board. In April 1994, after the pilot was ranked number one in its time slot the night it aired (and number twenty-two for any program aired that week) in the United States, CBS bought the seven episodes for its 1994–95 season, paying 70 per cent of their $1.5-million-each tab.

Five months later, in late October, CBS ordered a further fifteen episodes of *Due South*, enough for a full season. While conventionally industrial in its financing, the series featured plenty of in-joke Canadian references, including a deaf, lip-reading wolf named Diefenbaker. It was also CTV's only Canadian drama series, industrial or indigenous, that fit John Cassaday's definition of a Big Event: a show that (at its peak) attracted more than two million viewers, making it the fifth-most-watched series in the country.

That November, CTV and Alliance hosted a gala schmooze-and-booze for *Due South* at the National Arts Centre in Ottawa. John Cassaday, Arthur Weinthal, Robert Lantos, the CRTC chairman Keith Spicer, and Heritage Minister Sheila Copps all toasted a Canadian success story. Despite Lantos's bitter reaction to the cancellation of *E.N.G.*, the CTV/Alliance partnership continued to flourish in the mid-1990s, as Cassaday and Lantos forged a friendship through their sons, both of whom played on Alliance's baseball team.

Unfortunately, about this time, Jeff Sagansky left CBS for Sony Pictures. Without a champion at the American network, *Due South* was cancelled after its first season. To Weinthal's credit, he kept it going for a second thirteen-episode season, even though CTV stood to lose money on it. He did so by raising the sum that CTV paid as a licence fee, thus triggering a higher level of financing from (among other sources) Telefilm's Broadcast Fund and the new $50-million Cable Production Fund. CTV also put more of its own money directly into the production budget.

Atlantis's futuristic *TekWars* suffered a similar fate at the hands of the USA Network (although eight new episodes, shot before the plug was pulled, were aired on CTV midway through its 1995–96 season). Only *Lonesome Dove* returned with a full slate of episodes, thanks to renewed financial commitments from its American syndicators.

At CTV's June launch of its 1995–96 season in Toronto's elegantly restored Winter Garden Theatre, screaming teenaged girls rushed the stage to promote a five-hour Beatles special, an ABC/CTV simulcast; Cynthia Dale of *Street Legal*, also known as the CBC news anchor Peter Mansbridge's significant other and Robert Lantos's ex-sister-in-law, took the spotlight to promote her new action-comedy *Taking the Falls*, developed by Alliance for CTV; and Diefenbaker (the lip-reading, law-enforcing wolf) made a brief appearance to mark the abbreviated return of *Due South*.

Four months later, in a last-minute reprieve, CBS picked up *Due South* to fill a hole in its fall schedule. But not for long. When the American network cancelled the series for a second time the following spring, CTV and Alliance refused to cobble together the requisite financing (without, Cassaday noted, "big bucks from elsewhere"). He didn't renew Alliance's *Taking the Falls*, either.

CTV's multi-media June preview of its 1996–97 season (again, held at the Winter Garden Theatre) rejoiced in the motto "Think Big," but the best that Cassaday could offer in the way of Canadian fare were three "Think Small" industrial drama series: the special-effects-laden *F/X: The Series*, from Fireworks Entertainment (a pale knock-off of a feature film that had at least been pre-syndicated in the States); the made-in-Vancouver *Poltergeist: The Legacy*, from Tony Allard's Pacific Motion Pictures and Trilogy, based on another feature film and pre-sold to MGM-TV and Showtime; and the made-in-Vancouver *Two*, from Telegenic and Stephen J. Cannell, which dealt with twin fugitives from the law, one good and one evil. "It's a question of us trying to find or acquire or develop the best Canadian shows we can, given financial restrictions," Arthur Weinthal said defensively. (And, to be fair, Weinthal had commissioned several distinctively Canadian kids' shows for CTV's Saturday-morning line-up, including *Bunch of Munsch*, *For Better or For Worse*, *Nilus the Sandman*, and *Bunnykins*.) As for the made-for-the-USA industrials, he added, "These programs are produced by Canadians through Canadian companies and are shot entirely in Canada."

In June 1996, while *Due South*'s sets were being dismantled or destroyed, and Paul Gross and his co-star David Marciano were in search of other employment opportunities, the program took home yet another honour. Having won the Gemini award as Best Drama Series for three seasons running (1993–94, 1994–95, and 1995–96), it was picked (over *NYPD Blue* and *ER*) as Best Continuing Series at the Banff Television Festival. "But if we're not continuing, should we even be in this category?" quipped Gross (who was acting as master of ceremonies), as Weinthal, Lantos, and a stageful of Telefilm representatives took their bows for supporting Diefenbaker and all who marched with him through the mean streets of Chicago.

☆

In the fall of 1994, just as American audiences were getting to know Gross's impossibly polite RCMP constable, CTV's shareholders finally triggered the conversion of their $14 million of debentures into equity. On September 29, the network transformed itself from a cooperative into a regular corporation. Seven large shareholders (Baton, WIC, Electrohome, CFCF, CHUM, Rogers Communications/Maclean Hunter, and Moffat) each held two million common shares; one very small shareholder (Newfoundland Broadcasting) retained 100.

Since Rogers Communications' $3-billion takeover of Maclean Hunter six months earlier, Ted Rogers had been telling anyone who'd listen that CTV was "going down the tubes" because of its internal conflicts of interest. "People should be trading properties around and solving the problem," he told the *Financial Post*. "If it isn't done there isn't much of a future for CTV." Although Rogers vowed to hang on to CFCN Calgary, Maclean Hunter's Ron Osborne continued to attend CTV board meetings on the station's behalf, while Rogers waited for the CRTC to announce its verdict on the takeover. The commission's December 19 decision put the Calgary affiliate in play, because approval of the Maclean Hunter acquisition was made contingent on Rogers's getting rid of it within a year — probably to another CTV shareholder, which would change the configuration of the new board.

At the same time, Electrohome's Bill McGregor announced his retirement, so CTV needed a new chairman. After seven fractious years on the board, an amazed and touched Doug Bassett was elected to succeed McGregor at the annual December meeting. "John Cassaday recommended me," Bassett says gratefully. "He phoned all the other directors before he asked me."

Unfortunately, CTV's latest financial crunch awaited his attention. This time, the problem was steep increases in airtime payments to the network's affiliates, increases that Doug Bassett had asked for. These payments would total $17.5 million in 1995–96 (of which $6.7 million would go to Baton for its eleven stations), and CHUM's Fred Sherratt foresaw a severe cash flow problem by 1997–98.

Out of necessity, John Cassaday had started looking at other options in the fall of 1994. With the help of Doug Cunningham, then with CIBC

Wood Gundy, CTV's management developed a reverse takeover proposal known as "the Gordian knot." This would have involved the shareholders putting their shares into a new company, which would then have made a bid for Baton Broadcasting. CTV's management put a value of about $10 million on each of the seven shareholders' equity interests. And, according to Gary Maavara, George Eaton had indicated that Telegram Corp. would tender its shares in Baton for the proposed price of $10.50 a share.

"The reverse takeover was . . . a creative solution," says John Pollock, "but it wasn't *the* solution. It was clear, though, that something had to be done." Fred Sherratt agrees on both counts, but adds that the takeover's proponents faced "the perennial question: 'Are you going to be able to sell it to WIC?'"

Apparently not, because the Gordian knot unravelled in the summer of 1995. At a CTV board meeting, held at a Winnipeg golf club to vote on resolutions that would enable the reverse takeover, WIC's Doug Holtby stood vehemently opposed. He claims that Cassaday had gone to solicit the support of the other six shareholders well in advance of the meeting, leaving WIC until the last minute. When Cassaday finally got around to calling him, Holtby blasted the network president, telling him that he was out of line. Moreover, he said, the reverse takeover scheme (and particularly the way that Cassaday had tried to peddle it) would set back CTV's shareholder relations by two or three years. "It was just John looking out for himself," Holtby said. In his view, the "very ambitious" Cassaday had struck an under-the-table agreement with George Eaton, which would have vaulted him ahead of Ivan Fecan for the top job. This scenario presumed that, having consummated the reverse takeover, Cassaday would have gone to Eaton and said, "See, I got you what you wanted." Fred Sherratt also thinks that when Cassaday made the takeover proposal, he "wanted to be the guy running Baton/CTV." Without Holtby's support, though, the concept was dead. "WIC just dug in and refused to budge," Sherratt remembers. "It didn't fly," Doug Bassett says, "so [Ivan and I] left the board meeting."

John Cassaday may have been trying to orchestrate the top job for himself, but his rival Ivan Fecan proved to be a deal maker in his own right, by secretly negotiating a strategic alliance with Bruce Cowie of Electrohome, which owned CKCO Kitchener. Their meetings lasted throughout the summer of 1995 and took place at a hotel in Toronto's western suburbs.

"I, for one, had to convince my wife I was going there for business reasons," Fecan jokes.

For quite some time, Electrohome's majority owner, John Pollock, had been feeling out WIC, Maclean Hunter/Rogers Communications, and CFCF Inc. about joining forces in some way or other. He contacted Baton as well, but matters went nowhere until George Eaton became interested in the idea and called him back. "It was obvious that the status quo was not going to carry Electrohome into the future," Pollock says. But Baton didn't have its act together. At last, the Eatons "took a hard look at Baton, whose share price had flatlined for five years. Once they decided to look at restructuring [it] and strengthening [its] management, a strategic alliance with Electrohome appeared to make sense."

The first discussions took place between Pollock and George Eaton, who reached a tentative agreement before assigning Fecan and Cowie (who'd succeeded Bill McGregor at Electrohome and once worked for Baton in Saskatchewan) to work out the specifics of structuring the alliance. "I was the new boy," Fecan says. "I could talk without being captive to history."

"I could not have done the [Electrohome] deal," Doug Bassett admits. "Ivan finalized it. Pollock didn't like me much. I'd lambasted his company and his team at the CRTC hearings [in 1992]." (Relations were certainly cool: even though Pollock owned a cottage near Bassett's on Lake Rosseau, the two men did not socialize.) When it came to thrashing out the details of the pact, Fecan and Cowie were aware of (though not bound by) all these bygone slights. "There was pride involved on both sides," Fecan explains. "That's why we only pooled certain assets. There was a long way to go to get around the pride issues."

Still, Fecan doesn't think the alliance would have come to pass if Baton hadn't had CFCN Calgary to put on the table. John Pollock and George Eaton had both made offers to Ted Rogers to buy it. Although Pollock and Rogers had a close relationship, having attended university together, Rogers seemed determined to sell to the Eatons, who'd helped him get his start and were "more than decent partners in Rogers Cable" until the regulators forced them to sell out. "I was always close to the Eatons," Rogers says. "They are real gentlemen."

Unfortunately, Rogers's swap of cable assets with Shaw Communications Corp. of Calgary meant that Shaw owned CFCN for "half a second." It took George Eaton and Fecan about that long to fly to Calgary, where they did a deal to pay J. R. Shaw and his son Jim Shaw Jr. their $75-million purchase price. The following day, the Baton contingent returned home "with Calgary in [their] pockets."

Under the terms of their strategic alliance, Baton would manage a joint venture known as Eastco, made up of Electrohome's CKCO Kitchener and Baton's independent stations in London and Wingham. CFTO, CJOH Ottawa, and Baton's northern Ontario CTV affiliates would play no part in the arrangement.

Conversely, Electrohome would manage Westco, another joint venture comprising Baton's six stations in Saskatchewan and CFCN Calgary, but not Electrohome's CFRN Edmonton. This meant that Electrohome would have to pay Baton $65 million for a 50 per cent stake in Westco.

Both the strategic alliance and the three-way swap were announced on September 29, 1995. If the CRTC approved the deals, Baton (thanks to a voting trust with Electrohome) would have control over three of CTV's eight votes, and its coverage area would grow to 61 per cent of English-speaking Canada.

Ivan Fecan had shown moxie as a deal maker, but how was he doing on the programming front? Several entries in BBS's 1994–95 season had a familiar industrial ring: the vampire/cop series *Forever Knight* from Toronto's Paragon Entertainment; an $11-million Canadian/German daytime soap opera titled *Family Passions*, which concerned two families, one North American and one German, who battle for supremacy in the auto industry; and *Robocop*, a $36-million Toronto-made series from Skyvision, spun off from the American feature film. None of these, however, could be laid at Fecan's doorstep. After participating in Baton's initial strategic review, he'd begun to set up a new development system, stealing his former colleague Suzanne Steeves from the CBC to serve as vice-president of production and distribution at BBS Productions (the renamed Glen-Warren Productions) and persuading Beverly Oda, a former CRTC commissioner, to become its senior vice-president of programming in late March 1995.

Like his NBC boss, Brandon Tartikoff, who'd stayed on top of the ratings game by signing the most talented American writer-producers to exclusive commitments, Fecan embarked on development deals with five to ten Canadian writers whom he'd worked with at the CBC. Prominent among them was Suzette Couture, otherwise known as "the queen of the true-life mini-series" for such outings as *Love and Hate, Conspiracy of Silence*, and *Million Dollar Babies* (the story of the Dionne quintuplets), which aired on the CBC and CBS networks in November 1994.

Fecan valued good writing highly. One of the lessons he'd learned at

NBC was "If it ain't on the page, it ain't on the stage." For example, when he read the first draft of *Love and Hate*, he called Couture to tell her that the script was extraordinary. She was shocked. "Heads of networks don't call writers," she says. Fecan ended that conversation with the promise, "You and I will be in business for a long time to come." When Fecan headed for Baton, Couture called him right away.

By the spring of 1995, Baton had formally optioned eight movies-of-the-week or mini-series. They included *Wild Geese*, an adaptation of Martha Osenso's novel by Suzette Couture; *Proof Positive*, an original script by Nancy Isaak, another of Fecan's former CBC writers; and *Golden Will: The Silken Laumann Story*, based on the injured rower's struggle for Olympic gold.

Still, Fecan disappointed his many admirers with Baton's 1995–96 season. His year and a half at Baton had resulted in nothing but a commitment to twenty-two more episodes of *Forever Knight*; *Camilla Scott*, a new afternoon talk show for teenagers; *BBS Master Control*, a block of children's cartoons; and *E-Now*, a bubbly entertainment magazine show that Fecan billed as a "modest effort" at building a star system in English-speaking Canada. Fecan had also decided that the *Dini Petty Show* would have more Canadian guests and forgo "much of the ubiquitous parade of American celebrities just passing through."

Late in 1995, Keatley-MacLeod Productions and Atlantis Communications (formerly Atlantis Films) pitched Fecan and his development team on *Cold Squad*, a series described as a cross between *Prime Suspect* and *The X-Files* that dealt with a group of police detectives in Vancouver who attempt to solve cases gone stale. It had already captured the interest of the Lifetime cable channel in the United States. "Ivan loved the idea," says Julia Keatley, its executive producer. "We always had his personal commitment." As a plus, Vancouver would be starring as itself for once, not as the stand-in for an American city.

In December 1995, fed up with Bay Street's continuing disdain for Baton's stock, the Eaton family launched an unexpected takeover bid for the 47 per cent of Baton that they didn't already own. At the time, they appeared to have deep pockets, thanks to the proceeds from huge real estate sales, but their retail empire was secretly in big trouble. T. Eaton & Co. would file for bankruptcy protection a little more than a year later.

"We were surprised by the [Eatons'] move . . . to quit retailing and focus entirely on broadcasting," joked a CanWest Global executive.

"Overnight, CTV became a harmonious and potent competitor. I guess they just needed a little competitive push."

The Eatons' takeover bid came about after Connor Clark & Co., an institutional investor that owned about 10 per cent of Baton's shares, indicated it would be interested in selling. Ted Rogers, who personally owned about 8 per cent of Baton, gave his approval. But the bid ran into a roadblock in early February, when two other institutional investors, the Ontario Municipal Employees Fund and the Ontario Hydro Pension Plan, objected to the Eatons' plan to buy them out and take Baton private. After hanging in through years of underperformance, they weren't about to give up their stakes now, when Baton finally looked as if it was on the road to a takeover of CTV. "We tried all kinds of things," Fred Eaton recalls — even John Cassaday's Gordian knot. The Eaton family had offered $11.25 a share, but their $150-million bid had expired in January 1996. Doug Bassett, Ivan Fecan, and Joe Garwood had stood to make over $1 million each from exercising roughly 350,000 stock options apiece.

In March 1996, at a public hearing in Vancouver into the Baton-Electrohome strategic alliance and the three-way swap between Rogers, Shaw, and Baton, the Baton-Electrohome team took up two-thirds of the seating room. The hearing's chairman, Fernand Belisle, tried to get Doug Bassett to describe the transactions himself, but after a brief introduction, Bassett handed off to Ivan Fecan and Bruce Cowie. One CRTC member commented that there had been "a great deal of trust exhibited between you two guys who have negotiated this most intricate deal. You've got me feeling [all] warm and fuzzy." Still, he wondered why Electrohome would let Baton control its CTV vote. Cowie replied that "Electrohome's expertise lies mostly in the management and operation of local television stations. . . . Baton, on the other hand, has an ongoing interest in CTV and in being a very influential participant in CTV. There was a natural trade-off, we think."

Asked whether CTV would now have one major decision-maker, Fecan replied that "three out of eight votes do not give us control of the network. . . . The network has mechanisms, program committees that all the affiliates are represented on, that really make the day-to-day strategic program decisions. [Now], there are a few less phone calls that CTV management needs to make. That is an improvement. It does not solve the problem that some feel exists, but it is a step in that direction."

This hearing represented the unveiling of Fecan's new team and was the first appearance before the CRTC at which he'd been "one of the authors of the deal." He remembers it as "a good test, because we knew our stuff." Afterwards, the Baton-Electrohome team commandeered most of the local restaurant Il Giardino to celebrate the seventieth birthday of Baton's chairman, Allan Beattie. Fecan keeps a photo of this occasion in his office. It shows the participants gazing up at a cluster of floating balloons.

Three months later, the CRTC officially blessed both the Baton-Electrohome alliance and Baton's purchase of CFCN Calgary. The latter transaction had cost $87 million, including $10 million for Calgary's network shares. But, thanks primarily to Ivan Fecan, Baton was just one vote away from controlling CTV.

18

The Threat of a Third Network
— 1993–96

As Baton moved ever closer to realizing its thirty-five-year-old dream, Izzy Asper renewed his fifteen-year-old ambition of building a coast-to-coast system of English-language television stations in major urban centres, a third national chain that would rival the CTV and CBC networks in reach but wouldn't involve the expense of servicing less populated areas. He still had hopes of incorporating WIC's stations into his plan. The death of WIC's founder, Frank Griffiths Sr., in the spring of 1994 and the subsequent Griffiths-Allard feud for control of his legacy presented an opportunity for a hostile bidder to seize control of WIC without having to buy the Griffiths shares.

Frank's death created havoc at WIC because his succession "lacked clarity," according to one of Griffiths's advisers. His widow, Emily, inherited sole authority over the family's control block of voting shares. She could do whatever she wished with them, without consulting her four children, WIC's board of directors, or its management. Of course, no one expected her to actually run WIC. Frank had made it clear in his hoarse whisper of a voice that he wanted Doug Holtby signed to a long-term contract, ensuring that he'd remain as president and CEO until age sixty-five. Unfortunately for Holtby, both Emily and the Allards had other plans.

The Allards had never forgiven their father, the late Doc Allard, for feeling that his children were incapable of running Allarcom Ltd. They resented the fact that Holtby had been put in charge of the family's broadcasting assets for a second time and wanted those assets back. "The Allards had a real dislike for Doug Holtby," WIC's former director Peter Paul Saunders says. "And [he wasn't] reporting to Emily the way she wanted him to."

Until his patron's death, Holtby had been happy at WIC. He got along well with Frank Griffiths, even though the WIC patriarch was already in poor health when Holtby arrived in 1989. "He kept going downhill," Holtby remembers. "There was diabetes, cancer, a stroke, a heart attack." In the final three years of Frank's life, Holtby drove to the Griffithses' West Vancouver home once a week to bring the WIC chairman up to date on the company's affairs. "His mind was always good," Holtby adds.

Frank also conducted board meetings at his home, because he was too ill to come into the office. Emily gained power as his health declined, becoming a director in 1993. After the Griffiths-controlled board appointed Frank Jr. vice-chairman of the company, the Allards and their representatives felt increasingly frustrated and shut out. Just before Christmas 1993, while Frank Jr. was in Edmonton visiting Harold and Cathy Roozen, the Allard family trust, Cathton, made its first takeover offer for WIC. Three months later, Cathton made a formal offer to buy enough of the Griffithses' voting A shares to bring the Allards' stake above 50 per cent.

Cathton's president, Robert Manning, met with Frank Jr. in Calgary and gave him a letter to take back to his dying father. "As a family-owned company ourselves, we understand the natural desire to build and then pass the fruits of our labors to our children and grandchildren," Manning wrote. "We are making this offer, however, because we have a serious concern about the future health and direction of WIC, if future control of the company were to lie with the trustees, rather than hands-on experienced and active board directors."

Frank Jr. replied on behalf of his father, saying that the Griffithses had "absolutely no interest" in selling. "My father although ill and bedridden, reacted angrily to the offer," he wrote. "With respect to your paragraphs about our family trust, it is absolutely none of Cathton's business as to what the trustees do or how they carry out their mandate, and equally it is none of our business to voice our opinions on how Cathton Holdings runs its affairs."

Manning immediately warned Frank Jr. that the Griffithses were "obliged to formally consider our offer and comply with the company's constitution. A visceral 'we will never sell' response is simply not permissible."

On April 7, three days after Cathton applied for a share conversion, arguing that the Griffithses had not reported Cathton's offer to WIC's secretary of the board, Frank Griffiths died at his home, surrounded by family and friends who'd gathered to celebrate the seventy-seven-year-old's induction into the Canadian Business Hall of Fame. (Frank Jr. was in Toronto to represent his father at the ceremonies.) Doug Holtby and Pat Quinn, the general manager of the Vancouver Canucks, visited Frank in his bedroom that evening. Later, Emily made a point of referring to Holtby as the company's "new chairman," adding that this was Frank's wish. She also asked Holtby to deliver a eulogy at the memorial service.

After the service, a small private ceremony took place aboard Frank's beloved boat *La Feline*, which was graciously lent for the occasion by its current owner, who'd bought it after Frank became house-bound. Observed by WIC's directors and senior officers, Emily scattered her husband's ashes in the waters of the bay overlooked by their home. ("It wasn't sad," says Allen Lambert. "It seemed appropriate.") One of the mourners asked Emily why she'd chosen that particular spot. "I wanted him to be somewhere where I could keep an eye on him," she quipped.

It wasn't long before Emily changed her mind about following her husband's wishes with respect to Doug Holtby. She pushed to have Frank Jr. succeed his father as chairman, but a special committee formed to consider the appointment rejected him. It was an open secret among the board members that Frank Jr. had threatened to pull all of WIC's accounts from the Toronto-Dominion Bank the year before if the bank wouldn't lend him the money to build his own multimillion-dollar house on the hill overlooking his parents' place. Holtby had to phone TD's chairman Dick Thomson and assure him that Frank Jr. didn't have that kind of clout. But the call wasn't necessary; Thomson knew all about Frank Jr.

Less than three weeks after Frank Griffiths's death, the Allards filed a petition in the B.C. Supreme Court to determine whether their rejected offer to buy the Griffithses' voting shares had triggered a coat-tails provision that would convert non-voting B shares into voting A shares, giving them the dominant position in WIC. (The Allards don't regret their actions, but they're sorry about the timing of their letter to Frank Griffiths. They claim to have had no idea that he was so close to death, since he'd been battling multiple illnesses for five years and had recovered time and time again.)

If the court declared in their favour, the Allards would own twice as many shares of WIC as the Griffithses, since they already owned more of the non-voting B shares. They asked a number of Bay Street institutional investors to join them in their lawsuit, but Bay Street declined, calling it a private feud.

Indeed, the suit had wide ramifications and was closely watched in various quarters. Ted Rogers said that the Griffiths-Allard court battle could benefit Canadian broadcasting as a whole if it wound up splitting WIC into two companies — one containing WIC's CTV affiliates and the other, its independent stations. (In mid-1994, when Rogers had criticized CTV's internal conflicts, he'd taken particular aim at WIC for having so many independents that competed directly with CTV's affiliates, and for making a two-year deal with CanWest Global to buy thirteen hours a week of American programming for its Alberta independent outlets.)

Even though the chances of the Allard lawsuit succeeding were remote, Emily Griffiths panicked. "This was a time of turmoil in her own life," the investment banker Edmund King recalls, "and she later felt that one advisor had let her down." That person was her estate lawyer, Lynn Waterman, who recommended that she settle with the Allards.

On the eve of the September 1994 court case, Emily Griffiths made a secret deal to sell the Allards a block of voting A stock, and Cathton dropped its lawsuit. After a WIC board meeting in Calgary, Cathton's Robert Manning put forward two resolutions: the automatic retirement of all directors (with the exception of Emily herself) over the age of sixty-five, and the election of Frank Griffiths Jr. and Harold Roozen as co-chairmen.

This meant lawyer Klaus Priebe would take a seat at the table next to his wife, Mary (who'd replaced her brother, Arthur Griffiths, on the WIC board that summer), and his mother-in-law Emily and brother-in-law Frank Jr.; Charles Allard and the Allards' estate lawyer Rod McLennan would join Robert Manning and Harold Roozen as the Allard family's representatives.

The idea of a co-chairmanship came as a double blow to Doug Holtby. When he insisted that WIC had a right to know what else was in the agreement reached between Emily Griffiths and the Allards, Holtby says he was told that "if he wanted to keep his job, he should mind his own business." But Holtby had other responsibilities. He wrote to Emily and Robert Manning, reminding them that he was required to keep the CRTC abreast of what was going on, because a change of ownership might jeopardize WIC's radio and television licences — but the families informed him that he'd better "start worrying about what the controlling shareholders want, not the CRTC."

"[Doug] had absolute responsibility to report to the CRTC if there was a significant change in ownership," argues Allen Lambert, one of the directors who'd been forced to retire from WIC's board. "And it was a significant change in ownership. He wasn't informed properly of the arrangement."

When it was revealed in February 1995 that the September agreement had given the Allards first right of refusal on the Griffithses' voting shares, two more ousted WIC directors (Sydney Welsh and Peter Paul Saunders) launched a lawsuit of their own the following month. It argued that, even if the Allards' first formal offer didn't trigger the conversion of WIC's non-voting B shares to voting A shares, the September deal did.

When they finally obtained a copy of the agreement, Saunders recalls, "our legal opinion said that the Allards were acting in concert with the Griffiths. They were acting in cahoots behind the board's back." He adds that he and Welsh brought the suit only "because we felt there was a real abuse of power."

Given these events, Doug Holtby, who continued to serve as WIC's chief executive, was in a difficult position. His own health began to suffer from the strain. By July 1995, the co-chairmanship of Frank Jr. and Harold Roozen had broken down, in part because the Griffithses still perceived the Allards as "evil" for launching their takeover bid when Frank Sr. was dying, and also because Frank Jr. and Roozen had stopped speaking to each other in March.

WIC's long-time investment banker Edmund King became chairman in their place, and Klaus Priebe was appointed deputy chairman. Frank Jr. was demoted to senior vice-president of human resources, but managed to hang on to his almost $400,000-a-year co-chairman's salary. (But Holtby didn't see Frank Jr. as WIC's major problem. The bulk of his headaches stemmed from the actions of Priebe and Roozen, the ambitious Griffiths and Allard sons-in-law.)

That summer, Holtby blocked CTV's reverse takeover of Baton Broadcasting. "Doug Holtby had tremendous influence within CTV . . . , but WIC was a complex arrangement," Baton's chairman Allan Beattie says. "We didn't know how to talk to [them]."

A month later, when the strategic alliance between Electrohome and Baton and the three-way swap between Baton, Rogers, and Shaw were announced, "WIC was on the sidelines," says Electrohome's John Pollock. "We weren't sure what they wanted. If the Griffiths and the Allards could have made up their minds . . . things might have been different. They didn't help WIC [to] play a major role at CTV. There were opportunities, [and] if they'd been more aggressive, they could have ended up being players, but Doug Holtby didn't have a mandate. We were willing to negotiate a strategic alliance with WIC."

Meanwhile, CanWest Global smelled blood. It interpreted WIC's reluctance to move out of its independent Alberta stations and into the Alberta CTV affiliates now owned by Baton and Electrohome as a signal that the company was paralyzed by the Griffiths-Allard feud. Now was the time to strike, when (as the Aspers thought) WIC wasn't protecting BCTV, its core asset.

"The greatest perceived threat to BCTV was a Global takeover of WIC," says Tony Parsons, BCTV's news anchor. "There was unrest and concern in the newsroom. We didn't know what was going on — whether Izzy Asper was going to be successful in a takeover bid. Communication between [us and WIC's] head office [was] lacking. We had to watch the wire services to find out whether . . . we [were part of] Global or WIC."

Izzy Asper had called Frank Griffiths Jr. on Sunday, November 12, 1995, to inform him that CanWest Global was about to launch a $636-million takeover bid for WIC the following day. "I was on a plane to visit our operations in Alberta when I returned his call," Frank Jr. later told the *Globe and Mail*. "It came out of left field. . . . I said, 'We need some time to think about this.'"

The Griffiths family met late Thursday to consider the offer. The consensus was that they wouldn't bite, and wouldn't entertain a higher offer, either. "There isn't any interest. Full stop. Period," Frank Jr. said. Late Friday, Doug Holtby joined them in rejecting CanWest's bid.

Asper was undeterred. He planned to piggyback on Sydney Welsh and Peter Paul Saunders's lawsuit. If the coat-tail provision was triggered, then CanWest's offer for non-voting B shares would give it control of WIC. A disingenuous Asper went so far as to suggest that the late Frank Griffiths would have welcomed CanWest's bid as a solution to WIC's present shareholder dispute. (But CanWest Global withdrew its bid the following January, after the B.C. Supreme Court ruled that the September agreement did not constitute a change of control at WIC, so there would be no conversion of the non-voting B shares.)

Stymied for what seemed like the umpteenth time in its efforts to get hold of WIC's independent Alberta stations, CanWest Global moved on to Plan B. Three years earlier, Asper had acquired MITV, a group of stations in the Maritimes, and expanded Global's signal into northern Ontario. The previous summer, he'd signed a deal to add CKMI, an English-language station in Quebec City, to the Global system. Now Asper hoped to fill in the major gap in his national coverage, by applying for new television licences in Calgary and Edmonton. If he got them, and if the Quebec City purchase went through, CanWest Global's geographic coverage of the English-language Canadian market would rise from 72 to 88 per cent.

To that end, Asper tried to rehabilitate his less than sterling reputation with the CRTC, which had given Global an abbreviated four-year licence (instead of the customary seven years) in 1992, for failing to air sufficient Canadian content. Now, Asper announced plans for a comprehensive national newscast and higher commitments to distinctively Canadian prime-time series, notably a version of *Jake and the Kid* and the Bay Street drama *Traders*.

WIC, meanwhile, took its own step towards becoming a national system, in a move that would expand its coverage of English-speaking Canada from 58 per cent to 72 per cent. In April 1996, it asked the CRTC for permission to extend its signal from CHCH Hamilton throughout Ontario, thereby challenging Baton and Global, which between them raked in fully 70 per cent of all the money spent by national advertisers on all the province's television stations. And for good reason. Ontario accounted for 30 per cent of Canada's population and 41 per cent of all television viewers nationwide. It also accounted for 65 per cent of the networks' expenditures on national rights to American entertainment programs. At this same time, WIC stepped up its own buying of national rights for shows that weren't provided to it by the network, successfully bidding for the upcoming season's best new prospect, the Brooke Shields sitcom, *Suddenly Susan*.

At the public hearings into WIC's Ontario expansion, CanWest Global's Jim Sward stood in for Izzy Asper, who was absent because he was busy launching an international share offering in New York. "He wanted to be here today," Sward confided. "He feels seriously threatened by the prospect of a 'super local station' that can shortcut what it has taken him twenty years to do. . . . It will make those of us who have taken the hard way — which we thought was the only way — look rather silly."

A month later, at the next round of specialty licence hearings in May 1996, WIC tried to lever its Vancouver news division into a regional channel. BCTV's suppertime *News Hour*, anchored by the extraordinarily popular Tony Parsons, routinely ranked as the most-watched program in the Vancouver-Victoria market. "News is our signature, news is our trademark," BCTV's president Ron Bremner told the commission. "We have been working very, very hard at branding the type of news that we do, the style that we do it in, the quality that we deliver it in, the way that we are perceived in the marketplace, and the marketing around that brand for many, many years."

Bremner conceded that *CTV National News* was the most-watched newscast in Canada, with 1.1 million viewers, but that was only 3.7 per cent of roughly 30 million people coast to coast. *News Hour*, on the other hand, was watched by 600,000 people, who represented 15 per cent of a potential audience of four million. Not only were those viewers the largest local news audience in Canada, they were the fourth largest such audience in North America, exceeded only by two stations in New York and one in Philadelphia.

WIC's argument was that it was ready to roll. In 1993, after BCTV's proposal for a national suppertime newscast had been turned down by the CTV board, WIC had launched *Canada Tonight* with Tony Parsons, an early-evening semi-national production that aired on its independent stations in Alberta and on CHCH Hamilton. By 1996, BCTV had opened five news bureaus across Canada and its state-of-the-art news facility in Burnaby had been redeveloped at a cost of more than $1.5 million. Although *Canada Tonight* didn't yet count as competition for *CTV National News*, the network newsroom perceived it, and more particularly BCTV's present application for a regional news channel, as a double-barrelled and malignant threat.

Elsewhere on the news front, Izzy Asper was busily preparing for the fall launch of *First National*, CanWest Global's own national suppertime newscast. It would be anchored in Toronto by the veteran broadcaster and native Albertan Peter Kent, supported by foreign bureaus in Washington, London, Tel Aviv, and Moscow. Asper put Kent front and centre at the July public hearings into the new Alberta licences — hearings at which Asper was slammed by his competition, who had no wish to see him parlay strength in Alberta into a new, more cohesive national "system."

"Global is pumped on regulatory steroids," John Cassaday told the *Financial Post*. "They have such regulatory advantages that they will win over time. Global's obligations should be the equal of [CTV's]." In the network's written intervention, Gary Maavara claimed that an expanded Global would be the equal of CTV in the minds of most major national advertisers without the responsibilities of a network licence. He said, "The lesson for CTV's owners is apparent. CTV should turn in its licence and establish a non-regulated 'system.'"

CTV urged the commission not to be fooled by Asper's late-blooming addition of two (count them, two) drama series to his lucrative line-up of simulcast American hit shows. Looking past the hype to the numbers, CanWest Global had spent only 26 per cent of its airtime revenues on Canadian programming in 1994–95, compared to CTV's 34 per cent (and would actually spend 5 per cent less the following season).

WIC, Baton, and Electrohome would also lose out if CanWest Global won the Alberta licences. Not only would WIC face two new competitors for its Calgary and Edmonton independent stations, it would no longer have the thirteen hours a week of those American shows that CanWest Global had been selling them.

These protests made at least some impression, but CanWest Global managed to mess up its application all on its own by trying to get the Calgary and Edmonton licences on the cheap, putting as little on the table as it thought it could get away with and making its "national" commitments conditional on CRTC approval of both its Alberta and Quebec applications. Furious at his team, Asper tried to salvage his dream of a "third national voice" by adding a last-minute benefits package that included $7 million a year for Alberta drama producers and $17 million annually for national expenditures on Canadian entertainment programming. The CRTC (and especially a rival applicant for the licences) viewed these figures with deep suspicion, which put Asper on the boil again. "We've challenged you as probably no one else has challenged the commission since CTV was licensed," Asper told the panel. "And I wish you all a hot, blazing Canadian summer."

Meanwhile, at WIC, ceaseless infighting continued to paralyze the decision-making process. In the late spring of 1996, the Griffithses and the Allards stood the sight of one another long enough to hold a united family meeting and decided that, since Doug Holtby wasn't taking their instructions, he'd have to go. WIC's former director Peter Paul Saunders sees a "pattern" at work here, starting with the untimely dismissal of Bill Hughes, followed by Ray Peters, and finally Holtby. But, like his predecessors, Holtby still had a year or so left on his contract. If the families wanted him out, they'd have to pay him to stay at home and mind his sizeable investment in the company.

Holtby says that he'd already decided he couldn't fight them any more. "They wanted to run management," says Allen Lambert. "[That] is not a proper role of directors, and it would have been improper of Doug Holtby to [take] decisions from [them]. They were all coming at him from different directions." In the assessment of Ray Peters (who'd been there and seen that), "Holtby got fed up with the families."

It seems to have taken several months to negotiate Holtby's departure, in part because he was going through a divorce and had to settle matters with his wife. But these discussions were kept extremely quiet. The July 2 announcement that he was "retiring" from WIC at the age of forty-nine stunned his closest colleagues, as well as the broadcasting community at large. WIC continued to pay Holtby $525,000 a year plus bonus and stock options for the remainder of his contract, which gave him plenty of time to oversee the construction of his new multimillion-dollar waterfront home in West Vancouver. "He wouldn't have got the settlement he got if it [weren't] for what Frank Griffiths had set up," says Allen Lambert. "[The two families] had to abide by the contract, but there was no desire to be generous to Holtby."

Still, Holtby left behind him a company (he considered it "a powerhouse") that seemed well-positioned to go forward. At the end of August, WIC received permission to extend its signal throughout Ontario, but didn't do so well with specialty licence applications. Turned down on its regional news service and the proposed Second City Comedy Channel, it had to be content with a consolation prize in the form of Teletoon, a channel that showed non-stop animated series.

Late that summer, Emily Griffiths fired Frank Jr., replacing him with her handsome son-in-law and new family favourite, Klaus Priebe. His wife, Mary, told the *Financial Post* that Frank Jr. was free to explore other possibilities because of "interference, management style, throwing his weight around, second-guessing, and bad-mouthing. It's sad, because he does know the business. He does have good ideas. If only he'd learned how to communicate effectively, without feeling he had to put down other people to make himself look good, he'd still be there today."

19

Vancouver
versus Montreal — 1996–97

Ivan Fecan faced hard choices in the fall of 1996. Either he could go all-out to win the first new television licence to be awarded in more than two decades in Vancouver, the second largest and fastest-growing market in English Canada, or he could make a play for CFCF-12 Montreal, when the "for sale" sign went up later that year. It was coming on the block because the Pouliot family had sold CFCF Inc., by then Quebec's second largest cable operator, its third largest French-language television network, and the owner of three television stations. CTV's English-language affiliate was the one thing that the new owners, Group Videotron Ltée, didn't want to keep.

If successful, CFCF-12's purchase would give Baton one more vote and enough shares to control CTV. The downside was that Montreal's English-language market wasn't growing at all. Its 750,000 people (a mere 4 per cent of English Canada) were an aging population, not the free-spending men and women in their twenties, thirties, and forties so coveted by advertising buyers. Add to this the pervasive political uncertainty that followed the previous year's referendum, and it's no surprise that advertisers preferred (in order) Toronto, Vancouver, Calgary, and Edmonton.

In contrast to Montreal, Vancouver represented coverage of 14 per cent of English-speaking Canada. As an added bonus, it vied with Toronto for the title of the third largest television and film production centre in the world, after Los Angeles and New York. Fecan had witnessed the early stages of this boom during the 1980s, when he'd come north to shepherd the filming of two NBC television movies.

"My friends and colleagues [from Vancouver] often use a railway metaphor," he later told the CRTC. "Historically, they say that Vancouver has been treated as the end of the line, a place to roll in eastern goods and imported ideas. We see it very differently, as a source of fresh and valuable work, a place of creative renewal and digital innovation, charting new socio-political waters. Yet much of what we see of Vancouver on Canadian television is quick hits on fish and lumber, or the city as a back-drop filling in for somewhere else on *The X-Files* or *Sliders*. We do not pretend to be experts on what Vancouver has to say, but we do know how to provide platforms for communities and creators to say it." Thus, the "end of the line" would become a starting point for Fecan's long-awaited renaissance in Canadian programming.

So far, developing a new programming strategy for Baton had proved an exercise in frustration for Fecan. Limited resources had cramped his accustomed style. He'd grown used to a pricier playing field — that is, the CBC, with its almost $1 billion in annual government appropriations. Another problem was that the BBS station group reached only 61 per cent of English-speaking Canada. "Reach translates into viewers," he explained, "and therefore into the revenues we need to amortize national licence fees. Reach also confers the ability to schedule and to promote [Canadian] programs, so that they find the audiences they need and deserve. We need a national infrastructure to pay for drama that [can't be paid] for by [reaching] only half the country."

Still, Fecan was doing what he could. Early in 1996, he'd asked Suzette Couture to develop a big-budget hour-long drama series that would serve as Baton's flagship offering, much as *Traders* had become CanWest Global's showcase. She came back with *The City*, a story of the clash between two neighbourhoods, rich and poor, in Toronto. Fecan loved it, so she and her partner, Pierre Sarrazin, began work on a pilot and a series bible.

Later that year, Fecan tried to lure *Royal Canadian Air Farce* and *This Hour Has 22 Minutes* away from the CBC, after the public broadcaster neglected to renew the Air Farce's contract, literally forgetting about its most popular show. The veteran comedy troupe appreciated Baton's bid, but at the last minute elected to remain with a national network. (Fecan did better at the specialty licence hearings in May, winning approval for The Comedy Network, as well as for two other cable channels, Outdoor Life, and Talk TV.)

As for drama, Fecan was pressing ahead with *Cold Squad*. His development team had been involved from the ground up, helping shape story ideas, reading every draft of the scripts, and picking up the slack when Lifetime, an American cable channel, backed out of the project after a change of management. Funding was reoriented for the more than $900,000-per-episode series, with Baton and Atlantis injecting more cash. As a result, the co-producer, Keatley-MacLeod, retained the American distribution rights, while Atlantis owned the rights for Canada and the rest of the world.

Fecan's first big movie-of-the-week, *Golden Will*, proved a major disappointment, however. CTV decided not to pick it up, and it aired (to very poor reviews) on BBS stations only in June 1996. At least Fecan recovered part of Baton's investment by using his connections to sell it south of the border to the Disney Channel.

☆

In August 1996, while on the links at the Toronto Golf Club, Doug Bassett told George Eaton that he was ready to hand the reins to his protégé. Bassett claims to have discussed this with no one, not even his wife, but friends had impressed upon him the necessity of an orderly transition at a public company. Apparently Eaton agreed that the timing was right. Late that month, Bassett announced that the forty-three-year-old Ivan Fecan would become president of Baton Broadcasting effective September 1, and its chief executive officer in December, following the annual shareholders' meeting. The fifty-six-year-old Bassett would then take the retiring Joe Garwood's place as Baton's vice-chairman, and would remain chairman of CTV. By then, Bassett had been Baton's CEO for fifteen years — five years longer than what he considered to be the optimum term. He'd hired Fecan because "Joe Garwood was older than I am, so Joe wasn't going to succeed me."

Fred Eaton supported this decision, but he must have wondered what the future held in store for his friend. He himself had handed the presidency of the T. Eaton Co. to his younger brother George in 1988, after the optimal ten years on the job. Then he'd stepped aside as chief executive officer and chairman, once again in favour of George, when Brian

Mulroney appointed him as High Commissioner in 1991. On his return home three years later, George had relegated him to the largely ceremonial post of vice-chairman of Eaton's of Canada.

"Douglas knew that one of his duties, as it is with every CEO, was to find a successor," Fred explains. "He hired Ivan. George was more involved in this, although I knew what was going on. [Then] I went and talked to [Ivan], and got to see what he was doing. I watched him perform. We all came to the conclusion that this was the man."

☆

Secure in his succession, Fecan's thoughts turned to the question of buying into either Vancouver or Montreal. One matter remained unresolved. The final closing of the Baton-Electrohome strategic alliance had been delayed three times since the CRTC had approved it in mid-1996, and Electrohome still owed $65 million for its half of Westco. The missed deadlines, however, led to a merger of the two companies. "When it came time to close the strategic alliance, it was not something [that Electrohome] was prepared to do," Fecan says. "After . . . all that time, [it] wasn't enough — in his heart, John Pollock knew it was the right thing. [So] Bruce Cowie and I worked it out until he was ready."

On September 19, Electrohome agreed to sell its broadcasting assets and CTV shares to Baton in exchange for Baton shares and $25 million in cash. If the CRTC approved the merger, Baton would then own 42.8 per cent of CTV and would operate a total of twenty-four stations in Ontario, Saskatchewan, and Alberta.

"Bruce Cowie [and I] went round and round," John Pollock explains. "The end result of sharing benefits was very complex; very few people understood it. In the end, we were better off to merge rather than continue in an increasingly complex alliance." Another factor drove the deal as well. "[This] was just before the Vancouver licence hearing," Fecan says, "[and] we felt we had to be in Vancouver."

At the outset, the new Vancouver licence seemed like a long shot for Baton-Electrohome. CHUM Ltd. was the odds-on favourite. A team from CITY, CHUM's independent Toronto station, had started their campaign almost two years in advance of the September 1996 public hearings, wining and dining Vancouver's elite. Their plan was to create a CITY clone — a lively, downtown, streetfront station, rather than a CFTO-like fortress in the suburbs. CHUM-CITY had succeeded in persuading the radio personality Pia Shandel, the author Peter C. Newman, the "Generation X" guru Doug Coupland, and the wheelchair athlete

Rick Hanson to join its advisory board. Other local celebrities, including Lilith Fair founder Sarah McLachlan, sent letters of support. And in an unprecedented and controversial move, British Columbia's NDP premier, Glenn Clark, publicly endorsed CHUM-CITY by appearing in a video that would be shown to the CRTC.

In addition to its late start, Baton-Electrohome had another strike against it. A rival applicant — Drew Craig, of Winnipeg's Craig Broadcasting — summed up the problem: "Why does Baton, now virtually in control of the CTV network, given that it has swallowed Electrohome, warrant a licence in Vancouver in competition with an existing CTV . . . affiliate? What public policy is served by approving this obvious conflict of interest?"

Craig was of course referring to WIC's BCTV, which lodged a protest of its own. Its submission to the CRTC stressed that it didn't want Baton-Electrohome (the "dominant force" within CTV) to operate an independent station that would compete with WIC's CTV affiliates (CHAN Vancouver and CHEK Victoria) in their own backyard.

Despite these roadblocks, Ivan Fecan exuded quiet confidence that his team would win. "I believe it will be either you or us," he told CHUM's Fred Sherratt. That, Sherratt says ruefully, meant that "Ivan thought he'd get it."

Baton-Electrohome had decided to take a different approach from CHUM-CITY's. It spent its money on wooing the CRTC rather than the city, in part because it felt that Fecan's reputation for supporting Canadian programming at the CBC had preceded him and would score brownie points with the regulator. "Look at what they put on the table," Sherratt says. "It was just what the commission wanted."

In short, Baton-Electrohome pledged to commit to two new thirteen-episode one-hour Canadian drama series, at least one of which (*Cold Squad*) would come from an independent British Columbia producer, as well as one twenty-six-episode half-hour family drama series from a similar source.

Baton-Electrohome also assured Vancouver's independent production community (which had thrived on servicing *The X-Files* and other Hollywood properties that wanted Vancouver to pass for Kansas City, New York, or Washington) that it was time for "the charade to end," and for Vancouver, and the west coast as a whole, to "proudly assume its identity." To facilitate this transition, it also proposed to launch *The Storytellers*, an anthology series of twenty original half-hour dramas. As well, independent producers would be expected to contribute half of the thirteen documentaries commissioned annually by Baton-Electrohome, which promised that all these programs would be aired on its twenty-four stations in prime time, thus "[showcasing] Vancouver to the rest of the country."

Even better, since Vancouverites resented having to fly to Toronto to get approval of their projects (a demeaning trek they referred to as the "$1,500 cup of coffee"), Baton-Electrohome also promised to establish a west-coast development office, run by a senior executive with full decision-making powers over $1.4 million in script development money. All together, Baton-Electrohome had committed to spending $72 million on Canadian programming over the course of a seven-year licence.

These proposals were enough to gain the support of Tony Allard, the president of Vancouver's Pacific Motion Pictures. This stance put him directly in conflict with his family's interests at WIC. Although Allard admired CITY, he and his partners had decided that Baton, which they expected would soon gain control of CTV, would be the best platform for his firm's dramatic productions. Allard also felt positively towards Ivan Fecan, because it was "refreshing to have a broadcaster who walked the talk." On balance, then (and out of what Allard termed pure self-interest), Baton was their pick, even though Allard thought that it was unlikely to win the licence.

CHUM-CITY couldn't match Baton's commitment to series drama. Its specialty and forte was "long-form drama" — that is, movies. As the country's largest television exhibitor of Canadian films, with more than 150 titles under licence, it pledged to commission new films from independent Vancouver sources. (In private, Fred Sherratt doubted that this would impress the commission, which he believed was "caught up in a time warp" and thought only "in terms of series programming.")

Ivan Fecan hoped that Sherratt was right. CHUM-CITY posed the biggest threat to his application, but he knew that the CITY model banked almost exclusively on movies to wave the Cancon flag. "We [continued] to support television series drama," he says. "So there were two distinct choices, and we fit more with the [CRTC's] thinking."

Baton-Electrohome went one better than CHUM-CITY in another important area. It had commissioned an Angus Reid Inc. survey that identified the issue of local control as of extreme importance to Vancouverites. They didn't want a transplanted Toronto station, not even a transplanted CITY. Baton-Electrohome therefore promised that the new Vancouver outlet would have a separate eight-member board of directors, at least four of whom would be recruited locally. Its choices were the well-known director Daryl Duke; the Simon Fraser University professor Dr. Catherine Murray; the impresario David Y. H. Lui; and the native affairs expert Calvin Helm. (Earlier, it had approached Carole Taylor, the former host of *Canada AM* and *W5*, but she was still with Ports Canada and prohibited, as a federal civil servant, from joining anyone else's board.)

☆

When the hearings got under way in the five-sailed convention complex known as Canada Place, conflict of interest charges flew thick and fast. CanWest Global told the CRTC's newly appointed chairwoman, Françoise Bertrand, that if Baton got the independent licence, its cooperative buying efforts with WIC and CTV would end; Baton, WIC, and CTV would compete to purchase the national rights for American shows, and Global (and other broadcasters) would be priced out of the market.

WIC's BCTV made a parallel objection, claiming that approval of Baton's application would give it national-rights buying clout second only to Global's. Approximately eighteen hours of BCTV's programming (two-thirds of which were American shows) currently belonged to Baton. With the exceptions of local news and hockey coverage, BCTV stood to lose most of the top non-CTV programs in its prime-time schedule: *Law & Order*, *Home Improvement*, *Melrose Place*, *Ellen*, *The Drew Carey Show*, and *Dr. Quinn, Medicine Woman*. If Fecan's group was licensed, BCTV could kiss them goodbye.

Fecan responded by pointing out that WIC had recently stepped up buying national rights on its own behalf, acquiring the Brooke Shields sitcom *Suddenly Susan*. He acknowledged that Baton supplied some of WIC's prime-time programming, but noted that WIC felt free to pick and choose what it wanted, at Baton's expense. For example, Baton had bought national rights to *Cosby*, which WIC had refused to carry. What good was paying for national rights if an entire province decided not to chip in? Fecan said that this was tantamount to "writing off British Columbia" — in other words, an inefficient use of Baton's finite resources.

Fecan concluded with the observation that CTV, Baton, and WIC's cooperative buying arrangement had worked well in the past, but that relationships change. The current arrangement was due to expire at year's end. "We hope to continue, should we be so fortunate as to be licensed, to work with WIC and CTV to continue in some way making sense of this bazaar in Los Angeles, where far too much Canadian money is left behind," he said. Beyond that, he made no guarantees.

☆

In early October 1996, the action shifted from Vancouver to Montreal, where potential buyers got a chance to examine the facilities at CFCF-12. Baton was among them, having hedged its bets by taking Montreal entertainment company Astral Communications as a potential partner in a joint bid that, if successful, would have given it four out of eight votes at the CTV boardroom table and a controlling equity interest in the network of 43 per cent. But Baton's costly merger with Electrohome had depleted its resources. When its bankers (the CIBC) said forget it, Baton could not proceed. "We kicked the tires, looked at the finances," Ivan Fecan says. "There were lots of strategic reasons to bid . . . , but at the end of the day there wasn't enough value."

"The situation in Montreal was so dramatically different," says Fred Eaton, comparing the city to what it had been eighteen years earlier, when Big John Bassett's attempt to purchase CFCF-12 had been thwarted by the CRTC. Baton's chairman, Allan Beattie, adds that there was justifiable concern about how much support existed for English-language television in Montreal. Besides, he feels, "the pricing seemed to be very aggressive. [CFCF-12] came up for sale in the midst of a whole raft of things. How much can you chew off?"

So, having kicked the tires, Baton retreated, leaving the field clear for WIC. Acquisition of CFCF-12 would give it two out of eight votes in the CTV boardroom and an equity interest of 28.6 per cent, but Jim Macdonald, the television division's new president, claimed that WIC didn't want to control the network. Rather, it saw CFCF-12 as a valuable asset in its own right, one that would increase WIC's coverage area to 75 per cent of English-speaking Canada (ahead of Baton and CanWest Global) and fill in one of the major gaps in its emerging national system.

The bidding process for CFCF-12 drew to a close at the end of November. The winner was a 70-30 joint venture between WIC and a subsidiary of the Caisse de dépôt et placement du Québec, which agreed to pay a minimum of $70 million. The price would go up by $30 million, though, if CanWest Global didn't get approval for its Quebec City television licence within two years. "I'm not sure why WIC went in as heavy as they did," a puzzled Fecan says.

Meanwhile, Izzy Asper was soldiering on, despite having suffered a major setback in the race for the next coast-to-coast television system. At the beginning of November, the CRTC announced its decision to award the new Alberta television licences to Craig Broadcasting. A month later, however, CanWest Global was in Quebec City for public hearings into its application, in partnership with TVA, to take control of the small English-language CBC affiliate in Quebec's capital, from which it hoped to feed its programming into Montreal, Sherbrooke, and other communities where a bigger English-speaking audience existed.

WIC's Jim Macdonald opposed Asper's scheme, since it once again involved skimming the cream from urban markets without the need to service smaller centres. "BCTV covers all the [provincial] interior with 113-odd transmitters," Macdonald said. "Those are not what we would call money-making contributors. There's a tremendous cost to the infrastructure." CTV's Gary Maavara mounted a similar protest. He called on Global to "step up to the plate" and provide the same benefits as did CTV in return for a network (or system, or whatever Asper wanted to call it). "We are happy," he said, "to compete on that basis."

In fact, CTV was having trouble competing with anyone. In the course of a directors' meeting late that fall, John Cassaday told the shareholders' group that something had to be done: "There is no more revenue in the system. If we are going to make CTV work, we are going to have to do something different." CTV could no longer operate as a separate entity in the old style of national networks; it needed a strong controlling shareholder in order to consolidate its infrastructure and cut costs so that it would have the money to buy and commission desirable and cost-efficient programming. "The way that CTV was operating was a huge improvement over what was there before Mr. Cassaday came to the organization," said Fecan. "[But] we felt that John had run out of every possible trick. [We] needed to take it to the next level." Fred Sherratt was even more colourful in his description: "I tell you, [John] had the lions jumping through the hoops for a long time. Often it was the same hoop that had to be jumped through two or three times. [But when] Baton [was] at the edge, it needed somebody to put it over the top. [This] needed to be done from Toronto. Agincourt was there; there was synergy going. And John didn't disagree with that."

☆

Baton's annual meeting on December 18, 1996, turned into a tribute to the departing Doug Bassett. Two years earlier, he and Susan had sold their Forest Hill mansion for $3.5 million to the Bay Street money manager Ira Gluskin. Their social standing diminished by lack of a prestigious address, they'd taken temporary rented digs near Ted Rogers. Apparently, Bassett had made some poor investments along the line, but he maintained his opulent summer cottage on Lake Rosseau — minus a few of his beloved boats — and his winter villa on the Caribbean island of Antigua.

With Brian Mulroney long gone from Ottawa and the Tories reduced to a table for two, Bassett's political clout had taken a dive as well. In 1994, he and Susan had hosted a $10,000-a-plate fundraising dinner for the new federal leader, Jean Charest, but the Conservatives were headed for the wilderness. Fred Eaton, one of the party's most ardent supporters, switched to Reform. The sole survivor was Big John's wife, Isabel, who'd failed to get elected on Kim Campbell's ill-fated ticket in 1993, but later won an Ontario provincial seat and served in Premier Mike Harris's government.

Perhaps most difficult for Doug to swallow was the loss of corporate power. His seats on several outside boards ended around the same time he moved out of CFTO, on the day of Baton's annual meeting, into a memorabilia-filled office in a nondescript tower in downtown Toronto, cut off from the company he'd managed for eighteen years. He remained chairman of CTV, saying that he was there as a "resource for Ivan," but felt it important that Fecan be free to manage Baton without the looming shadow of a former CEO.

Bassett's backers think he doesn't get enough credit for his contributions to Baton's eventual takeover of CTV. "It was quite a legacy that Douglas left," Brian Mulroney says. "[He] was a builder, like his father. By the time he left, Baton was a huge bloody thing." "Douglas had vision," adds *Sunday Edition*'s Mike Duffy. "[He] laid the groundwork for the expansion. He just ran into roadblocks from the [other shareholders] which were more difficult than even he, with all of his background . . . , imagined. [He] also laid the groundwork with the Eatons. In the end, they stayed the course as a result of his work. [For] more than five years [they] spent money and amassed debt without a nickel's return on their investment, as they took Doug's advice to be patient and wait for the [CTV] deal to mature."

WIC's new chief executive officer, John Lacey, was shocked in December of 1996 when a group of arbitrageurs from New York's Oppenheimer & Co. demanded that WIC be dismantled and sold off piece by piece. Eric Rosenfeld, one of the New York contingent, led a shareholders' revolt at WIC's annual meeting on January 8, 1997. In a special (and in the end, fruitless) ballot, the majority of the non-voting B shareholders voted to dissolve WIC because they felt slighted by the Griffiths and Allard families. "Can you just repeat that?" a stunned Lacey asked the scrutineer. "I think you got it backwards." The united families easily shot down the rebels' motion, because they controlled the company through their voting A shares. "You have absolutely no desire to hear the views of the B shareholders," Rosenfeld told them. Frank Griffiths Jr. attended the meeting, sitting several rows back and on the opposite side of the room from his estranged mother, Emily. Doug Holtby was also present, off in his own corner.

WIC's management received another blow at month's end, when the CRTC awarded Baton the licence for the new Vancouver station. This meant that Baton would soon control twenty-five outlets and cover 75 per cent of English-speaking Canada, slightly behind WIC, whose coverage area was 76 per cent but which owned only ten television stations.

Perhaps the commission wished to ensure a level of parity among Canada's three largest station groups, because it approved, at this same time, CanWest Global's application to take over (and relaunch as an independent) the Quebec City station, giving Izzy Asper and Co. 77 per cent coverage, and keeping the Winnipeg mogul's hopes of a national system alive.

By early February, Ivan Fecan and Bruce Cowie were hanging out in a Vancouver hotel room, suffering through the birth pangs of their new station, which was expected to begin broadcasting that fall. Baton-Electrohome had already optioned land in the suburbs, but a real estate agent fortuitously informed the two men that the landlord of a renovated building that used to house the Vancouver Public Library needed a new tenant in place of one who'd just taken a walk. Its upper floors were available at a more reasonable rent than the $200-per-square-foot lease price that the main-floor tenants, Virgin Records and the Planet Hollywood restaurant, were shelling out.

Ivan Fecan went up to the third floor of the heritage-class Modernist building overlooking the corner of Robson and Burrard, and surveyed the passing scene. "For twenty-four hours I sat and watched," he said. "And there [were] always people there. [I] thought: this is where I want to be, because this is where all the different worlds [of Vancouver] mix." To top it off, a former co-worker, the ex-head of finance at the CBC, now happened to run the CBC Pension Fund, which owned the building and would approve the lucky tenant. Fecan knew that the entire sequence of events was destiny — and Vancouver Television had its brand new home.

20

And That's the Kind of Takeover It's Been — 1997–98

At the beginning of 1997, Ivan Fecan assembled the final piece of the puzzle that enabled Baton to achieve its dream of assuming control of CTV. He did so by looking unexpectedly eastward. The previous summer, Fecan had asked Fred Sherratt if CHUM would be interested in dealing off its Atlantic affiliates. Sherratt was born and raised in Truro, Nova Scotia, and had begun his career in radio there while still in high school. He'd managed these stations for twenty-five years and saw them as "a big piece of [his] life's work." He replied that he felt such a deep emotional tie to them that it was difficult to give them up. He agreed that a solution had to be found to make Baton CTV's single controlling shareholder, but he didn't want to "sell the Maritimes" to do it.

Over lunch at the Granite Club in Toronto that January, Fecan suggested to Sherratt that there might be another way to do a deal. Perhaps each had something the other wanted. The two men developed the concept of swapping properties of equal value: Baton's London, Wingham, Wheatley, and Pembroke, Ontario, stations for CHUM's three Maritime CTV affiliates (and their CTV shares), its Saint John station, and the Atlantic Satellite Network. This would put Baton over the top at CTV, expand its national reach to 84 per cent of English-speaking Canada, and give CHUM a presence in London and the Ottawa Valley. Besides,

Baton could well afford to give up four of its Ontario outlets, which amounted to duplicate coverage because it owned the equivalent of two regional networks in the province, thanks to Doug Bassett and Joe Garwood's buying spree.

"Baton suffered from too deep pockets," argues Electrohome's John Pollock. "It worked out in the end, but they spent a lot more money than they should have." Fecan agreed, but liked the result. "It all kind of fit," he says. Eight months earlier, he'd convinced the CRTC to end the Pembroke station's CTV affiliate status, since it "wasn't doing particularly well." Now, it had become "a valuable chip for CHUM" — or, in the words of Baton's chairman, Allan Beattie, "trade bait."

Fecan and Sherratt continued their negotiations in secret, usually at CHUM's Toronto offices on Sunday mornings. Fecan, who lived a little to the south, brought the cappuccino. Sherratt, who lived a little to the east, supplied the bagels. Shortly after the CRTC announced its decision to award the new Vancouver licence to Baton, however, they had to vary this leisurely schedule and wrap matters up by phone. (Sherratt later said that he "misread" the situation in Vancouver, because he didn't think that Baton "had a hope" of getting the licence, given that CTV's ownership situation remained unresolved.) Then, having finalized all the details, Baton and CHUM released the news of their swap on February 25 — the day before the T. Eaton Co. sought bankruptcy protection.

☆

Baton's financial health wasn't robust either. Its stock had hit a low of $6.90 in early 1997, after suffering the corporate ignominy of being de-listed from the Toronto Stock Exchange Composite 300 Index. In February, it cut 154 jobs at its Ontario stations because of increased competition from WIC, which was broadcasting its OnTV signal throughout the province.

In April, however, it was WIC's turn to react to the prospect of competing head to head with Baton in Vancouver. Its chairman, Ed King, and its CEO, John Lacey, arrived by helicopter at BCTV's Burnaby studios, to break the news that 51 (out of roughly 280) jobs would be "gradually eliminated" at WIC's British Columbia stations, while another 44 positions would be cut throughout Alberta, where Craig Broadcasting would shortly be launching two new outlets.

Earlier that week, one WIC executive had found a new home. Ivan Fecan had recruited Jon Festinger, WIC's general legal counsel, to manage Baton's new Vancouver station. The long-time lawyer, apprehensive about jumping from corporate work to a more creative function, had phoned WIC's former CEO Doug Holtby to ask his advice. Holtby told him to "just do it," because there wasn't any school where Festinger could go to learn the requisite skills. That same month, the mercurial Emily Griffiths resigned as a WIC director, declaring that she was seventy-five years old and wanted to be less directly involved in WIC's affairs.

Meanwhile, CanWest Global had recently pushed its holdings in WIC up to 15 per cent of the non-voting B shares from a little less than 10 per cent. Izzy Asper made it known that he wanted to be at the table if WIC came "up for grabs," so as to get at its Alberta stations. He was disappointed that his federal Liberal friends — notably Finance Minister Paul Martin — had failed him in February, dismissing his appeal against the CRTC's decision to award the new Alberta licences to Craig Broadcasting. To atone for this lapse, the Chrétien cabinet issued an order-in-council, suggesting that the CRTC consider licensing "one or more new national networks." Since there were now (either by accident or design) three private broadcasting groups or systems (CanWest Global, Baton, and WIC) that reached roughly equal audiences of English-speaking Canadians, the commission duly scheduled a round of network hearings for the late autumn.

Back at CTV, John Cassaday had seen the writing on the wall. Ivan Fecan was on track for his job, and there wasn't room for both of them in the organization. To Cassaday's disgust, Fecan's supporters were waging a whisper campaign against him, primarily on the grounds that he was to blame for the lack of indigenous Canadian drama in CTV's schedule. Cassaday hadn't helped his cause by replacing the retiring Arthur Weinthal with Gary Maavara in January. A talented entertainment lawyer who'd done well with the network's operations, sports, and public affairs, Maavara was short on development or programming experience. His appointment as group vice-president of programming was taken as an insult by most independent producers.

Maavara didn't see what the fuss was about. He acknowledged that Weinthal, over his thirty-year career, had been instrumental in building Canada's independent production community, but Maavara considered that this job was over and done with. He would select shows, rather than developing them. His priority would be American and Canadian programs with broad appeal for CTV's middle-of-the-road audience.

Consistent with the network's recent focus, four industrial dramas waved the Cancon flag in CTV's 1997–98 schedule: *FX: The Series* (returning, courtesy of Fireworks Entertainment); *Police Academy: The Series*, from Paul Bronfman's Protocol Entertainment; *La Femme Nikita*, also from Fireworks; and *John Woo's Once a Thief*, from the ubiquitous Alliance.

Once a Thief had a mildly interesting genesis. The project started rolling when Alliance approached Arthur Weinthal, after a deal with Global came undone. Weinthal looked at the made-in-Vancouver pilot movie, directed by the Hong Kong chopsocky legend John Woo, and decided that it was a good action-adventure, whose hip young triumvirate of law enforcement agents would score with viewers in the States and overseas. He therefore agreed that CTV would put up more money than usual. Gary Maavara also believed in *Once a Thief*. "Every aspect of it is great," he said. "It's well written, well directed, well acted, well cast." The pilot movie (which, unlike the individual shows, merited some of this praise) would air first, and the series would debut later in September.

Maavara's buying trip with John Cassaday and Arthur Weinthal (who acted in a consulting capacity) to Los Angeles that May proved a bit of a bust. Almost all of their picks, including an American version of the Robbie Coltrane vehicle *Cracker*, would not last the season. They did, however, manage to return with the rights to a Big Event — the $40-million special-effects extravaganza *Merlin*, the most expensive mini-series ever made.

By the beginning of June, the tension between John Cassaday and Ivan Fecan had escalated into extreme hostility. Observers noted (but Fecan later denied) that the pair didn't say a word to each other as they stood side by side in CTV's newsroom during the network's scattered coverage of the federal election.

Three days later, on June 5, CTV's gala launch of its fall season at Toronto's Bluma Appel Theatre was highlighted by the amazing resurrection of *Due South*. CTV and Alliance, together with the BBC (on which *Due South* had ranked as the number one foreign program), a German broadcaster, and several American syndicators, pooled financing for twenty-six more episodes. Half would be shown in 1997–98, and half the following season. Paul Gross cemented his status as a renaissance man by collecting a $2-million pay cheque to executive-produce, act in, and occasionally script the series. Baton's talk show host Camilla Scott would return as Gross's boss and love interest, but his co-star David Marciano was out, except for guest appearances. He was replaced by Callum Keith Rennie, and a smarter, better-trained dog assumed the role of Diefenbaker. Gary Maavara called *Due South*'s new 7 p.m. Sunday time slot "a jewel" and hoped that it would result in even better ratings than the series had realized the previous season, when it had pulled in 1.2 to 1.3 million viewers on Thursdays at eight o'clock, despite being pitted against Global's simulcast of *Friends.*

This launch was the last such waltz for John Cassaday, although he kept his impending departure quiet for a day or so. Instead, the erstwhile food executive informed the *Toronto Star* that "programming is product. You have to position yourself, as McDonald's did when they changed to hard french-fries from soft. What matters is what people want, particularly in the entertainment business, where specialty channels are competing with free TV, satellites . . . , even bowling alleys."

Rather than mount a gala of its own, Baton called personally on media buyers that same week, dispensing individual boxed lunches and word of a mixed bag of programming. Fecan's buying trip to Los Angeles had yielded four new American pick-ups that wouldn't last the season. He had, however, snared the comedy-drama *Ally McBeal.* Fecan found its almost unclassifiable blend of fantasy and reality so intriguing that he bid on it even though he couldn't simulcast it anywhere except Vancouver, because it aired during CTV's network service time on Monday nights. This meant that Baton had to swallow the cost of its so-called "national" rights, but the risk paid off when the show started making headlines.

Unfortunately, Fecan ran into even greater trouble with his slate of Canadian shows. Eight months earlier, Heritage Minister Sheila Copps had merged Telefilm's Broadcast Fund with the Cable Fund and injected an extra $100 million in taxpayers' dollars. The result — the $200-million Canada Television and Cable Production Fund — was known throughout the broadcast community as "Sheila's money." But too many independent producers rushed to get a piece of it, and an instant cash crunch threatened most of Baton's promised Cancon offerings from its Vancouver station. *Cold Squad* was among the first to suffer. Despite a partially successful bout of last-minute haggling, it received nowhere near the $4 million it had been expecting to go towards its initial thirteen episodes, which pushed their appearance back to mid-season.

Also scheduled to be broadcast from Vancouver was a sketch comedy series created by Bob Robertson and Linda Cullen, the CBC's *Double Exposure* radio team; a mid-morning talk show hosted by the former CBC radio chat maven Vicki Gabereau (who told the *Financial Post* that she'd "got an offer from a good friend"); and a Sunday morning political commentary series chaired by the *Globe and Mail*'s former west-coast columnist, Robert Mason Lee.

Finally, for airing on the BBS stations, Fecan had chosen repeats of the first season of *The X-Files*. They would serve as a useful lead-in to Baton's latest industrial Canadian drama series from Atlantis, *Gene Roddenberry's Earth: Final Conflict*, based on a long-dormant concept from the creator of *Star Trek*.

As for the competition, WIC had aggressively outbid Global for the new Kirstie Alley series, *Veronica's Closet*, which would follow *Seinfeld* in NBC's Thursday line-up. Global, for its part, had three hot prospects: *Dharma & Greg*, *South Park*, and *Dawson's Creek*. Otherwise, its Cancon schedule was heavy with the usual industrial suspects, except for the returning *Traders*.

On June 27, in something of an anti-climax following the fall previews, John Cassaday announced his resignation. After more than seven years in charge of CTV, he planned to leave at the end of August to take up his new position as president and CEO of Shaw Media, Shaw Communications' new broadcasting division. He cited the conclusion of CTV's new shareholder and affiliate agreements, its successful coverage of two Olympic Games, and its successful bid for three new specialty licences, including CTV News 1, as the major achievements of his presidency. He also took satisfaction in having aired *E.N.G.* and *Due South*.

A disingenuous Ivan Fecan later professed not to understand why Cassaday jumped ship. "We would have made an interesting team," he said. "We did agree on a lot of issues."

Doug Bassett hosted a moving-on party for Cassaday at the Toronto Club, attended by most of CTV's former directors. Doug Holtby called Bassett from Vancouver to say how touched he'd been to receive an invitation.

John Lacey, Holtby's replacement as WIC's CEO, had hinted at the CRTC hearing into its purchase of CFCF-12 Montreal that WIC saw its television division as a third network capable of leaving CTV and going it alone when the current affiliation agreement expired in September 1999. To make up for the shows that used to be provided by CTV, it would step up its bidding for national rights to American and Canadian programming and put more resources into *Canada Tonight*, the national newscast anchored by Tony Parsons.

WIC Television's president, Jim Macdonald, told the commission that "most people recognized CTV for its news," but credited an individual affiliate, not the network, for entertainment programs. For example, if Montrealers tuned in to *Spin City* or *ER*, they'd say they were watching CFCF-12. Indeed, they were watching CTV, but they didn't think of it that way. News was "very different," Macdonald said. "People watch Lloyd Robertson or Sandie Rinaldo. They say: 'I watched the *CTV News*.'"

WIC Television knew that branding was all-important and intended to use the two years that remained in its affiliation agreement to build brand identification of its own, starting with *Canada Tonight*. It was doing well, but posed no threat to *CTV News* as yet. "The numbers [a daily viewership of 700,000] aren't great past Alberta," conceded Parsons. Nonetheless, he felt that adding a new station in Quebec would give it both increased coverage and added credibility. "Everyone would like to see it go as a national program," he said, adding that he expected WIC to "put more money into it if the WIC stations disaffiliated." That eventuality seemed to move somewhat closer when, five weeks later, the CRTC approved WIC and the Caisse's purchase of CFCF-12.

In preparation for their proposed takeover of CTV, Ivan Fecan and his team endured two weeks of mock inquisition by an ersatz CRTC. Baton's lead counsel, Kathy Robinson, and her legal cohorts drilled the executives in a studio at CFTO that had been set up to look like the Outaouais Room in Hull. As Fecan puts it, the legal team "ran a boot camp" and there were "people playing commissioners who asked every rotten question." Media consultant Pauline Couture (cousin of screenwriter Suzette Couture), who'd come on board during the Baton-Electrohome strategic alliance hearing, wrote thirty to forty drafts of their presentation. "It was the last piece, the most important, what we'd been working for in one form or another for thirty-eight years," Fecan says. "This would not be the one to blow."

Strangely enough, no one formally intervened against the takeover in advance of the July 15 and 16 hearings, although CanWest Global asked to appear so as to express concerns about the way the CRTC made its decisions. Even more surprising than the lack of protest was a letter in favour of the takeover, penned by WIC's retired president, Ray Peters. It seemed to stem from the fact that Peters knew and admired Fecan, whom he'd met while co-chairing a federal task force in 1990–91.

Peters began by lauding Fecan's "proven credentials" and credited him and his hand-picked management team with "a dramatic change in direction" at CTV — but couldn't resist taking a few shots at his old foes. Having mentioned his twenty-year-long fight against Baton's seizing control of the network, he explained that his opposition had been "rooted in two major concerns." First, he'd doubted that the previous management team at Baton/CFTO was capable of running CTV. Second, he'd taken issue with Baton/CFTO's "stated objective" to centre the bulk of the network's Canadian production in Toronto. By contrast, he commended Fecan for setting up the new regional development office in Vancouver and committing to a similar office in Halifax.

But all was not to Peters's liking. He went on to complain that Baton/CFTO still dominated CTV's news and public affairs programming. When he was chairman of CTV's executive committee, "a portion of the sixty-five hours of [CTV's] programs was produced in the regions." This wasn't as much as he wanted to see, but at least some effort was being made, despite the Baton/CFTO group's power grabs. Now, however, "the network has been reduced to only forty hours of CTV programming per week," seventeen of which (that is, *Canada AM*, *W Five*, and *CTV News*) "reflect the social, political, economic and cultural views of [Ontario], with programs originating from the studios of Baton/CFTO."

On July 15, the first day of the public hearings, the CRTC worked through the Baton-Electrohome merger, the Baton-CHUM swap, and the transfer of CHUM's equity interest in CTV to Baton, giving it control of CTV.

To support the merger, Baton put $10 million in benefits on the table, including $6 million that would fund the creation of Baton Signature Presentations, a nationwide programming initiative designed to provide additional financing for movies-of-the-week and mini-series that addressed provocative social issues. Bruce Cowie cited as an example the story of Sheldon Kennedy, the young hockey player who'd recently come forward to expose his sexual abuse by a trusted coach. (The other $4 million would go towards improvements in news operations.)

To bolster the Baton-CHUM swap, Baton proposed to spend $2.25 million on a Halifax development office, and an extra $14 million on new independent Atlantic Canada productions for *The Storytellers* series, as well as for documentaries.

Finally, for the privilege of taking over CTV, Baton pledged to allot $1 million to a Baton Canadian Literature Fund, which would aid independent producers in bringing Canadian novels to the screen. This struck the commission as inadequate, but Baton argued that it had already spent almost half a billion dollars on various acquisitions, including benefits of more than $125 million. Enough was enough.

With regard to quantity, Baton's application was supported by what looked like a cast of hundreds. Besides Ivan Fecan and his front-line team, the main panel included both John Cassaday and Lloyd Robertson. A perfectly starched Doug Bassett sat quietly in the audience all by himself until his daughter Jennifer joined him after lunch. He did not participate in the CTV presentation, which kicked off at four o'clock. CHUM's Fred Sherratt began by announcing that "CTV needs the kind of efficiencies and synergies that this proposal offers. It needs them now and Baton is the best party to do it."

A deeply tanned John Cassaday went on to describe Baton's takeover as the best guarantee of a strong and vibrant network. "CTV could have a wonderful future," he predicted. "It has a trusted reputation, [thanks to] its various brand names, [which] can now be expanded over an entire 126-hour schedule. It has [a] news gathering [operation] which will be further enhanced by a closer working relationship with local newsrooms owned by its new parent. [Finally], it will now have the buying and scheduling clout to ensure that the best Canadian and [American] programs are on CTV. Baton has seized the initiative made possible by the new shareholders' agreement and has the most significant synergy with CTV. Our team has accomplished a great deal, but I would be concerned about CTV's ability to survive in the absence of approval of this transaction."

In honeyed tones, Lloyd Robertson — who closed each evening newscast with the phrase "And that's the kind of day it's been" — informed the commissioners that the news division welcomed Baton's takeover, because a single controlling shareholder satisfied a need for stability and clarity of focus. "At *CTV News*, we have speculated for some time now that Baton Broadcasting might gain majority control of CTV," he said. "And we have concluded that a move to one major owner would be a positive development.

"When I arrived at CTV twenty-one years ago, there were ten owners," he continued. "[Then some] of the smaller organizations . . . merged with larger companies. Others sold their assets and moved on. At one point, everybody else was in as a network owner, and Baton was out. Then, before we knew it, Baton was back in. Naturally, these moves, and the attendant publicity about chaos [at], and the possible collapse [of], CTV caused some nervousness in the news division. We watched as regional news networks grew within our system, in some cases reaching national proportions. We wondered whether our owners might one day simply declare us redundant, [which] might have made economic sense for them."

Fortunately for Robertson and the news division, the "network managed to survive. And, as it turns out, our owners did not desert the news." Robertson credited this to Baton's special relationship with the news division, the home of *CTV National News* for more than thirty years and *Canada AM* for almost twenty-five.

Ivan Fecan said that Baton was like the "fifty-year-old actor in a hit movie, [who'd] spent thirty years in summer theatre doing everything that prepared [him] for that moment." He reiterated that Baton had spent almost half a billion dollars hoping to become that sort of "overnight success." He promised to use Baton's development process to "create a string of popular Canadian programs that [would] take their place in the Top Ten." But, in order to do so, Baton had to "free up money that can go on the screen," by consolidating the twin infrastructures of Baton and CTV as quickly as possible. The only exception would be national news. "We're not taking anything away from news. News is very important," Fecan stressed, at which point Lloyd Robertson looked sideways at his new boss and laughed.

The next day, July 16, the commissioners were treated to the case for the prosecution. "This is historic, unique, never-seen-before stuff," Global Television's president Jim Sward said of the Baton-CHUM swap. "It is a big deal. It is an outstanding business deal that these parties have woven together. [Speaking as something] of a student of business deals, this goes down as one of the most elegant [and] artful [in] recent memory. . . . The 's' word — survival — has been used a lot. [We've heard about the] survival of CTV, [the] survival of local programming, [the] survival of prime-time Canadian drama, the survival of the Canadian broadcasting system. [But] there is no issue of survival. Things have never been better than they are today. . . . CTV is an incredibly powerful force today, compared to what it was ten years ago."

Sward reminded the commission that CanWest Global had asked for, but had been turned down on, its own national station chain. "Baton is asking for this privilege for the first time," he said. "This is [a] unique privilege. It is asking [you] to put [control] of a coast-to-coast service of 126 hours a week [into] one ownership hand. Is it a competitive advantage? You bet it is."

Sward pointed out that Baton's stock, which had hit a low of $6.90 at the beginning of the year, now traded at $13. "The market place bets that [you] will approve this [takeover], and [that] it will mean tens and tens of millions of dollars of asset value to Baton," he explained.

Shortly after lunch, Baton replied to Sward's intervention. Ivan Fecan spoke with barely suppressed fury, charging that "Global sees this as a business deal, pure and simple. We see it as a lot more." Under Baton's stewardship, Fecan said, CTV would assume its rightful place as a "showcase" for distinctive Canadian drama. As his career path proved, he believed in and had actively promoted Canadian talent of every kind. Others knew that he put his money where his mouth was. Hadn't the commission received more than 1,500 letters in support of Baton's takeover from artists such as Rita MacNeil and Ashley MacIsaac; producing/writing teams such as Pierre Sarrazin and Suzette Couture and Wayne Grisby and Barbara Samuels; and Canadian publishers such as Avie Bennett and Anna Porter?

Baton, he claimed, had the "guts" to assume "all of the risks and responsibilities of a network," including the tens and tens of millions of dollars it would have to spend on Canadian programming. Unlike Global, it would no longer hide behind the word "system." Fecan invited the CRTC, when it got around to the upcoming third network hearings, to compare Global's commitments in this regard with the combined commitments of CTV and its affiliates. "I suspect you will find that it is a very different . . . number," he said, adding that he looked forward to competing with Global "on a more level playing field."

Next, Fecan took issue with Sward's contention that Baton's profits had never been higher. "[Last year], we made a couple of million dollars," he said. "Electrohome — not much more. CTV is break-even. Global made $50 million profit on its Canadian operations. [They've been] quoted [as] saying that they think it might go as [much] as 30 per cent [higher] this year. They can do that, I guess, because they have the thinnest infrastructure. They can do that, I guess, because they control all 126 of their hours, something they wish to deny us."

As for stock prices, Fecan admitted that Baton's "was $13 yesterday." But ten years earlier, before it started "on the road to CTV," its shares had traded at $15. During that decade, CanWest Global's stock had enjoyed phenomenal growth.

Finally, Fecan wondered how Sward could allege that CTV's "survival" wasn't an issue. Five of its directors had said that it *was*. How would Sward know differently? "We have not seen Mr. Sward in our boardroom," Fecan remarked, in a tone that suggested that he wouldn't welcome Sward's appearance if it happened.

☆

On Thursday, August 28, Ivan Fecan flew to Los Angeles to attend a memorial service for his former NBC boss, Brandon Tartikoff. Fecan knew that Tartikoff had been battling Hodgkin's disease, a usually fatal form of cancer, since his early twenties. It had twice gone into remission after rounds of chemotherapy — the second time, just before Fecan had joined Tartikoff's team in 1985. Then, in 1997, Tartikoff's wife, Lilly, told Fecan that it had returned.

Fecan phoned Tartikoff at once. "We had a great conversation, and he pitched me on his current project," Fecan later wrote. The project was "a satire on network television." In keeping with the subject matter, Tartikoff had named his latest company after the character played by Peter Finch in the film *Network* — the half-crazed anchorman Howard Beale, who screams out, "I'm mad as hell and I'm not going to take it any more!" Baton had planned to broadcast the feature, and Paul Bronfman's Protocol Entertainment had agreed to be its Canadian producer.

When Tartikoff died on Wednesday, August 27, the *Globe and Mail* asked Fecan to write a tribute piece. Initially, he didn't want to do it. "Frankly, I was scared of it," he explains, "but I talked to Sandra about it and I became obsessed with it. It was good for therapy."

The *Globe* published Fecan's tribute on the front page of its arts section that Friday. In it, Fecan confessed that he'd been "devastated" by the news. "Brandon was my mentor, my friend, and the brother I never had," Fecan wrote. He considered it ironic that he was flying to California while "awaiting the CRTC decision on Baton's control of CTV, a subject we had discussed excitedly and which, if it happens, will certainly be an important achievement in my career — a career for which Brandon can take a large part of the credit. Or blame. Before I left to catch my plane, I looked at the T-shirt from my second year at NBC. It said: 'That Championship Season II.' It was. And I cried."

Afterwards, the savagely satirical *Frank* magazine, whose tastelessness sometimes knows no bounds, questioned how close Fecan's friendship with Tartikoff had been, calling his tribute "posthumous brown-nosing." *Frank* had become a regular conduit for those who nursed personal vendettas against Fecan. It also floated the rumour that Tartikoff had backed a rival comedy channel, not Fecan's, at the time of the 1996 specialty-licence sweepstakes. In fact, Tartikoff had sent a letter supporting The Comedy Network. It was Lorne Michaels, the executive producer of *Saturday Night Live*, who'd written on behalf of both The Comedy Network and WIC's Second City Comedy Channel. As for the relationship between the two men, Fecan says that, as with any friendship, "there were strong times, and different times when you drift apart."

☆

Scarcely had Fecan touched down in Los Angeles when he heard that Baton had received approval of its network takeover. At Baton's headquarters, the celebrations were rather low-key, considering that this was the culmination of more than thirty-five years of schemes and dreams, plots and convoluted counterplots. "There wasn't a champagne party," Fred Eaton recalls, "but everyone was happy that the goal had finally been achieved. It was the best thing that could have happened."

At a whirl of social events around Toronto, Doug Bassett beamed with pride. "It was terrific. It was exciting," he crows. "Everybody was happy — everybody but Izzy!" (The CRTC had blocked Asper's coast-to-coast system, which didn't stop him from branding Global as a de facto network that fall, by means of a recurring series of promotional spots with a distinctive crescent moon icon. The word "Global" also replaced the individual call letters for each of the CanWest Global stations.)

But, like Fecan's, Bassett's joy was tempered by personal tragedy. "We were going through a tough time," he says. His daughter Debbie had suffered a broken neck in Antigua and was recuperating at the Bassetts' Toronto home. Meanwhile, Big John was bed-ridden as well, as a result of complications that arose after heart surgery. Senator Finlay MacDonald, who'd spoken in favour of the Baton-CHUM swap at the acquisition hearings, called to congratulate his friend on Baton's takeover of CTV. Big John's nurse explained that her patient was sleeping, so MacDonald wrote a letter instead.

Almost all of the credit for the takeover went to Fecan. *Sunday Edition*'s Mike Duffy called it an "amazing coup" on his part. Doug Bassett agreed: "Ivan made the dream come true."

☆

On the Sunday following the CRTC's decision, the world mourned the death of Princess Diana in a Paris car crash, while Lloyd Robertson and Valerie Pringle flew to London to cover the funeral. That same weekend, in an odd though appropriate coincidence, Alliance's *The Sweet Hereafter* opened the Toronto Festival of Festivals. Directed by Atom Egoyan, it told the story of a small town's attempts to cope with the aftermath of a fatal schoolbus accident.

Egoyan and Robert Lantos arrived by stretch limousine in front of the Hummingbird Centre, where they were accosted by Carla Collins, the wise-cracking, white-blonde host of Baton's *E-Now* entertainment program, who solicited their opinion of the newly laid red carpet.

A minute later, Collins collared Ivan Fecan. "We're asking everybody tonight," she said gamely. "You've been down a lot of red carpets in your illustrious career. How does this [one] hold up?"

"The *best*," Fecan replied.

"Why is it the best?" Collins asked.

"Because we own the movie for broadcast," Fecan replied with a laugh.

☆

By mid-September, Fecan was back out west, poised to invade a $200-million advertising market and counting the minutes until he could cut the ribbon for Vancouver Television's high-tech, fully digital studios. In search of sets for the newscast and other shows, Fecan had recruited Rick Ulfers, a Hollywood designer who'd come up with wonderfully inventive treatments such as *Breakfast Television*'s giant breakfast plate, with a piece of toast, fried egg, strawberries, fork, and knife.

There was some question, though, whether VTV would be ready in time for its September 22 debut. "You bet we're going to make it," promised Fecan, as he led reporters through the under-construction station. "We may be [wearing] hard hats [when] we sign on, but we'll be here and we'll be broadcasting."

The night before its 6 a.m. launch, VTV's staff gathered at the Hotel Vancouver for a celebratory dinner with Fecan, John Pollock, and Doug Bassett, who told a local CRTC official that Vancouver Television would be the model for all Baton's outlets.

But *Gabereau Live!*, the first daily network television show ever to emanate live from Vancouver, got off to a rocky start the next morning, amid a background of echoing hammers that threatened to drown out the conversation. (It hit its stride the following month when Gabereau interviewed David Duchovny, star of *The X-Files*, shortly after he'd offended Vancouverites by telling NBC's late-night host Conan O'Brien that the city received "400 inches" of rain a day. Gabereau gave the sheepish Duchovny no quarter; he subsequently decamped to more arid settings in California.)

Having had a chance to examine VTV's site, format, and overall ambience, CITY's resident guru, Moses Znaimer, accused Ivan Fecan of stealing the CITY concept lock, stock, and barrel. "I know when I'm borrowing from someone else," says Fecan (who'd in fact played a role in developing *CityPulse*, Znaimer's local newscast). "CITY doesn't do community news bureaus. Yes, we have live eyes [rooftop cameras]. Yes, we have ethnic reporters. [These things aren't] exclusive to CITY." Like CITY, though, VTV frequently escaped the studio to stage live performances on the Burrard Street sidewalk.

Mid-October marked the launch of CTV News 1, The Comedy Network, Outdoor Life, and the History Channel. The network had hired fifty additional staff for its twenty-four-hour headline-news service on basic cable, which was immediately criticized for its lack of fresh items and a preference for lightweight features. Satirists went to town on its revolving set, which rotated forty-five degrees every fifteen minutes. Rick Mercer of *This Hour Has 22 Minutes* weighed in with a sketch about a pretty-boy news anchor who gets so dizzy that he vomits into a paper bag on camera. Luba Goy from *Royal Canadian Air Farce* portrayed CTV News 1's anchor Leslie Jones as helplessly spinning in her chair. "Everything revolves," the faux Jones said. "What goes around comes around and around and around." (Fecan left the set alone for the first season, but told CTV's news director Henry Kowalski to put more hard items into each News 1 segment.)

At the end of October, Daryl Duke resigned from VTV's board, claiming that Baton had misrepresented what its members would be empowered to do. "We were directors of bubbles, of nothing," he claimed. "Vancouver Television as a company didn't exist." The latter statement was correct, because when Baton and Electrohome merged, VTV was folded into the new company, and in fact no longer existed as a separate legal entity. Duke and the three other local members were invited to remain, but in a purely advisory capacity. John Pollock says that Baton-Electrohome had been "sincere" in recruiting them, but that the arrangement hadn't worked out. "They thought they would be management and run the show," he said. "You can't have the board trying to manage the business. . . . To think [that] Daryl Duke would tell the Eatons how to spend their money!" In retrospect, Pollock thinks that they ought to have been signed on as advisers only, because changing their mandate mid-stream was "bad optics." Naturally, the local press (and particularly the CBC) jumped on the story as yet another example of insular Torontonians riding roughshod over Vancouverites.

☆

The week that Baton gained control of CTV, Ivan Fecan and his team flew to Ottawa, to attend the CRTC's hearings into the possibility of licensing a third national network. CanWest Global viewed these hearings as its chance to shine, the result of the pressure it had brought to bear on the Liberal government. Unfortunately, matters went immediately awry, when the Friends of Canadian Broadcasting passed out a chart of Global's prime-time schedule, with its few home-grown programs coloured patriotic red, and called upon Asper to "get more red" in future.

But no such luck. Global's president, Jim Sward, proceeded to blurt out during his Q&A session that there might not be another season of Global's showcase Canadian drama series, *Traders*. "We probably cannot do it next year," he said, "because two of the stars and three of the writers are headed [to] bigger productions in the United States."

The next morning, Fecan took the microphone, armed with a proposal he said would create a "level playing field" for Baton, CanWest Global, and WIC. He suggested that each of the station groups be required to air at least seven hours a week of Canadian music, drama, and variety in prime time, and that each devote 30 per cent of its airtime revenues to Canadian programming. In 1996–97, Baton/CTV had done so, spending 33 per cent, or $147 million. Global lagged far behind, with only 18 per cent, or $67 million.

Then, having taken the obligatory swing at Global's skimming the cream in major urban centres while CTV was required to service less populated areas, Fecan retired to the Chateau Laurier and got ready to attend to other, even more pressing duties.

In order that CTV's consolidation could proceed, Baton needed to buy out the 43 per cent of CTV still held by minority shareholders. Within a week of the CTV closing, Fecan had flown to Winnipeg to try to persuade Randy Moffat to sell Moffat Communications' two million common shares, representing 14.3 per cent of CTV, to Baton for $10 million. "Randy was noncommittal, his usual methodical and thoughtful self," Fecan recalls. Two or three days later, Fecan met with WIC's chief executive, John Lacey. At the time, Lacey wasn't keen to sell Baton WIC's four million common shares, representing 28.6 per cent of CTV. He cautioned Fecan against moving too quickly in integrating the CTV and Baton operations, reminding him of the minority shareholders' rights. In fact, unlike Moffat, Lacey didn't think that the two structures should necessarily be merged at all.

Soon, however, both Moffat and Lacey made up their minds to sell. Moffat in particular felt that it was imperative to move with speed. He phoned Fecan at the Chateau Laurier on Tuesday, November 4, just before the third-network hearings began. Baton's board met by telephone the next day, and Doug Bassett, as CTV's chairman, called a full-scale board meeting for that Friday afternoon in Ottawa. By Thursday night, six million of CTV's common shares were sold. Fecan and Moffat "shook hands on the phone" and Lacey agreed as well, subject to approval by the WIC board. Baton had agreed to pay $14 million to Moffat and $28 million to WIC, a $12-million premium on the value of those shares that had been set by CTV in 1995. Baton said the premium reflected CTV's interests in four new specialty services: 100 per cent of CTV News 1; 12 per cent of the History Channel; 40 per cent of CTV Sportsnet (the regional sports channel, then unlaunched); and 60 per cent of CTV Direct (the pay-per-view sports channel, ditto).

At the Friday afternoon board meeting, held in the offices of Osler Hoskin & Harcourt, Fecan was unanimously elected president and CEO of the CTV Television Network, and Tom Peddie returned to his former position of chief financial officer.

Early the following week, Lacey got WIC's approval, and the share transaction closed the day after Remembrance Day, enabling Fecan's team, as he put it, to "move down the road in a timely fashion." Fecan also felt that the negotiations had been fair.

But one minority shareholder — Newfoundland Broadcasting — remained unaccounted for. Fecan had a harder time persuading the Stirlings to sell their 100 common shares than he'd experienced in getting the Moffats and the Griffithses and Allards to part with their six million. (Perhaps the Stirlings were brooding on what might have been. If they — like the other seven shareholders — had invested $2 million in two million common shares in 1993, they'd have realized a 700 per cent return on their money too.) "They'd been in CTV a long time," Fecan says. "They had a lot of emotional issues." Be that as it may, the Stirlings relented, and their 100 shares cleared before Baton's annual meeting.

As soon as Baton had virtually 100 per cent of CTV, Fecan put his own people in place: Suzanne Steeves, as senior vice-president of CTV sports and the new specialty channels; Susanne Boyce, as senior vice-president of original programming; and Beverly Oda, as senior vice-president of industry affairs. Steeves (at present the only woman heading a North American sports network) moved quickly, signing the National Hockey League to a four-year cable broadcast agreement on Sportsnet, which was slated to debut in October 1998.

Baton, meanwhile, cancelled CTV's lease at the Eaton Centre and made plans to move the network's headquarters out to the CFTO complex in Agincourt. It also began consolidating CTV's staff of 450 with Baton's full-time staff of 1,600.

CTV's senior vice-president of programming, Gary Maavara, had expected to spend part of American Thanksgiving watching football games on his office television set, as he'd tried to do throughout his ten years at the network. Instead, he was among the casualties in Baton's mass firing of CTV management that took place that day. The network's entire corporate communications department went down for the count, as did Tom Peddie, the chief financial officer; Gail Morrell, the director of programming; Peter O'Neil, the corporate secretary and director of public affairs and strategic planning; and two other vice-presidents. Security guards escorted them from the premises and seized their mail. Maavara never got to see his Christmas cards.

Fecan takes offence at this Scrooge-like depiction of the layoffs. He claims that the managers themselves had asked to be turfed quickly if they were going to be turfed at all, rather than spend the holidays in limbo and doubt. "We offered fair packages," he says, "and every single one of them accepted."

Besides, Fecan points out that some CTV managers survived the consolidation, such as Doug Beeforth, the vice-president of sports; Rita Fabian, the vice-president of marketing; and Allan Morris, the chief engineer (whom Baton laid off its own engineer to retain). And to the general relief of the national newsroom, Henry Kowalski, formerly CTV's vice-president and general manager of news, became senior vice-president of news for the combined companies. Still, everyone knew that more layoffs were on the way, and hundreds more jobs on the line. In Fecan's words, "That's what you have to do, to transfer money onto the screen."

Ivan Fecan, dressed in a dark suit and red power tie, with his silvered locks trimmed to a fashionable length, enjoyed a day of triumph at the Baton annual meeting on December 17, 1997. "Ladies and gentlemen, welcome to our home," he began his shareholders' address. "As you made your way to Studio 6, . . . you were able to see what a remarkable transformation this modest television station is undergoing. . . . [The] fiscal [year] 1997 transformed us from an important regional player into a truly national broadcaster, with an unparalleled group of broadcast assets." He then proceeded to enumerate them all, before acknowledging the "wisdom" of Baton's chairman Allan Beattie, and thanking Doug Bassett for recruiting him in the first place and for "providing a first-class platform upon which to build."

To shield the sensitive Fecan from the rigours of a media scrum,

Baton's corporate communications staff had decreed that questions be asked from microphones provided in Studio 6, thus ensuring that everyone could hear.

In response to a sceptical scribe who wondered if CTV Sportsnet was "viable" without a cable contract, Fecan nimbly paraphrased Big John Bassett's 1961 response to the Board of Broadcast Governors. When the CBC had demanded that he hand back the rights to his CFL football games, the feisty patriarch had replied, "I have no sponsors and I have no network and I have no microwave, but I do have the rights, and I'm gonna exercise them."

Fecan replied in kind: "To quote the honourable Big John's line, we don't have cable contracts, we don't have staff, and we don't have the facilities, but we do have the rights, and we're going to exercise them!" The studio audience (with the exception of the one-upped journalist) erupted into laughter.

Afterwards, at the shareholders' luncheon with Baton/CTV's stars, Fecan stood by himself in the entranceway, removed from the glad-handing inside. His reluctance to be in the limelight likely had much to do with the fact that he'd been savaged by the media at the end of his CBC tenure.

George Eaton played coy with journalists, too, although he couldn't get past Brenda Dalglish, then with the *Financial Post*. She asked him whether he supported Fecan's emphasis on financially problematic made-in-Canada offerings. "It's a calculated business decision, which was quite clear in the selection of Ivan as CEO," Eaton replied. "[He's] a terrific programmer and I believe that he can produce excellent programming here and sell it into the States."

Fred Eaton, never one to pass up a good schmooze-and-booze, showed the family flag by bopping around the room, paying court to Vicki Gabereau and anyone else who happened to cross his path. "It was a great party!" he recalls with enthusiasm. John Craig Eaton, for his part, introduced Thor, who ran the Eaton Hall Farm horse stables, as the "smart brother."

The four Eatons gave no hint that they were about to wave goodbye to Baton, the company their father had co-founded almost forty years earlier. Fred won't say when the brothers decided to sell, except that they did so "after the CTV takeover." The reason had to do with "family planning."

And no wonder. The T. Eaton Co. Ltd. had just emerged from bank-ruptcy protection and the two eldest brothers, John Craig and Fred, apparently wanted to cash out of their only big investment that was thriving. Baton's stock price, which had stagnated below $10 for the past decade, had more than tripled in value over the course of 1997. The Eatons' stake in Baton had rebounded from a low of less than $100 million in value to a rewarding $375 million on the public markets.

Ivan Fecan says that he knew the Eatons "were looking at every option, rethinking a whole bunch of things. [Insolvency] qualifies as a life-changing situation." The possibility that they'd want to sell out of Baton "played out over the holidays and into January."

During this period, the Eaton family's investment bankers "canvassed all over the place," Fred Eaton recalls. By the fourth week of January 1998, however, several media companies, including Torstar Corp., had rejected the opportunity of buying the family's stake for almost $400 million. So, at 4 a.m. on January 27, in the Toronto offices of Osler Hoskin & Harcourt, after a seven-hour meeting of the Baton board, the Eaton brothers agreed (George in person, and Fred by phone) to have their shares included in Baton's own public share offering. Three and a half hours later, Newcrest Capital presented the issue to the other firms in the syndicate. Ivan Fecan, who exercised 475,000 stock options to include his shares in the float, was so excited by the night's events that after only an hour's sleep, he hopped in his Mercedes, drove downtown to Newcrest's trading floor, and watched the 9:30 a.m. opening.

"What an incredible world!" marvels Fecan, ever on the watch for dramatic settings. (A pity that Global's Jim Sward spotted it three years earlier, resulting in *Traders*.) "This was my first time on Bay Street. I went from thinking of raising equity for Baton [in May], to selling half the company. It was a wild ride."

The bonanza offering raised $107 million for Baton, enabling it to pay down some of its debt, and $336 million for the Eatons, sub-divided into four parcels, one for each of the brothers. Why did they sell their shares? Fred Eaton remarks the best answer to that question is a "wonderful quote" attributed to Paul Desmarais when he sold his stake in Consolidated Bathurst to Chicago's Stone Container Corp. According to Eaton, Desmarais replied, "Because Mr. Stone gave me so much money."

The Baton offering also raised $8 million for Ivan Fecan, before tip and tax. The Eatons had made a deal with him that, if they sold out of Baton, he could immediately convert his $8-a-share stock options and hit the road. Bay Street money managers, however, had warned Newcrest that they wouldn't buy into the Baton issue if Fecan wasn't running the show. To ensure that he stayed on, Baton's board offered him 650,000 new options to replace the ones he'd be exercising early, as well as a new, long-term contract renewable until age sixty-five, and a multimillion-dollar golden parachute. As one resolutely unidentified source told the *Financial Post*, "Bay Street bought Fecan a network."

"Ivan is a very capable strategist and programmer," explains John Pollock, whose family company, Electrohome, became Baton's largest single shareholder, with 16 per cent of the stock. "In the last year and a half, under rapidly changing conditions, Ivan earned his spurs. He earned the respect of everyone who knows him. I give him full credit."

What would Fecan do with his instant millions? Irritated by the question, he takes refuge in the fact that he's "hardly alone here. A lot of money has been made in the broadcasting sector in the past year." He points to Jim Sward at Global and John Lacey at WIC, the man with the $3.8-million pay packet. "No one's interested in what they made!" Fecan grumbles.

After all, his $8-million financial score started melting away at once. Deduct the cost of the investment receipts, and it's down to "$6 million and change." Deduct capital gains tax, and it's down to $4 million. Deduct the $1 million or so he paid for 50,000 Baton shares, and that leaves a measly $3 million. Mind you, he's "not complaining." But what did he do with the leftovers? "We burnt the mortgage, that's what we did!" he cries.

In fact, as 1998 drew to a close, Fecan and Sandra Faire slapped down $2.25 million for a 5,000-square-foot home in Rosedale, with four marble fireplaces and a huge swimming pool overlooking a ravine. Then they engaged an architect to aid them in a $1-million-plus renovation of the ninety-two-year-old property, once the abode of John Craig Eaton. Thus, as noted by the *Globe and Mail*, the self-made Fecan had managed to acquire "another piece of the family legacy."

Rivals at CanWest Global had somewhat maliciously predicted that Fecan would take the money and fly south, where he'd have a shot at running a "real" television network (or, at the least, a Hollywood production company). Sandra Faire shot down this scenario. "We thought about it carefully," she says. "We expect to be here nine to ten years."

They're going to be interesting times. The heat was on Fecan immediately, now that ownership of Baton/CTV had shifted away from Eaton family patronage to a widely held and mostly institutional shareholder base. Bay Street money managers, whose principal task is to maximize shareholder value, called the shots on 75 per cent of Baton's stock. What if they expected Fecan to make the kind of money Canwest Global did? It was Canada's most profitable broadcaster by far, largely because it simulcast the most American shows and spent proportionately much less on Canadian programming than its competitors.

Would Fecan be forced to abandon his plans of Canadianizing CTV's prime time, now that the Eatons had cashed in their chips? His friends have no doubt that he can run a profitable network, but caution that if he can't realize his dream of presenting quality Canadian dramas five nights a week, his "heart won't be in it."

21

Global
versus CTV—1998–99

Ivan Fecan loves television. He watches everything, from quality dramas to schlock, consuming enormous amounts of programming on a daily basis. As a boy who grew up in the television age, he's always been a fan. But not everyone loves Ivan Fecan. In the small and incestuous world of Canadian broadcasting, he's always attracted the jealousy and scepticism of those who characterize him as a highly overrated self-promoter. His own fans disagree. After they work through the phrase "very intense," they fondly refer to him as their "creative dictator." Fecan's intimates have come to know what one describes as his "wicked sense of humour," too. Creative talents recognize a kindred spirit. They've gravitated to Fecan throughout his career, and he in turn has made them feel at home.

Several of Fecan's former protégés followed him to Agincourt — or, as Fecan likes to think of it, "Burbank North." CBC's former head of operations, Suzanne Steeves, led the migration. The veteran producer Susanne Boyce, who many people mistake for Vicki Gabereau ("and I don't dissuade them"), soon followed, taking Steeves's place as CTV's senior vice-president of programming. She calls Fecan "Ivanski." He calls her "Boycey." Ed Robinson, once a variety programmer at the public corporation, heads up The Comedy Network; Carol Hay, formerly in program development at the CBC and currently CTV's head of dramatic development. She reports to Bill Mustos, who ran the Cable Production Fund for two years and now serves as CTV's vice-president of dramatic programming.

To transform CFTO's dark and gloomy executive suite into CTV's network headquarters and Toronto regional development office, Fecan asked that the station's second floor be renovated into a wide-open space with light wood panelling, large skylights, overhead television screens, an espresso bar, and a floor-to-ceiling glass wall overlooking the national news centre. His office, a room minimally decorated with black-and-white photographs of Sandra Faire, contains the latest in high-tech gadgets, from the requisite TV-VCR combination to a flat-panel computer monitor. His desk is glass, his chair leather, and his fridge stocked with bottled water. From his window, he looks across to the building that houses the sports specialty channels, with its circular control room. Indeed, Fecan brought the entire station complex into the future, consolidating its master control facilities and installing fully automated digital equipment that could deliver fourteen separate signals simultaneously. All these investments cost nearly $50 million.

Like Baton's founder, Big John Bassett, Fecan's informality belies his authority. Like his predecessor, Doug Bassett, he's a control freak, involved in every detail of the Agincourt upgrade. Unlike either Bassett, though, he reads outlines and draft scripts, approves casting, looks at rough cuts, and sorts through contracts and licence-fee arrangements. He believes in development, arguing that it's important to spend money early on, to take losses before a series goes to air. Doug Bassett cites his "commitment to Canada and the Canadian broadcasting system," which is demonstrably true. But Fecan adds a vital qualification: "People don't watch flags," he says. "They watch good shows."

The fourth Friday in January 1998, marked the debut of his development team's first drama series out of the gate, the uneven but laudable *Cold Squad*, from Keatley-MacLeod Productions and Atlantis Films (a division of Atlantis Communications). In the two years since Fecan had given the series the green light, the Vancouver police procedural had run into nothing but problems. Telefilm had refused to support it, but "Baton went to bat for us," says Julia Keatley. "It put its full weight behind [the project]." Baton kicked and screamed until the government agency committed to fund eleven episodes, not the usual thirteen. By then, however, several key writers and directors had been hired away by other shows. Even worse, *Cold Squad*'s first few instalments looked weak — so Fecan's team hit upon a scheme that would enable the series to build an audience and survive. They delayed its launch until January 1998 and ran the fifth episode first, holding the shakier ones in reserve until the CBC began its coverage of the Winter Olympics in Nagano, Japan, when viewers and critics were occupied elsewhere. This strategy worked. The eleven instalments attracted hundreds of thousands more viewers on Friday nights than *Traders* drew to Global on Thursdays. Not only did *Cold Squad* win in its time slot against the American newsmagazine *20/20* (an ABC/Global simulcast), it was the only new Canadian series to appear among the top twenty shows nationwide that spring.

The 1998–99 season would mark the first year that Baton made the programming decisions for the 40 hours a week of CTV's network service carried by affiliated outlets, and the 126 hours a week of service on Baton owned and operated stations. Ivan Fecan planned to air a slate of five Canadian drama series — among them, the $1-million-an-episode *The City* from Sarrazin-Couture Productions, which was slated to begin prioduction that summer. "It's a social drama set in Rosedale and Regent Park [in Toronto]," he enthused. "It's really gritty, with fabulous writing."

Baton/CTV was willing to supply more financing for *The City*, over and above its 20 per cent licence fee, in exchange for international distribution rights. But, had it done so, Sarrazin-Couture would have lost its Telefilm funding. Telefilm specifically excluded Canadian broadcasters from its list of "acceptable" distributors (even though no Canadian distributors, almost all of which were affiliated with independent Canadian production companies, were willing to contribute enough money to bring *The City*'s production values up to international standards). Fortunately, the quality of Suzette Couture's scripts attracted the attention and financial participation of the Pearson Co., a British media firm. Otherwise, *The City* might have died in the development stage.

As it was, *The City* wasn't scheduled to begin airing until mid-season, but *Cold Squad* would be back in the fall, along with several unseen episodes of *Due South* and a new series from Alliance Communications. This was *Power Play*, the story of an NHL franchise in Hamilton, Ontario.

"Ivan has a vision for what he wants to do," *Cold Squad*'s executive producer Julia Keatley says. "We're very lucky to have someone like that on the private side. . . . You need volume, so that [viewers] don't say, 'Oh, that's the token Canadian show.' As a program maker, I want to be in [the same] roster as [*The City*]. Whether the system can afford it is another matter."

Other original Canadian projects expected to be aired in 1998–99 included three movies funded in part by Baton/CTV's $6-million Signature Presentation Fund: *The Sheldon Kennedy Story*, another Sarrazin-Couture production penned by Couture, who worked closely with Kennedy on the script; *Class Rebellion at Burger High*, the story of a teenager who attempts to unionize a fast-food chain, starring Sarah Polley; and *Proof Positive*, the story of a young woman whose lover deliberately infects her with HIV, written by Nancy Isaak.

Also about to move into production was the CTV-commissioned *Hard Times: The David Milgaard Story*, about a wrongfully convicted prisoner and his devoted mother, who fought for his release. Add to this a raft of documentaries from western and Atlantic Canada, and Fecan's team seemed to be well on its way to the revitalization of CTV's Canadian content.

"Ivan represents a sea change at CTV," says Suzette Couture, who hadn't even bothered pitching projects to the network during John Cassaday's regime, because of its reputation as a boys' club and a "home for industrial programming."

Even so, a gloating Izzy Asper was happy to take advantage of CTV's dismal performance at the 12th Annual Gemini Awards in March 1998 to get in a dig at Ivan Fecan. "Step up to the plate and join us in producing quality Canadian programming," Asper challenged, a few days after the awards were handed out for 1996–97. Indeed, CTV had managed to win only five Geminis, compared to Global's eleven. Even more galling, the coveted prize for Best Drama Series (which had been awarded in nine out of twelve previous seasons to the CTV/Alliance productions *Due South*, *E.N.G.*, and *Night Heat*) had found a new home, going instead to the Global/Atlantis production *Traders*. (Fecan didn't rise to Asper's bait. He remains convinced that Global looks upon *Traders* and its other indigenous shows as a "tax" for operating in Canada. "They don't truly believe in Canadian programming," he argues. As a result, he sees Global's development effort as minimal at best, much like CTV's before he took control.)

Not long after CTV's poor showing at the Geminis, Fecan and Sandra Faire (who'd been nominated for the variety program *Amanda Marshall*) flew to California for their first vacation in more than a year. "It was a holiday — really!" he protests. "We walked the beach every day in Santa Barbara." They also attended the Oscars for the first time, compliments of the ABC network. A record 6.6 million Canadians watched the ABC-CTV simulcast of the seventieth annual Academy Awards on March 23, up 32 per cent from the previous year, thanks to a "big boat" and two Canadian-born directors.

From "nosebleed seats," Fecan and Faire looked on as Atom Egoyan of *The Sweet Hereafter* lost the best-director statuette to James Cameron of *Titanic*, who later proclaimed himself "king of the world." Two tickets to the Governor's Ball meant that they were better placed to brave the who-are-you? stares of the Hollywood studio chiefs. "You've got to do it once," Fecan declares of the Oscars, red carpet and all.

Others contend, by the way, that the California "vacation" consisted largely of Fecan's phoning Toronto several times a day. If so, his purpose was twofold. First, he wanted to check on CTV's attempts to obtain the broadcasting rights to subsequent Olympic Games. (But Suzanne Steeves's team couldn't match a phenomenal $160-million joint bid from the CBC and NetStar Communications' The Sports Network (TSN), which will see them providing Canadian coverage of the next five summer and winter contests.) And second, Fecan wanted to stay abreast of the takeover battle for WIC.

Just before Christmas 1997, Emily Griffiths had confided to Tony Allard at a Vancouver Canucks hockey game that she was sick of owning WIC. Rumours swirled as she engaged an investment banker to shop the Griffiths family's voting stake. CanWest Global, which by then owned almost one-third of WIC's non-voting B shares, made her a handsome offer in early March, naming a price of $67.50 for each voting A share and $34 for each non-voting B share, contingent on the Aspers getting a majority of WIC's board seats and the right to appoint a new chairman. On March 13, Emily opted instead for an offer of $61 for each voting A share and $39 for each non-voting B share from Shaw Communications Corp. of Calgary. This worked out to $91 million, about $3 million more than CanWest Global's offer, since the Griffithses had twice as many non-voting shares. In a tricky bit of manoeuvring designed to avoid a transfer of control (which would have triggered the coat-tail provision and converted WIC's non-voting shares into voting shares), Emily's investment banker sold some of the Griffithses' voting shares to Shaw, and some to the Allard family, who had first right of refusal on the Griffithses' voting block. That gave both parties less than 50 per cent of the voting A shares, but left CanWest Global with 0.04 per cent and virtually no voting power.

Thus, after more than four decades, the Griffiths family was out of Canadian broadcasting. Emily, who probably enjoyed excluding Asper from the WIC boardroom, embarked on a round-the-world cruise with millions of dollars in her purse, while Asper raged publicly that the "secret deal" between the Griffithses, the Shaws, and the Allards was abusive to WIC's minority shareholders. Having complained long and loud to securities regulators and mounted several court challenges, Asper was back at it again on March 23, when CanWest Global made a $39-a-share takeover bid for all of WIC's voting and non-voting stock. In mid-April, Shaw countered with a $43-a-share bid for the 85 per cent of WIC's non-voting stock it didn't own. Shaw emerged as WIC's majority shareholder at the end of May, with 52 per cent of the total equity, compared to CanWest Global's 44 per cent. After CanWest's efforts to get the courts to overturn the "secret deal" stalled, it only remained for the two adversaries to carve up WIC's parts between them.

In mid-April, Fecan's plans for Baton/CTV's first combined season had suffered a major setback, when three home-grown drama series (*The City*, *Cold Squad*, and *Power Play*) didn't receive their top-up dollars from the Canada Television and Cable Production Fund, thanks to a tangled web of bureaucratic red tape. The trouble was that, before independents such as Sarrazin-Couture Productions could tap into "Sheila's money," their projects had to be approved by Telefilm itself. This year, however, Telefilm dragged its heels, and the April 14 deadline came and went — as did the money, which was allocated on a first-come, first-served basis to the producers who weren't using Telefilm money. Telefilm eventually approved the three Baton/CTV series, but a family drama series from British Columbia, four new TV movies (including *The Sheldon Kennedy Story*), eleven documentaries from western and Atlantic Canada, and the political satire *Double Exposure* were all rejected for funding by the government agency.

Meanwhile, the Cable Production Fund borrowed against future years' fundings in order to underwrite the victims of the deadline fiasco. On April 28, this bailout plan saved *Cold Squad*, *Power Play*, and *The City*. But first-come, first-served meant exactly that. Suzette Couture paid a security guard $11 an hour to stand in line, paperwork in hand, and get his hands on the cheque, which amounted to about 15 per cent of *The City*'s total production costs for thirteen $1-million episodes. (The rest was covered by Telefilm's contribution, Baton/CTV's 20 per cent licence fee, and the distributor, the Pearson Co.)

"I'd love to go to eighteen to twenty episodes," Fecan said. But the money wasn't there for distinctively Canadian series in quantity. This held true across the board. The thirteen already produced but as yet unseen episodes of *Due South* were joined by only fifteen new instalments of *Cold Squad* and thirteen of *Power Play*. By contrast, CTV's two industrial Canadian series (Atlantis Films' *Gene Roddenberry's Earth: Final Conflict* and *Nikita*, from Fireworks Entertainment) both would air twenty-two episodes in 1998–99, because American syndicators and cable networks had paid most of their tab through pre-sale agreements.

Both were popular south of the border. *Earth: Final Conflict* had topped the American syndication market for new shows in 1997–98, and even Fecan was an unabashed fan of *Nikita*. Its star, the Australian actress Peta Wilson, got lots of attention from the American entertainment press — including the dubious distinction of being named to *People* magazine's list of the worst-dressed celebrities in the United States, where *Nikita* was the USA Network's number one show. Fecan was less enamoured of CTV's other industrial dramas, *FX: The Series* and *Once a Thief*. He killed the pair of them, claiming that *Once a Thief* "didn't get the numbers." (But some of its episodes drew more than one million viewers, enough for the series to qualify as a Canadian hit.)

The truth was that Fecan wanted to make room in CTV's schedule for bigger and better indigenous Canadian dramas. The reality was that he couldn't afford them. Thus, *Earth: Final Conflict* and *Nikita* remained part of the program mix. "My dreams are far greater than the public money available," Fecan admits. At the height of the Television and Cable Production Fund snafu, Suzette Couture sent him a letter, outlining her pride at what he was trying to do at CTV, and her disappointment that "bureaucratic bungling" had "let him down." Fecan, for his part, calls the entire sequence of events a "disconnect" between what the system aspires to be, and what it can accommodate.

A day before the funding bailout, Baton/CTV's patriarch, John W. H. Bassett, died at home with his family, six weeks after his release from hospital, where the surgeons had "cut big hunks out of his heart." Amid the outpouring of tributes, both Fred Eaton and Ted Rogers claimed him as their "second father." Rogers recalls meeting him in a hospital corridor some months earlier, sitting in a wheelchair pushed by his youngest son, Matthew. "You look good," Rogers said. "Compared to what?" the unsinkable Bassett roared. Comparisons were useless; no one would see his like again.

On April 30, outside St. Paul's Anglican Church in mid-town Toronto,

Doug Bassett chatted amiably with the pallbearers — the Florida-tanned Fred, George, John Craig, and Thor Eaton; the paler-than-pale press baron Conrad Black; and the old-school journalist Peter Worthington. The coffin was draped in a Canadian flag.

Inside, the church was standing-room-only, overflowing with representatives of the political, publishing, and broadcasting worlds who'd come to pay their last respects. Two former prime ministers (Joe Clark and John Turner) were in attendance. Mila Mulroney appeared on behalf of her husband, who couldn't break a previous commitment to meet with a visiting head of state. Other dignitaries included Ontario's premier, Mike Harris; Ontario's lieutenant governor, Hilary Weston, and her husband Galen; Ken Thomson; Bobby's widow Ethel Kennedy; and Big John's widow, Ontario's Minister of Culture, Isabel Bassett. Lloyd Robertson, Mike Duffy, and Pamela Wallin joined Murray Chercover, John Cassaday, and Knowlton Nash. Ivan Fecan and Sandra Faire sat well to the back. "It was my first society funeral," said Faire. In a company statement, Fecan said that Big John "took great pride in living to see Baton assume 100 per cent ownership of the network."

The Baton-owned CTV launched its new fall season with an afternoon gala for media buyers at the Toronto Convention Centre on June 10. It began, appropriately enough, in the John W. H. Bassett Theatre, with a slick multi-screen display of video clips from returning shows and new American pilots, as well as filmed interviews with the executive producers of the new Canadian drama series, and live appearances by Canadian stars such as *Cold Squad*'s Julie Stewart, *L.A. Doctors*'s Rick Roberts, and the ever-popular Lloyd Robertson. As master of ceremonies, Mike Bullard warned the buyers that they had a choice between "ten more episodes of *Once a Thief*, or this opening." His boss (or "what's his name," as Bullard insisted on calling him) was subjected to rigorous scrutiny. In Bullard's close-to-the-bone words, "If he wasn't head of the network, he'd be one of those hard-core unemployed, who watches television twenty-four hours a day."

Then Mr. Television himself emerged on stage. "Welcome to CTV!" Fecan announced. "Not BBS, not Baton, not Baton-Electrohome, but — at last — the new CTV." He then proceeded to list the new CTV's strengths:

- "CTV is number one overall." Fecan claimed the spring 1998 ratings crown for CTV, as the only English-Canadian broadcaster to increase its audience share (to 15.7 per cent from 15.5 per cent, a little less than one out of every seven viewers). Global's share had dropped to 6.2 per cent, although it still boasted seven of the ten most-watched programs in the Toronto-Hamilton market, led by *Seinfeld*, *The X-Files*, *Friends*, and *Frasier*. Global also claimed fourteen of the top twenty shows, with *Dharma & Greg* making the final cut in its rookie season at number twenty. Baton/CTV, by contrast, aired only three of the top ten (*ER*, *Law & Order*, and *Jeopardy*) and six of the top twenty, although *Ally McBeal* had debuted at number thirteen, making it Toronto-Hamilton's hottest new show. (Nationwide, it made the top ten, ranked number five in its first season.)

- "CTV is number one in news." Earlier that year, CTV had refuted the CBC's inaccurate claim that *The National* was Canada's most-watched single newscast by taking out full-page newspaper ads that demonstrated that CTV attracted more viewers around the clock, as follows: *Canada AM* walked all over the *CBC Morning News* (337,000 to 42,000); CTV's local noontime newscasts handily defeated *CBC Midday* (537,000 to 113,000); its local early-evening newcasts led the CBC's by a gratifying margin (1.7 million to 468,000); and — in a closer contest — *CTV National News* edged out *The National* (1.2 million to 991,000). Then it was back to domination as usual, with CTV's late-night local newscasts outpacing the CBC's (451,000 to 152,000). Fecan went on to hint that the sixty-four-year-old Lloyd Robertson wouldn't necessarily retire when his contract was up in 1999. "Lloyd is anchor for life," he proclaimed. "Lloyd is the bedrock of CTV, and we want him to stay in that seat for as long as he feels comfortable."

- "CTV has the top two Canadian drama series, *Due South* and *Cold Squad*, and the strongest new Canadian drama series, [*The City*] and *Power Play*." Fecan called *The City* "a contemporary *Upstairs Downstairs*."

- "CTV has the number one U.S. drama: *ER*." NBC had agreed to pay a staggering US$13 million an episode to renew *ER* in 1998, up from US$2 million four years earlier, having panicked over losing its big Thursday night money-maker *Seinfeld*. Fortunately, CTV had signed a long-term renewal deal with the Hollywood supplier, Warner Bros. Television, just before NBC sent the price sky-high.

- "CTV has the most talked-about comedy: *Ally McBeal*." Viewership for the Fox-CTV simulcast climbed to almost two million in Canada, and *Time* magazine chose Ally's portrayer Calista Flockhart to illustrate a cover story on the death of feminism. (The spate of "is-she-or-isn't-she-anorexic" stories were still to come; but there's no such thing as bad publicity.)

- "CTV has cracked late night with the incomparable Mike Bullard." Fecan had learned a lesson in how not to launch a show from the *Ralph*

Benmergui fiasco at CBC. "It's best to play it on a self-deprecating basis," he suggests. *Open Mike with Mike Bullard* debuted on The Comedy Network with little fanfare, and slowly built an audience before moving up to full network status. Bullard would open his second season in a new home, the Masonic Temple in downtown Toronto.

- "CTV is the new force in sports with CTV Sportsnet and Outdoor Life." Fecan boasted that Sportsnet had "stunned the old boys' club" with its NHL hockey deal. Outdoor Life, meanwhile, would be refocused in its second year to suit a target audience Fecan called "generation extreme."

- "CTV is Canada's major integrated broadcaster." As Fecan stated, "We are now, for the first time in thirty-seven years, a fully . . . unified network speaking with one voice. With interests in seven specialty channels, ownership of ASN (a satellite network), . . . and more, this is the powerhouse that is now CTV."

According to Fecan, the upcoming season was going to be the best ever for home-grown drama, but local operations had paid the price. The next round of layoffs resulting from the consolidation of the CTV and Baton infrastructures, ordered on May 13, cut an additional 334 positions by the end of August, gutting local news in several regions. Attrition and early retirement would take care of 126 jobs. Another 105 were axed in Toronto, 41 in the Maritimes, and 12 at the newly opened VTV, thus freeing up more money for the "new CTV's" national programming.

Which of course included the latest and most hyped from Hollywood. At the Los Angeles screenings of network pilots, Ivan Fecan, Bruce Cowie, and Susanne Boyce had picked up the rights to four new prime-time dramas and three situation comedies, topped by *Felicity* (described by Fecan and everybody else as "Ally McBeal goes to college") and *Sports Night*, about a cable television show vaguely akin to ESPN's *Sports Center*. Continuing the John Cassaday tradition of CTV as the home of the Big Event, the Baton/CTV team also renewed the rights to its huge American awards-show package, anchored by the Oscars, and purchased rights to the next big mini-series, *Stephen King's Storm of the Century* and *Tom Clancy's Net Force*. They also won the exclusive Canadian rights to *Titanic*, which will rise again as an NBC simulcast.

All these and more had to find places in the schedule, which Fecan began to describe in more detail for his attentive audience. He calls this exercise "playing the squares," but he had no need of a display board with magnetic cards. Like Brandon Tartikoff, Fecan had mastered this multi-dimensional game of tic-tac-toe, responding to competitors' programs, ratings, and time slots as he shifted Baton/CTV's pieces around, and could have done it blindfolded. The exercise was to cram CTV's prime time with six Canadian drama series as well as *W Five* and *Double Exposure*; seven new American shows and *Dateline NBC*; nine returning American programs in addition to the syndicated hits *Jeopardy* and *Wheel of Fortune*; and one other American sitcom, *Veronica's Closet*, which had migrated from WIC, just as Baton had shifted its rookie hit *Ally McBeal* to CTV midway through the previous season.

Many of Fecan's choices had been made to counter what his arch-rival Global was up to. Asper's team had returned from Los Angeles with the rights to *Jessie*, the new half-hour comedy in NBC's post-*Seinfeld* Might-As-Well-See Thursday line-up; *That 70s Show*, a retro-sitcom comfortably sandwiched between *The Simpsons* and *The X-Files* in Fox's Sunday line-up; and several other wait-and-see sitcoms and dramas. Global's only maple-leaf-imprinted drama series would be twenty-two episodes of *Traders*, minus a couple of stars and the original writing team. Global had poached money from other projects in order to fund five additional instalments after Telefilm balked at backing more than seventeen. Its two industrial drama series (*The Outer Limits* and *Psi Factor*) would return by mid-season. The adult-oriented cartoon show *Bob & Margaret*, from Nelvana Ltd., would debut when one of the new American series was cancelled. Global also planned to air a made-in-Canada version of *The Addams Family*.

In response, Fecan had taken several what-the-hell-was-he-thinking-about? swings at Baton/CTV's schedule. First, he'd decided to put reruns of *The Drew Carey Show* up against first-run episodes of *Frasier* (a Fox-Global simulcast), the heir to *Seinfeld*'s throne on Thursday nights. ("When in doubt, punt," Fecan quipped.) He'd also scheduled more non-entertainment American programming in prime time, such as the news magazine *Dateline* on Friday nights at nine, and the so-called reality shows, *Cops* and *America's Most Wanted*, on Saturdays between eight and ten o'clock. *Double Exposure* wound up at 6:30 p.m. on Saturdays to make way for *Gene Roddenberry's Earth: Final Conflict* at 7 p.m. and *Nikita* at 10 p.m. Then Fecan put the new season's most talked-about show, *Felicity*, in the seven o'clock family viewing hour on Sundays, replacing *Due South*, which moved to 8 p.m. on Wednesday nights. *Power Play* would debut at eight o'clock on Thursdays. *Cold Squad* returned at 10 p.m. on Fridays, and *The City* would take the ten o'clock slot on Tuesdays midway through the season, sharing this time period with *W Five*, whose season had been cut back when it lost more than 200,000 viewers in 1997–98. CTV's Valerie Pringle and Baton's Tom Clark would co-host the truncated public affairs show.

Following Fecan's presentation, CTV's senior vice-president of sales, Gary Greenway, observed that it was "highly unusual" for the network's CEO to be "so involved with the schedule." Then Bullard instructed Fecan to "bring the car around," and the crowd headed down the hall to CTV's Program Fair, a veritable extravaganza of interactive exhibits where the buyers could mingle with assorted stars, watch a snowboarding demonstration courtesy of Outdoor Life, and gorge themselves on a roast beef buffet.

At a nearby press conference, Fecan informed the assembled journalists that Baton/CTV's broadcasting operations would operate henceforth under the CTV brand. "Over a period of time," he said, "Baton Broadcasting will disappear and be replaced by CTV. We're just not sure right now whether it will be CTV Inc. or CTV Television Broadcasting Ltd. or whatever. But we're not going to come this far and then not reclaim the brand."

In mid-August, it was Ivan Fecan's turn to invite Izzy Asper to step up to the plate and deliver Canadian programming, when the Gemini nominations for 1997–98 were announced. (The industry had requested that the Geminis be moved to fall 1998 from spring 1999, to make the awards more relevant and timely, and to coincide with both the CRTC's review of its Canadian television policies and the launch of everybody's new season.) Baton came off looking good. *Cold Squad* received eight nominations, including one for best dramatic series. Both Dini Petty and Vicki Gabereau were named in the talk-show category, and Sandra Faire had a shot at the best variety program award for Rita MacNeil's *Celtic Celebration*. At CTV, *Due South* garnered ten nominations. It and *Once a Thief* were up for best dramatic series as well. *Canada AM*'s Valerie ("don't-call-me-perky") Pringle was in the running for best host of a news or information series. All together, Baton/CTV received fifty-five nominations as compared to Global's twelve.

Nominations were well and good — but within a week, Izzy Asper struck back where it really counted. On August 18, CanWest Global announced that it had reached a $950-million preliminary deal with Shaw to buy WIC's eleven television stations, including the Alberta outlets. If approved, this purchase would fill in a vital blank, extending Global's reach from British Columbia to Nova Scotia and qualifying it as Canada's largest private television system.

Fecan expressed himself "delighted" that Asper had finally realized his dream but couldn't resist referring to the expanded Global system as a "de facto network" — an implicit demand that it be subject to more stringent Canadian content rulings. Predictably, this infuriated Asper, and the two men engaged in a slanging match, conducted through the pages of *Canadian Business* magazine.

Six weeks later, Asper lumbered into the Outaouais Room in Hull, on the second-to-last day of the CRTC's month-long hearings, called to review Canadian television policies in general. Fecan was at the microphone, calling for "some kind of equivalence" when it came to regulating the three major station groups. Asper took his seat at the rear of the room, coughing and spluttering while he angrily flipped the pages of the CTV Group's explanatory pamphlet. Then — having engaged Fecan and Allan Beattie in what appeared to be a more or less amicable chat — he took his place in the spotlight as an unexpected member of the CanWest Global panel.

Global Television's president Jim Sward led off their submission, railing against CTV's request for a more equitable regulatory framework. "We all have the same rules and we all make different choices about where we are going to go with our enterprise," he said. "At the end of the day, we all end up in different places. If, by your choices, over the last two years or ten years, you are in a hole, you dug it." (No one had to wonder who, in Sward's view, the excavator was. Earlier, he had informed the *Globe and Mail* that "CTV is on a very personal mission. [They] must be driven by debt, or something. [I think] they're saying, 'We want the commission to bring everybody up to our level of mistakes.'")

Sward, on the other hand, didn't want the CRTC to bring anybody up; he certainly had no wish to see Global's spending on Canadian programming raised to CTV's level. That, he said, wasn't "this commission's business," especially when dealing with the private sector. "We all got to where we are on our own; we are responsible for it," he repeated. "If it's good, good — if it's not, it's our job to fix it. God bless private enterprise! That's the juice that makes it work. If we start to play around with that, [to] compromise it, stop it, take the excitement out of it for the entrepreneurs by coming [in] and looking to level it, then we are not going to have the energy and the commitment and drive that have built the broadcasting system the way it is today. I'm sorry — [this] is a bit of a soapbox issue with me."

"Well, let me get you back on track," interrupted the CRTC's vice-chairwoman Andrée Wylie. "The train you are on is regulated. It has been regulated from the start, and it has worked very well for most parties in some ways, less well in others."

In fact, despite Sward's soapbox utterances, regulation had worked very well for CanWest Global. Like the CTV Group, it was part of a privileged class of Canadian broadcasters, protected by legislation from direct American competition and American ownership, and licensed to make money from a public resource (the Canadian airwaves) by rebroadcasting American shows, meanwhile contributing as little as possible in the way of Canadian programming in return. No one could seriously maintain that Global would exist today if the American networks had been allowed to set up shop in Canada at the dawn of the television age.

No one, that is, except Izzy Asper, who'd always considered regulation to be a corporate straitjacket. Having defended Global as a major contributor to "good Canadian programming," he lit out after CTV, which he accused of spreading "mischievous, ill-founded disinformation" concerning that contribution. Reciting a garbled mish-mash of percentages, he urged the commission to ignore the "invidious comparisons" that CTV and its "propagandists" had been leaking to the press. "They have twenty-five stations, and we have eight," he said. "They reach 98 per cent of Canada, and we reach 79 per cent." (These figures didn't include the proposed purchase of WIC's television division.) "We are quite confident [that] the commission knows the difference between [self-serving] hyperbole and . . . hard facts."

Later, Fecan (whose ears and neck reddened while listening to Asper's rant) fielded questions in the lobby. He said that CTV had chosen to take the high road, and CanWest Global, the low. Further, he thought that Asper would come to rue his intemperate remarks, among them his portrayal of independent producers (particularly the newly merged Alliance-Atlantis, now the twelfth-largest production company in North America) as "socialists," who wanted to redistribute wealth from his pockets to theirs.

But Asper's wealth was momentarily on the wane. CanWest Global's shares, like those of other broadcasters, had plunged by 40 per cent over the summer of 1998, as growing fears of an economic downturn battered the world's stock markets. To add salt to his wounds, an unfavourable tax ruling from Revenue Canada had killed Shaw-Global's preliminary agreement to carve up WIC. (The parties quickly returned to the bargaining table — and a new deal seemed to be in the offing.) For the moment, CTV remained Canada's largest private television network.

Meanwhile, Ivan Fecan had successfully energized the CTV logo, with a campaign spearheaded by an eye-catching fall promotional spot that depicted red, blue, and green silk streamers unfurling across the country. These symbolized the network's programming strengths. From now on, the colour red and the circle surrounding the letter "C" would be associated with entertainment; the colour blue and the cube surrounding the "T," with news and public affairs; and the colour green and the triangle surrounding the "V," with sports. A wide selection of Canadian and American stars appeared inside the appropriate geometrical shape, and the closing words "CTV: Canadian Television" harked back — either by accident or pleasing design — to Spence Caldwell's original name for his network.

At the CTV Sports Group, the Big Event of fall 1998 was the launch of CTV Sportsnet on October 9 — a boon to a potential six million cable viewers from sea to sea. Four separate feeds meant that masochistic Vancouverites could watch the Canucks lose, while Ottawa fans followed the fortunes of the Senators. Other options included PGA golf, and English and Italian league soccer. Fecan bragged that, within two months, Sportsnet had become the nation's second-most-watched specialty channel, at least among consenting adults in prime time, next to TSN.

At CTV's National News Service, Lloyd Robertson signed a new seven-year contract in mid-December, thus staking out the anchor desk until well into the next millennium. On the chat-show front, Mike Bullard agreed to stay behind his desk for another two years. "Lloyd and Mike — the Yin and Yang of CTV," joked Fecan.

Bullard's success was one of few bright spots in a bleak fall season bereft of breakout American hits. The much-touted *Felicity* failed to register with anyone except young women — a sought-after demographic group, but scarcely numerous enough to pay the freight. This morose college drama failed to place among the top thirty shows in the Toronto-Hamilton and Vancouver-Victoria markets. "It's important to remember that television viewers aren't bound to the same timetable as Bay Street," Fecan later instructed Baton's institutional shareholders, counselling patience on their part, and reminding them that *Ally McBeal* didn't become a hit until midway through its first season. Ratings were even worse for Canadian series. Many fans of *Due South* hadn't followed it to its new time slot on Wednesday nights; *Power Play* struggled vainly against *Friends* on Thursday nights; and *Cold Squad*'s second season didn't attract as many viewers as its first. Fecan's team responded by shuffling *Due South* and *Power Play* around in the second half of the season, and promoting VTV's *Double Exposure* to network prime time, following *Power Play* on Thursday nights. *The City* (Fecan's best hope for a Great Canadian Drama Series of his own) would kick off in early

March with a two-hour Sunday night movie, before settling into its regular time slot on Tuesday nights. It was more of a soap opera than anything that smacked of vérité, although *The City*'s large cast of Toronto characters featured one self-made, self-promoting real estate developer, who resembled none other than a young Ivan Fecan.

In early November, at the Canadian Association of Broadcasters' conference in Vancouver, Fecan had offered up his vision of CTV five years down the line. He predicted that it would place several Canadian shows (of which the network would own significant pieces) among the nation's most-watched programs. That seemed unlikely as the bad numbers started landing for fall 1998, and critics began stepping up their attacks on the government's cultural policies in general and the CRTC's devotion to Cancon in particular.

Indeed, some observers wondered whether Fecan would be around, at least in his present position, in 2003. The consensus as the year's end drew closer was that someone had targeted Baton for a takeover bid. More than one-third of its outstanding shares had traded since early October, as the stock price rebounded from its summer plunge to the $22 range. Fecan believed that arbitrageurs were behind the share runup, playing the difference between Baton's share price and the current trading value of its instalment receipts (held by the Eatons and other investors from Baton's early 1998 share offering, and scheduled to close in February 1999). Some Bay Street analysts were cautiously recommending the stock, in part because there was light at the end of the tunnel. CTV was chipping away at Global's ratings lead. And CTV would hang onto all its affiliates in 1998–99 because both its network licence and affiliation agreement had been renewed for another year, until August 31, 2000.

On balance, then, Fecan could approach Baton's annual meeting on December 18 with a sense of guarded optimism. This gathering — held at CTV's new Downtown Studios in the Masonic Temple (a one-time venue for rock concerts, and the Rolling Stones' rehearsal hall in advance of their Bridges to Babylon tour) — was lower key than the previous year's conclave in Agincourt. For one thing, no CTV stars were on hand to mingle with the Bay Streeters. For another, Fecan's flowing locks had finally been cut back to approved corporate length.

In his shareholders' address, Fecan chose to touch upon three objectives — reducing costs, strengthening schedules, and building "a new corporate culture." He must have said the right thing. Although Baton's $6-million net income in 1997–98 was less than double what he'd spent on his new home, the shareholders approved a generous stock-option package for him and his management team.

Doug Bassett and Fred Eaton represented Baton's founding families at the annual meeting. Thus, it was entirely appropriate that the boyhood friends moved and seconded the motion that Baton be renamed CTV Inc. — proof positive that Baton had finally won its decades-long struggle to control the network, even though it still didn't own the CTV-affiliated stations in Victoria, Vancouver, Winnipeg, Montreal, or St. John's. Meanwhile, the broadcasting industry still hummed with change. CanWest Global was trying to hammer out a new deal with Shaw to purchase WIC's television division, which included the CTV affiliates in British Columbia and Quebec; however, rumblings in Ottawa suggested that the CRTC would once again thwart Izzy Asper's dream of making Global the country's biggest private television system, by turning down such a takeover.

In early February, the CTV-Global battle for television supremacy took another unexpected turn when CTV Inc. trumped its arch-rival by topping Global's offer for control of NetStar Communications Inc., the country's largest specialty channel company. Bay Street applauded CTV's $409-million bid for 68 per cent of the owner of TSN (to be renamed ESPN Canada) and the Discovery Channel Canada, but stopped short of a standing ovation because of concerns about CTV's resulting debt load and the approvals process: would the Competition Bureau and the broadcasting regulator allow CTV to control both of Canada's rival sports networks? Even if CTV was forced to sell off Sportsnet, the deal had the potential to make CTV the country's television powerhouse for the new millennium.

Did the founders foresee how big it would become? Will the network continue to snowball in size and strength, or will it collapse under its own weight? For news of what the future may hold for these and other television cliffhangers, we'll have to stay tuned.

Sources

Unless otherwise attributed, quotations come from either author interviews or the official transcripts of public hearings.

Books

Auletta, Ken. *Three Blind Mice: How the TV Networks Lost Their Way*. New York: Random House, 1991.

Black, Conrad. *A Life in Progress*. Toronto: Key Porter, 1993.

Block, Alex Ben. *Outfoxed*. New York: St. Martin's Press, 1990.

Cameron, Stevie. *On the Take: Crime, Corruption and Greed in the Mulroney Years*. Toronto: Macfarlane, Walter & Ross, 1994.

Carter, Bill. *The Late Shift: Letterman, Leno & the Network Battle for the Night*. New York: Hyperion, 1994.

Clark, Andrew. *Stand and Deliver: Inside Canadian Comedy*. Toronto: Doubleday, 1997.

Ellis, David. *Networking: How Are Canada's English TV Networks Performing?* Toronto: Friends of Canadian Broadcasting, 1991.

———*Split Screen: Home Entertainment and New Technologies*. Toronto: Friends of Canadian Broadcasting, 1992.

Fitzgerald, James. *Old Boys: The Powerful Legacy of Upper Canada College*. Toronto: Macfarlane, Walter & Ross, 1994.

Fleming, James. *Circles of Power: The Most Influential People in Canada*. Toronto: Doubleday, 1996.

Forsey, Eugene. *A Life on the Fringe*. Don Mills: Oxford University Press, 1990.

Francis, Diane. *Controlling Interest: Who Owns Canada?* Toronto: Macmillan, 1986.

Frank, Anne. *Telling It: Writing for Canadian Film and Television*. Toronto: Doubleday Canada, 1996.

Fraser, John. *Telling Tales*. Toronto: Collins, 1986.

Frum, Linda. *The News Makers: Behind the Cameras with Canada's Top TV Journalists*. Toronto: Key Porter, 1990.

Goodman, Eddie. *Life of the Party: The Memoirs of Eddie Goodman*. Toronto: Key Porter, 1988.

Hardin, Herschel. *Closed Circuits: The Sellout of Canadian Television*. Vancouver: Douglas & McIntyre, 1985.

Hehner, Barbara, and Andra Sheffer. *Making It: The Business of Film & Television Production in Canada*. Toronto: Doubleday Canada, 1995.

Kirck, Harvey, with Wade Rowland. *No One Calls Me Mr. Kirck*. Toronto: Collins, 1985.

Manera, Tony. *A Dream Betrayed: The Battle for the CBC*. Toronto: Stoddart, 1996.

McDonald, Marci. *Yankee Doodle Dandy*. Toronto: Stoddart, 1996.

McQueen, Rod. *The Eatons: The Rise and Fall of Canada's Royal Family*. Toronto: Stoddart, 1998.

Nash, Knowlton. *Prime Time at Ten*. Toronto: McClelland & Stewart, 1987.

——*The Microphone Wars: A History of Triumph and Betrayal at the CBC*. Toronto: McClelland & Stewart, 1994.

——*Cue the Elephant!* Toronto: McClelland & Stewart, 1996.

Newman, Peter C. *Renegade in Power: The Diefenbaker Years*. Toronto: McClelland & Stewart, 1973.

——*The Canadian Establishment: The Old Guard*. Toronto: McClelland & Stewart, 1975.

——*The Canadian Establishment: The Acquisitors*. Toronto: McClelland & Stewart, 1981.

——*The Canadian Revolution, 1985–1995: From Deference to Defiance*. Toronto: Viking, 1995.

——*Titans: How the New Canadian Establishment Seized Power*. Toronto: Viking, 1998.

Peers, Frank W. *The Public Eye: Television and the Politics of Canadian Broadcasting, 1952–1968*. Toronto: University of Toronto Press, 1979.

Pevere, Geoff, and Greig Dymond. *Mondo Canuck: A Canadian Pop Culture Odyssey.* Toronto: Prentice Hall, 1996.

Sawatsky, John. *Mulroney: The Politics of Ambition.* Toronto: Macfarlane, Walter & Ross. 1991.

Sexton, Rosemary. *The Glitter Girls.* Toronto: Macmillan, 1993.

——*Confessions of a Society Columnist.* Toronto: Macmillan, 1995.

Skene, Wayne. *Fade to Black: A Requiem for the CBC.* Vancouver: Douglas & McIntyre, 1993.

Siggins, Maggie. *Bassett: His Forty Years in Politics, Publishing, Business and Sports.* Toronto: James Lorimer & Co., 1979.

Smith, Denis. *Rogue Tory: The Life and Legend of John G. Diefenbaker.* Toronto: Macfarlane, Walter & Ross, 1995.

Sonmor, Jean. *The Little Paper That Grew.* Toronto: Toronto Sun Publishing, 1993.

Stanton, Raymond. *Visionary Thinking: The Story of Canada's Electrohome.* Kitchener: Canadian Corporate Histories, 1997.

Stewart, Andrew, and William H. N. Hull. *Canadian Television Policy and the Board of Broadcast Governors, 1958–1968.* Edmonton: University of Alberta Press, 1994.

Stursberg, Peter. *Mister Broadcasting: The Ernie Bushnell Story.* Toronto: Peter Martin and Associates, 1971.

Tartikoff, Brandon. *The Last Great Ride.* New York: Turtle Bay Books, 1992.

Thomas, Dave. *SCTV: Behind the Scenes.* Toronto: McClelland & Stewart, 1996.

Tinker, Grant, and Bud Rekeyser. *Tinker in Television.* New York. Simon & Schuster, 1994.

Weir, Austin. *The Struggle for National Broadcasting in Canada.* Toronto: McClelland & Stewart, 1965.

Articles

Adilman, Sid. "CBC-TV executive quits for offer he couldn't refuse," *The Toronto Star*, June 12, 1986.

——"TV's top survivor still delivers 'the eyeballs,'" *The Toronto Star*, March 2, 1996.

Ashley, Lynda. "Top gun," *Broadcaster*, February 1988.

Barber, John. "Box top," *Flare*, April 1988.

Best, Patricia. "Broadcast blues," *Financial Times of Canada*, May 9, 1988.

Boone, Mike. "CBC schedule is in the hands of a child of the television age," Montreal *Gazette*, November 10, 1987.

Brehl, Robert. "2 WIC families rebuff rebellion," *The Toronto Star*, January 9, 1997.

——"CanWest bid highest for WIC A shares," *The Globe and Mail*, July 17, 1998.

Brewster, Todd. "The shows that changed America: 60 years of network television," *Life*, April 1999.

Chisholm, Patricia, with Luke Fisher and Ross Laver. "Tycoon of the Tube: Canada's most ambitious broadcaster launches a $636-million takeover bid," *Maclean's*, November 27, 1995.

Corelli, Rae. "CTV's bitter family feud," *Maclean's*, March 23, 1987.

——"The decline of a dynasty," *Maclean's*, March 10, 1997.

Cowan, Jennifer. "Hot Couture: Suzette Couture, queen of the mini-series, couldn't have written a better script for herself," *Saturday Night*, October 1994.

CTV Anniversary Anecdotes, *Broadcaster*, October 1991.

CTV 30th Anniversary, *Playback*, July 5, 1991.

Dalglish, Brenda. "Let's make a deal," *Maclean's*, October 2, 1995.

——"Family feud sees WIC's Frank Griffiths fired by his mother," *Financial Post*, September 18, 1996.

——"Ivan Fecan's new season," *Financial Post*, June 20–22, 1998.

Davis, Ted. "Power player," *Broadcaster*, August 1990.

——"Cassaday close up," *Broadcaster*, September 1990.

——"From Caldwell to Cassaday," *Broadcaster*, October 1991.

——"Requiem for a Heavyweight?" *BC Business*, July 1997.

DeMont, John. "A global vision: Izzy Asper plans a national TV network," *Maclean's*, February 5, 1990.

Dwyer, Victor. "Shakeup at CTV: A new president makes his mark on a network," *Maclean's*, July 23, 1990.

——"Fine-tuning CTV," *Maclean's*, February 10, 1992.

Enchin, Harvey. "Marketing whiz turns his skills to running CTV," *The Globe and Mail*, February 12, 1990.

——"CTV wars over as deal signed," *The Globe and Mail*, January 23, 1993.

——"Dynasty vs Dynasty: CanWest goes after WIC," *The Globe and Mail*, November 18, 1995.

Fecan, Ivan. "TV legend Tartikoff never feared risks," *The Globe and Mail*, August 29, 1997.

Festinger, Jonathan B. "Mapping the electronic highway: A survey of domestic and international law issues," *U.B.C. Law Review*, 1995.

Fleming, James. "The captain's call letters," *Report on Business Magazine*, October 1990.

Goddard, Peter. "CBC Variety chief's young image refreshing," *The Toronto Star*, February 29, 1984.

Greenspon, Edward. "The off-camera drama at CTV," *Report on Business Magazine*, June 1987.

Greenwood, John. "Masters of compromise," *The Financial Post Magazine*, April 1992.

Heller, Liane. "These clans 'pull together,'" *The Toronto Star*, April 24, 1984.

Hubbard, Jaimie. "CTV network boss tuned into business," *Financial Post*, June 28, 1990.

Hume, Mark, and David Baines. "The rise and fall of the Griffiths empire," *The Vancouver Sun*, November 16–18, 1996.

Johnson, Brian D. "Inside stories," *Maclean's*, April 17, 1995.

Kirby, Blair. "CTV puts a circus in a studio and comes up with a winner," *The Globe and Mail*, April 15, 1978.

Knelman, Martin. "Into the network soup," *Toronto Life*, March 1991.

Landsberg, Michele. "TV Women: How they're doing in male-chauvinist TV-Land," *Chatelaine*, May 1974.

Mallet, Gina. "Top guns: Of all the shootouts in Hollywood North *Night Heat* is one of the few that's on target," *Toronto*, May 1987.

Mazurkewich, Karen. "Ivan Fecan: 'I had several major goals . . . ,'" *Playback*, January 4, 1993.

———"Ivan Fecan unplugged," *Playback*, January 3, 1994.

———"Shaking things up at Mother Corp.," *Playback*, January 3, 1994.

Macfarlane, David. "The boy in the box: Wunderkind Ivan Fecan," *Toronto*, March 1989.

McCullough, Michael. "Line of dissent: The Griffiths Family saga," *The Financial Post Magazine*, May 1997.

McElgunn, Jim. "The longest-running saga in Canadian TV," *Marketing*, October 2, 1995.

McFarland, Janet. "CanWest leaps ahead of CTV: Becomes Canada's biggest private broadcaster with deal for 11 TV stations," *The Globe and Mail*, August 19, 1998.

McGugan, Ian. "Eaton's on the Brink," *Canadian Business*, March 1996.

McLaughlin, Gord. "Jumping from Mother Corp.," *Financial Post*, May 31, 1997.

McQueen, Rod. "The mogul," *Toronto Life*, October 1987.

———"Passing the Baton," *Financial Post*, April 29, 1995.

Melnbardis, Caroline. "Encounter: John Cassaday," *The Financial Times of Canada*, March 26, 1990.

Milan, Luis. "Risen from the Red," *Broadcaster*, April 1994.

Murphy, Dan. "Who the hell is Ivan Fecan?" *The Province*, March 16, 1997.

Newman, Peter C. "The nation's business: From dynastic myth to mere mortals," *Maclean's*, March 10, 1997.

Partridge, John. "Western patriarch faces old-fashioned showdown," *The Globe and Mail*, November 2, 1991.

———"Grand auctioneer puts CTV shares under the hammer," *The Globe and Mail*, February 7, 1992.

———"CTV members waver on Baton," *The Globe and Mail*, February 22, 1992.

———"Bid to reshape CTV ownership collapses," *The Globe and Mail*, February 22, 1992.

———"Baton, CTV raise divorce question," *The Globe and Mail*, April 14, 1992.

———"CTV reaches new deal," *The Globe and Mail*, August 29, 1992.

———"Baton fears larger CTV board," *The Globe and Mail*, September 3, 1992.

———"Baton accepts CTV terms," *The Globe and Mail*, September 26, 1992.

———"CTV close to new plan for running network," *The Globe and Mail*, October 1, 1992.

———"CTV status remains bottled up," *The Globe and Mail*, November 28, 1992.

Pitts, Gordon. "Striving to lead Eaton chain back to glory," *Financial Post*, April 20, 1992.

Riches, Hester. "The new challenge for TV's boy wonder," *The Toronto Star*, October 23, 1985.

Saunders, Doug. "Mr. Television: He likes to watch," *The Globe and Mail*, April 11, 1998.

———"Chaos in the culture industry," *The Globe and Mail*, April 25, 1998.

———"Will Canada still be a TV star?" *The Globe and Mail*, September 23, 1998.

Scott-Atkinson, David. "Douglas the 'invisible' Bassett is now heir apparent to an empire," *Marketing*, August 29, 1977.

Sears, Val. "Profit-minded CTV under regulatory gun," *The Toronto Star*, April 6, 1987.

Siklos, Richard. "Channel-hopping," *The Financial Times of Canada*, August 13, 1990.

———"High drama as CTV gets new cast, script," *Financial Post*, February 17, 1992.

———"Alliance's Lantos looks due south," *Financial Post*, October 27, 1994.

Schofield, John. "The widening rift at CTV," *Maclean's*, February 24, 1997.

Suchard, Derek "The history of a television giant," *Playback*, July 8, 1991.

A Tribute to Murray Chercover, *Playback*, July 9, 1990.

Vale, Allison. "Baton metamorphosis a 'work in progress,'" *Playback*, April 10, 1995.

————"Arthur Weinthal: skeds, buys and videotape," *Playback*, January 29, 1996.

Vlessing, Etan. "Pip Wedge bids adieu to the CTV," *Playback*, January 31, 1994.

Waal, Peter. "Your move, Ivan," *Canadian Business*, September 11, 1998.

Waldie, Paul. "Majority owner rejects CanWest bid," *The Globe and Mail*, September 18, 1995.

Walker, Dean. "Doug Bassett: A TV son gets star billing," *Executive*, September 1983.

Wells, Jennifer. "The big picture," *Report on Business Magazine*, October, 1992.

————"Izzy's dream," *Maclean's*, February 19, 1996.

————"The Empire Strikes Out," *Maclean's*, March 10, 1997.

Wong, Jan. "Lunch with Fred Eaton: The emperor wears his own clothes," *The Globe and Mail*, May 15, 1997.

Young, Pamela. "A lean, mean alternative," *Maclean's*, November 3, 1986.

Zerbasias, Antonia. "CTV's struggle for survival," *The Toronto Star*, July 24, 1994.

————"Remote control," *The Toronto Star*, March 2, 1997.

Other

Canadian Communications Foundation. *The History of Canadian Broadcasting*. Web Page: www.rcc.ryerson.ca/schools/rta/ccf/

Report of the Fowler Commission. *Royal Commission on Broadcasting*, 1957.

Report of the Fowler Committee. *Committee on Broadcasting*, 1965.

Report of the Task Force. *Broadcasting Policy*, 1986.

Report of the Task Force. *The Economic Status of Canadian Television*, 1991.

Working Group on Canadian Programming and Private Television. *The Future of Canadian Programming and the Role of Private Television: Keeping Canada on the Information Highway*, March 1995.

Canadian Association of Broadcasters. *Canadian Television: A World of Success*, 1998.

Index